NEGIMA! 25

Ken Akamatsu

TRANSLATED AND ADAPTED BY
Alethea Nibley and Athena Nibley

LETTERING AND RETOUCH BY
Steve Palmer

BALLANTINE BOOKS • NEW YORK

Negima! volume 25 is a work of fiction. Names, characters, places, and incidents are the products of the author's imagination or are used fictitiously. Any resemblance to actual events, locales, or persons, living or dead, is entirely coincidental.

A Del Rey Manga/Kodansha Trade Paperback Original

Published in the United States by Del Rey, an imprint of The Random House Publishing Group, a division of Random House, Inc., New York.

Publication rights arranged through Kodansha Ltd.

First published in Japan in 2009 by Kodansha Ltd., Tokyo

ISBN 978-0-345-51882-8

Printed in the United States of America

www.delreymanga.com

9 8 7 6 5 4 3 2 1

Translators/adapters: Alethea Nibley and Athena Nibley
Lettering and retouch: Steve Palmer

Honorifics Explained

Throughout the Del Rey Manga books, you will find Japanese honorifics left intact in the translations. For those not familiar with how the Japanese use honorifics and, more important, how they differ from American honorifics, we present this brief overview.

Politeness has always been a critical facet of Japanese culture. Ever since the feudal era, when Japan was a highly stratified society, use of honorifics—which can be defined as polite speech that indicates relationship or status—has played an essential role in the Japanese language. When addressing someone in Japanese, an honorific usually takes the form of a suffix attached to one's name (example: "Asuna-san"), is used as a title at the end of one's name, or appears in place of the name itself (example: "Negi-sensei," or simply "Sensei!").

Honorifics can be expressions of respect or endearment. In the context of manga and anime, honorifics give insight into the nature of the relationship between characters. Many English translations leave out these important honorifics and therefore distort the feel of the original Japanese. Because Japanese honorifics contain nuances that English honorifics lack, it is our policy at Del Rey not to translate them. Here, instead, is a guide to some of the honorifics you may encounter in Del Rey Manga.

-*san*: This is the most common honorific and is equivalent to Mr., Miss, Ms., or Mrs. It is the all-purpose honorific and can be used in any situation where politeness is required.

-*sama*: This is one level higher than "-san" and is used to confer great respect.

-*dono*: This comes from the word "tono," which means "lord." It is an even higher level than "-sama" and confers utmost respect.

-*kun*: This suffix is used at the end of boys' names to express familiarity or endearment. It is also sometimes used by men among friends, or when addressing someone younger or of a lower station.

-chan: This is used to express endearment, mostly toward girls. It is also used for little boys, pets, and even among lovers. It gives a sense of childish cuteness.

Bōzu: This is an informal way to refer to a boy, similar to the English terms "kid" and "squirt."

Sempai/Senpai: This title suggests that the addressee is one's senior in a group or organization. It is most often used in a school setting, where underclassmen refer to their upperclassmen as "sempai." It can also be used in the workplace, such as when a newer employee addresses an employee who has seniority in the company.

Kohai: This is the opposite of "sempai" and is used toward underclassmen in school or newcomers in the workplace. It connotes that the addressee is of a lower station.

Sensei: Literally meaning "one who has come before," this title is used for teachers, doctors, or masters of any profession or art.

Anesan (or *nesan*): A generic term for a girl, usually older, that means "sister."

Ojōsama: A way of referring to the daughter or sister of someone with high political or social status.

-[blank]: This is usually forgotten in these lists, but it is perhaps the most significant difference between Japanese and English. The lack of honorific means that the speaker has permission to address the person in a very intimate way. Usually, only family, spouses, or very close friends have this kind of permission. Known as *yobisute,* it can be gratifying when someone who has earned the intimacy starts to call one by one's name without an honorific. But when that intimacy hasn't been earned, it can be very insulting.

A Word from the Author

Presenting *Negima!* volume 25! Finally, the Negi Party vs. Fate Party battle begins! Now is the time to show the fruits of their training.

At any rate, the enemies have very powerful pactio cards, too, so it will become almost the first artifact vs. artifact battle in the history of Negima. (*There was just a little bit of that at the school festival.) What does destiny hold for the partners!?

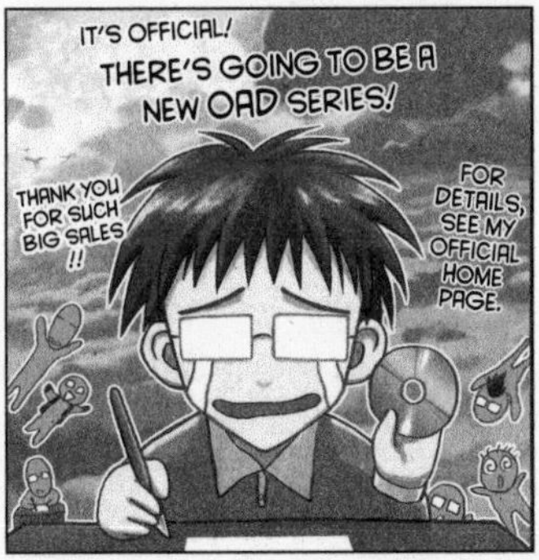
IT'S OFFICIAL!
THERE'S GOING TO BE A NEW OAD SERIES!
FOR DETAILS, SEE MY OFFICIAL HOME PAGE.
THANK YOU FOR SUCH BIG SALES !!

...And now I have a big announcement!! It was so popular that they've already decided to make a new OAD series! The next one will be a tinge different than what we've seen until now! For details, see my official home page! (^^)

Ken Akamatsu
www.ailove.net

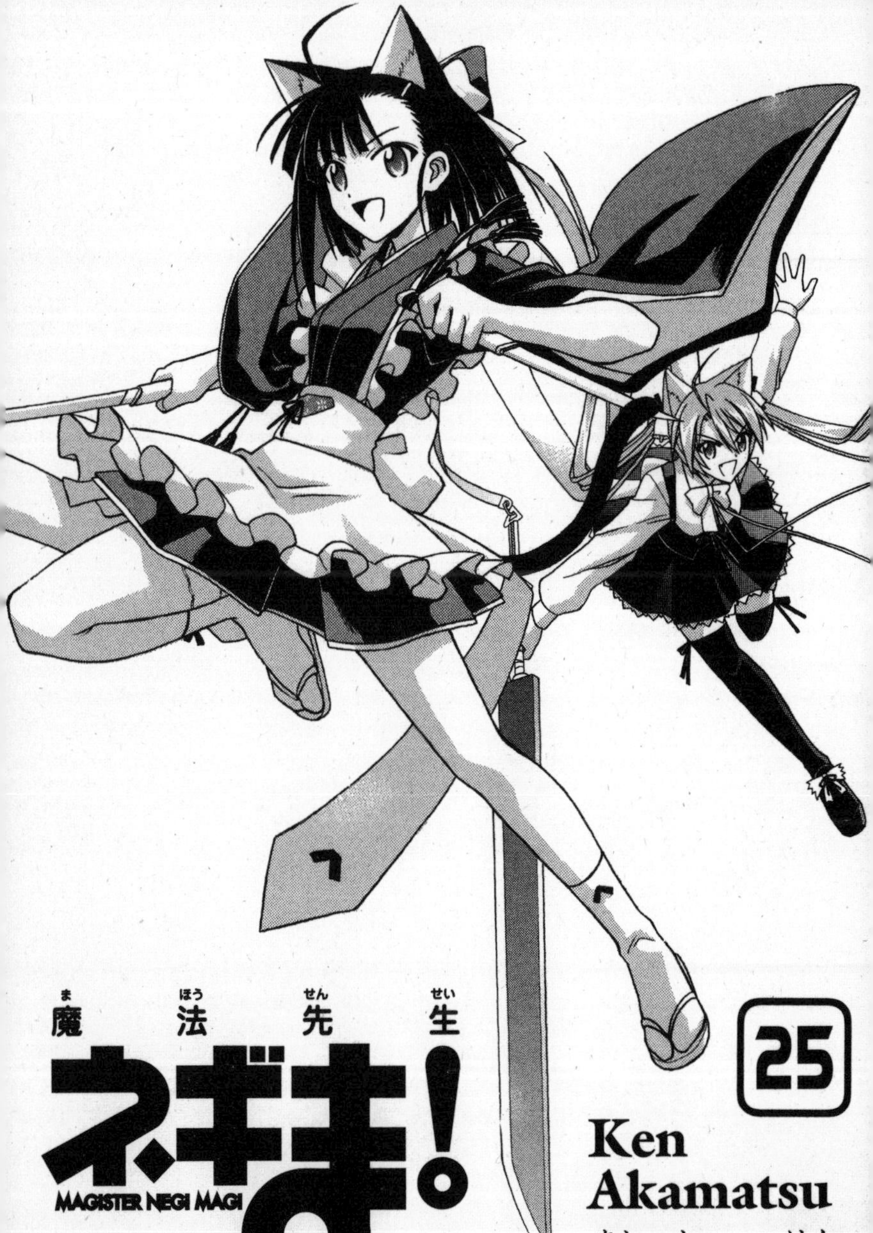

魔法先生ネギま!

MAGISTER NEGI MAGI

25

Ken Akamatsu

赤松健

CONTENTS

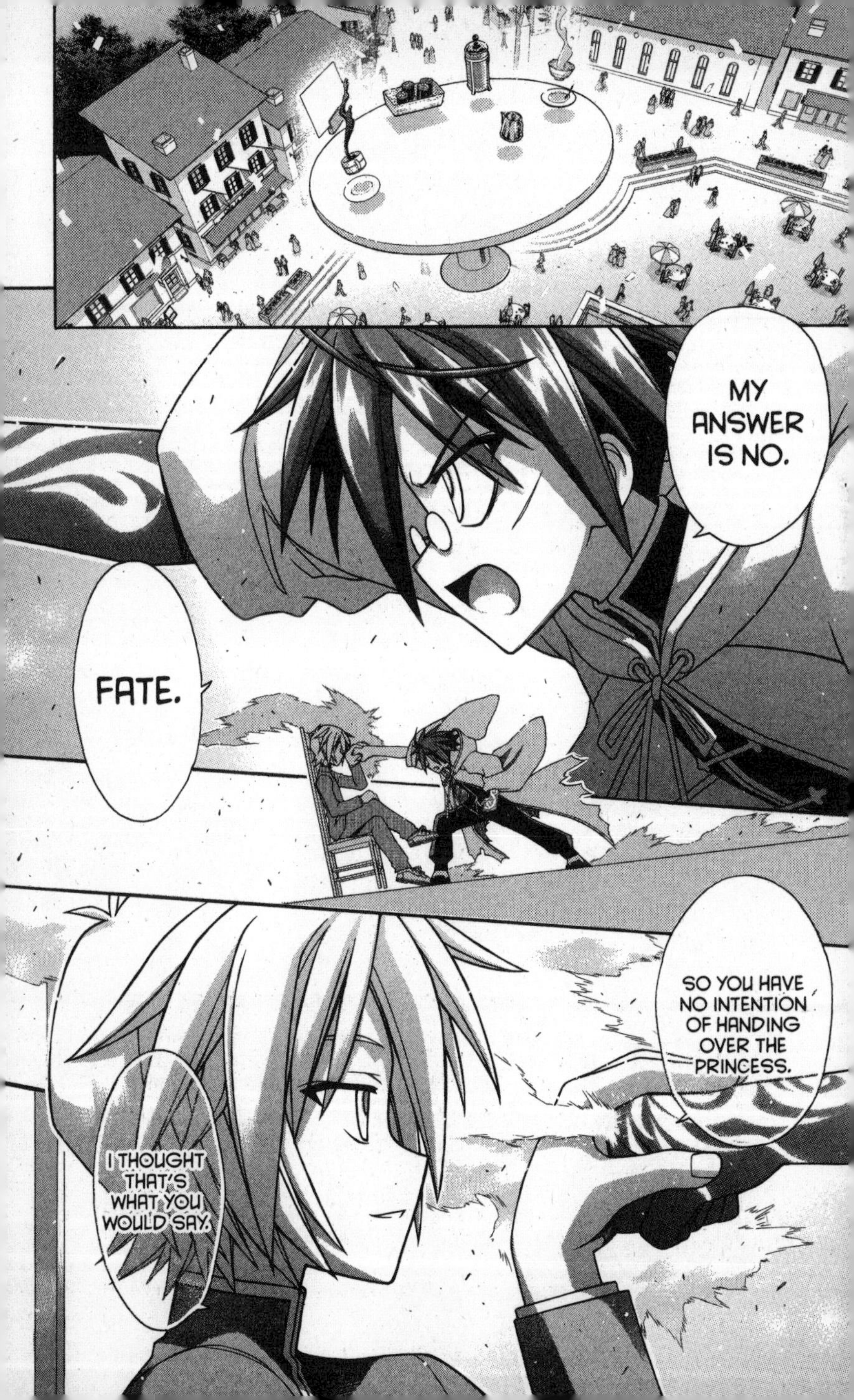
MY ANSWER IS NO.
FATE.
SO YOU HAVE NO INTENTION OF HANDING OVER THE PRINCESS.
I THOUGHT THAT'S WHAT YOU WOULD SAY.

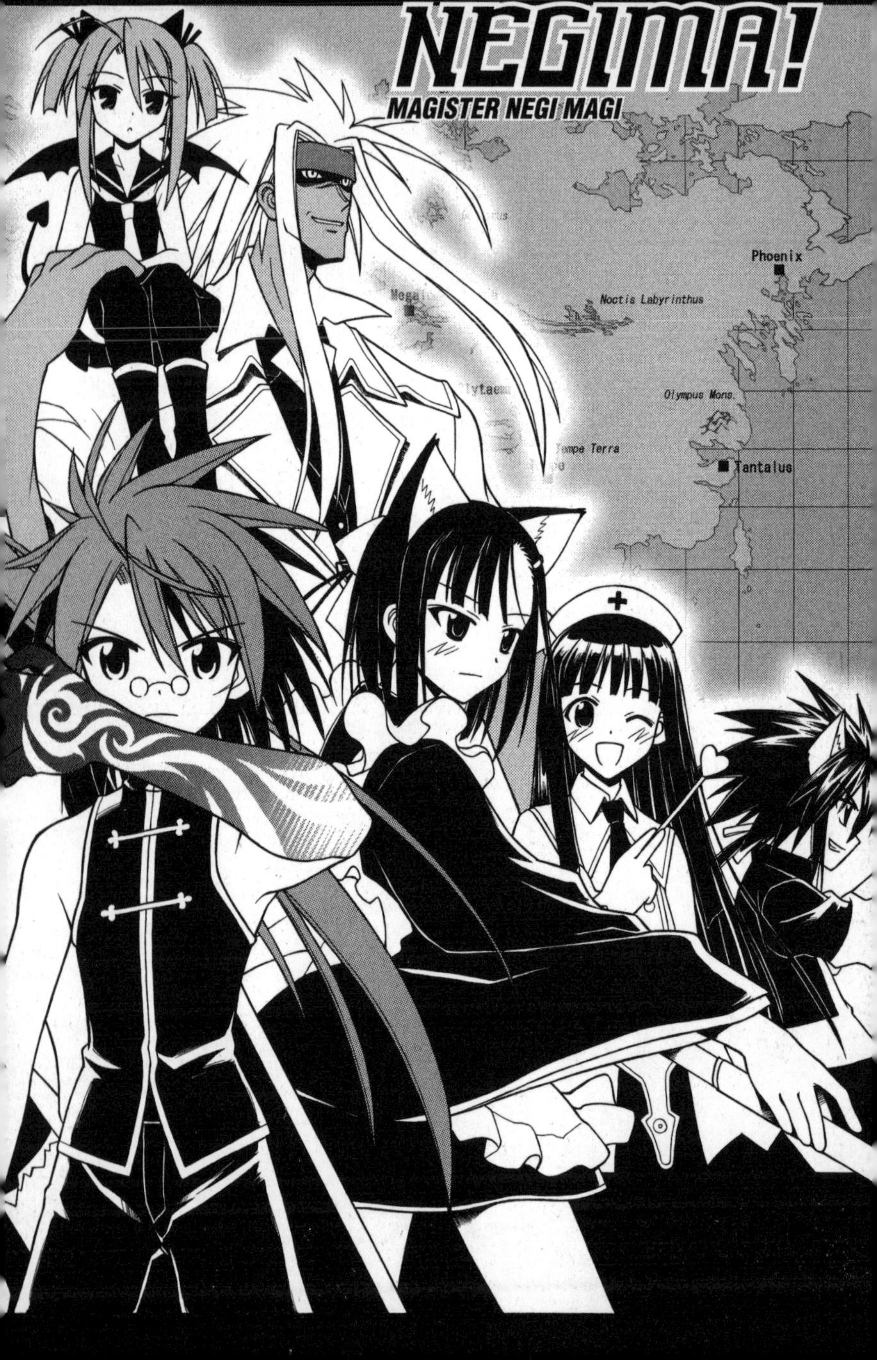
NEGIMA!
MAGISTER NEGI MAGI
Phoenix
Noctis Labyrinthus
Olympus Mons.
Tempe Terra
Tantalus

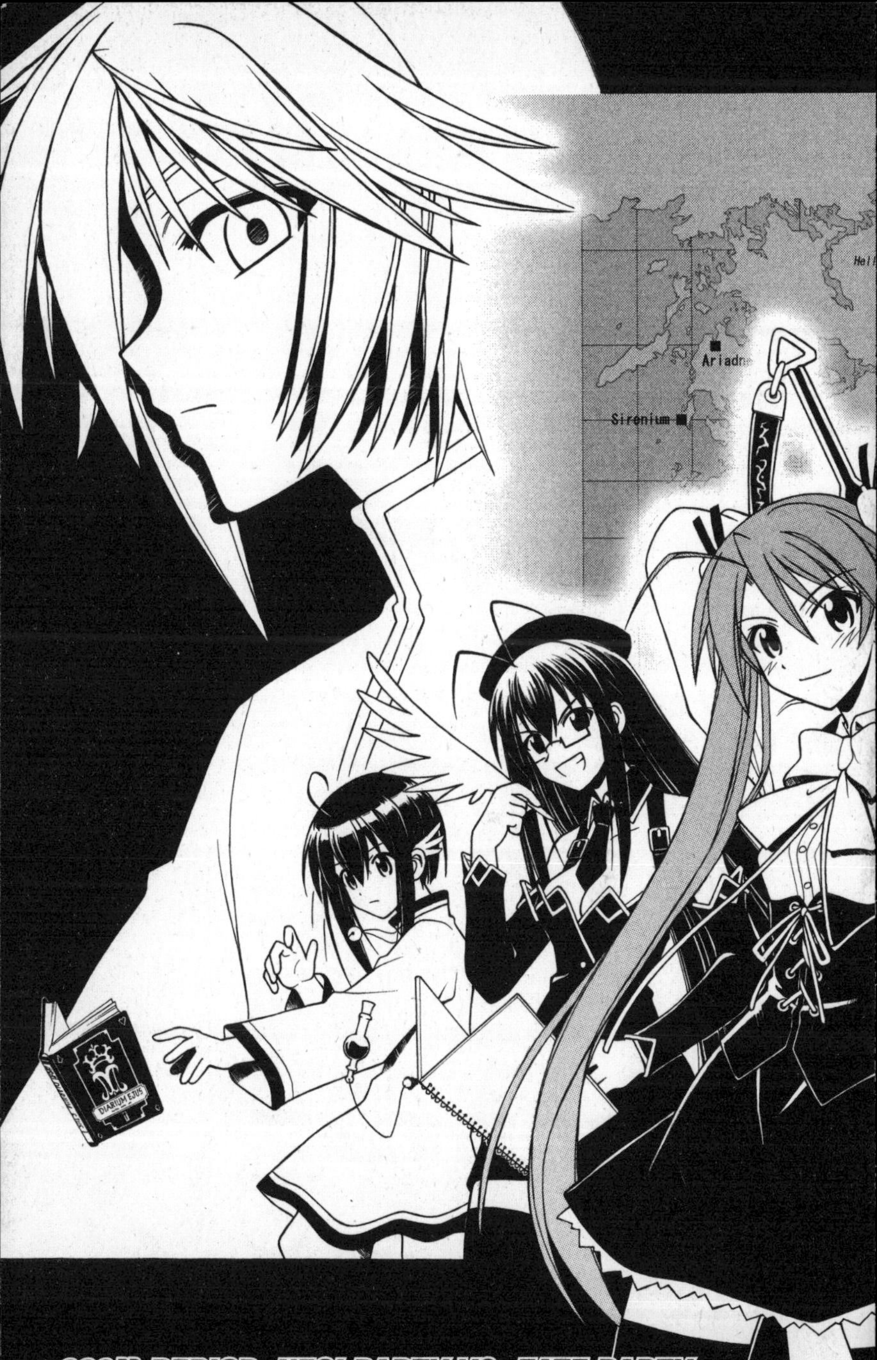
Sirenium
DIARIUM EJUS

223RD PERIOD: NEGI PARTY VS. FATE PARTY

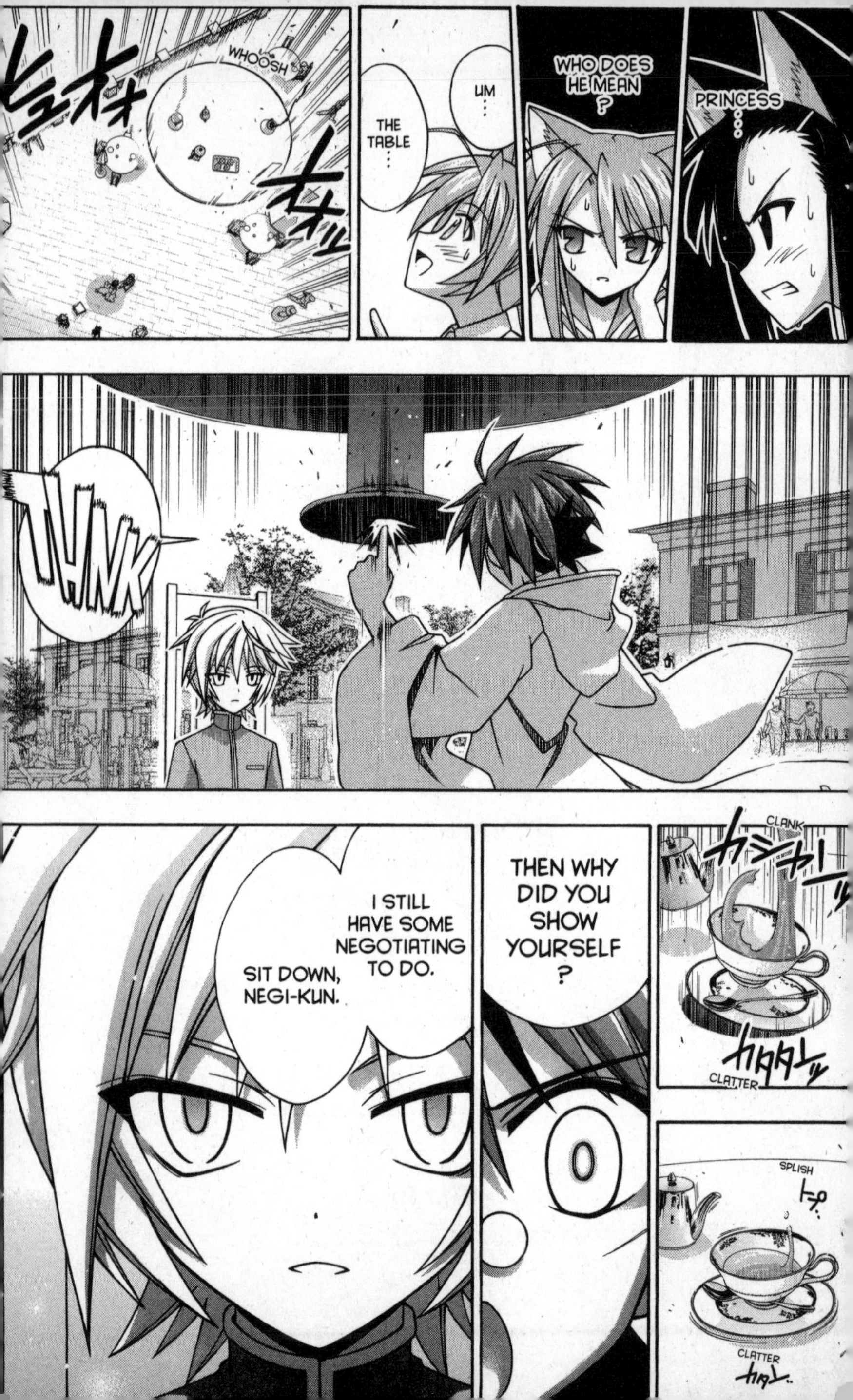
PRINCESS...
WHO DOES HE MEAN?
UM...
THE TABLE...
WHOOSH
THNK
CLANK
CLATTER
SPLISH
CLATTER
THEN WHY DID YOU SHOW YOURSELF?
I STILL HAVE SOME NEGOTIATING TO DO.
SIT DOWN, NEGI-KUN.

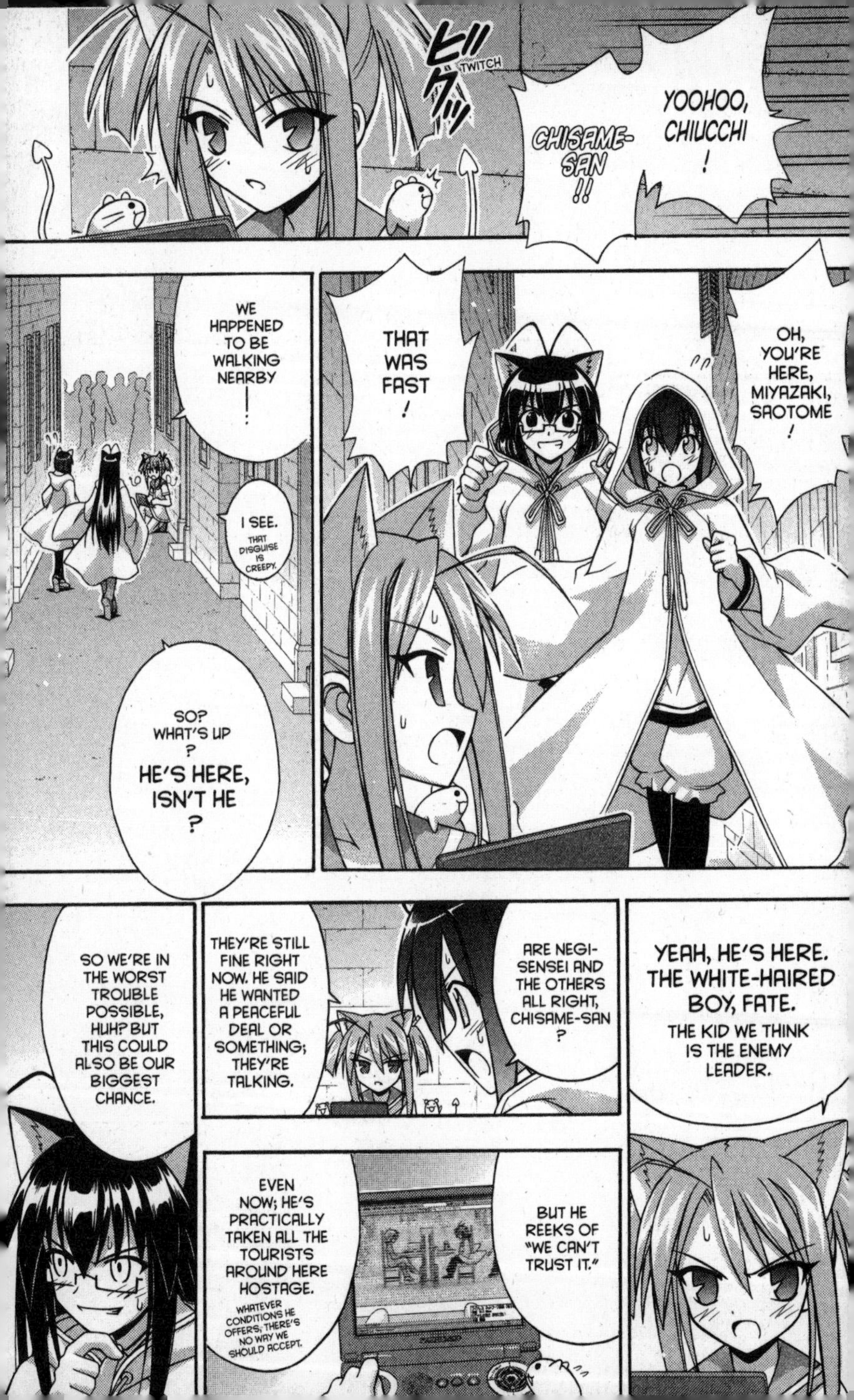

TWITCH
YOOHOO, CHIUCCHI!
CHISAME-SAN!!
OH, YOU'RE HERE, MIYAZAKI, SAOTOME!
THAT WAS FAST!
WE HAPPENED TO BE WALKING NEARBY!
I SEE. THAT DISGUISE IS CREEPY.
SO? WHAT'S UP? HE'S HERE, ISN'T HE?
YEAH, HE'S HERE. THE WHITE-HAIRED BOY, FATE. THE KID WE THINK IS THE ENEMY LEADER.
ARE NEGI-SENSEI AND THE OTHERS ALL RIGHT, CHISAME-SAN?
THEY'RE STILL FINE RIGHT NOW. HE SAID HE WANTED A PEACEFUL DEAL OR SOMETHING; THEY'RE TALKING.
BUT HE REEKS OF "WE CAN'T TRUST IT."
EVEN NOW; HE'S PRACTICALLY TAKEN ALL THE TOURISTS AROUND HERE HOSTAGE.
WHATEVER CONDITIONS HE OFFERS; THERE'S NO WAY WE SHOULD ACCEPT.
SO WE'RE IN THE WORST TROUBLE POSSIBLE, HUH? BUT THIS COULD ALSO BE OUR BIGGEST CHANCE.

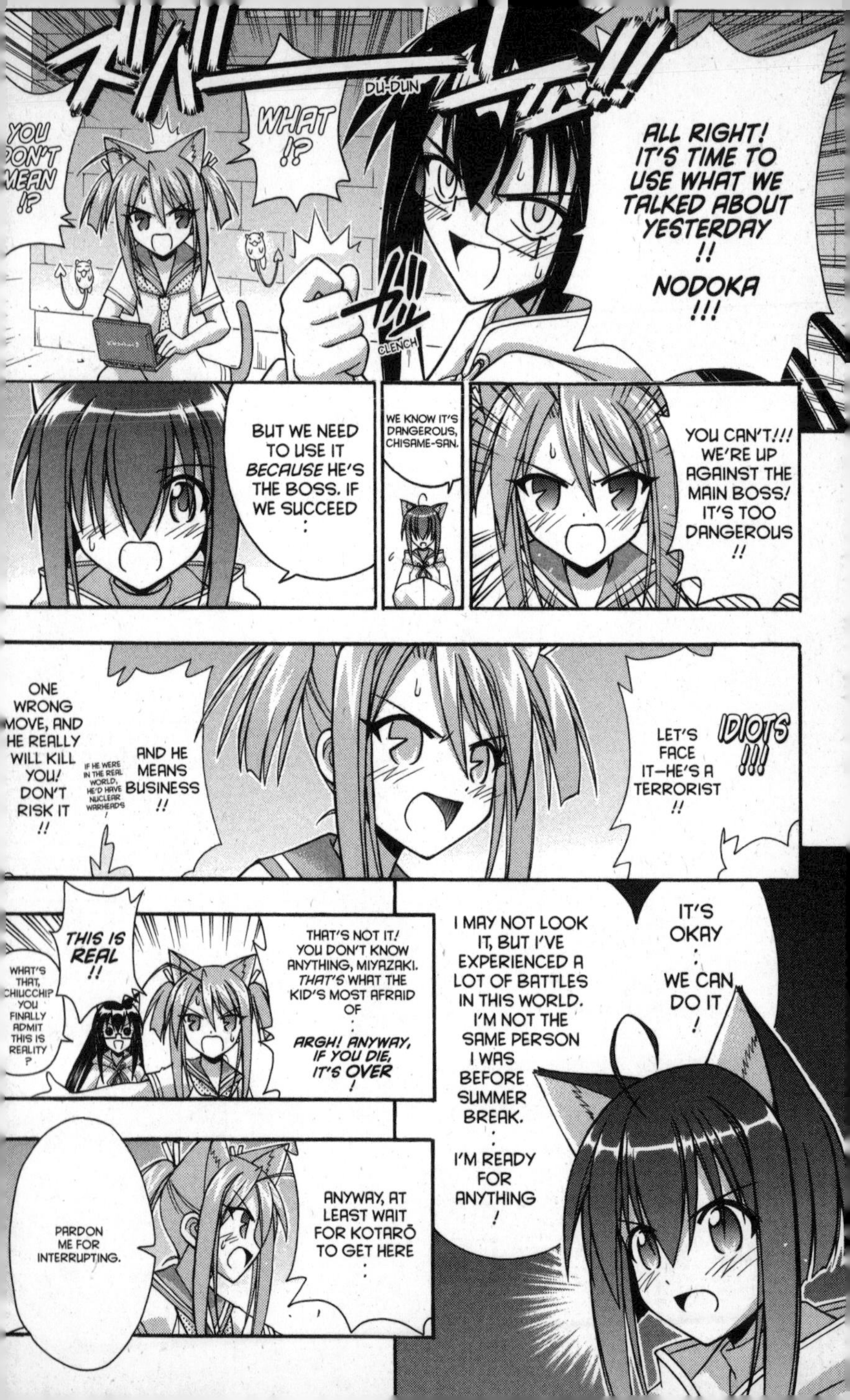

ALL RIGHT! IT'S TIME TO USE WHAT WE TALKED ABOUT YESTERDAY !! NODOKA !!!
DU-DUN
CLENCH
WHAT !?
YOU DON'T MEAN !?
YOU CAN'T!!! WE'RE UP AGAINST THE MAIN BOSS! IT'S TOO DANGEROUS !!
WE KNOW IT'S DANGEROUS, CHISAME-SAN.
BUT WE NEED TO USE IT *BECAUSE* HE'S THE BOSS. IF WE SUCCEED :
IDIOTS !!!
LET'S FACE IT—HE'S A TERRORIST !!
AND HE MEANS BUSINESS !!
IF HE WERE IN THE REAL WORLD, HE'D HAVE NUCLEAR WARHEADS !
ONE WRONG MOVE, AND HE REALLY WILL KILL YOU! DON'T RISK IT !!
IT'S OKAY : WE CAN DO IT !
I MAY NOT LOOK IT, BUT I'VE EXPERIENCED A LOT OF BATTLES IN THIS WORLD. I'M NOT THE SAME PERSON I WAS BEFORE SUMMER BREAK. : I'M READY FOR ANYTHING !
THAT'S NOT IT! YOU DON'T KNOW ANYTHING, MIYAZAKI. *THAT'S* WHAT THE KID'S MOST AFRAID OF : ARGH! ANYWAY, IF YOU DIE, IT'S OVER !
THIS IS REAL !!
WHAT'S THAT, CHIUCCHI? YOU FINALLY ADMIT THIS IS REALITY ?
ANYWAY, AT LEAST WAIT FOR KOTARŌ TO GET HERE :
PARDON ME FOR INTERRUPTING.

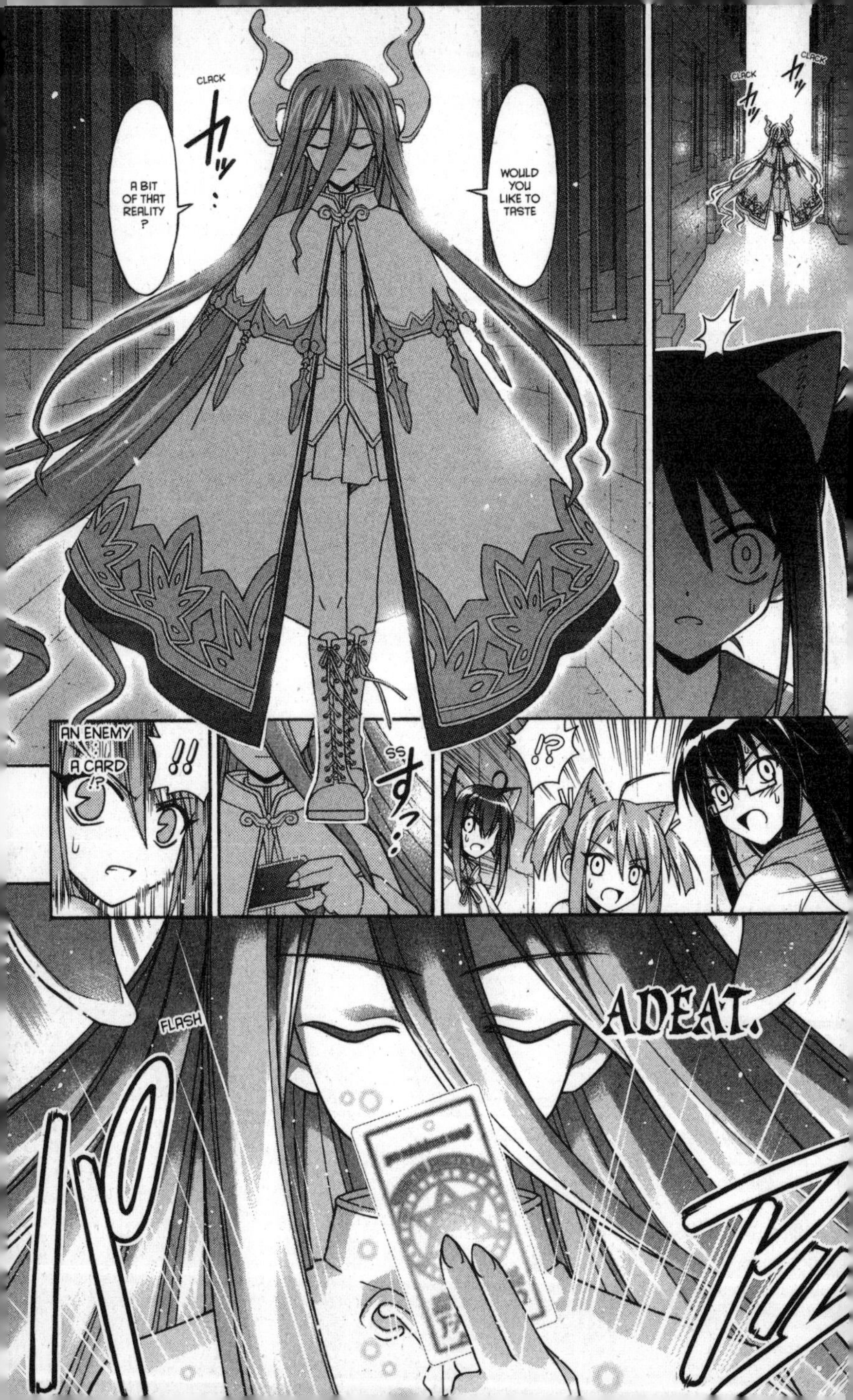
CLACK
CLACK
WOULD YOU LIKE TO TASTE
CLACK
A BIT OF THAT REALITY?
!?
AN ENEMY A CARD !?
!!
SS
ADEAT.
FLASH

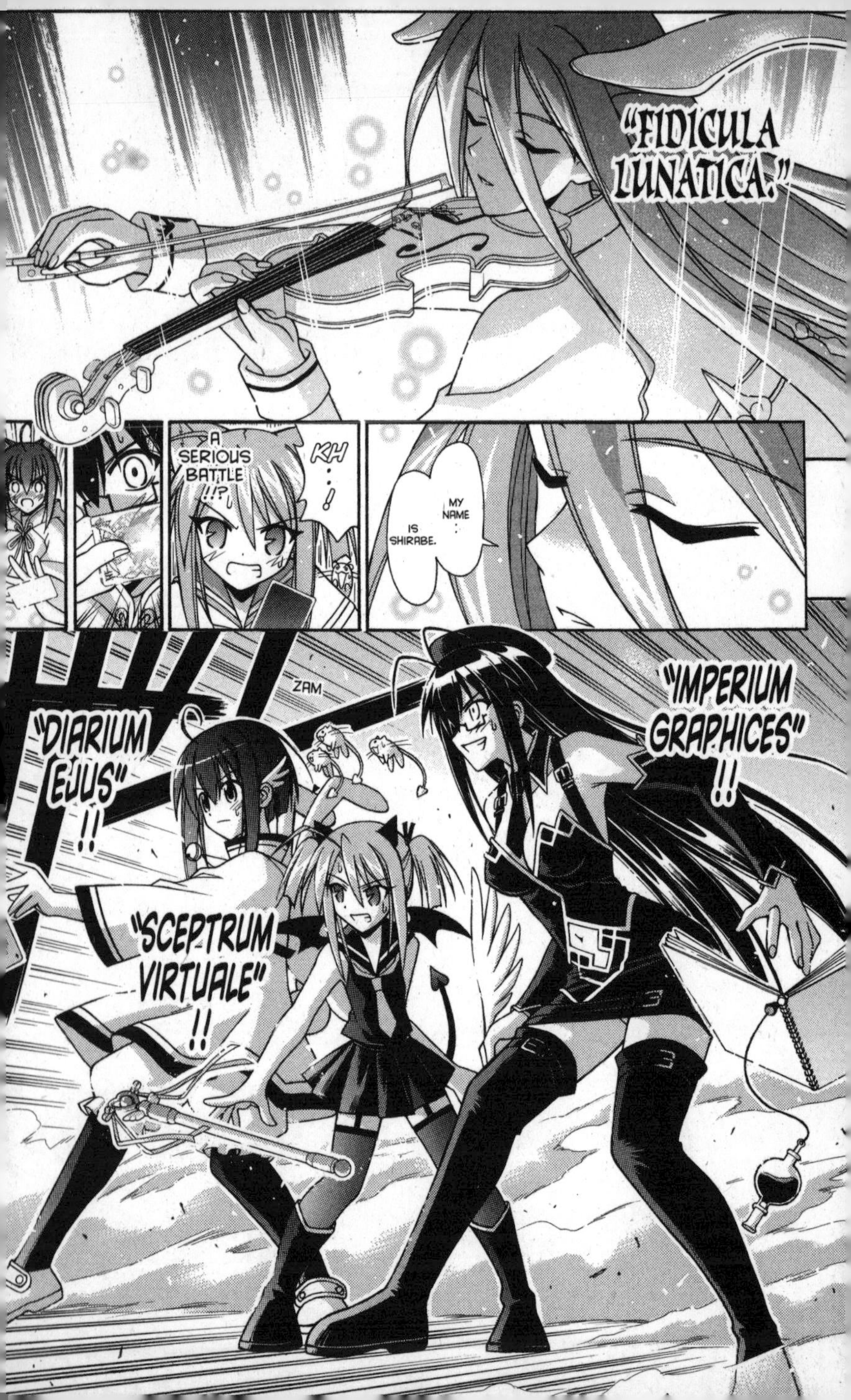
"FIDICULA LUNATICA."
MY NAME : IS SHIRABE.
KH . . . !
A SERIOUS BATTLE !!?
"IMPERIUM GRAPHICES" !!
ZAM
"DIARIUM EJUS" !!
"SCEPTRUM VIRTUALE" !!

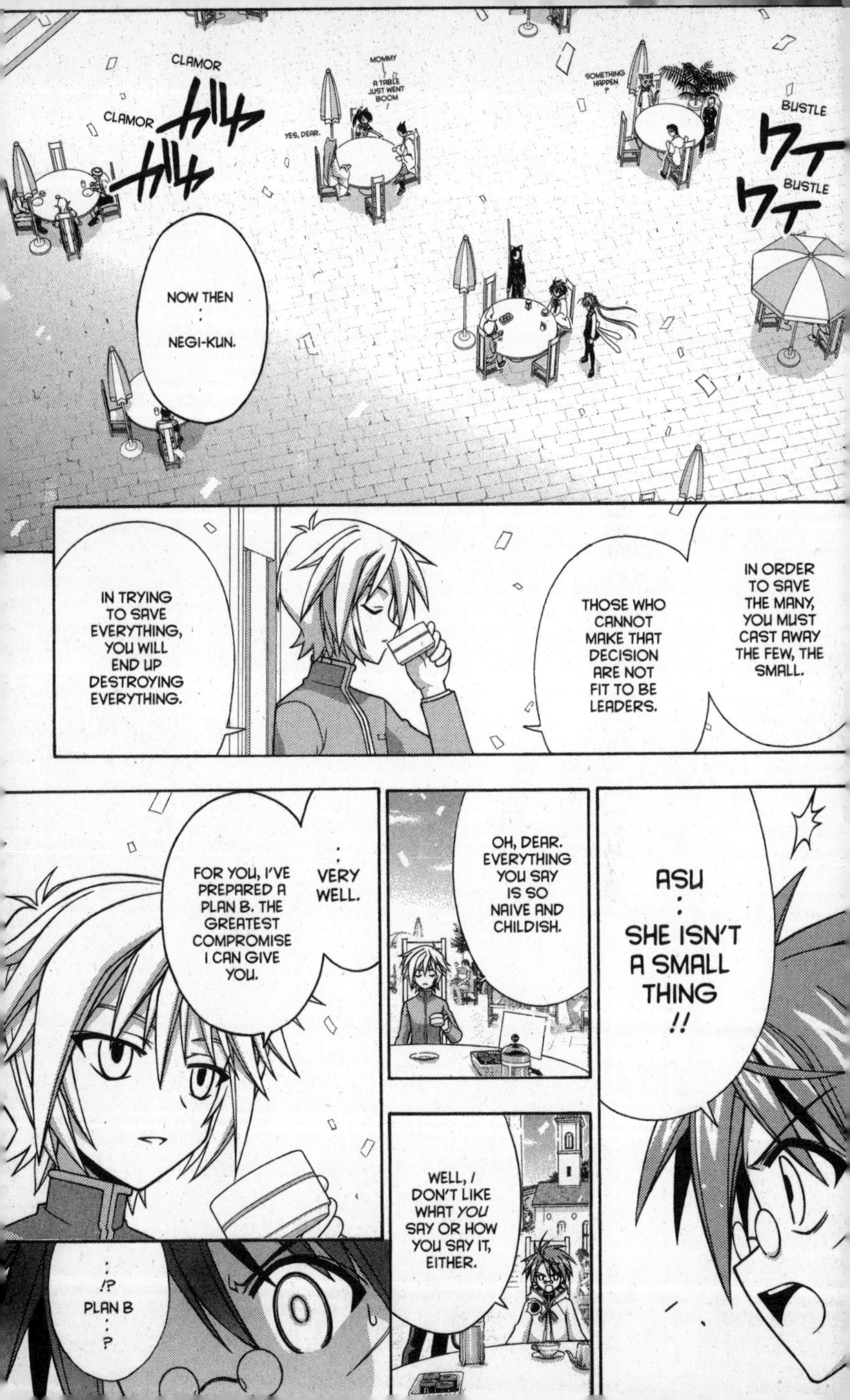
BUSTLE
ワイ
BUSTLE
ワイ
SOMETHING HAPPEN?
MOMMY! A TABLE JUST WENT BOOM
YES, DEAR.
CLAMOR
ガヤ
CLAMOR
ガヤ
NOW THEN : NEGI-KUN.
IN ORDER TO SAVE THE MANY, YOU MUST CAST AWAY THE FEW, THE SMALL.
THOSE WHO CANNOT MAKE THAT DECISION ARE NOT FIT TO BE LEADERS.
IN TRYING TO SAVE EVERYTHING, YOU WILL END UP DESTROYING EVERYTHING.
ASU : SHE ISN'T A SMALL THING !!
OH, DEAR. EVERYTHING YOU SAY IS SO NAIVE AND CHILDISH.
WELL, I DON'T LIKE WHAT *YOU* SAY OR HOW YOU SAY IT, EITHER.
: VERY WELL.
FOR YOU, I'VE PREPARED A PLAN B. THE GREATEST COMPROMISE I CAN GIVE YOU.
. . !? PLAN B . . . ?

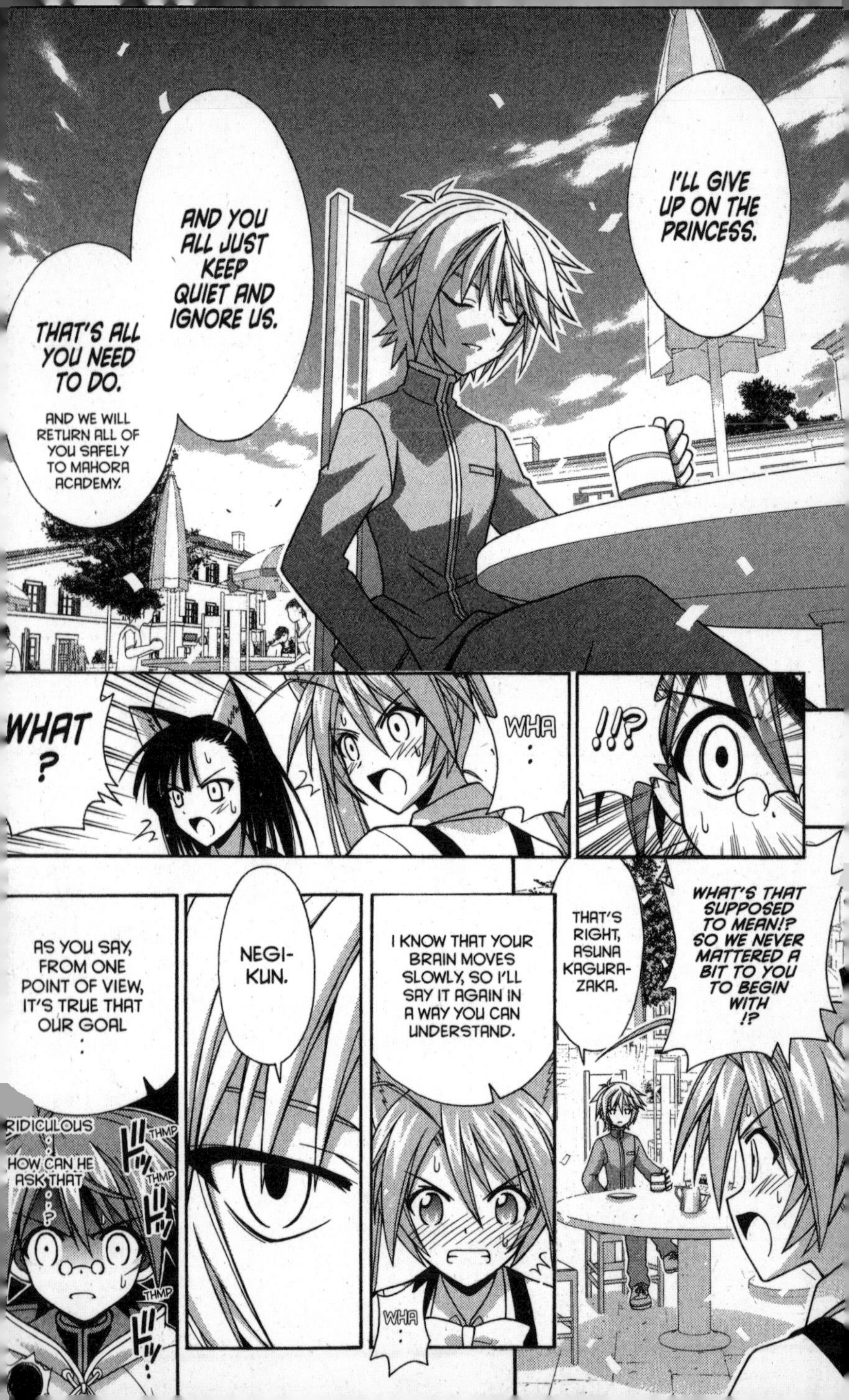
I'LL GIVE UP ON THE PRINCESS.
AND YOU ALL JUST KEEP QUIET AND IGNORE US.
THAT'S ALL YOU NEED TO DO.
AND WE WILL RETURN ALL OF YOU SAFELY TO MAHORA ACADEMY.
!!?
WHA :
WHAT ?
WHAT'S THAT SUPPOSED TO MEAN!? SO WE NEVER MATTERED A BIT TO YOU TO BEGIN WITH !?
THAT'S RIGHT, ASUNA KAGURA-ZAKA.
I KNOW THAT YOUR BRAIN MOVES SLOWLY, SO I'LL SAY IT AGAIN IN A WAY YOU CAN UNDERSTAND.
WHA :
NEGI-KUN.
AS YOU SAY, FROM ONE POINT OF VIEW, IT'S TRUE THAT OUR GOAL :
RIDICULOUS ...
HOW CAN HE ASK THAT ...?
THMP
THMP
THMP

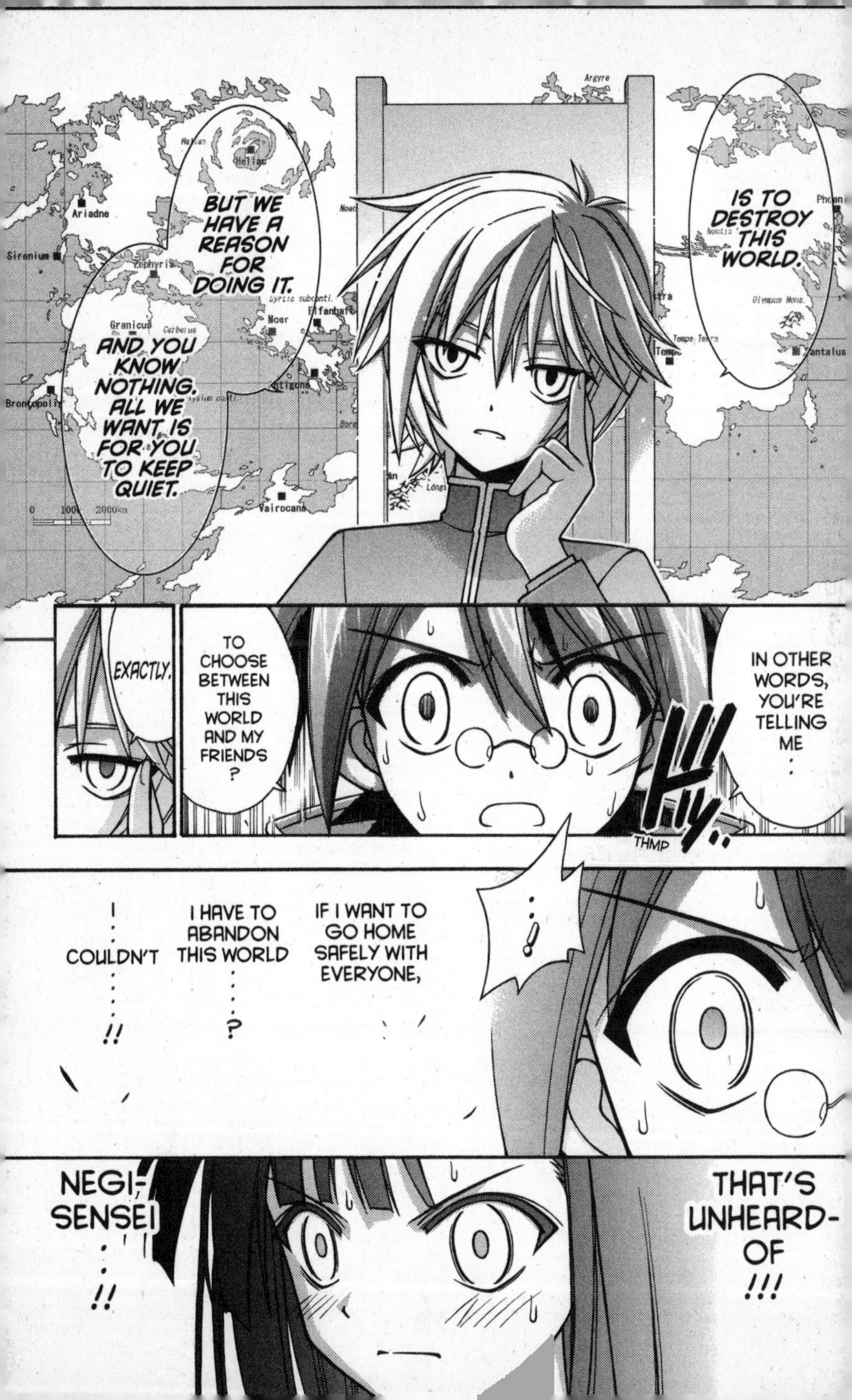
IS TO DESTROY THIS WORLD.
BUT WE HAVE A REASON FOR DOING IT.
AND YOU KNOW NOTHING. ALL WE WANT IS FOR YOU TO KEEP QUIET.
Argyre
Ariadne
Sirenium
Zephyria
Granicus
Vairocana
Tantalus
IN OTHER WORDS, YOU'RE TELLING ME ...
THMP
TO CHOOSE BETWEEN THIS WORLD AND MY FRIENDS?
EXACTLY.
...!
IF I WANT TO GO HOME SAFELY WITH EVERYONE,
I HAVE TO ABANDON THIS WORLD ....?
I ... COULDN'T ....!!
THAT'S UNHEARD-OF!!!
NEGI-SENSEI ...!!

YOU SHOULD ACCEPT FOR NOW!
THERE'S NO GUARANTEE THEY'LL KEEP THEIR PROMISE.
BUT ANYWAY, IF WE GIVE IN TO HIS DEMANDS, WE CAN GET OUT OF THIS HOSTAGE SITUATION!
SENSEI...
YOU ONLY HAVE TO *PRETEND* TO ACCEPT!!
IT WOULD BE BEST TO FIRST BUY SOME TIME AND GET HELP FROM RAKAN-SAN AND THE MILITARY...
NO, WAIT! SOME-THING'S NOT RIGHT.
IT CAN'T BE THAT EASY.
IF THEY JUST WANTED TO PRESENT THESE OVERLY KIND DEMANDS, THERE WOULD BE NO POINT IN THIS BOY TAKING THE TIME TO SEE US.
WHAT IF, FOR EXAMPLE, HE HAS A POWERFUL MAGIC ITEM OR ARTIFACT THAT FORCES THE FULFILLMENT OF A PROMISE?
IN THAT CASE, WE WOULD HAVE TO ANSWER HIM HONESTLY.
NO, I GET THE FEELING THAT THESE DEMANDS WERE SET UP FROM THE BEGINNING JUST TO DRIVE NEGI-SENSEI INTO A CORNER.
EITHER WAY, I SENSE A STRANGE ATTACHMENT TO NEGI-SENSEI IN THIS BOY'S ACTIONS.
NEGI-SE...
WHAT REASON DO YOU HAVE TO HESITATE, NEGI-KUN?

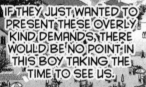

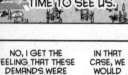

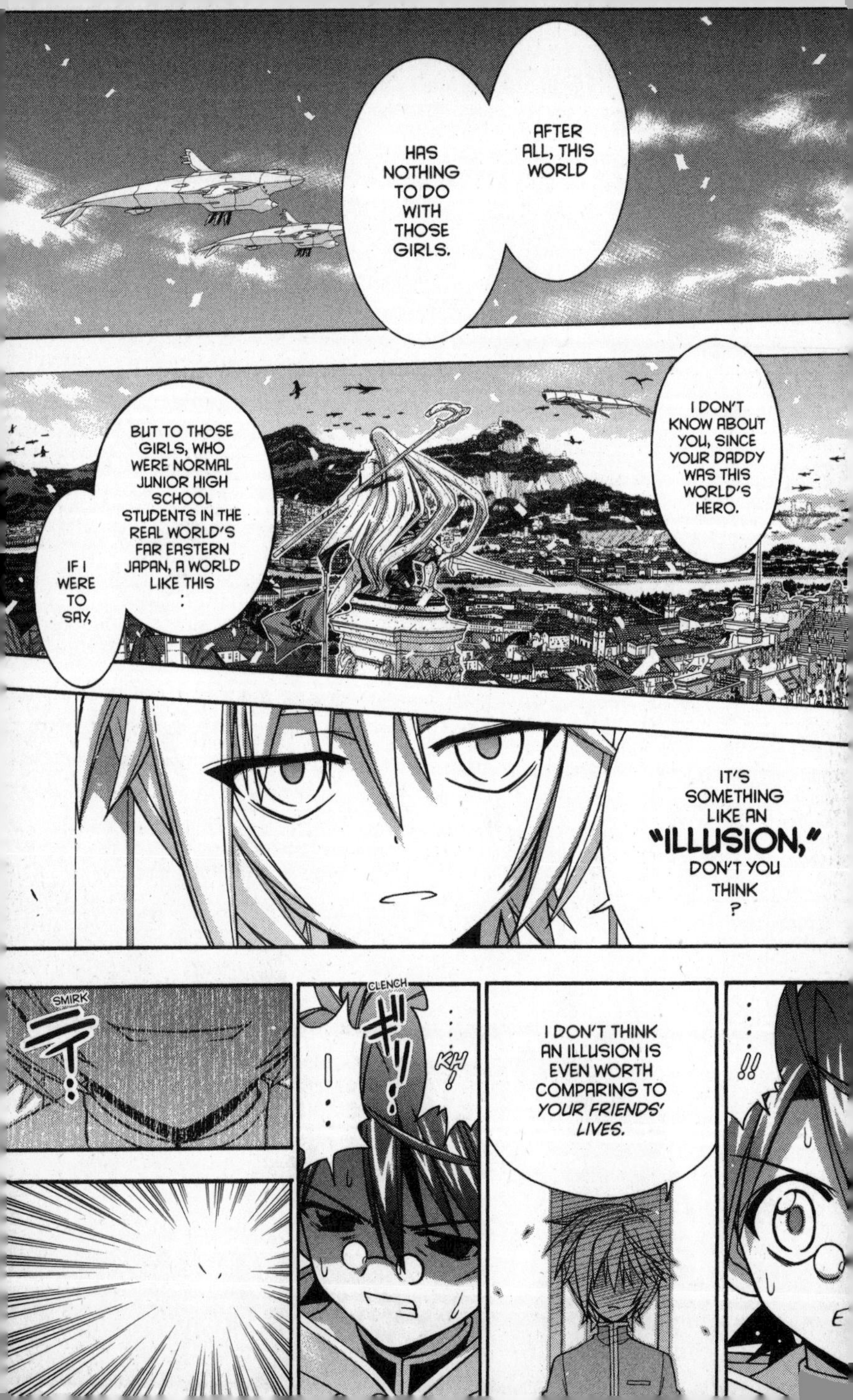
AFTER ALL, THIS WORLD
HAS NOTHING TO DO WITH THOSE GIRLS.
I DON'T KNOW ABOUT YOU, SINCE YOUR DADDY WAS THIS WORLD'S HERO.
BUT TO THOSE GIRLS, WHO WERE NORMAL JUNIOR HIGH SCHOOL STUDENTS IN THE REAL WORLD'S FAR EASTERN JAPAN, A WORLD LIKE THIS :
IF I WERE TO SAY,
IT'S SOMETHING LIKE AN "ILLUSION," DON'T YOU THINK ?
.....!!
I DON'T THINK AN ILLUSION IS EVEN WORTH COMPARING TO *YOUR FRIENDS'* LIVES.
CLENCH
ギリッ
KH!
.....
...!
SMIRK
ニィ

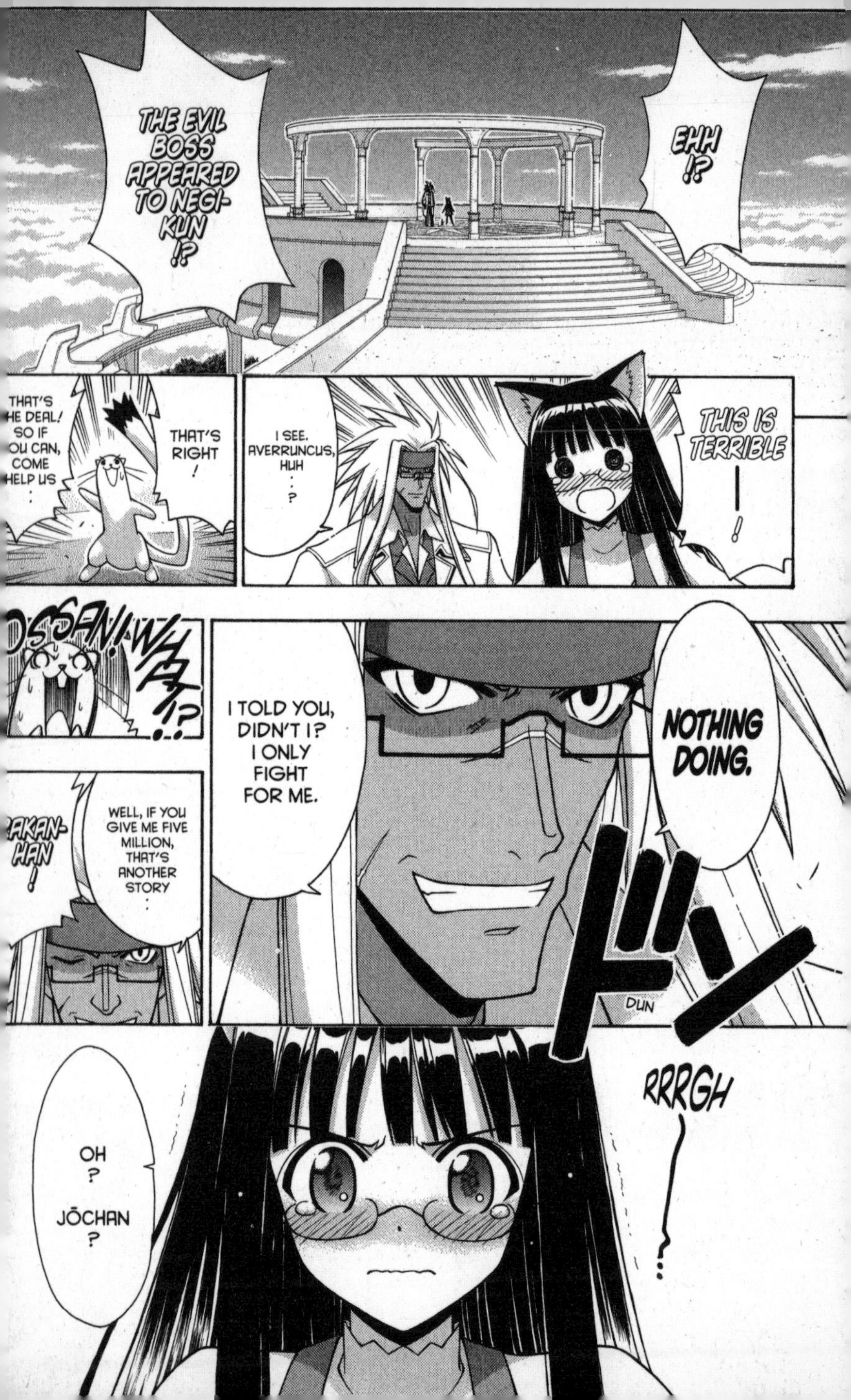
EHH !?
THE EVIL BOSS APPEARED TO NEGI-KUN !?
THIS IS TERRIBLE !
I SEE. AVERRUNCUS, HUH . . ?
THAT'S RIGHT !
THAT'S HE DEAL! SO IF OU CAN, COME HELP US . .
NOTHING DOING.
I TOLD YOU, DIDN'T I? I ONLY FIGHT FOR ME.
DUN
OSSAN! WHAT!?
AKAN-HAN !
WELL, IF YOU GIVE ME FIVE MILLION, THAT'S ANOTHER STORY . .
RRRGH . . .
OH ? JŌCHAN ?

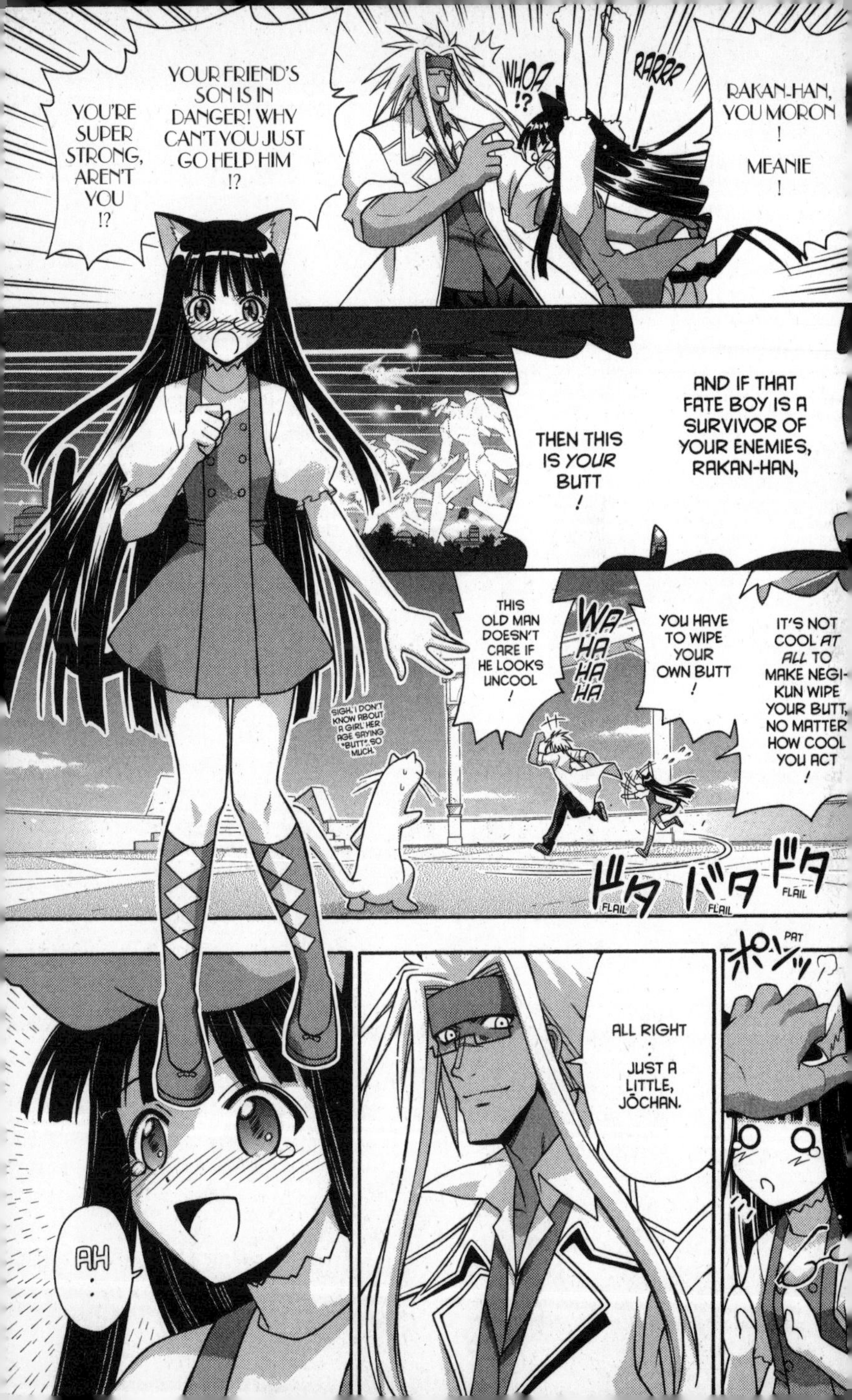
RAKAN-HAN, YOU MORON !
MEANIE !
RARRR
WHOA !?
YOUR FRIEND'S SON IS IN DANGER! WHY CAN'T YOU JUST GO HELP HIM !?
YOU'RE SUPER STRONG, AREN'T YOU !?
AND IF THAT FATE BOY IS A SURVIVOR OF YOUR ENEMIES, RAKAN-HAN,
THEN THIS IS *YOUR* BUTT !
IT'S NOT COOL *AT ALL* TO MAKE NEGI-KUN WIPE YOUR BUTT, NO MATTER HOW COOL YOU ACT !
YOU HAVE TO WIPE YOUR OWN BUTT !
WA HA HA HA HA
THIS OLD MAN DOESN'T CARE IF HE LOOKS UNCOOL !
SIGH, I DON'T KNOW ABOUT A GIRL HER AGE SAYING "BUTT" SO MUCH.
ドタ FLAIL バタ FLAIL ドタ FLAIL
ポンッ PAT
ALL RIGHT . JUST A LITTLE, JŌCHAN.
AH . .

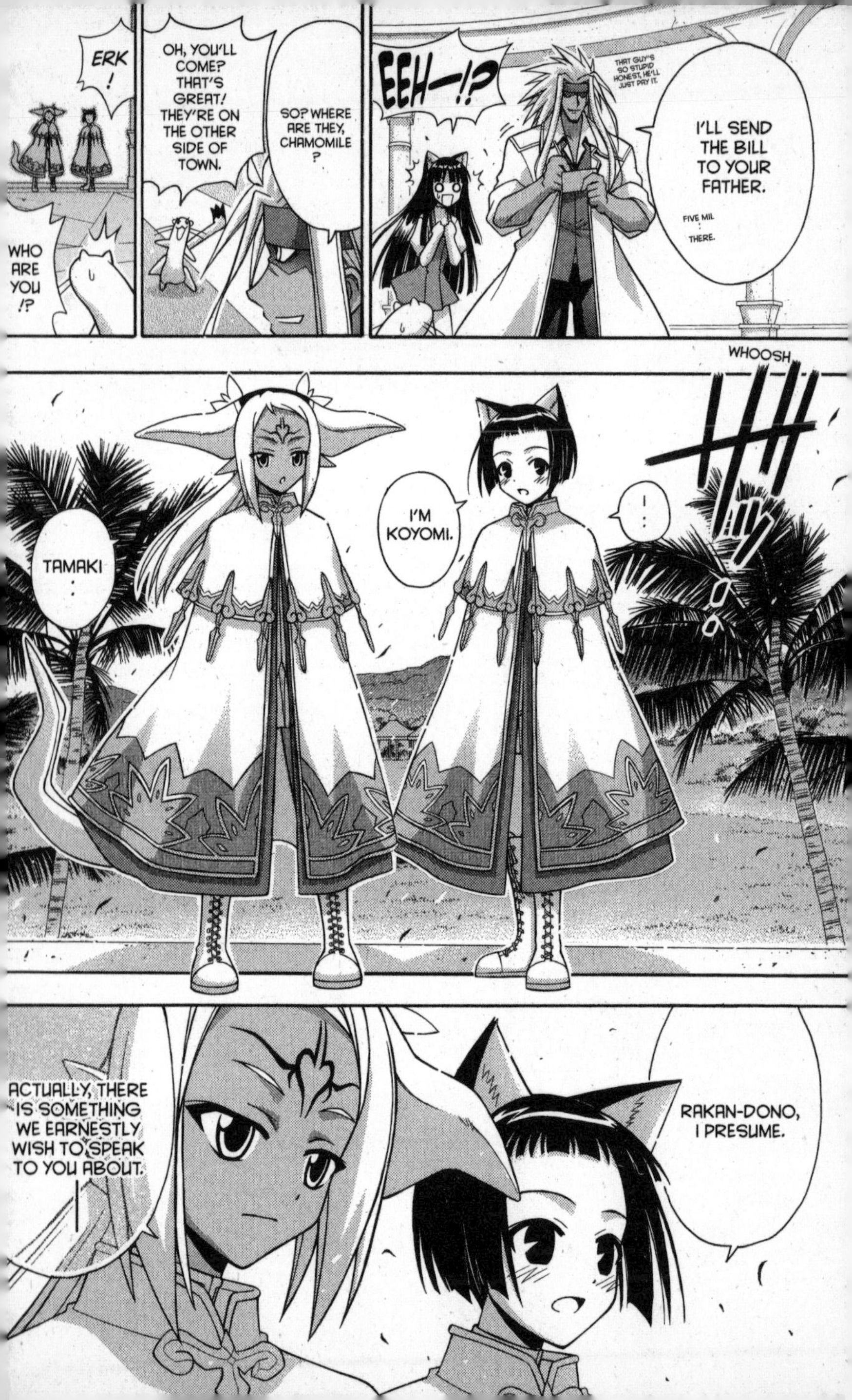

I'LL SEND THE BILL TO YOUR FATHER.
THAT GUY'S SO STUPID HONEST, HE'LL JUST PAY IT.
EEH—!?
FIVE MIL : THERE.
SO? WHERE ARE THEY, CHAMOMILE ?
OH, YOU'LL COME? THAT'S GREAT! THEY'RE ON THE OTHER SIDE OF TOWN.
ERK !
WHO ARE YOU !?
WHOOSH
! . .
I'M KOYOMI.
TAMAKI . .
RAKAN-DONO, I PRESUME.
ACTUALLY, THERE IS SOMETHING WE EARNESTLY WISH TO SPEAK TO YOU ABOUT.

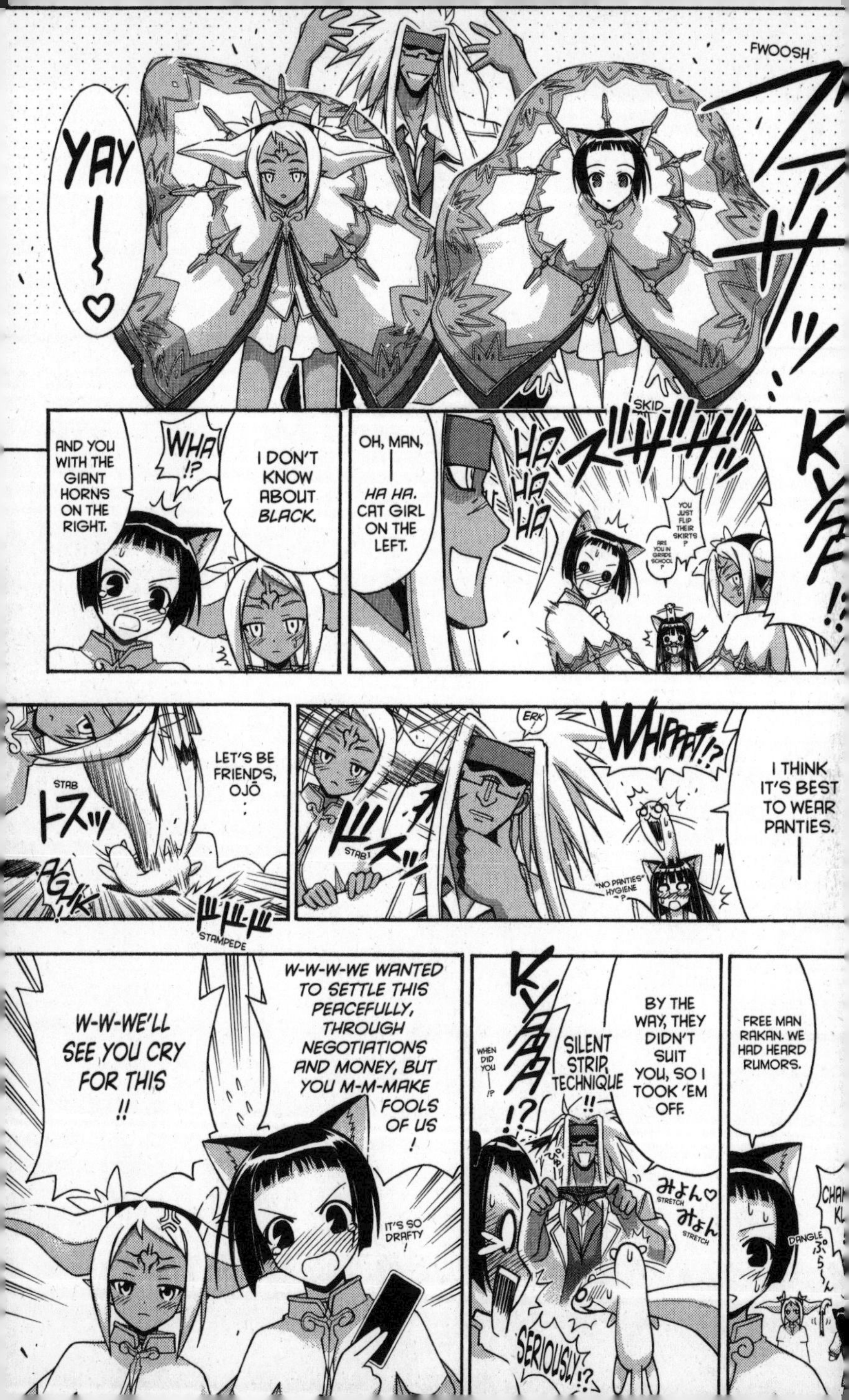
FWOOSH
ファサッ
YAY!~♡
KYAA!!
SKID
ズザザザ
HA HA HA
OH, MAN, — HA HA. CAT GIRL ON THE LEFT.
YOU JUST FLIP THEIR SKIRTS!?
ARE YOU IN GRADE SCHOOL!?
I DON'T KNOW ABOUT BLACK.
WHA!?
AND YOU WITH THE GIANT HORNS ON THE RIGHT.
I THINK IT'S BEST TO WEAR PANTIES. —
WHAAT!?
ERK
"NO PANTIES" HYGIENE...?
STAB
ドスッ
LET'S BE FRIENDS, OJŌ
STAB
トスッ
AGHK!
ドドドド
STAMPEDE
FREE MAN RAKAN. WE HAD HEARD RUMORS.
DANGLE
ぷら~ん
BY THE WAY, THEY DIDN'T SUIT YOU, SO I TOOK 'EM OFF.
SILENT STRIP TECHNIQUE!!
KYAAA!?
WHEN DID YOU—!?
みょん♡
STRETCH
みょん
STRETCH
SERIOUSLY!?
W-W-W-WE WANTED TO SETTLE THIS PEACEFULLY, THROUGH NEGOTIATIONS AND MONEY, BUT YOU M-M-MAKE FOOLS OF US!
IT'S SO DRAFTY
W-W-WE'LL SEE YOU CRY FOR THIS!!

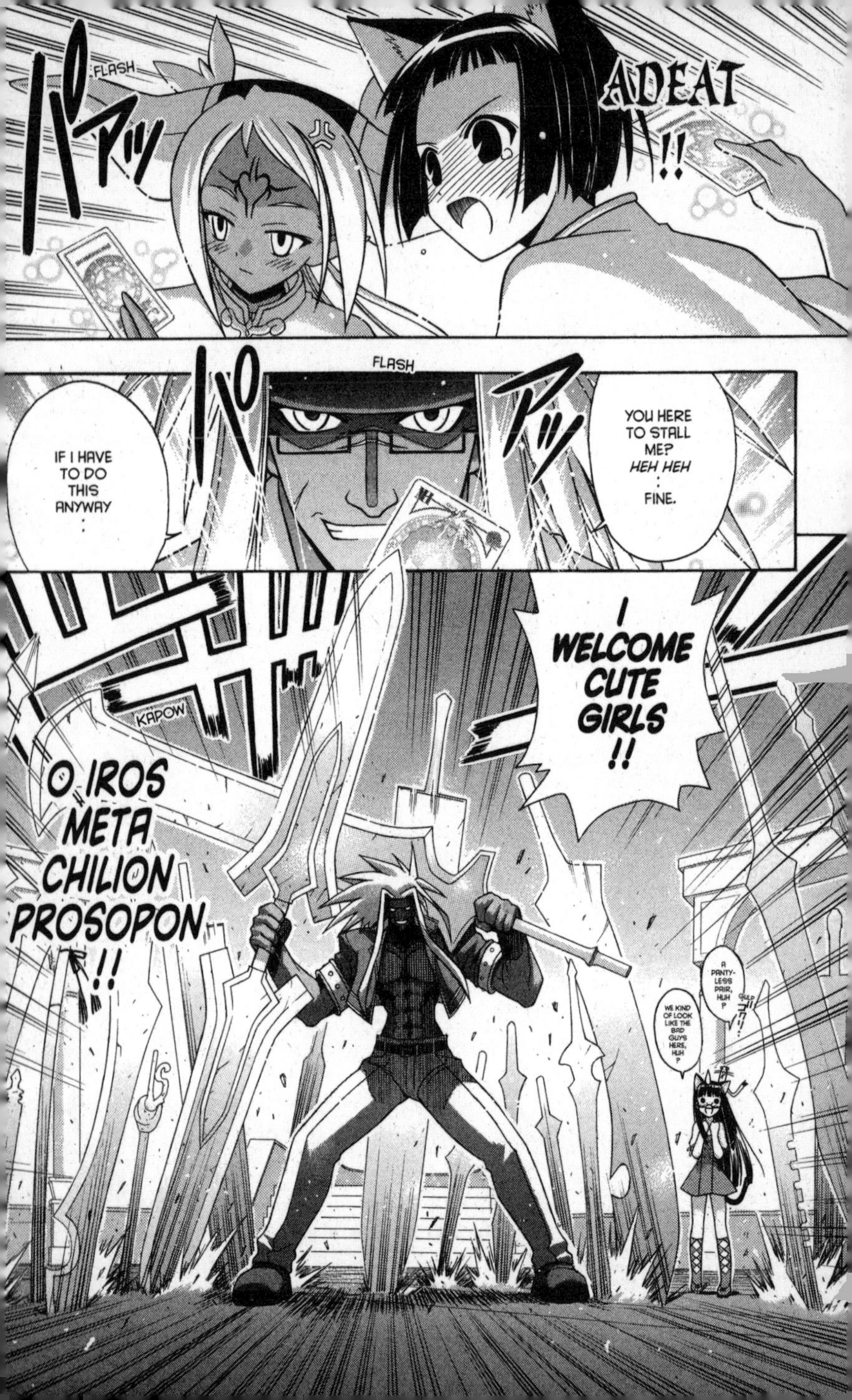
ADEAT!!
FLASH
YOU HERE TO STALL ME? HEH HEH : FINE.
FLASH
IF I HAVE TO DO THIS ANYWAY :
I WELCOME CUTE GIRLS!!
KAPOW
O IROS META CHILION PROSOPON!!
A PANTY-LESS PAIR, HUH?
GULP
WE KIND OF LOOK LIKE THE BAD GUYS HERE, HUH?

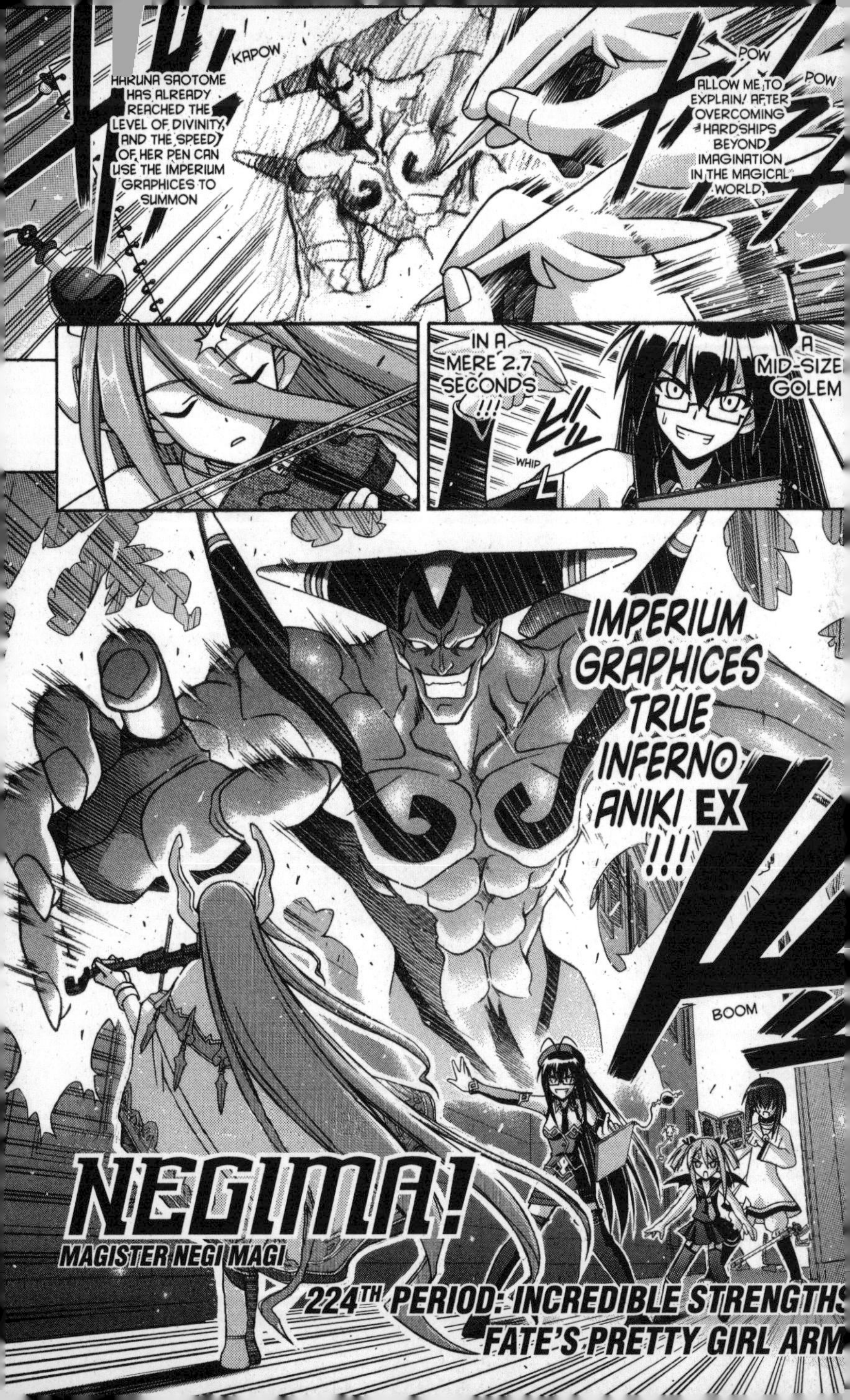
POW
POW
ALLOW ME TO EXPLAIN! AFTER OVERCOMING HARDSHIPS BEYOND IMAGINATION IN THE MAGICAL WORLD,
KAPOW
HARUNA SAOTOME HAS ALREADY REACHED THE LEVEL OF DIVINITY, AND THE SPEED OF HER PEN CAN USE THE IMPERIUM GRAPHICES TO SUMMON
A MID-SIZE GOLEM
IN A MERE 2.7 SECONDS !!!
WHIP
IMPERIUM GRAPHICES TRUE INFERNO ANIKI EX !!!
BOOM
NEGIMA!
MAGISTER NEGI MAGI
224TH PERIOD: INCREDIBLE STRENGTHS
FATE'S PRETTY GIRL ARM

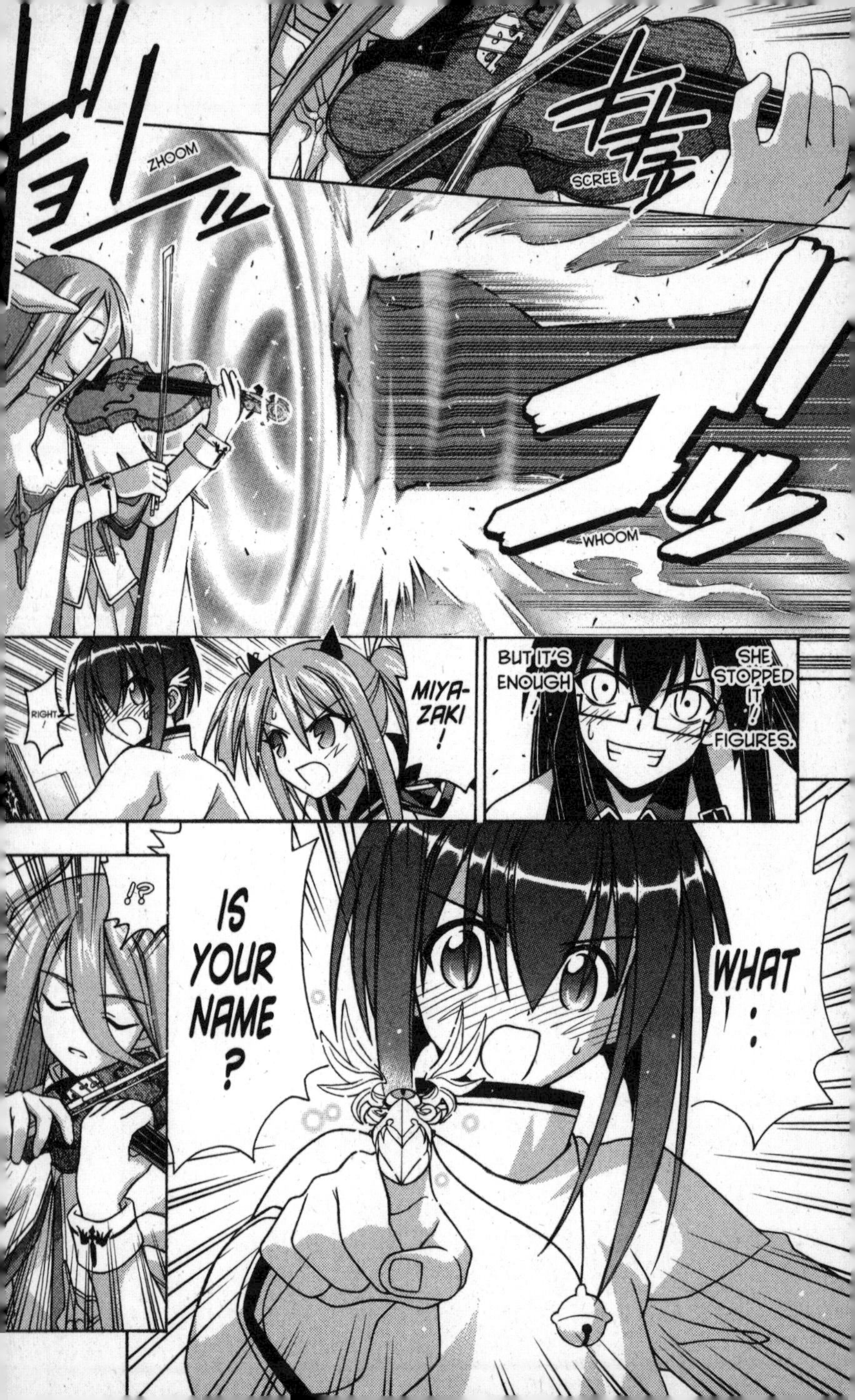
SCREE
ZHOOM
WHOOM
SHE STOPPED IT!
BUT IT'S ENOUGH
FIGURES.
MIYA-ZAKI!
RIGHT!
WHAT
IS YOUR NAME?
!?

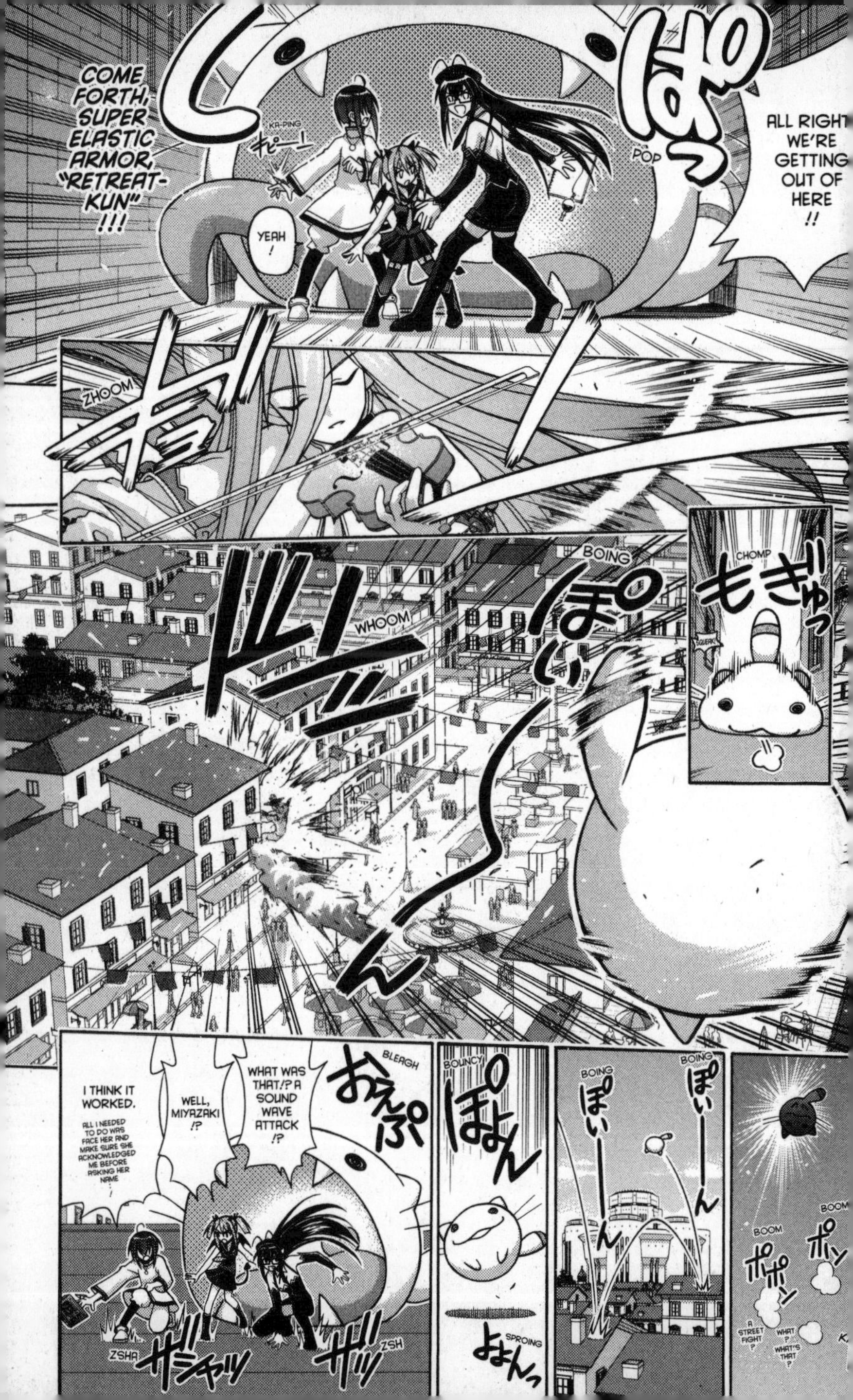
ALL RIGHT WE'RE GETTING OUT OF HERE !!
POP
ぱっ
KA-PING
キピーン
COME FORTH, SUPER ELASTIC ARMOR, "RETREAT-KUN" !!!
YEAH !
ZHOOM
CHOMP
もぎゅっ
SQUEAK
BOING
ぽい
WHOOM
ド
BOOM
ポン
BOOM
ポポン
A STREET FIGHT ?
WHAT ? WHAT'S THAT ?
BOING
ぽいーん
BOING
ぽいーん
BOUNCY
ぽよん
SPROING
よよんっ
BLEAGH
おえっぷ
WHAT WAS THAT!? A SOUND WAVE ATTACK !?
WELL, MIYAZAKI !?
I THINK IT WORKED.
ALL I NEEDED TO DO WAS FACE HER AND MAKE SURE SHE ACKNOWLEDGED ME BEFORE ASKING HER NAME ...!
ZSH
ザッ
ZSHA
ザシャッ

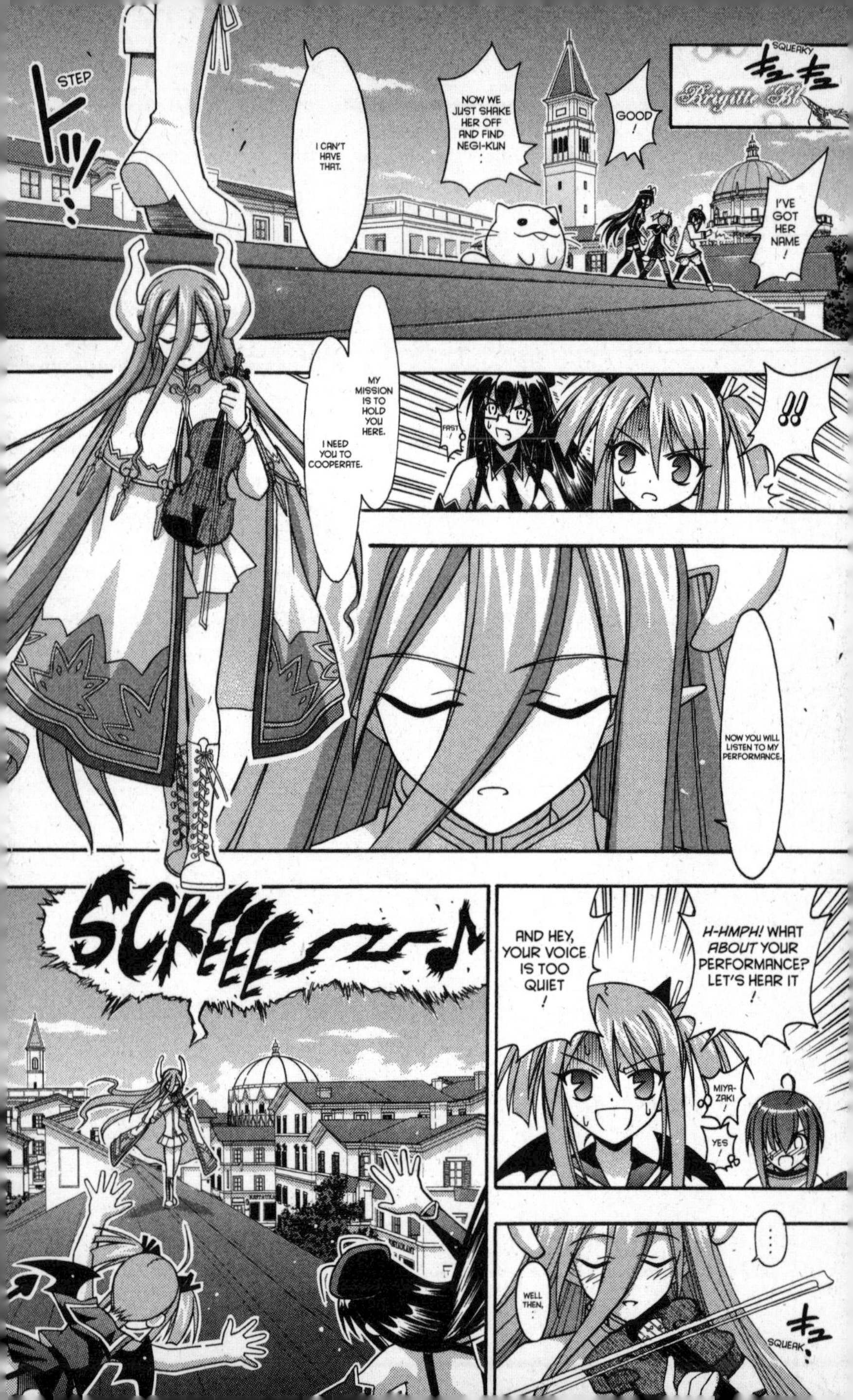
SQUEAKY
Brigitte Bl
I'VE GOT HER NAME!
GOOD!
NOW WE JUST SHAKE HER OFF AND FIND NEGI-KUN...
I CAN'T HAVE THAT.
STEP
MY MISSION IS TO HOLD YOU HERE.
I NEED YOU TO COOPERATE.
!!
FAST!
NOW YOU WILL LISTEN TO MY PERFORMANCE.
H-HMPH! WHAT ABOUT YOUR PERFORMANCE? LET'S HEAR IT!
AND HEY, YOUR VOICE IS TOO QUIET!
MIYAZAKI!
YES!
...
WELL THEN, ...
SQUEAK
SCREEEE♪

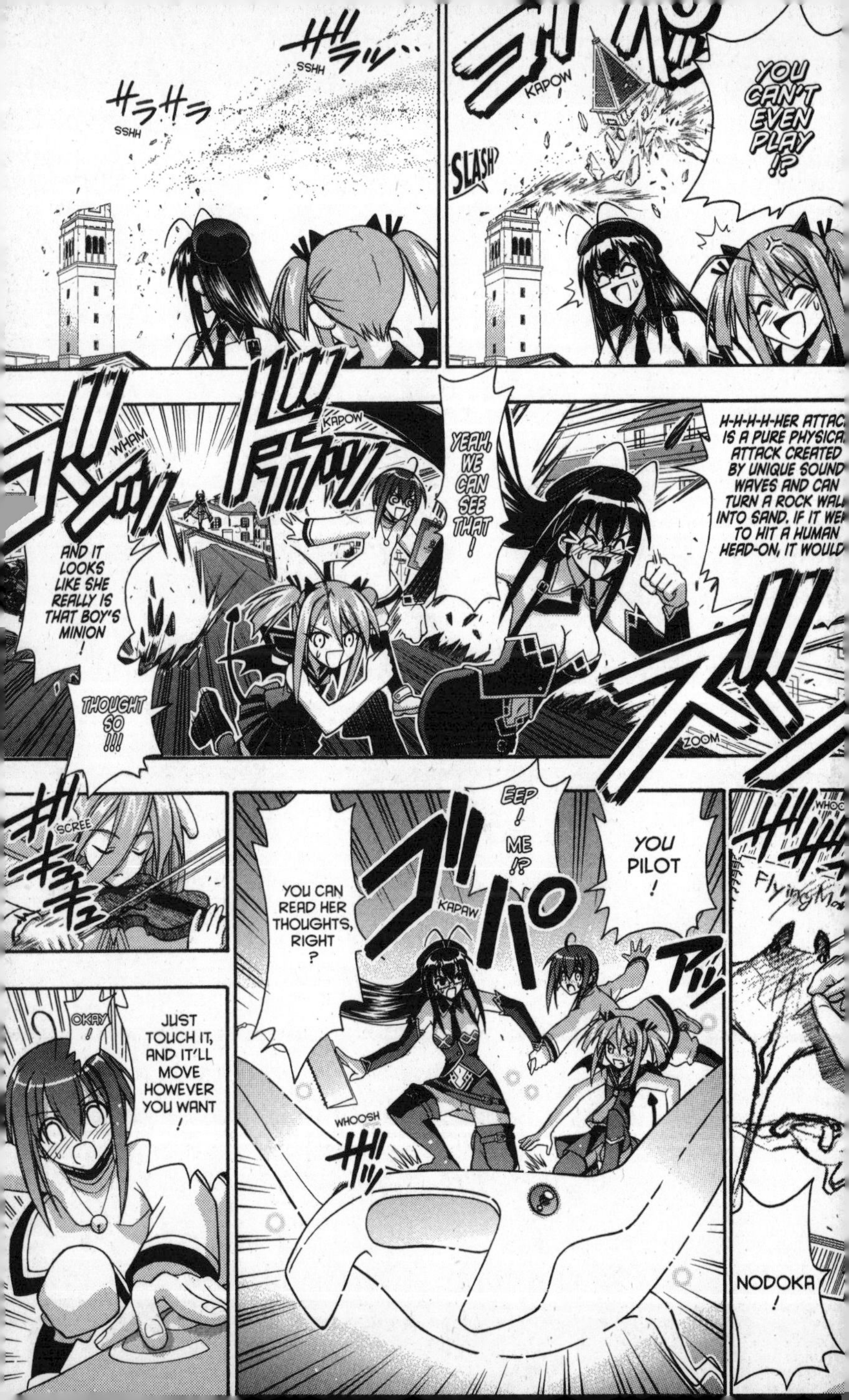
KAPOW
SLASH
YOU CAN'T EVEN PLAY !?
SSHH
SSHH
H-H-H-H-HER ATTAC IS A PURE PHYSICA ATTACK CREATED BY UNIQUE SOUND WAVES AND CAN TURN A ROCK WAL INTO SAND. IF IT WE TO HIT A HUMAN HEAD-ON, IT WOULD
ZOOM
YEAH, WE CAN SEE THAT !
KAPOW
WHAM
AND IT LOOKS LIKE SHE REALLY IS THAT BOY'S MINION !
THOUGHT SO !!!
NODOKA !
YOU PILOT !
EEP ! ME !?
YOU CAN READ HER THOUGHTS, RIGHT ?
KAPAW
WHOOSH
SCREE
OKAY !
JUST TOUCH IT, AND IT'LL MOVE HOWEVER YOU WANT !

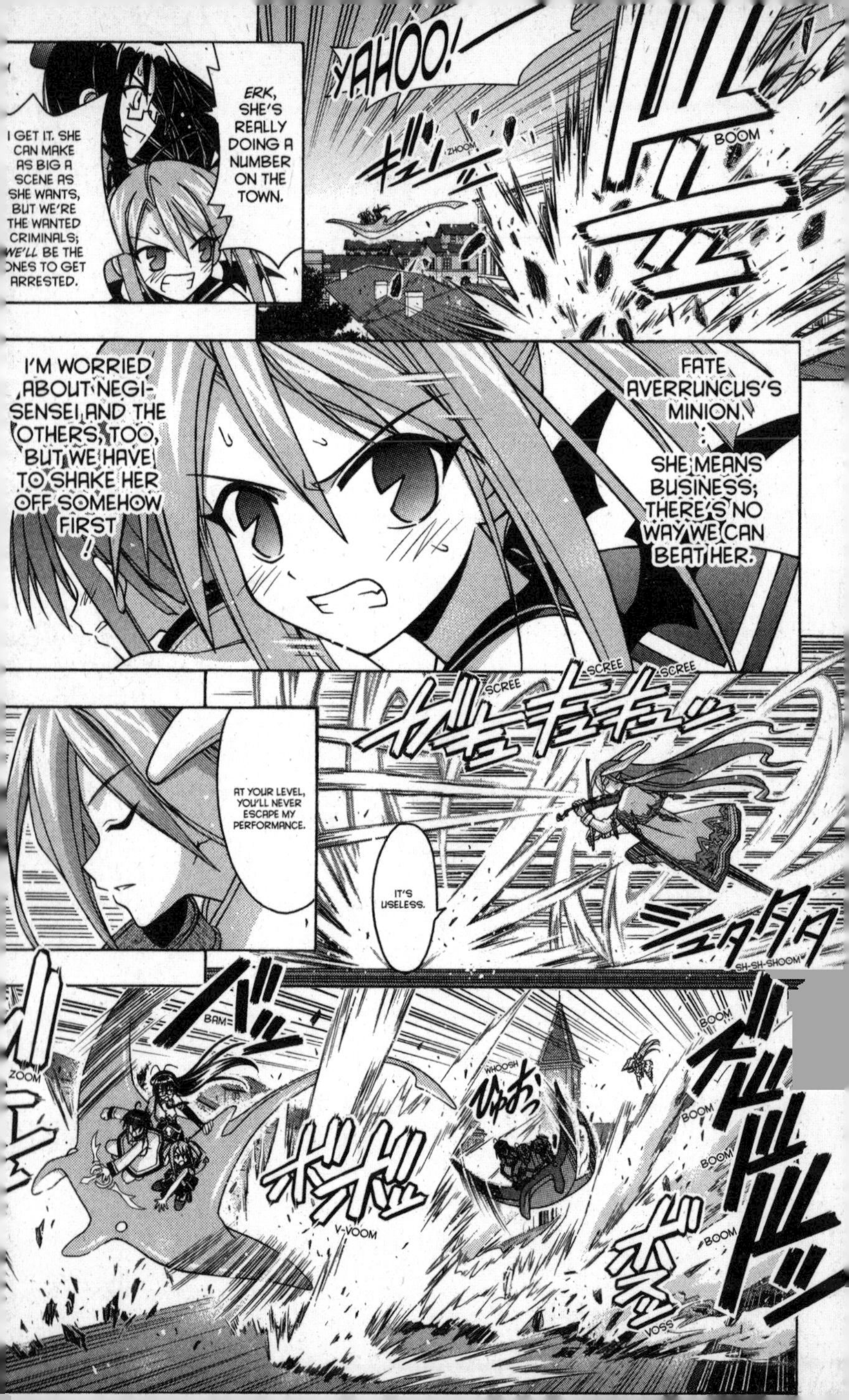
YAHOO!
ZHOOM
BOOM
ERK, SHE'S REALLY DOING A NUMBER ON THE TOWN.
I GET IT. SHE CAN MAKE AS BIG A SCENE AS SHE WANTS, BUT WE'RE THE WANTED CRIMINALS; WE'LL BE THE ONES TO GET ARRESTED.
FATE AVERRUNCUS'S MINION...
SHE MEANS BUSINESS; THERE'S NO WAY WE CAN BEAT HER.
I'M WORRIED ABOUT NEGI-SENSEI AND THE OTHERS, TOO, BUT WE HAVE TO SHAKE HER OFF SOMEHOW FIRST!
SCREE
SCREE
SCREE
SH-SH-SHOOM
AT YOUR LEVEL, YOU'LL NEVER ESCAPE MY PERFORMANCE.
IT'S USELESS.
BOOM
BOOM
BOOM
BOOM
VOSS
WHOOSH
V-VOOM
BAM
ZOOM

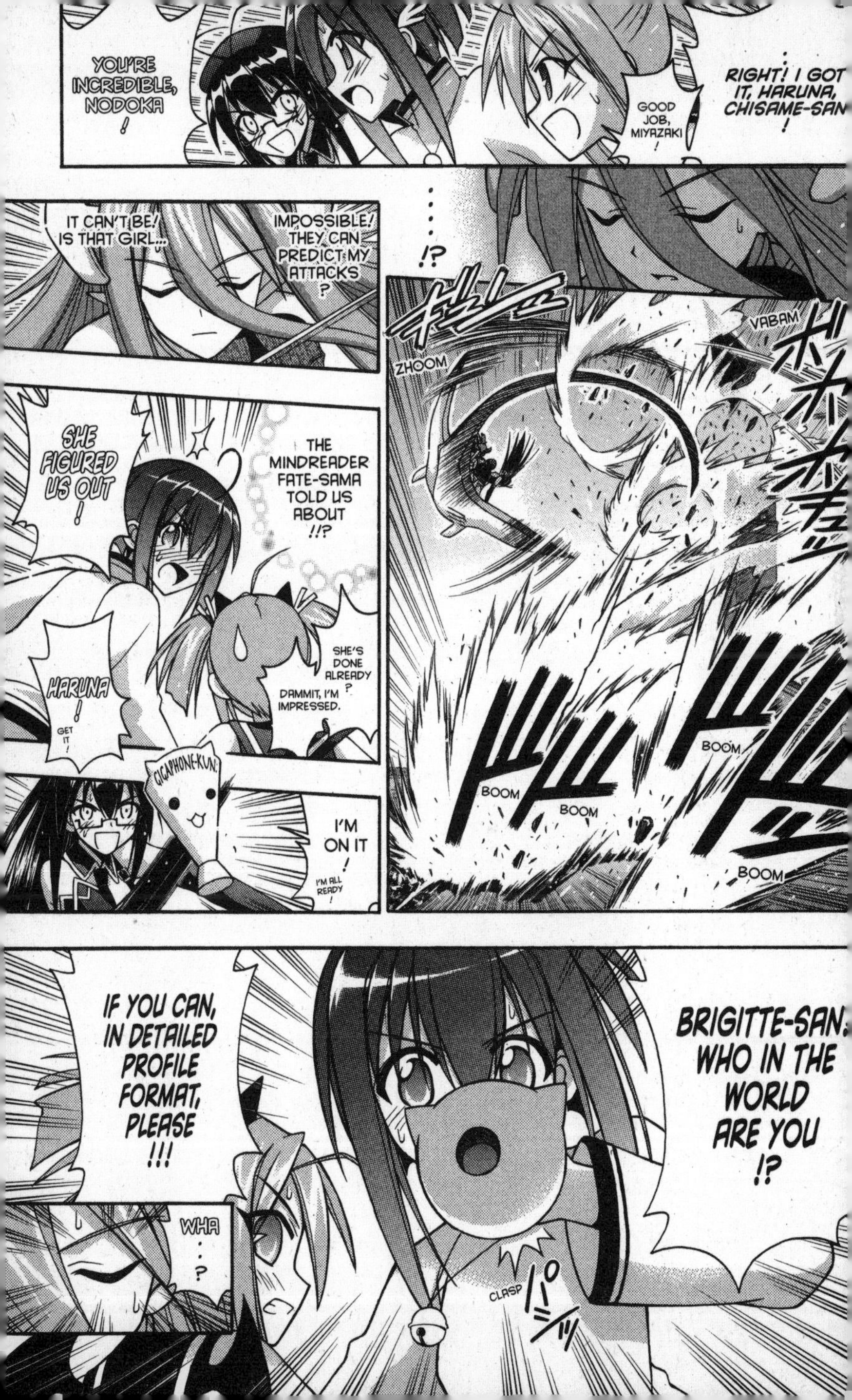
RIGHT! I GOT IT, HARUNA, CHISAME-SAN!
GOOD JOB, MIYAZAKI!
YOU'RE INCREDIBLE, NODOKA!
...!?
ZHOOM
VABAM
BOOM
BOOM
BOOM
BOOM
IMPOSSIBLE! THEY CAN PREDICT MY ATTACKS?
IT CAN'T BE! IS THAT GIRL...
THE MINDREADER FATE-SAMA TOLD US ABOUT!!?
SHE FIGURED US OUT!
SHE'S DONE ALREADY?
DAMMIT, I'M IMPRESSED.
HARUNA!
GET IT!
I'M ON IT!
I'M ALL READY!
GIGAPHONE-KUN
BRIGITTE-SAN: WHO IN THE WORLD ARE YOU!?
IF YOU CAN, IN DETAILED PROFILE FORMAT, PLEASE!!!
CLASP
WHA...?

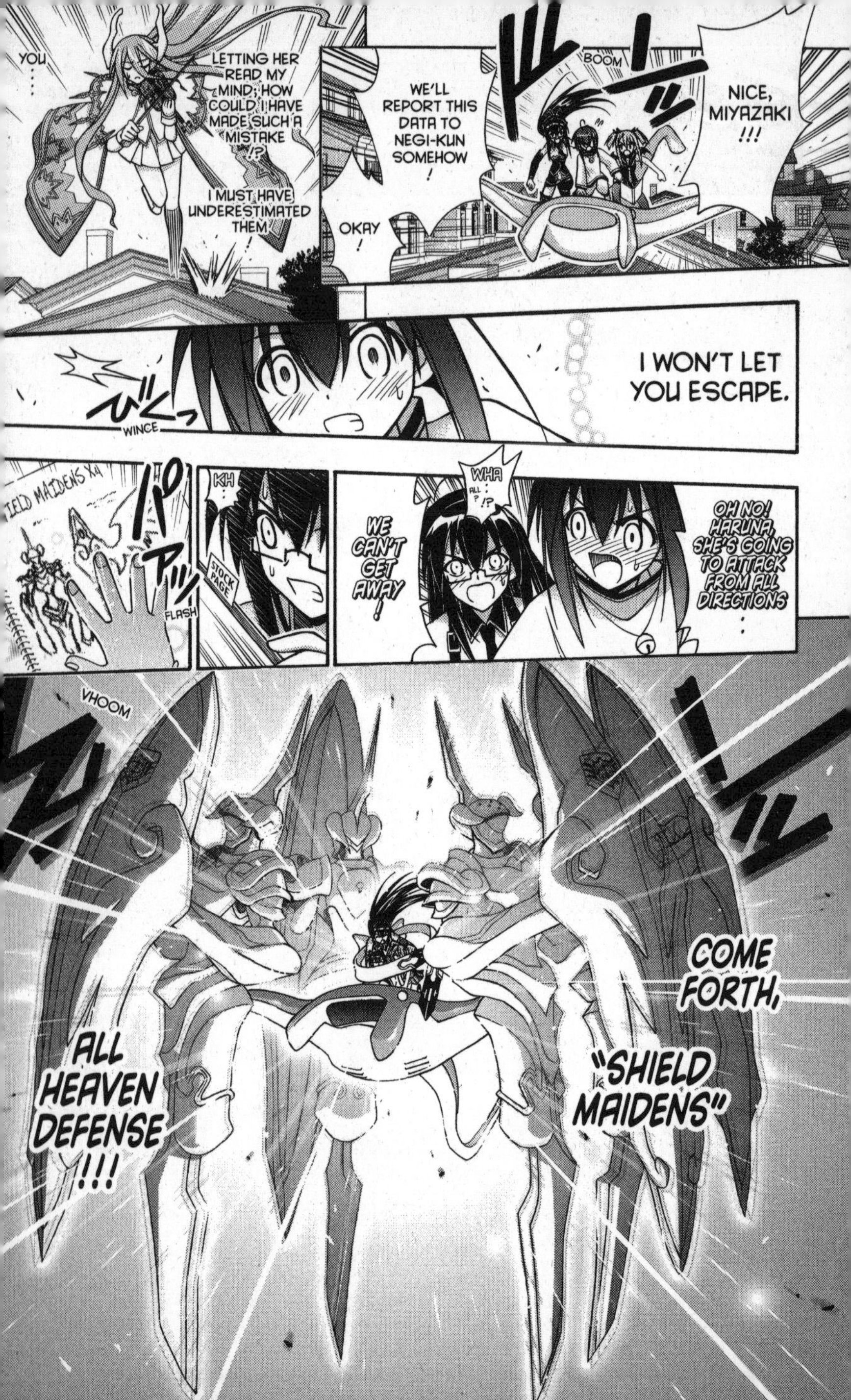
BOOM
NICE, MIYAZAKI!!!
WE'LL REPORT THIS DATA TO NEGI-KUN SOMEHOW!
OKAY!
YOU...
LETTING HER READ MY MIND; HOW COULD I HAVE MADE SUCH A MISTAKE!?
I MUST HAVE UNDERESTIMATED THEM!
I WON'T LET YOU ESCAPE.
WINCE
OH NO! HARUNA, SHE'S GOING TO ATTACK FROM ALL DIRECTIONS...
WHA...!?
ALL...?
WE CAN'T GET AWAY!
KH...
STOCK PAGE
FLASH
SHIELD MAIDENS X4
VHOOM
COME FORTH,
"SHIELD MAIDENS"
ALL HEAVEN DEFENSE!!!

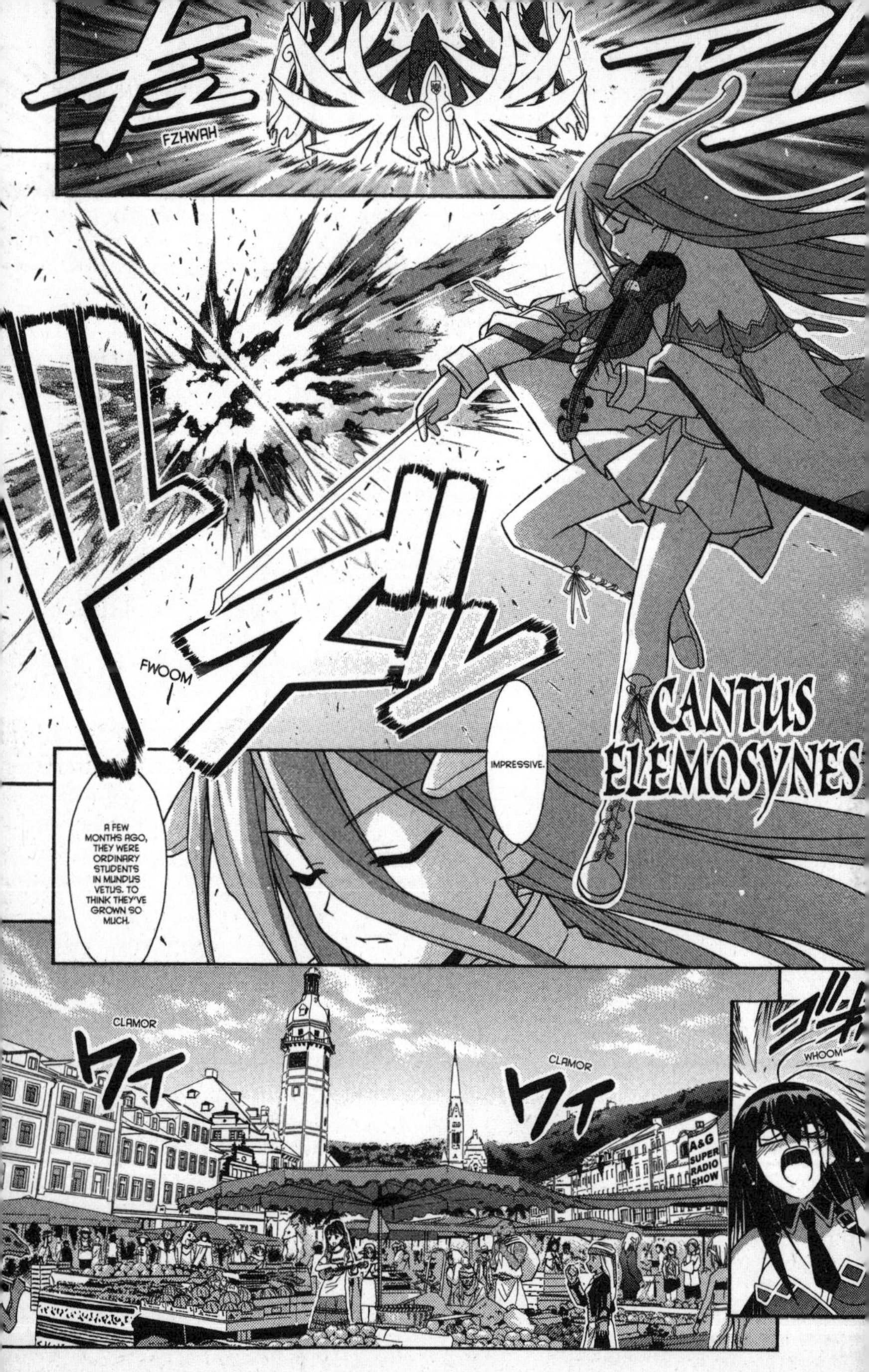
FZHWAH
FWOOM
CANTUS ELEMOSYNES
IMPRESSIVE.
A FEW MONTHS AGO, THEY WERE ORDINARY STUDENTS IN MUNDUS VETUS. TO THINK THEY'VE GROWN SO MUCH.
WHOOM
CLAMOR
CLAMOR
A&G SUPER RADIO SHOW

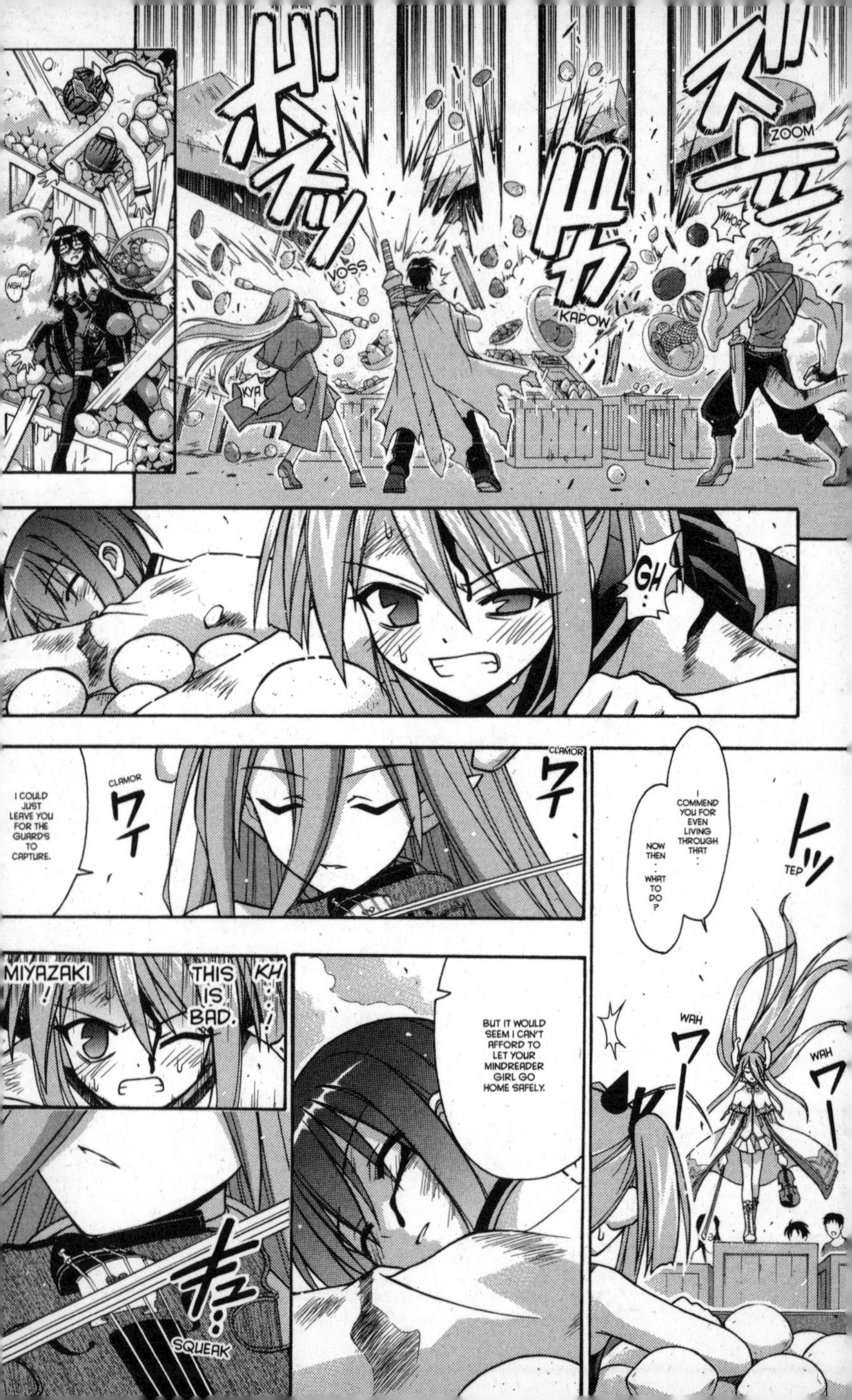
ZOOM
WHOA!
KAPOW
VOSS
KYA!
UGH
NGH
GH..!
TEP
I COMMEND YOU FOR EVEN LIVING THROUGH THAT..
NOW THEN... WHAT TO DO?
WAH
WAH
CLAMOR
CLAMOR
I COULD JUST LEAVE YOU FOR THE GUARDS TO CAPTURE.
BUT IT WOULD SEEM I CAN'T AFFORD TO LET YOUR MINDREADER GIRL GO HOME SAFELY.
KH..!
THIS IS BAD.
MIYAZAKI!
SQUEAK

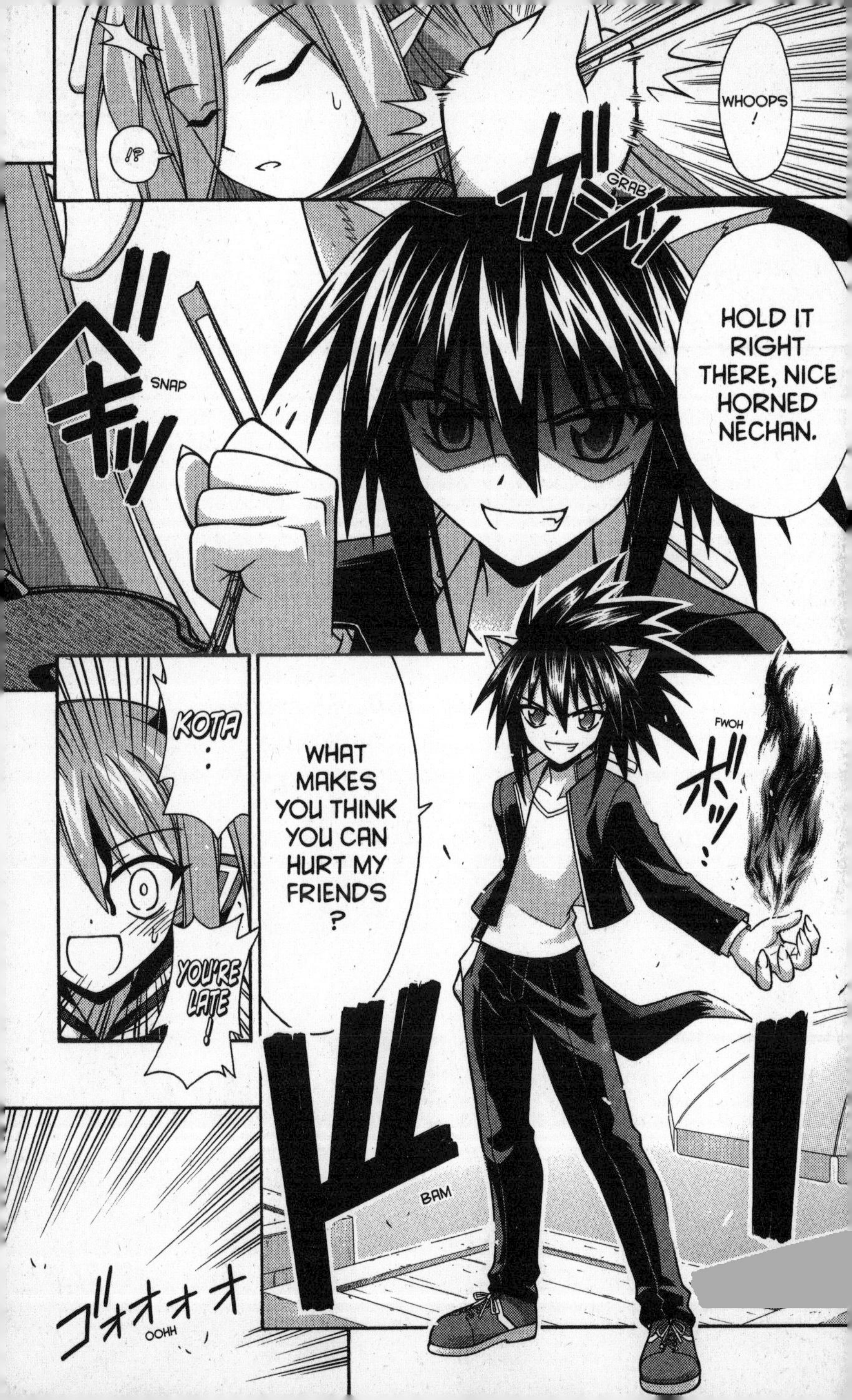
WHOOPS!
!?
GRAB
HOLD IT RIGHT THERE, NICE HORNED NĒCHAN.
SNAP
FWOH
WHAT MAKES YOU THINK YOU CAN HURT MY FRIENDS?
BAM
KOTA...
YOU'RE LATE!
OOHH

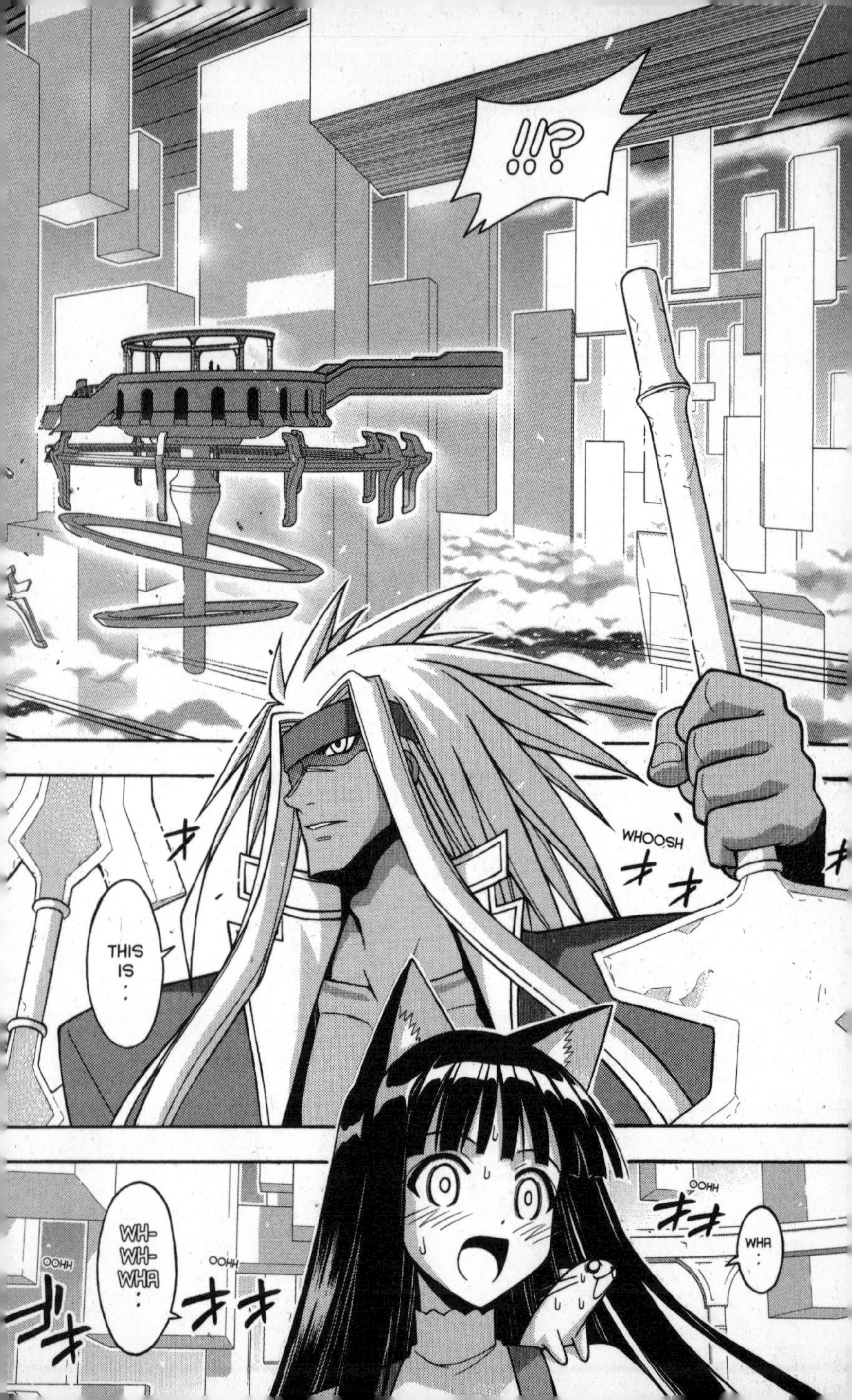
!!?
WHOOSH
THIS IS...
OOHH
WHA...
WH-WH-WHA...
OOHH
OOHH

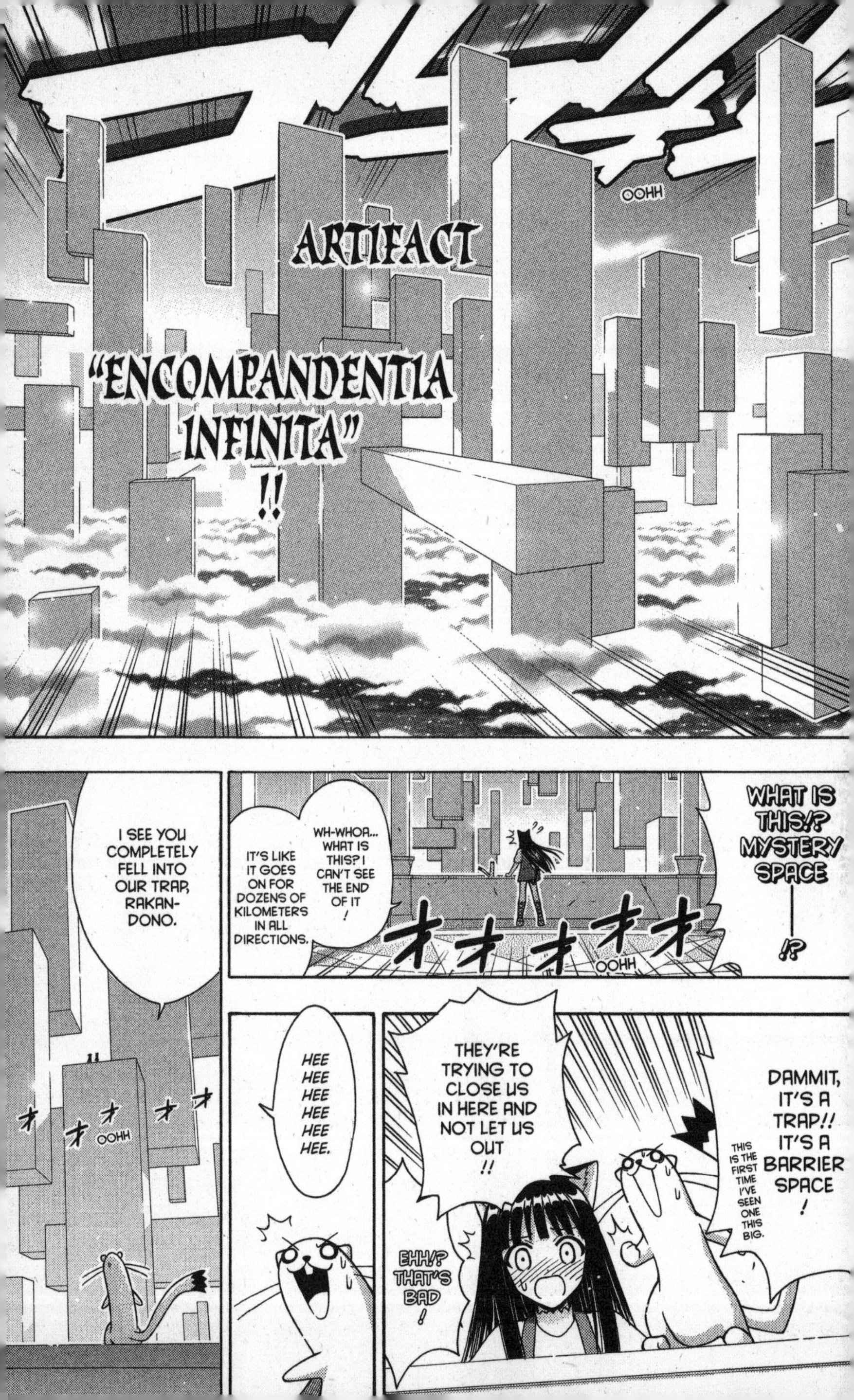
OOHH
ARTIFACT
"ENCOMPANDENTIA INFINITA" !!
WHAT IS THIS!? MYSTERY SPACE ——!?
WH-WHOA... WHAT IS THIS? I CAN'T SEE THE END OF IT!
IT'S LIKE IT GOES ON FOR DOZENS OF KILOMETERS IN ALL DIRECTIONS.
OOHH
DAMMIT, IT'S A TRAP!! IT'S A BARRIER SPACE!
THIS IS THE FIRST TIME I'VE SEEN ONE THIS BIG.
THEY'RE TRYING TO CLOSE US IN HERE AND NOT LET US OUT!!
EHH!? THAT'S BAD!
HEE HEE HEE HEE HEE HEE.
I SEE YOU COMPLETELY FELL INTO OUR TRAP, RAKAN-DONO.
OOHH

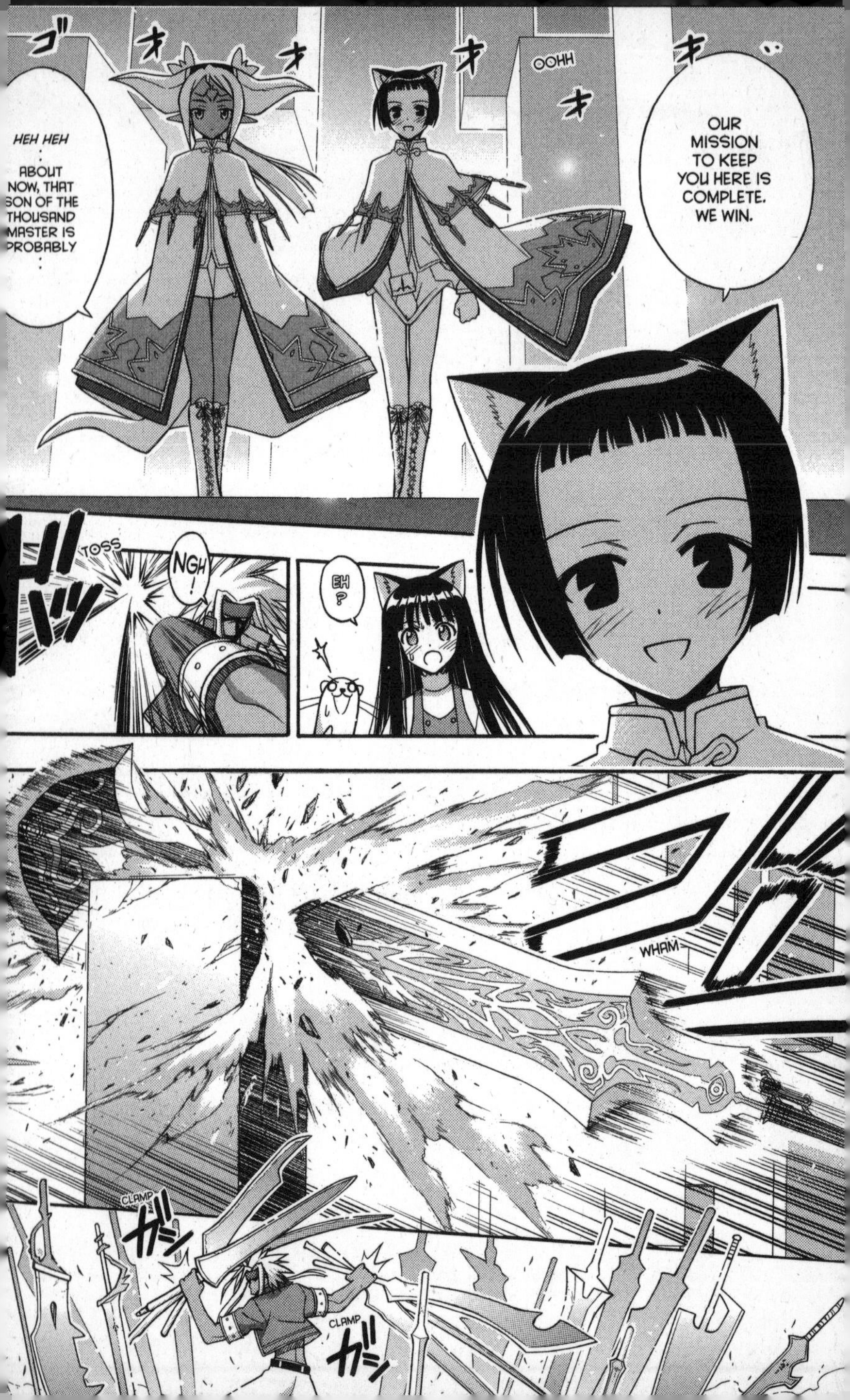

OUR MISSION TO KEEP YOU HERE IS COMPLETE. WE WIN.
OOHH
HEH HEH : ABOUT NOW, THAT SON OF THE THOUSAND MASTER IS PROBABLY :
EH ?
NGH !
TOSS
WHAM
CLAMP
CLAMP

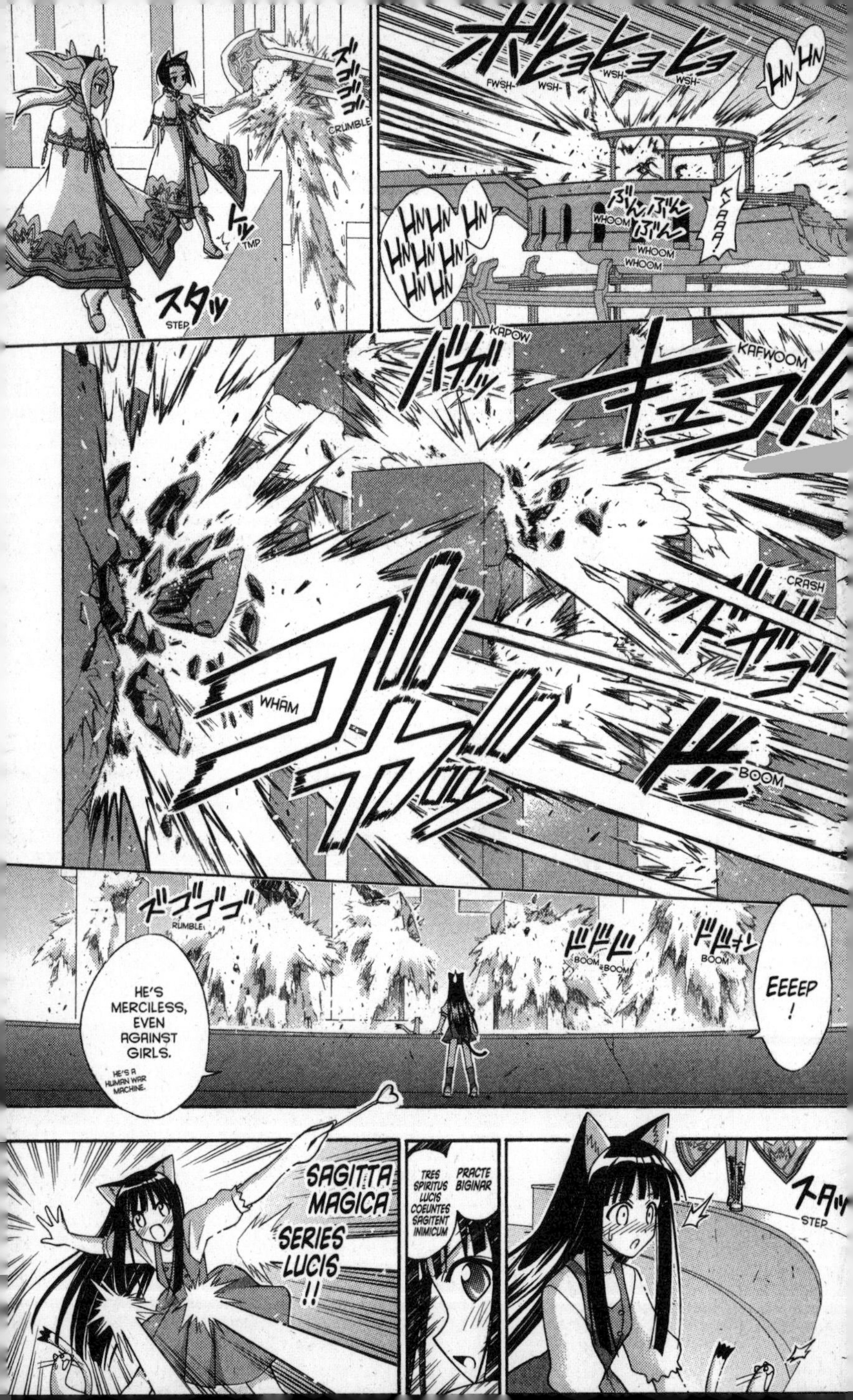

ボヒュヒュヒュ
FWSH- WSH- WSH- WSH-
HN HN
KYAAA!
ぶんぶんぶん
WHOOM WHOOM WHOOM
HN HN HN HN HN HN HN HN HN
ズゴゴゴ
CRUMBLE
トッ
TMP
スタッ
STEP
キュブ!!
KAFWOOM
バガッ
KAPOW
ボガゴ
CRASH
ドッ
BOOM
ゴバッ
WHAM
EEEEP!
ドドオン
BOOM
ドドド
BOOM BOOM
ズゴゴゴ
RUMBLE
HE'S MERCILESS, EVEN AGAINST GIRLS.
HE'S A HUMAN WAR MACHINE.
スタッ
STEP
PRACTE BIGINAR
TRES SPIRITUS LUCIS COEUNTES SAGITENT INIMICUM
SAGITTA MAGICA
SERIES LUCIS!!

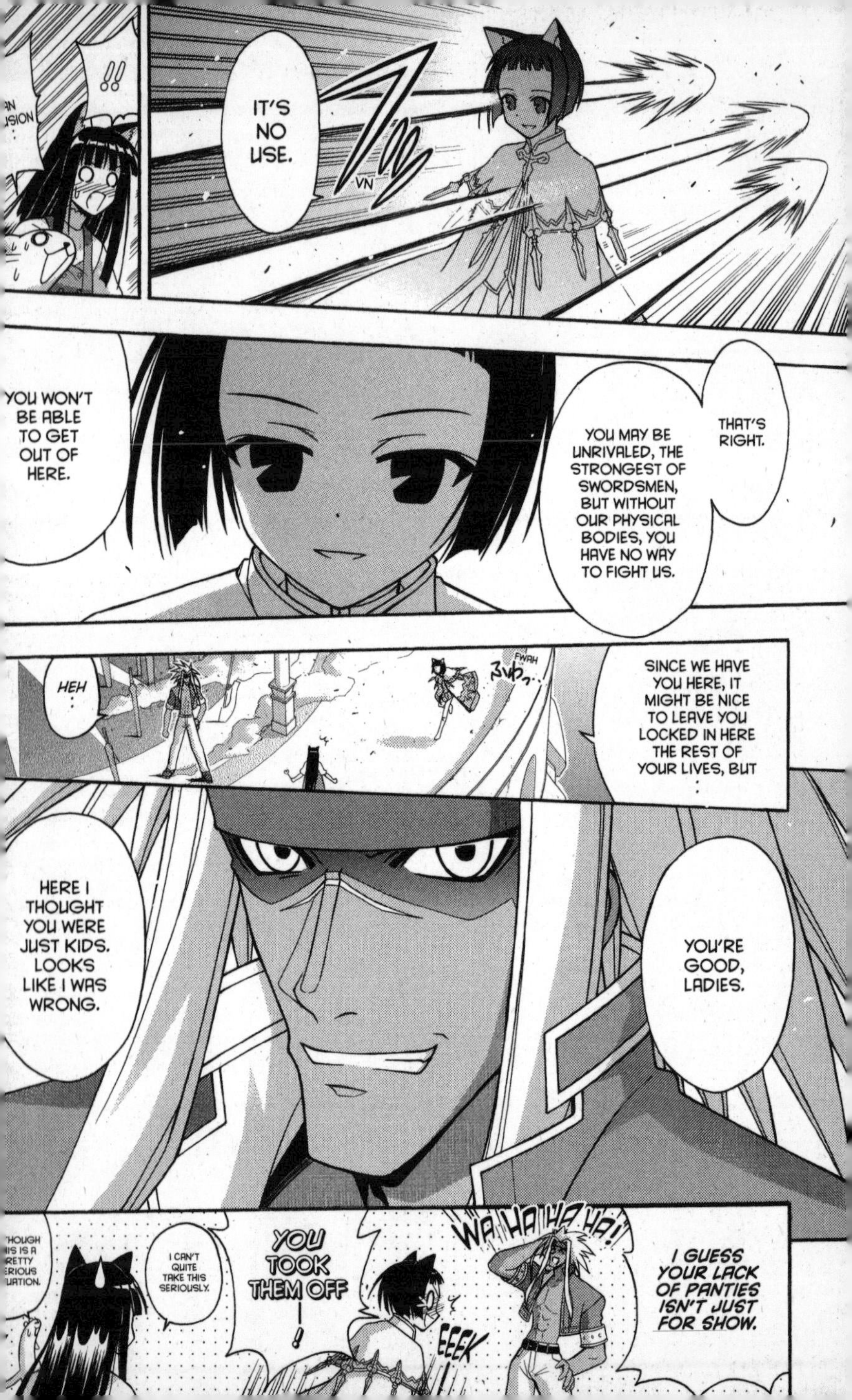
IT'S NO USE.
VN
!!
THAT'S RIGHT.
YOU MAY BE UNRIVALED, THE STRONGEST OF SWORDSMEN, BUT WITHOUT OUR PHYSICAL BODIES, YOU HAVE NO WAY TO FIGHT US.
YOU WON'T BE ABLE TO GET OUT OF HERE.
SINCE WE HAVE YOU HERE, IT MIGHT BE NICE TO LEAVE YOU LOCKED IN HERE THE REST OF YOUR LIVES, BUT...
FWAH
HEH...
YOU'RE GOOD, LADIES.
HERE I THOUGHT YOU WERE JUST KIDS. LOOKS LIKE I WAS WRONG.
I GUESS YOUR LACK OF PANTIES ISN'T JUST FOR SHOW.
WA HA HA HA!
YOU TOOK THEM OFF!
EEEK!
I CAN'T QUITE TAKE THIS SERIOUSLY.

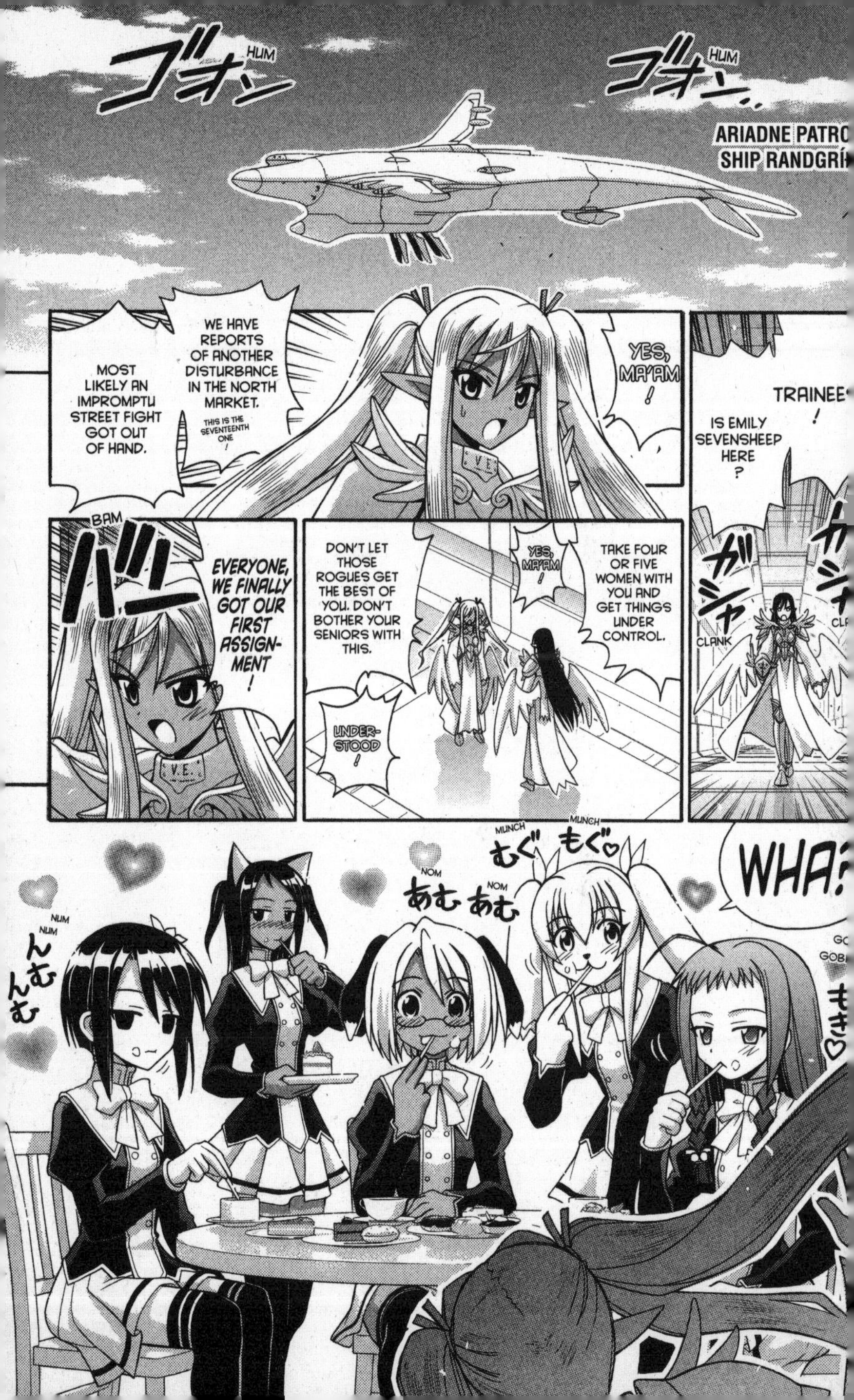
HUM
HUM
ゴオン
ゴオン…
ARIADNE PATRO
SHIP RANDGRÍ
TRAINEE!
IS EMILY SEVENSHEEP HERE?
YES, MA'AM!
WE HAVE REPORTS OF ANOTHER DISTURBANCE IN THE NORTH MARKET.
THIS IS THE SEVENTEENTH ONE!
MOST LIKELY AN IMPROMPTU STREET FIGHT GOT OUT OF HAND.
CLANK
ガシャ
ガシャ
CL
TAKE FOUR OR FIVE WOMEN WITH YOU AND GET THINGS UNDER CONTROL.
YES, MA'AM!
DON'T LET THOSE ROGUES GET THE BEST OF YOU. DON'T BOTHER YOUR SENIORS WITH THIS.
UNDER-STOOD!
BAM
バン
EVERYONE, WE FINALLY GOT OUR FIRST ASSIGN-MENT!
WHA?
GO
GOB
もき♡
MUNCH
むぐ
MUNCH
もぐ♡
NOM
あむ
NOM
あむ
NUM
NUM
んむ
んむ

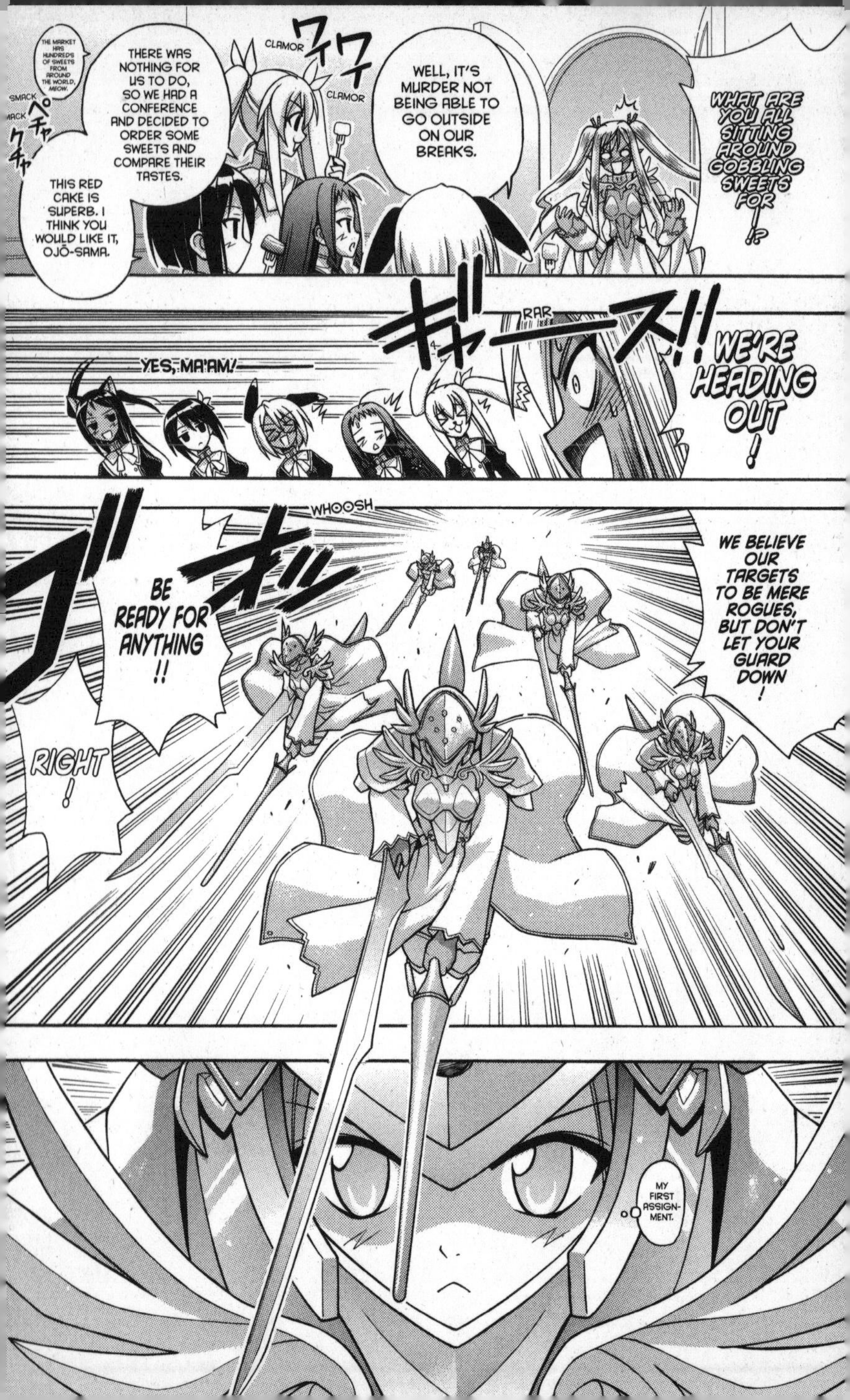
WHAT ARE YOU ALL SITTING AROUND GOBBLING SWEETS FOR ...!?
WELL, IT'S MURDER NOT BEING ABLE TO GO OUTSIDE ON OUR BREAKS.
CLAMOR
ワイワ
CLAMOR
THERE WAS NOTHING FOR US TO DO, SO WE HAD A CONFERENCE AND DECIDED TO ORDER SOME SWEETS AND COMPARE THEIR TASTES.
THE MARKET HAS HUNDREDS OF SWEETS FROM AROUND THE WORLD, MEOW.
SMACK
ペチャ
クチャ
SMACK
THIS RED CAKE IS SUPERB. I THINK YOU WOULD LIKE IT, OJŌ-SAMA.
WE'RE HEADING OUT!
ギャース!!
RAR
YES, MA'AM!
WE BELIEVE OUR TARGETS TO BE MERE ROGUES, BUT DON'T LET YOUR GUARD DOWN!
WHOOSH
ゴオッ
BE READY FOR ANYTHING!!
RIGHT!
MY FIRST ASSIGNMENT.

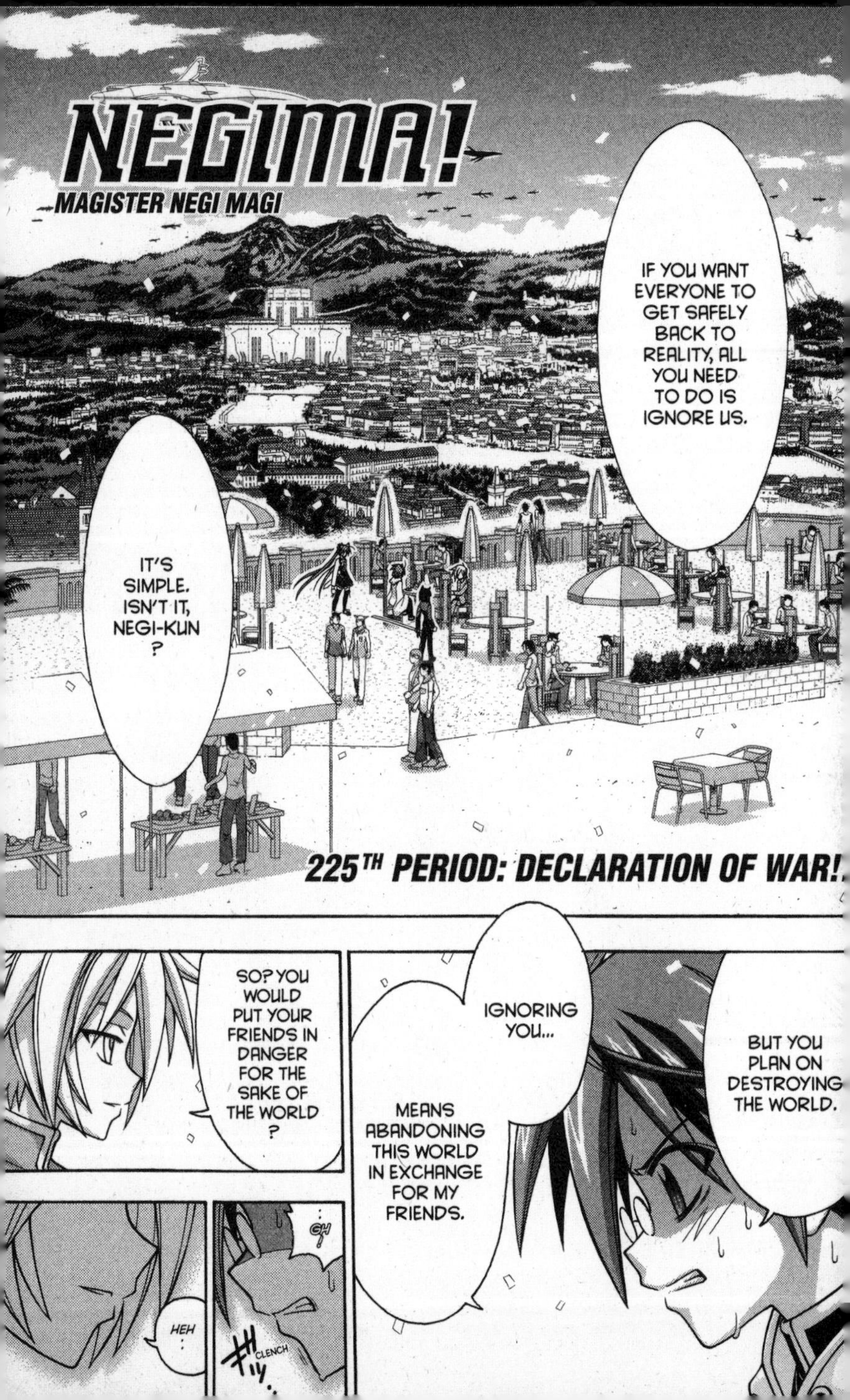
NEGIMA!
MAGISTER NEGI MAGI
IF YOU WANT EVERYONE TO GET SAFELY BACK TO REALITY, ALL YOU NEED TO DO IS IGNORE US.
IT'S SIMPLE. ISN'T IT, NEGI-KUN?
225TH PERIOD: DECLARATION OF WAR!
BUT YOU PLAN ON DESTROYING THE WORLD.
IGNORING YOU...
MEANS ABANDONING THIS WORLD IN EXCHANGE FOR MY FRIENDS.
SO? YOU WOULD PUT YOUR FRIENDS IN DANGER FOR THE SAKE OF THE WORLD?
GH!
CLENCH
HEH...

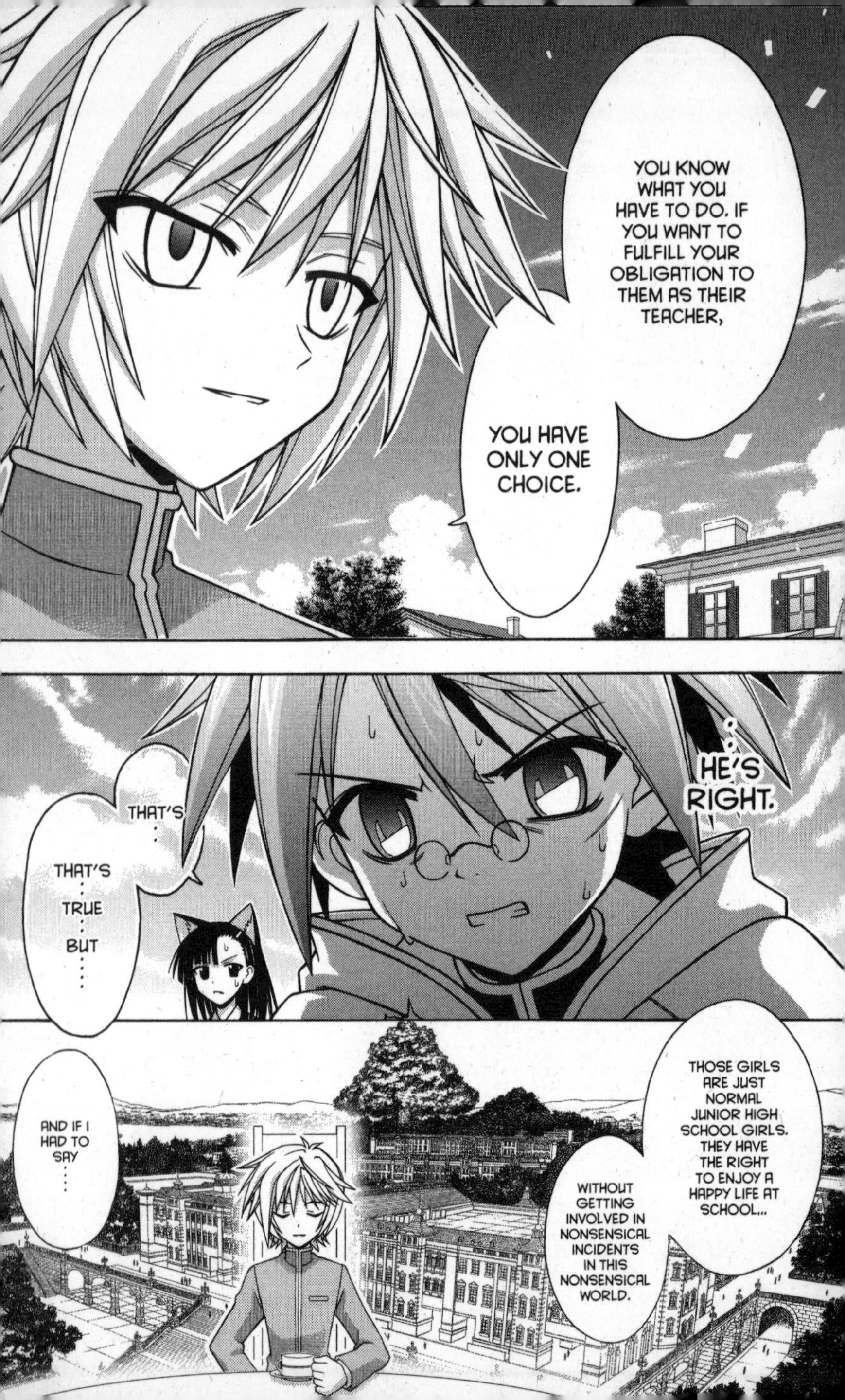
YOU KNOW WHAT YOU HAVE TO DO. IF YOU WANT TO FULFILL YOUR OBLIGATION TO THEM AS THEIR TEACHER,
YOU HAVE ONLY ONE CHOICE.
HE'S RIGHT.
THAT'S... THAT'S... TRUE... BUT...
THOSE GIRLS ARE JUST NORMAL JUNIOR HIGH SCHOOL GIRLS. THEY HAVE THE RIGHT TO ENJOY A HAPPY LIFE AT SCHOOL...
WITHOUT GETTING INVOLVED IN NONSENSICAL INCIDENTS IN THIS NONSENSICAL WORLD.
AND IF I HAD TO SAY...

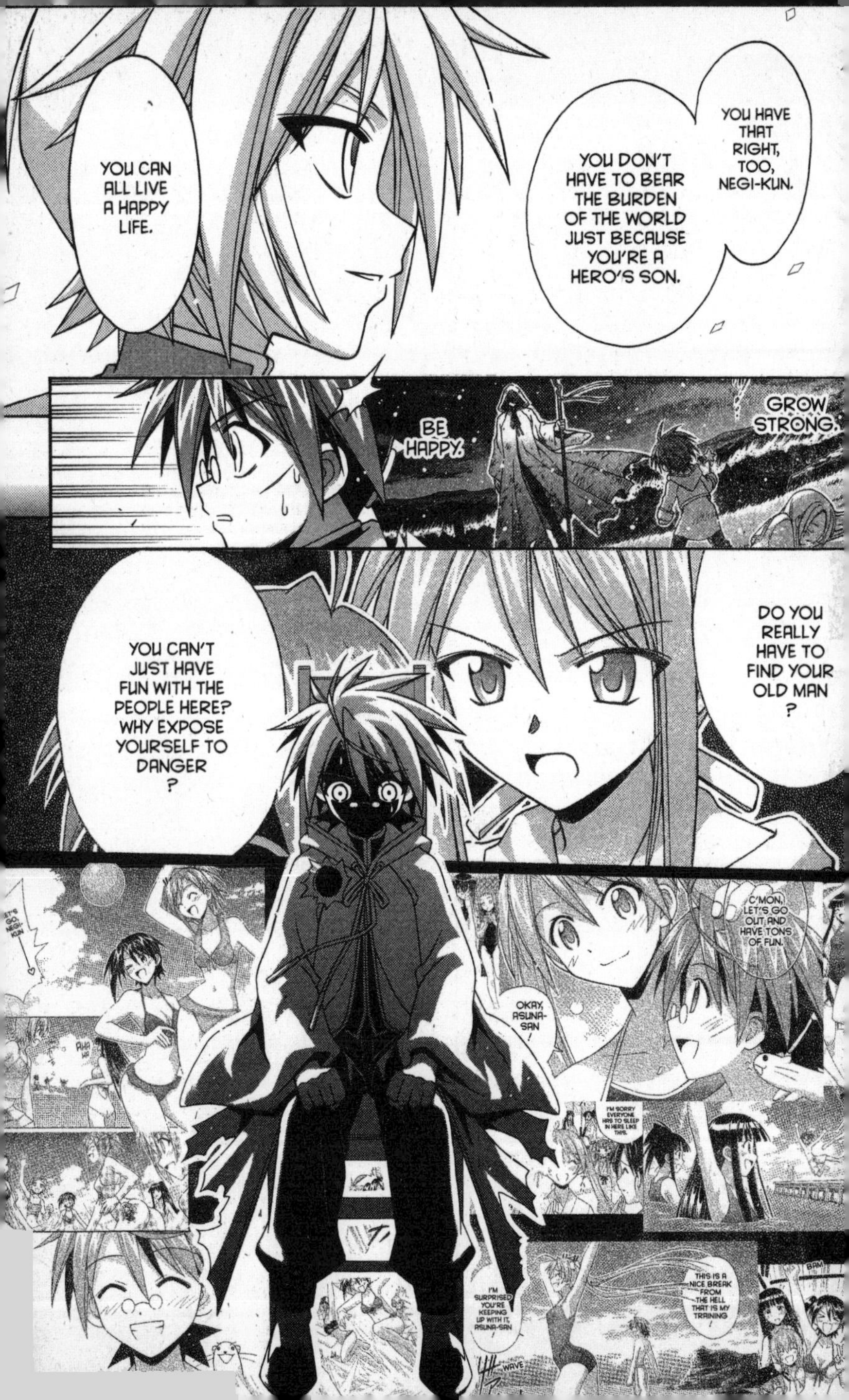
YOU HAVE THAT RIGHT, TOO, NEGI-KUN.
YOU DON'T HAVE TO BEAR THE BURDEN OF THE WORLD JUST BECAUSE YOU'RE A HERO'S SON.
YOU CAN ALL LIVE A HAPPY LIFE.
GROW STRONG.
BE HAPPY.
DO YOU REALLY HAVE TO FIND YOUR OLD MAN?
YOU CAN'T JUST HAVE FUN WITH THE PEOPLE HERE? WHY EXPOSE YOURSELF TO DANGER?
C'MON, LET'S GO OUT, AND HAVE TONS OF FUN.
OKAY, ASUNA-SAN!
LET'S GO, NEGI-KUN ♡
AHA HA
I'M SORRY EVERYONE HAS TO SLEEP IN HERE LIKE THIS.
BAM
THIS IS A NICE BREAK FROM THE HELL THAT IS MY TRAINING!
I'M SURPRISED YOU'RE KEEPING UP WITH IT, ASUNA-SAN!
WAVE

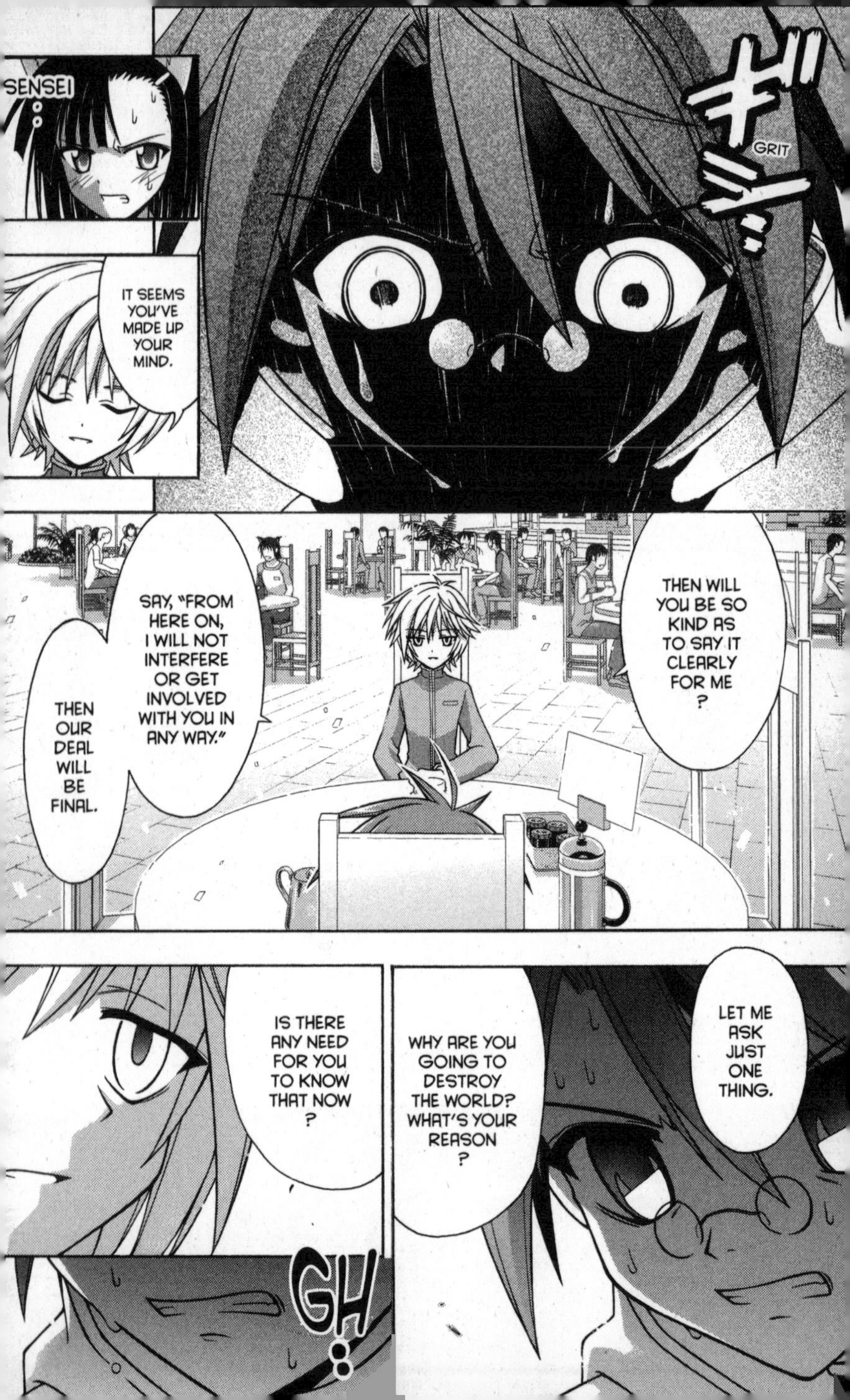
GRIT
SENSEI...
IT SEEMS YOU'VE MADE UP YOUR MIND.
THEN WILL YOU BE SO KIND AS TO SAY IT CLEARLY FOR ME?
SAY, "FROM HERE ON, I WILL NOT INTERFERE OR GET INVOLVED WITH YOU IN ANY WAY."
THEN OUR DEAL WILL BE FINAL.
LET ME ASK JUST ONE THING.
WHY ARE YOU GOING TO DESTROY THE WORLD? WHAT'S YOUR REASON?
IS THERE ANY NEED FOR YOU TO KNOW THAT NOW?
GH!..

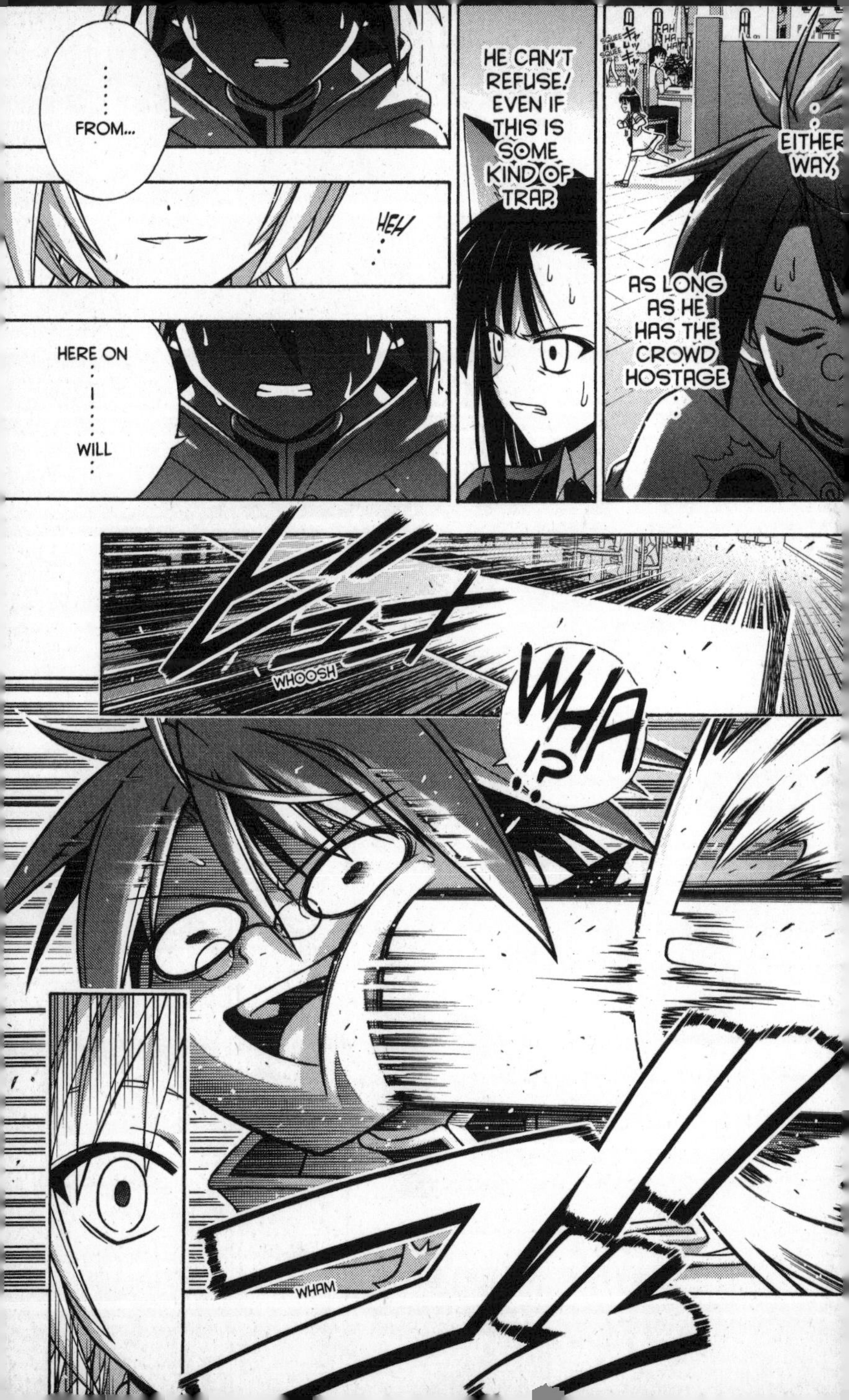
SQUEE
SQUEE
AH HA HA
...EITHER WAY,
AS LONG AS HE HAS THE CROWD HOSTAGE
HE CAN'T REFUSE! EVEN IF THIS IS SOME KIND OF TRAP.
......FROM...
HEH...
HERE ON... I... WILL...
WHOOSH
WHA!?
WHAM

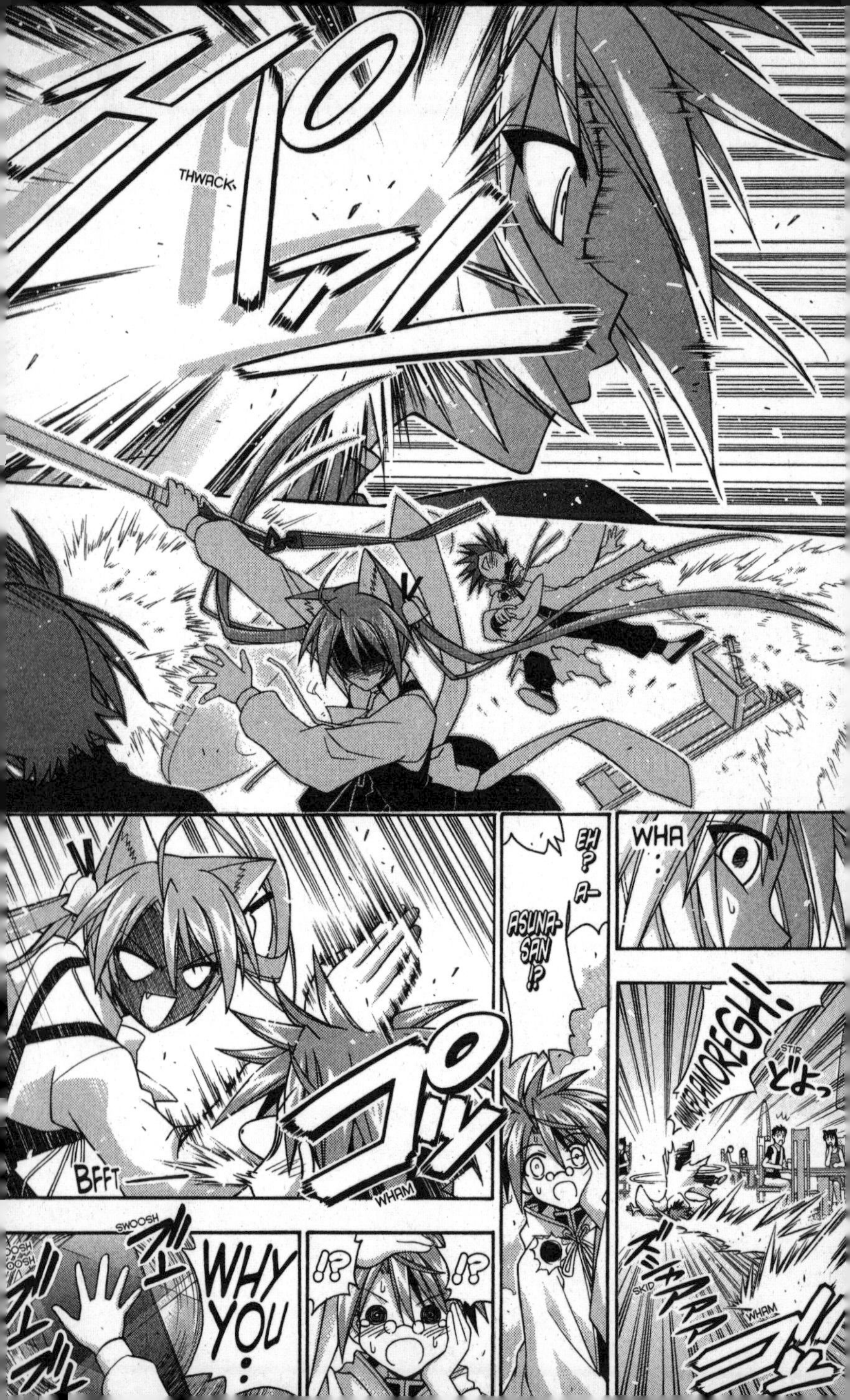
THWACK
WHA...
EH? A-
ASUNA-SAN!?
BFFT
WHAM
MOREGH!
STIR
SKID
WHAM
!?
!?
SWOOSH
WHY YOU...
OOSH
OOSH

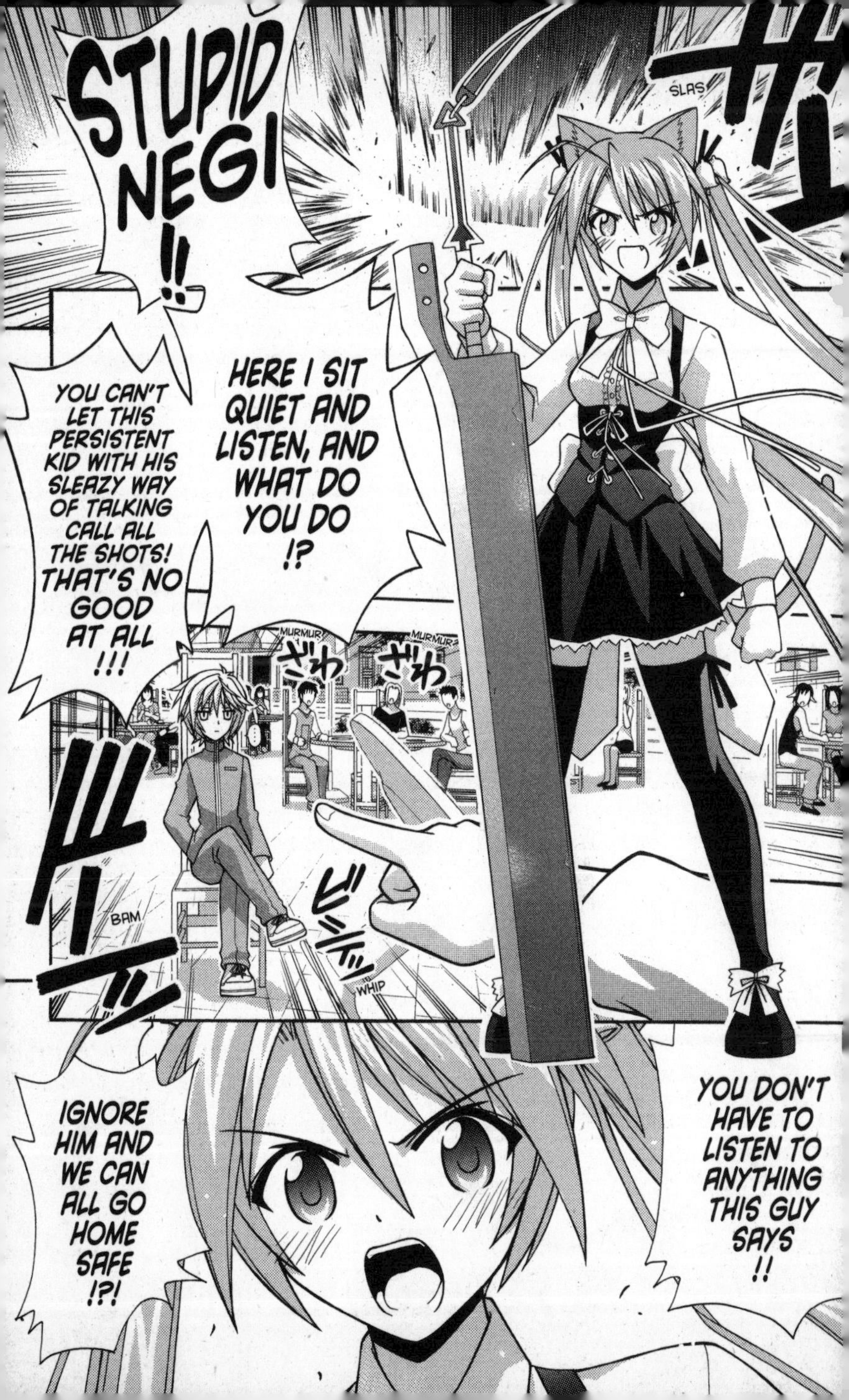
SLAS
STUPID NEGI !!
HERE I SIT QUIET AND LISTEN, AND WHAT DO YOU DO !?
YOU CAN'T LET THIS PERSISTENT KID WITH HIS SLEAZY WAY OF TALKING CALL ALL THE SHOTS! THAT'S NO GOOD AT ALL !!!
MURMUR
MURMUR
BAM
WHIP
YOU DON'T HAVE TO LISTEN TO ANYTHING THIS GUY SAYS !!
IGNORE HIM AND WE CAN ALL GO HOME SAFE !?!

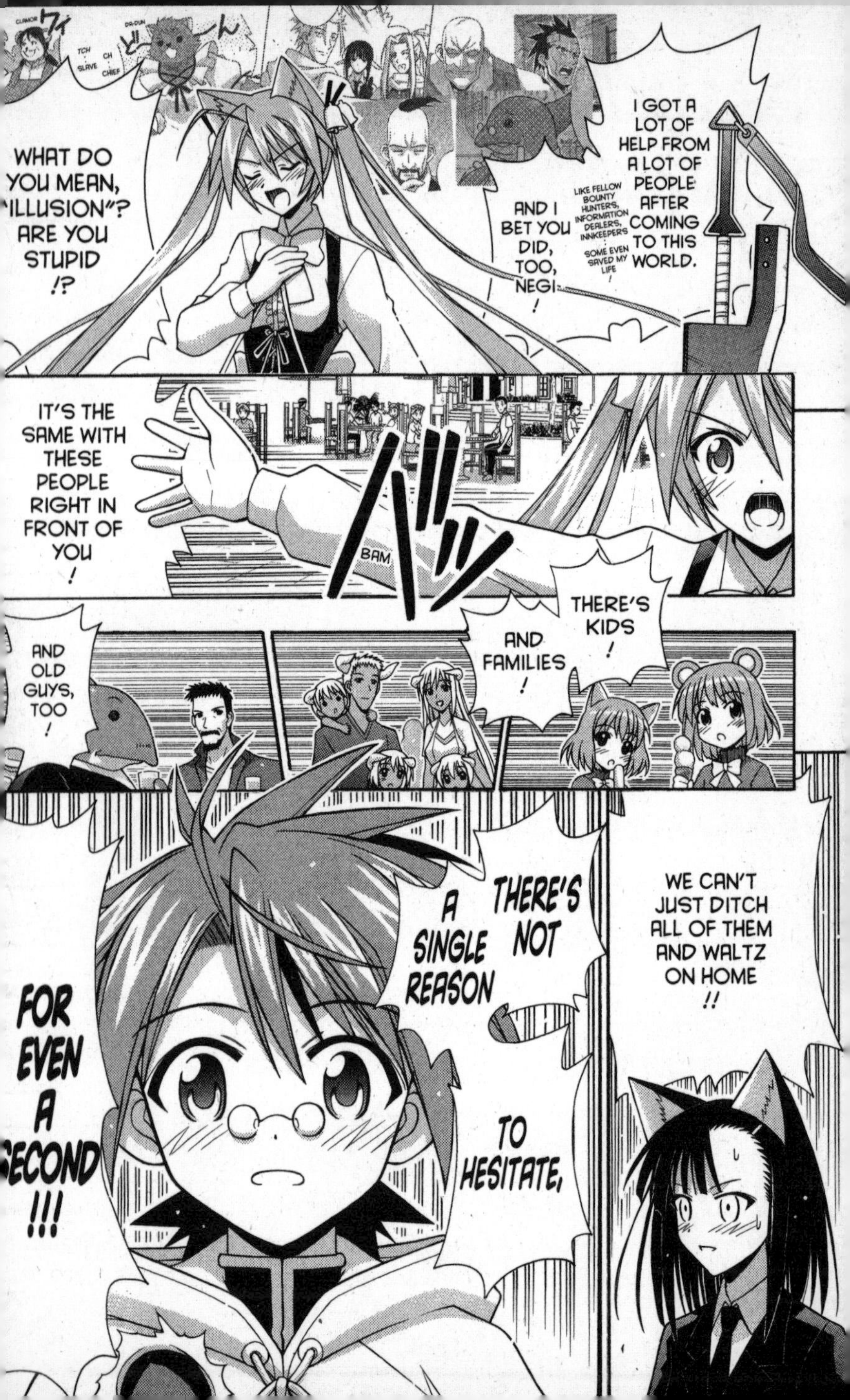
CLAMOR
DA-DUN
TCH
SLAVE
CH
CHIEF
I GOT A LOT OF HELP FROM A LOT OF PEOPLE AFTER COMING TO THIS WORLD.
LIKE FELLOW BOUNTY HUNTERS, INFORMATION DEALERS, INNKEEPERS... SOME EVEN SAVED MY LIFE!
AND I BET YOU DID, TOO, NEGI!
WHAT DO YOU MEAN, "ILLUSION"? ARE YOU STUPID!?
IT'S THE SAME WITH THESE PEOPLE RIGHT IN FRONT OF YOU!
BAM
THERE'S KIDS!
AND FAMILIES!
AND OLD GUYS, TOO!
WE CAN'T JUST DITCH ALL OF THEM AND WALTZ ON HOME!!
THERE'S NOT A SINGLE REASON TO HESITATE,
FOR EVEN A SECOND!!!

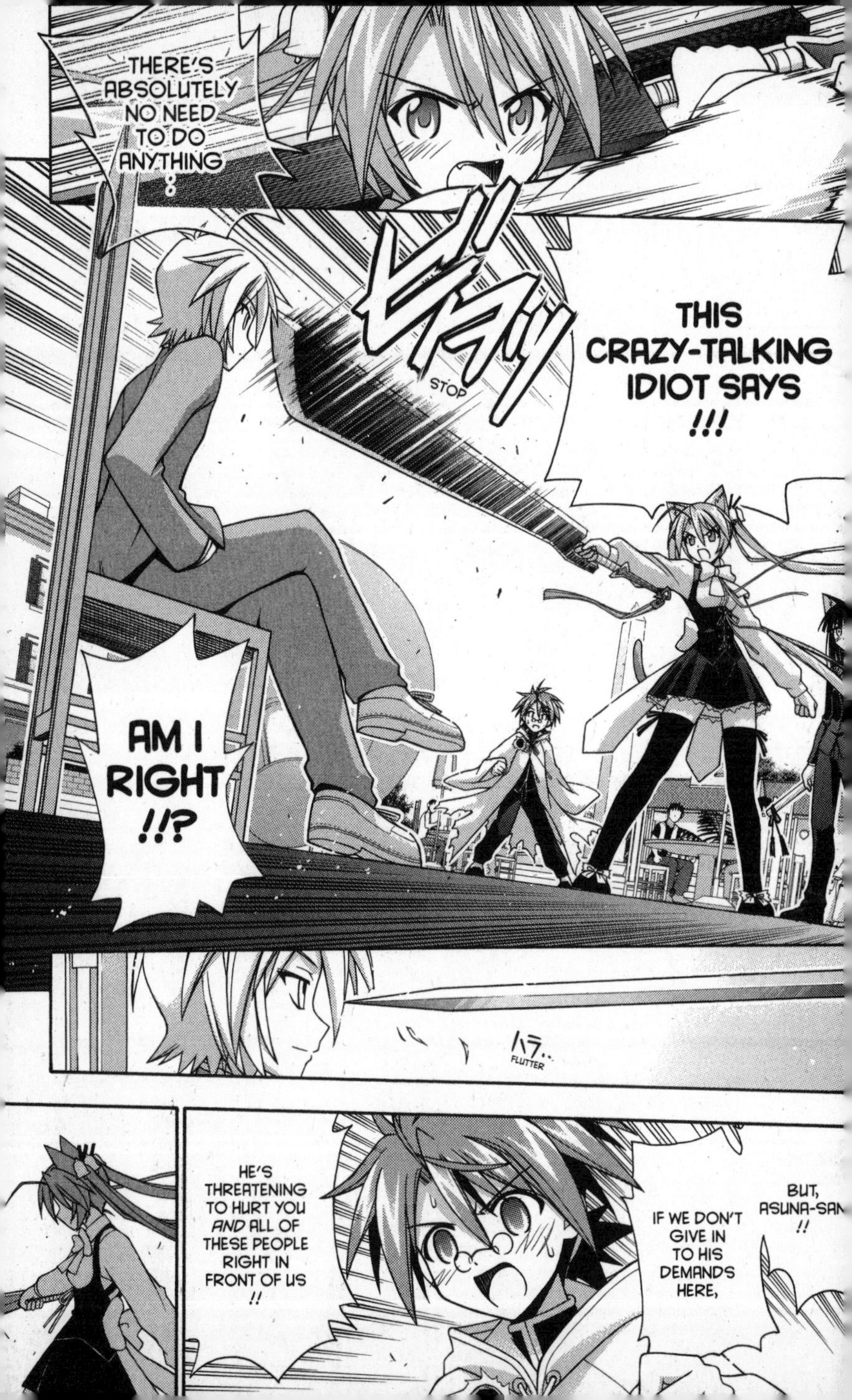
THERE'S ABSOLUTELY NO NEED TO DO ANYTHING⁈
STOP
THIS CRAZY-TALKING IDIOT SAYS!!!
AM I RIGHT!!?
FLUTTER
BUT, ASUNA-SAN!!
IF WE DON'T GIVE IN TO HIS DEMANDS HERE,
HE'S THREATENING TO HURT YOU AND ALL OF THESE PEOPLE RIGHT IN FRONT OF US!!

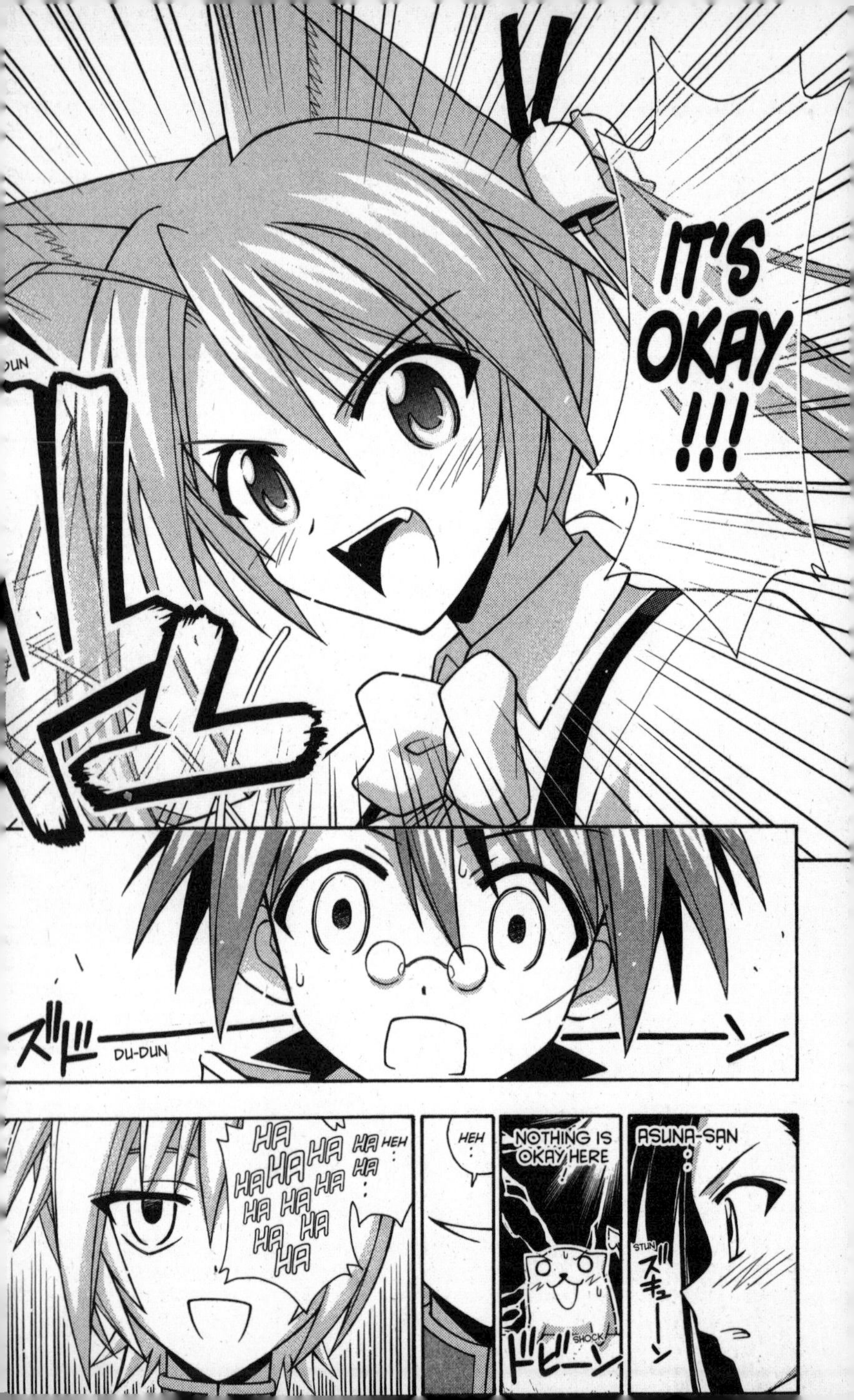
IT'S OKAY !!!
DUN
ズドドーーーーン
DU-DUN
HEH
HEH
HA HA HA HA HA HA HA HA HA HA HA HA HA HA
NOTHING IS OKAY HERE
ドビーン
SHOCK
ASUNA-SAN
ズギューーン
STUN

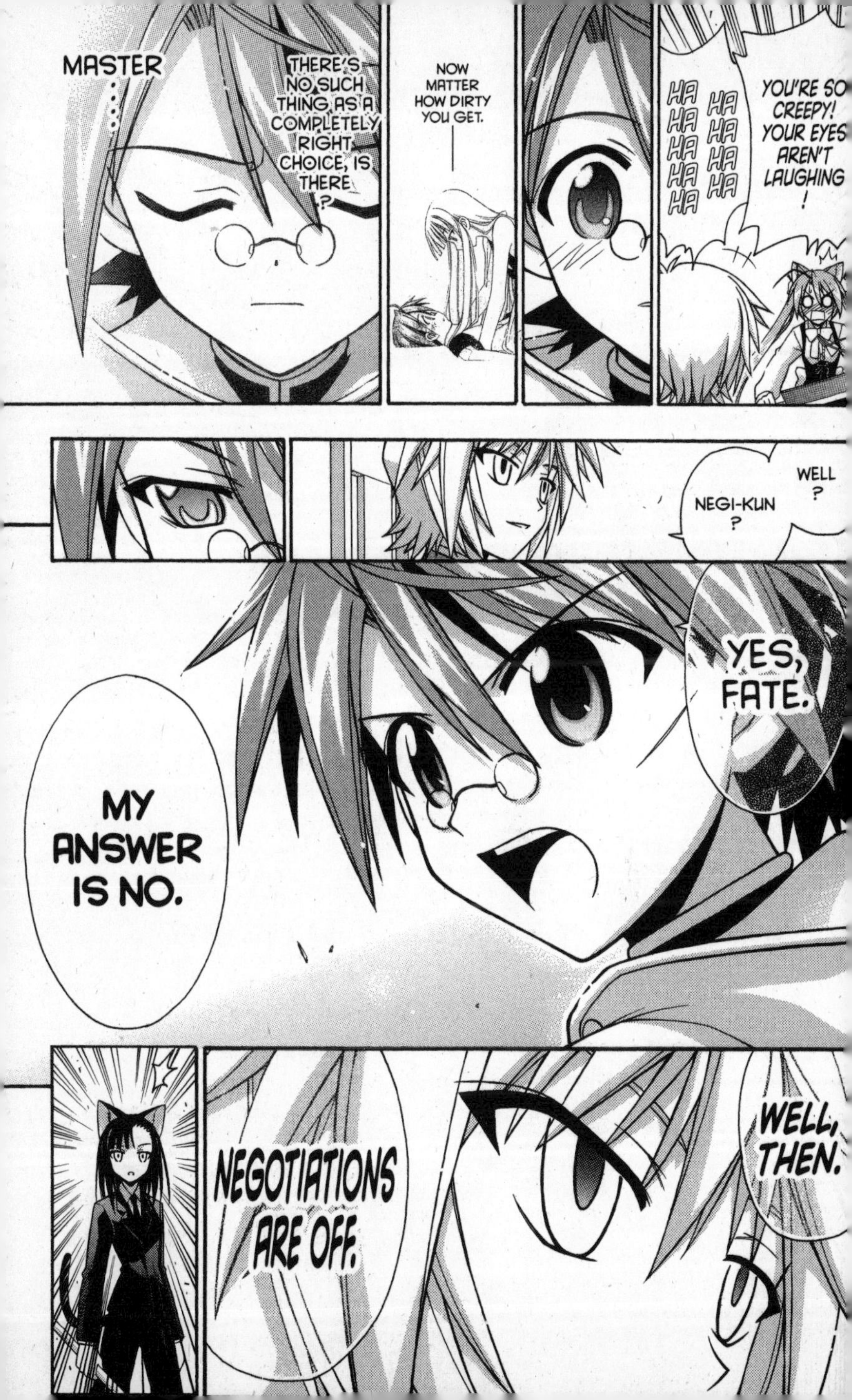
YOU'RE SO CREEPY! YOUR EYES AREN'T LAUGHING!
HA HA HA HA HA HA HA HA HA
NOW MATTER HOW DIRTY YOU GET.
THERE'S NO SUCH THING AS A COMPLETELY RIGHT CHOICE, IS THERE?
MASTER.....
WELL?
NEGI-KUN?
YES, FATE.
MY ANSWER IS NO.
WELL, THEN.
NEGOTIATIONS ARE OFF.

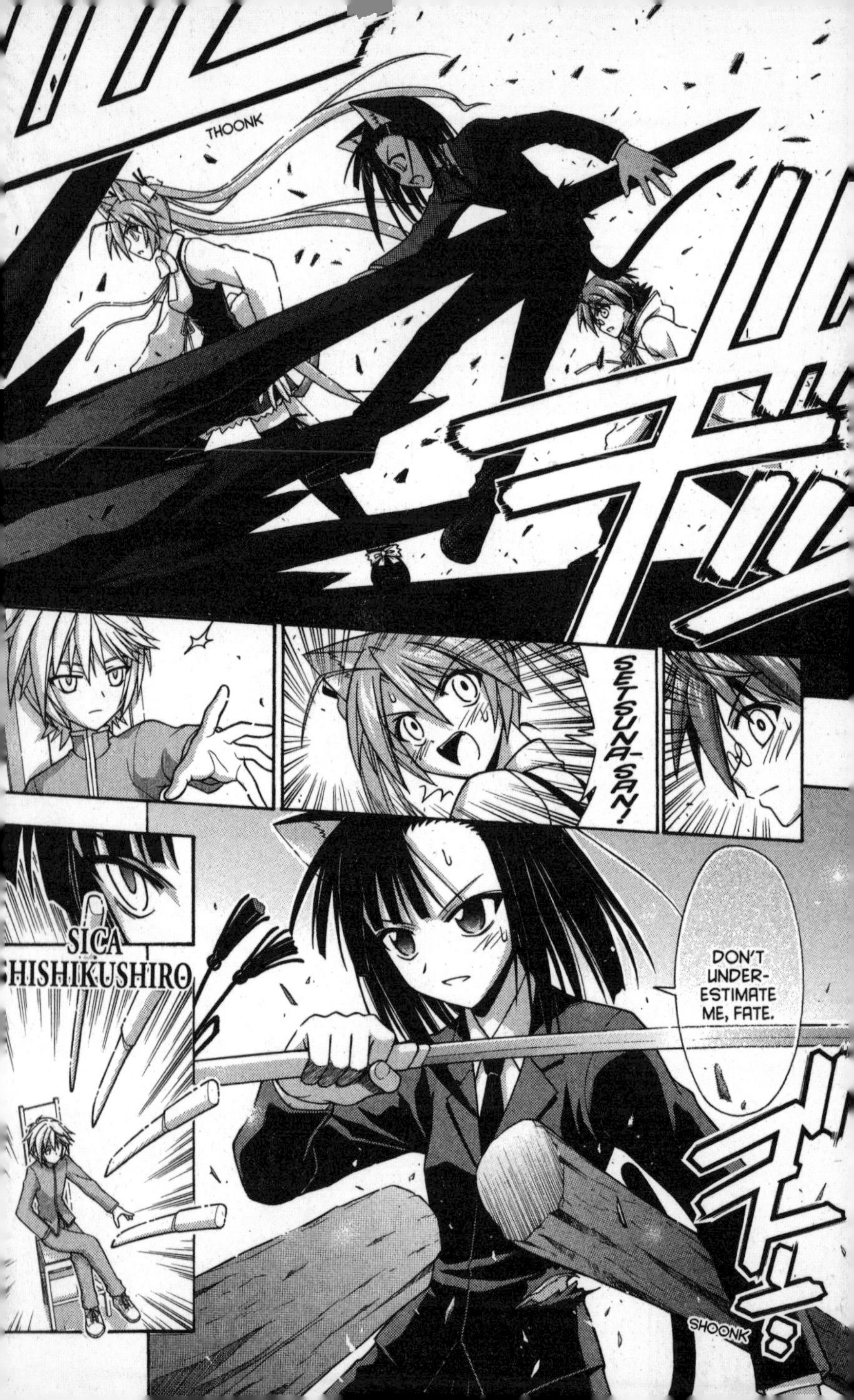
THOONK
SETSUNA-SAN!
DON'T UNDER-ESTIMATE ME, FATE.
SICA HISHIKUSHIRO
SHOONK

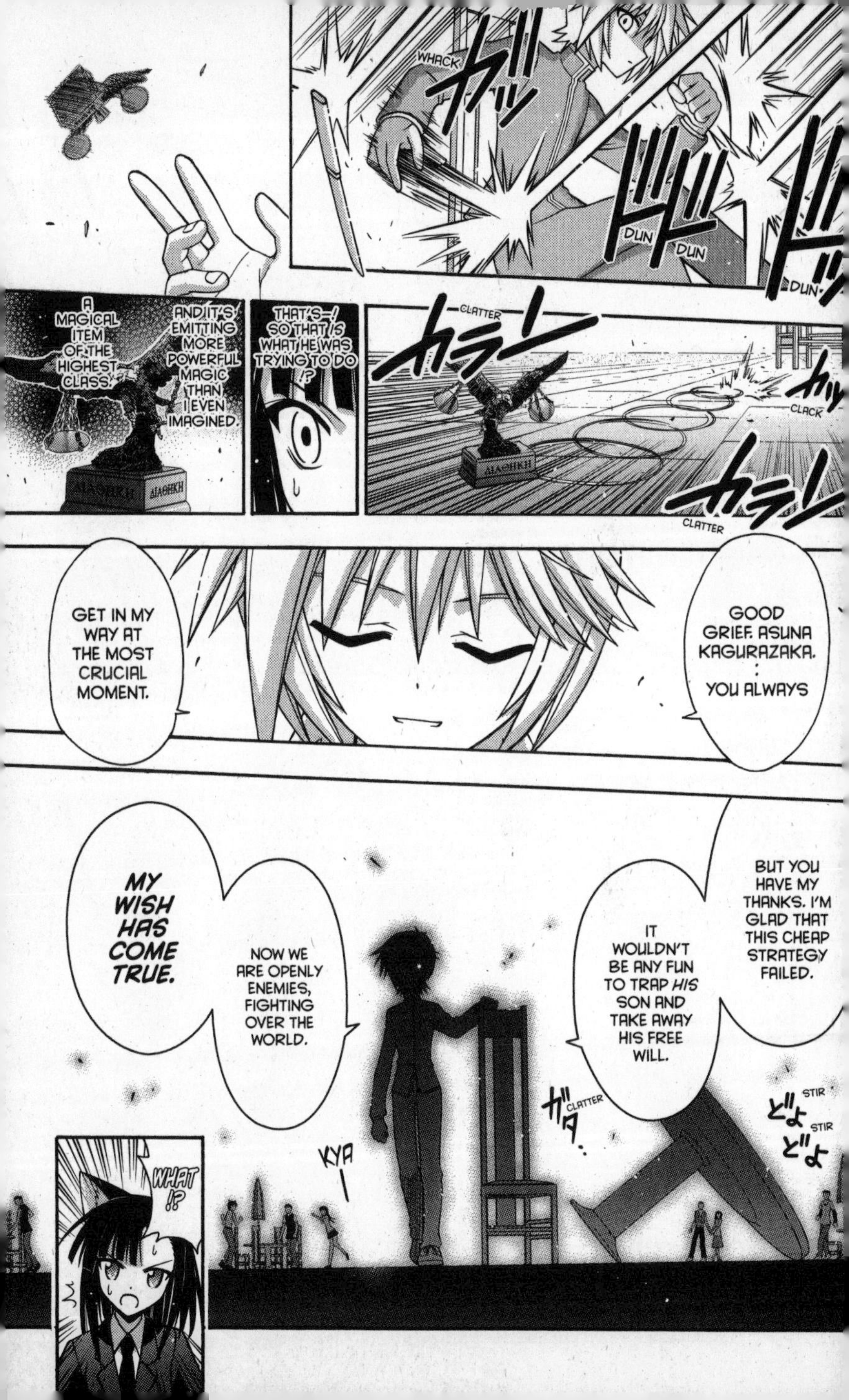

WHACK
DUN
DUN
DUN
CLATTER
CLACK
CLATTER
THAT'S—! SO THAT IS WHAT HE WAS TRYING TO DO!?
AND IT'S EMITTING MORE POWERFUL MAGIC THAN I EVEN IMAGINED.
A MAGICAL ITEM OF THE HIGHEST CLASS.
GOOD GRIEF. ASUNA KAGURAZAKA. : YOU ALWAYS
GET IN MY WAY AT THE MOST CRUCIAL MOMENT.
BUT YOU HAVE MY THANKS. I'M GLAD THAT THIS CHEAP STRATEGY FAILED.
IT WOULDN'T BE ANY FUN TO TRAP HIS SON AND TAKE AWAY HIS FREE WILL.
NOW WE ARE OPENLY ENEMIES, FIGHTING OVER THE WORLD.
MY WISH HAS COME TRUE.
STIR STIR
CLATTER
KYA
WHAT!?

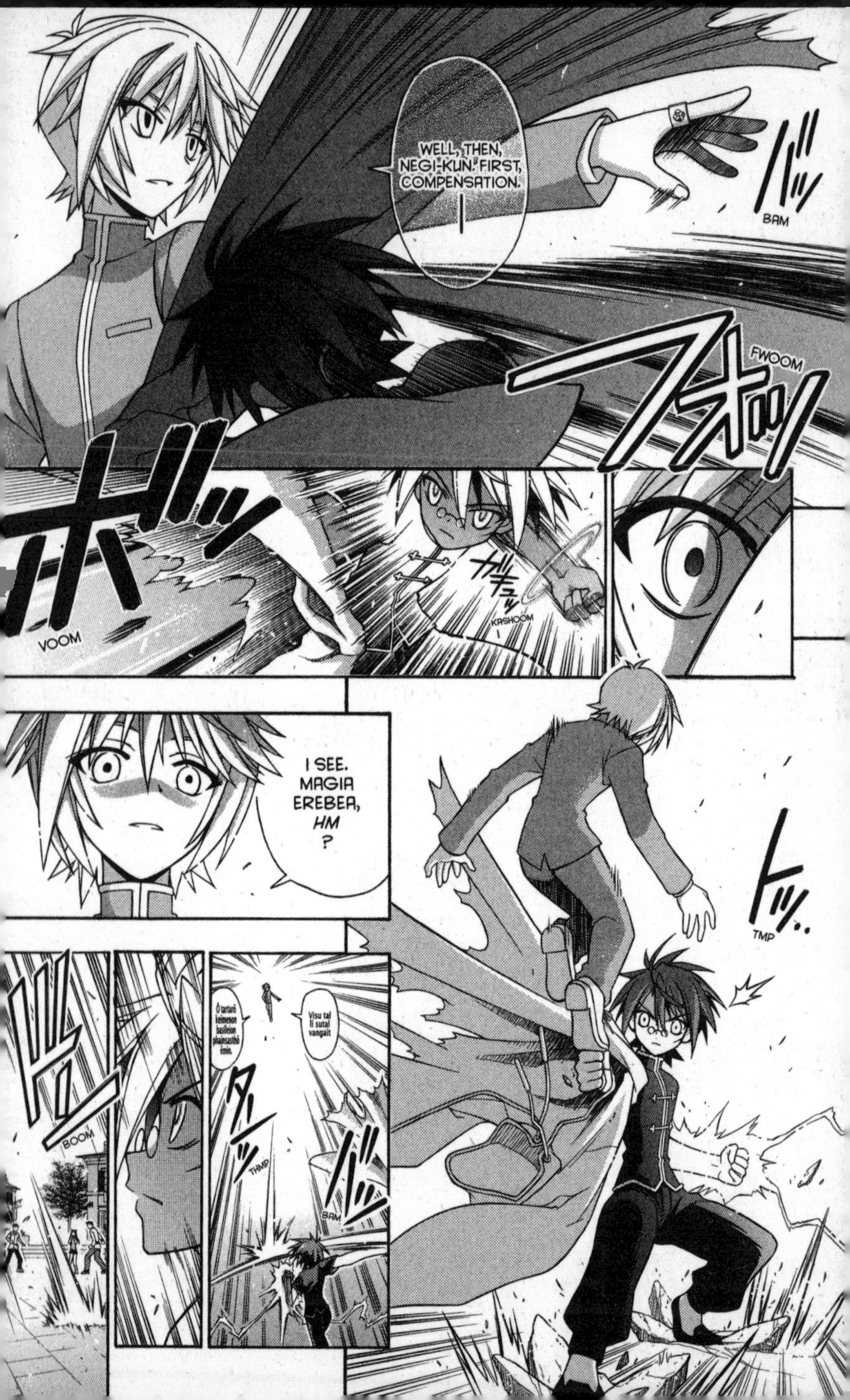
WELL, THEN, NEGI-KUN. FIRST, COMPENSATION.
BAM
FWOOM
KASHOOM
VOOM
TMP
I SEE. MAGIA EREBEA, HM?
Visu tal li sutal vangait
Ô tartarô keimenon basileion phainsasthô ĕmin.
BAM
THMP
BOOM

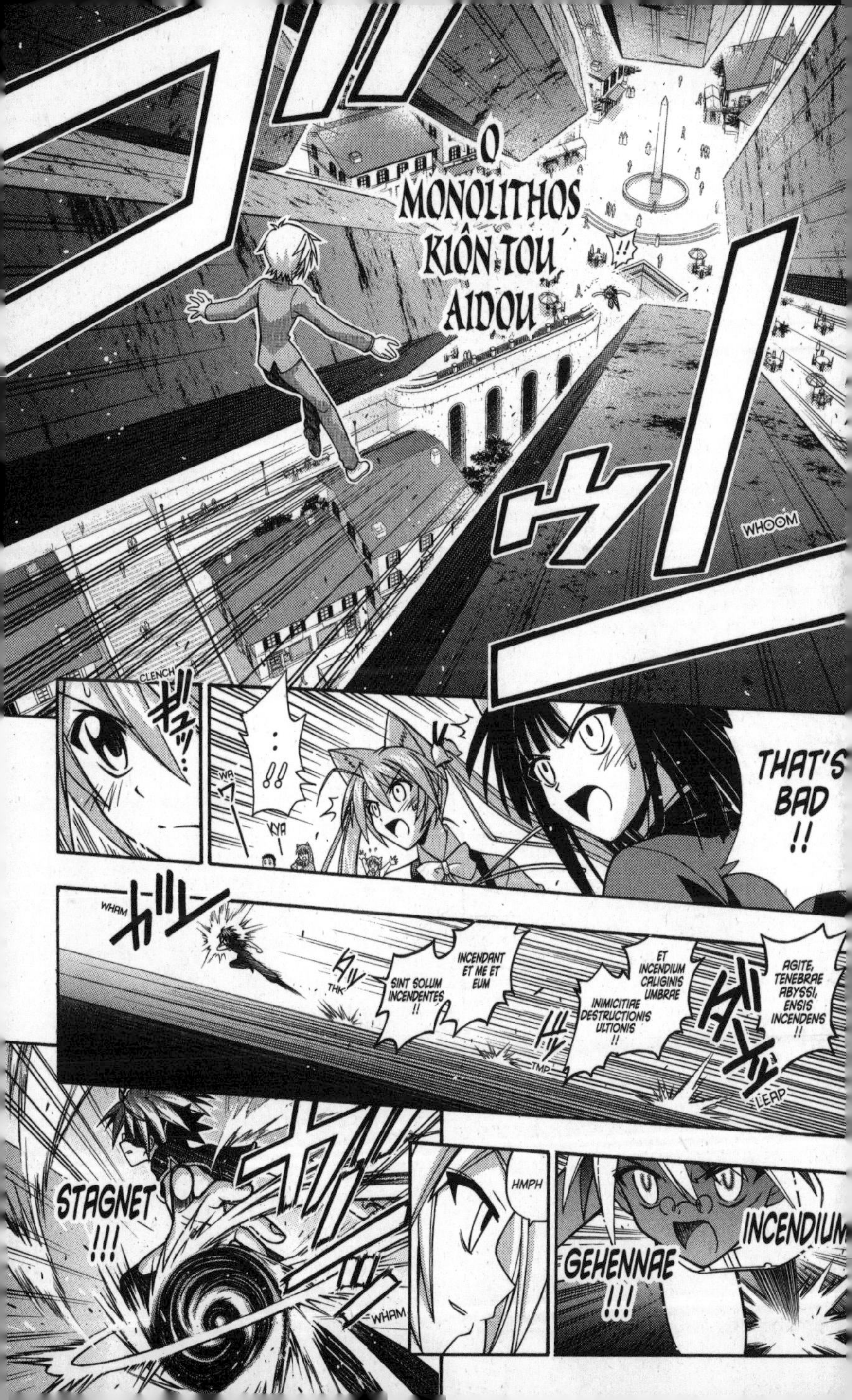
O MONOLITHOS KIÔN TOU AIDOU
!!
WHOOM
CLENCH
THAT'S BAD !!
... !!
WA
KYA
WHAM
AGITE, TENEBRAE ABYSSI, ENSIS INCENDENS
LEAP
ET INCENDIUM CALIGINIS UMBRAE
INIMICITIAE DESTRUCTIONIS ULTIONIS !!
TMP
INCENDANT ET ME ET EUM
SINT SOLUM INCENDENTES !!
THK
INCENDIUM
GEHENNAE !!!
HMPH
STAGNET !!!
WHAM

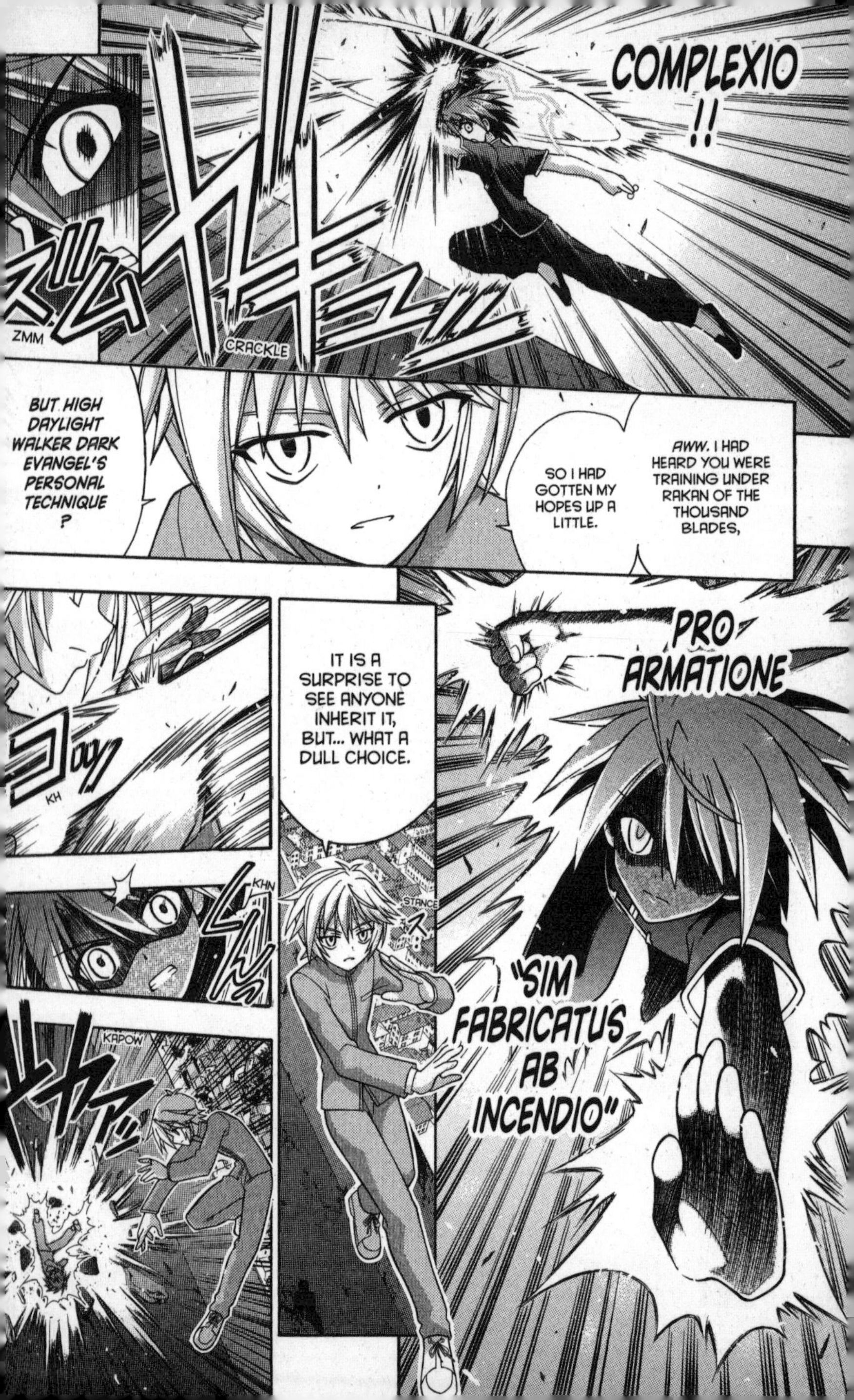
COMPLEXIO !!
CRACKLE
ZMM
AWW. I HAD HEARD YOU WERE TRAINING UNDER RAKAN OF THE THOUSAND BLADES,
SO I HAD GOTTEN MY HOPES UP A LITTLE.
BUT HIGH DAYLIGHT WALKER DARK EVANGEL'S PERSONAL TECHNIQUE ?
PRO ARMATIONE
"SIM FABRICATUS AB INCENDIO"
IT IS A SURPRISE TO SEE ANYONE INHERIT IT, BUT... WHAT A DULL CHOICE.
STANCE
KH
KHN
KAPOW

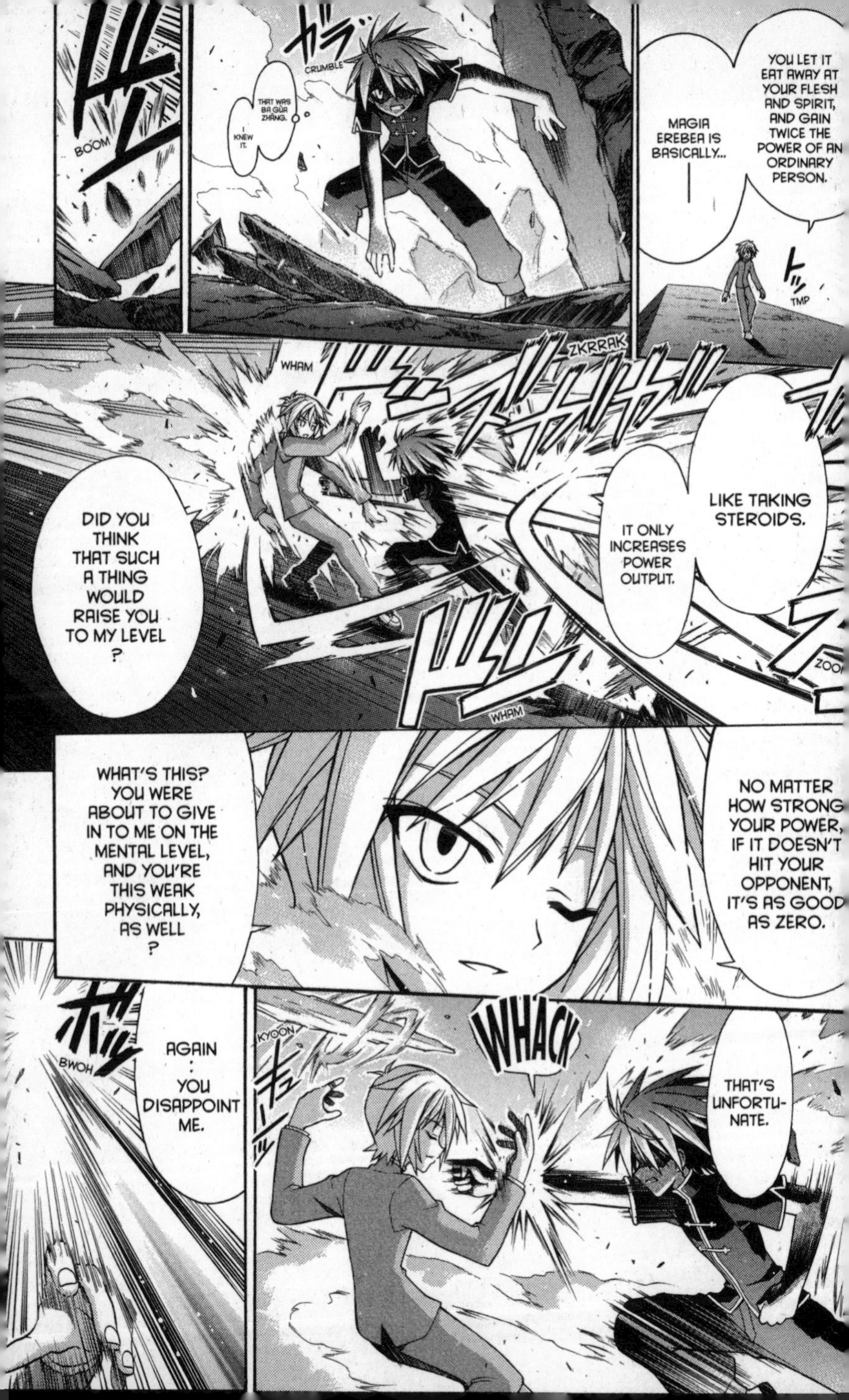
MAGIA EREBEA IS BASICALLY...
YOU LET IT EAT AWAY AT YOUR FLESH AND SPIRIT, AND GAIN TWICE THE POWER OF AN ORDINARY PERSON.
TMP
CRUMBLE
THAT WAS BA GUA ZHANG.
I KNEW IT.
BOOM
LIKE TAKING STEROIDS.
IT ONLY INCREASES POWER OUTPUT.
ZOOM
ZKRRAK
WHAM
WHAM
DID YOU THINK THAT SUCH A THING WOULD RAISE YOU TO MY LEVEL?
NO MATTER HOW STRONG YOUR POWER, IF IT DOESN'T HIT YOUR OPPONENT, IT'S AS GOOD AS ZERO.
WHAT'S THIS? YOU WERE ABOUT TO GIVE IN TO ME ON THE MENTAL LEVEL, AND YOU'RE THIS WEAK PHYSICALLY, AS WELL?
THAT'S UNFORTUNATE.
WHACK
KYOON
AGAIN: YOU DISAPPOINT ME.
BWOH

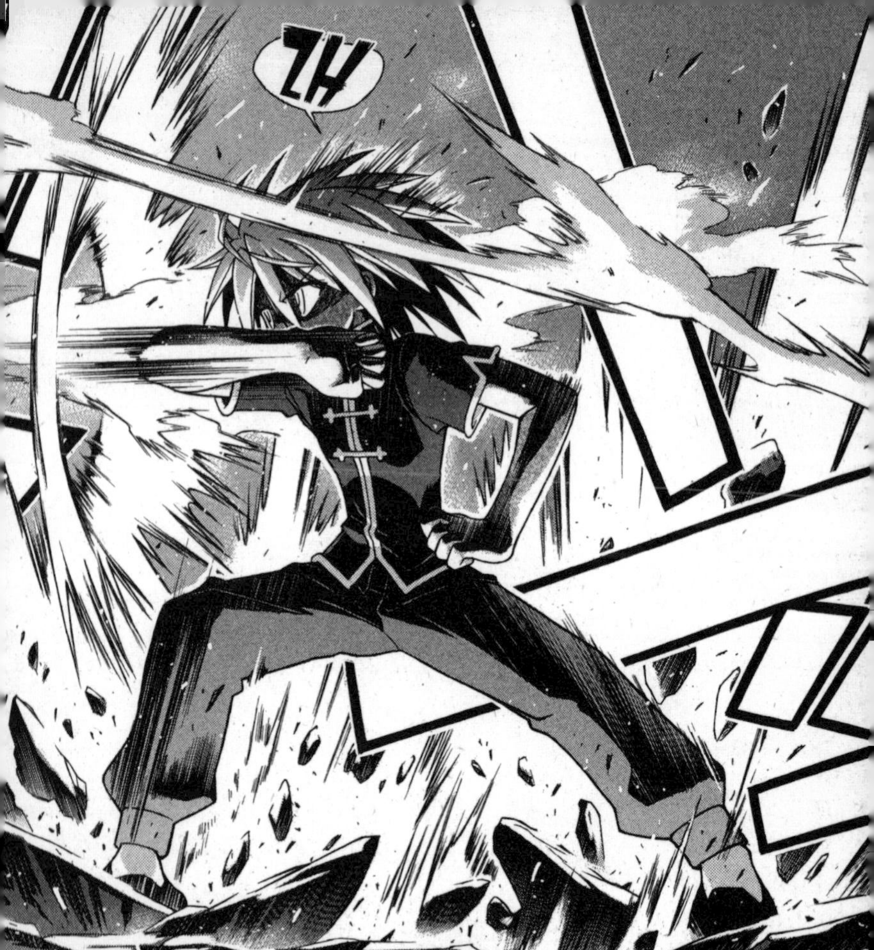
ZH
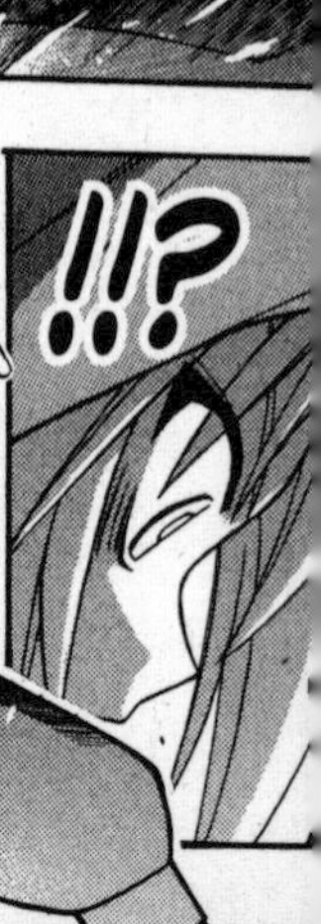
!!?
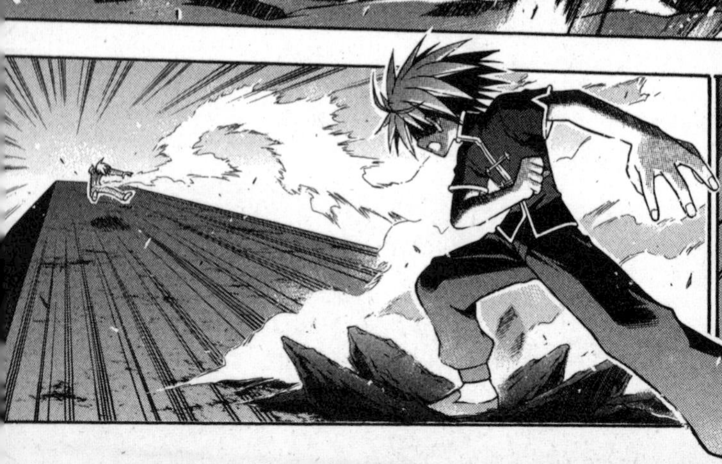

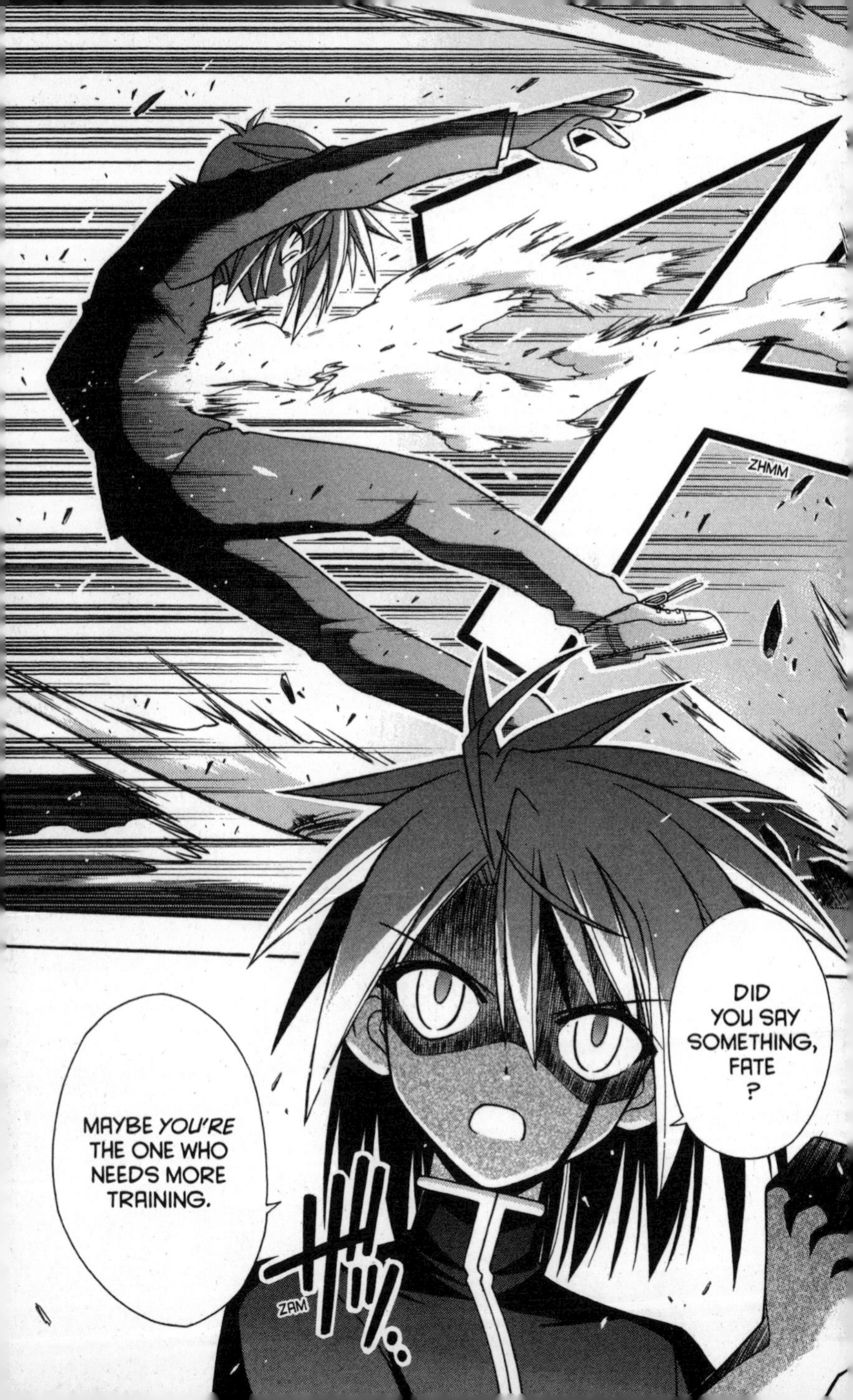
ZHMM
DID YOU SAY SOMETHING, FATE ?
MAYBE *YOU'RE* THE ONE WHO NEEDS MORE TRAINING.
ZAM

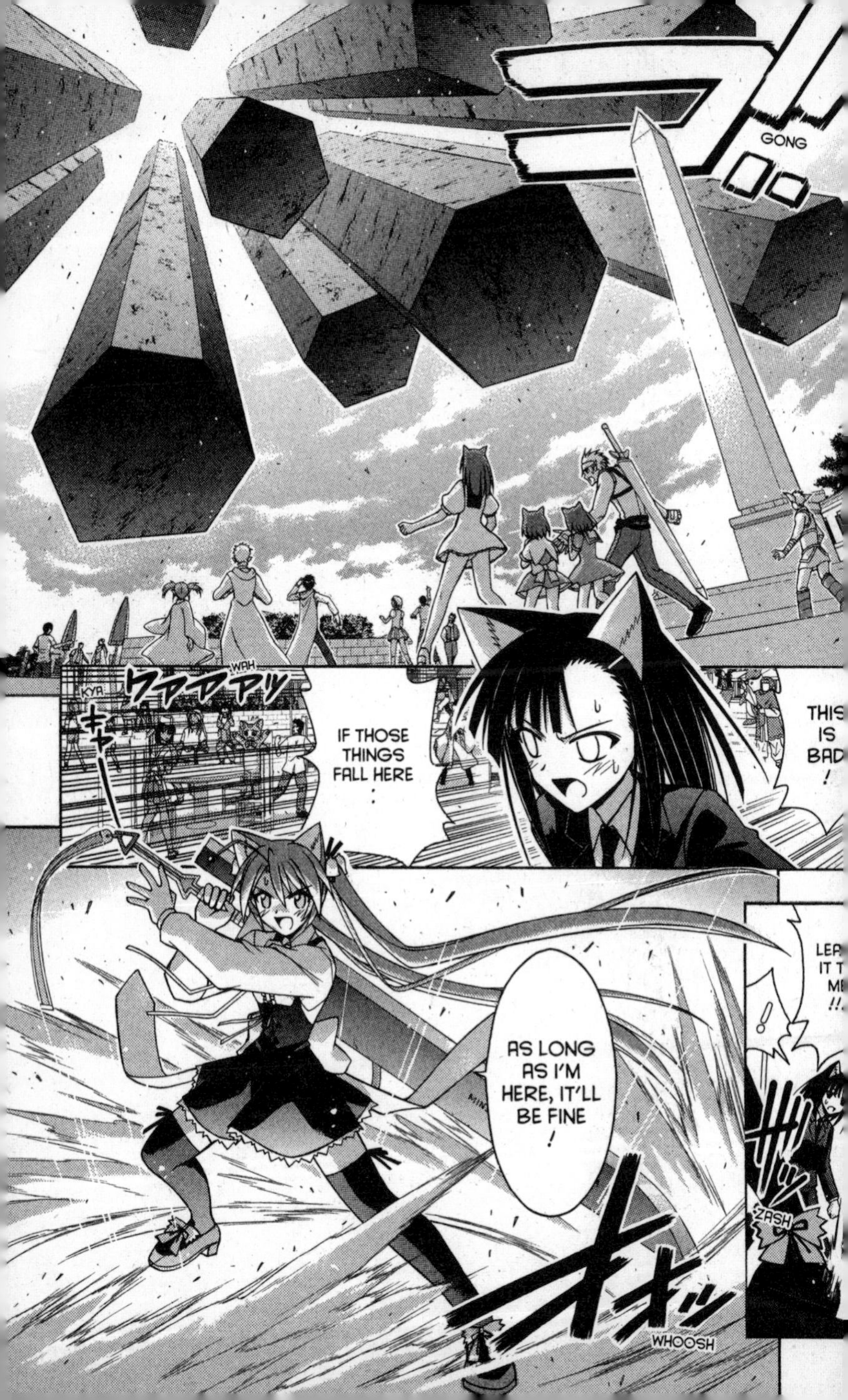
GONG
WAH
KYA
IF THOSE THINGS FALL HERE
THIS IS BAD!
LEA IT T ME!!
AS LONG AS I'M HERE, IT'LL BE FINE!
ZASH
WHOOSH

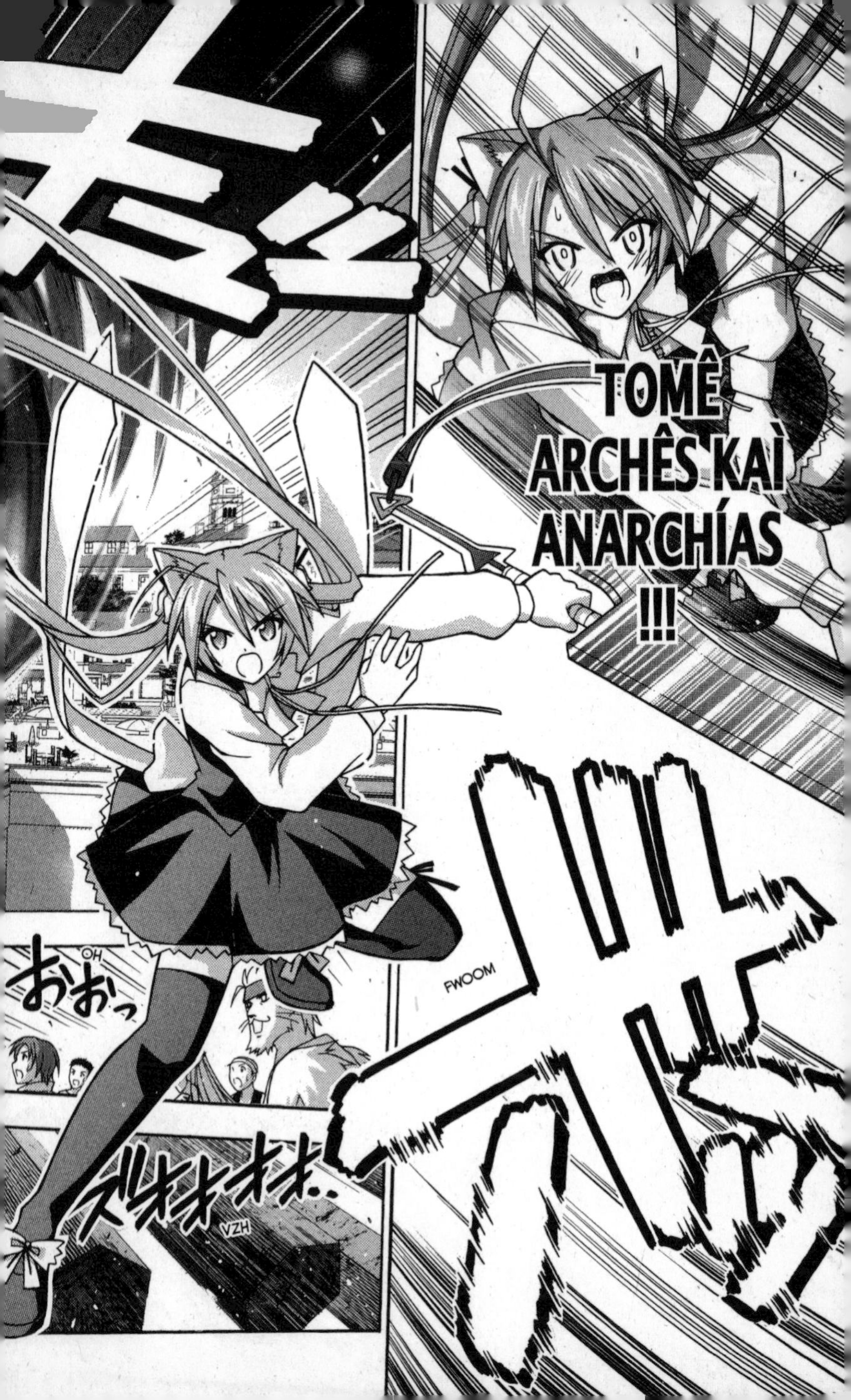
TOMÊ ARCHÊS KAÌ ANARCHÍAS !!!
FWOOM
OH
VZH

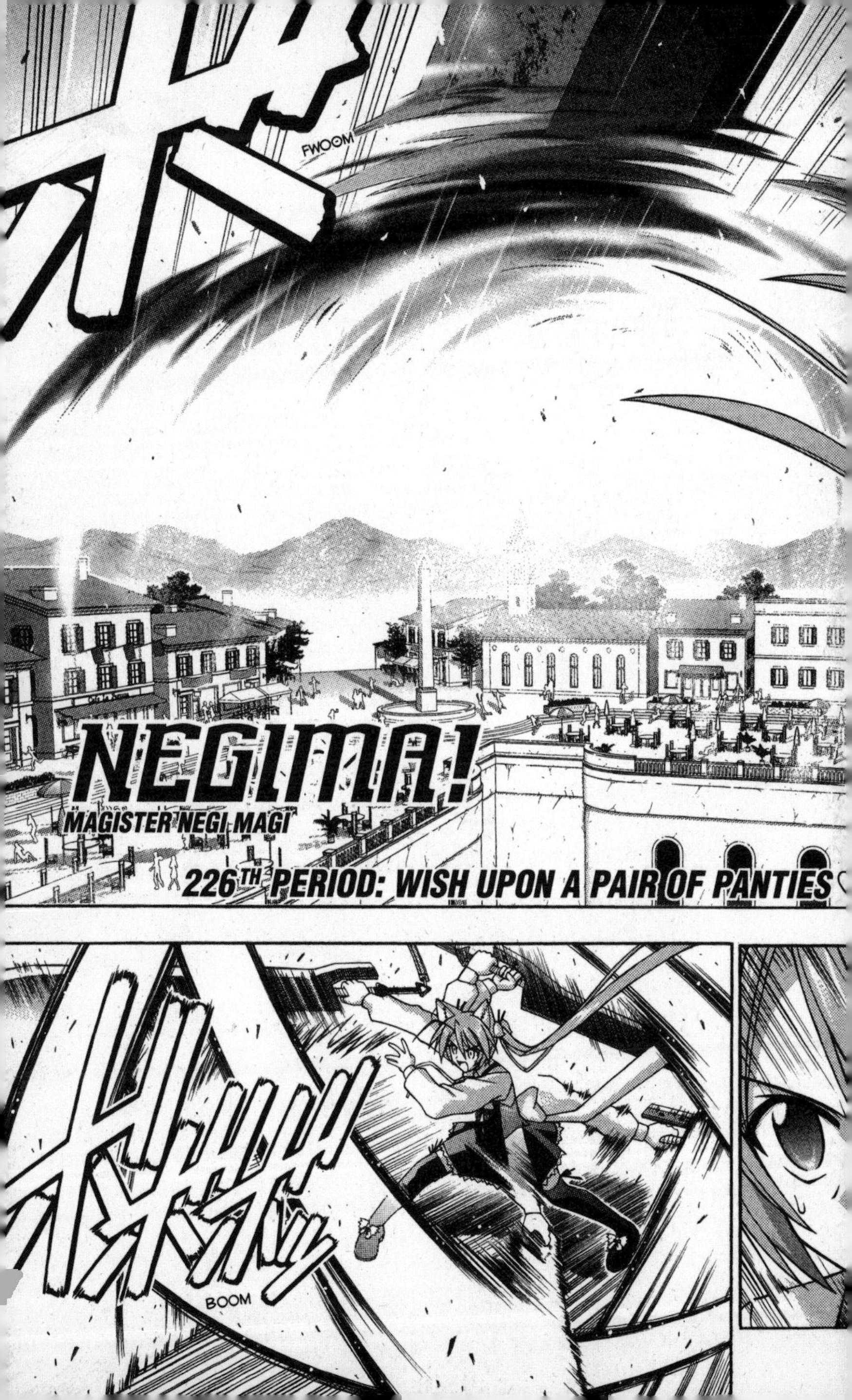
FWOOM
NEGIMA!
MAGISTER NEGI MAGI
226TH PERIOD: WISH UPON A PAIR OF PANTIES
BOOM

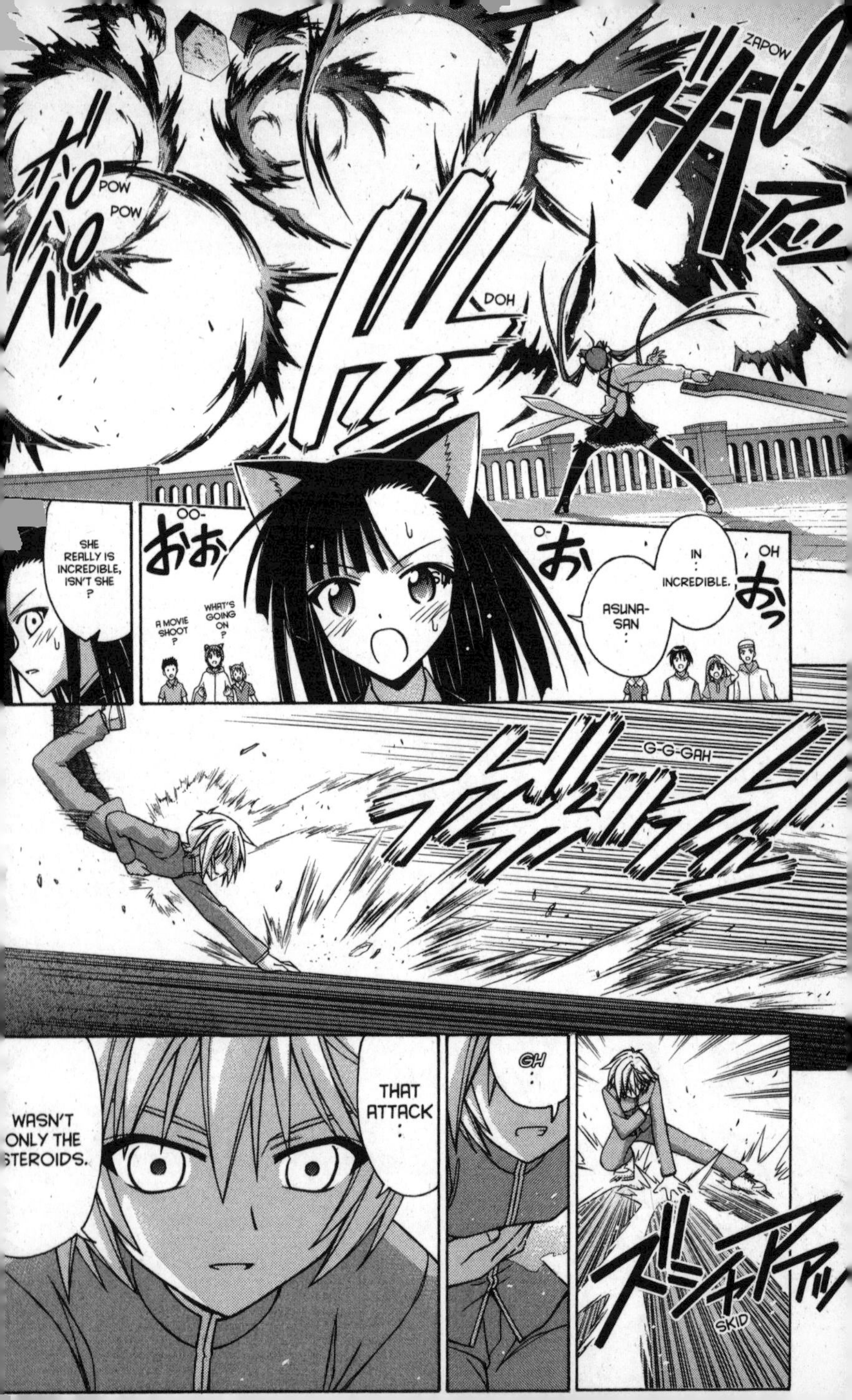
ZAPOW
DOH
POW
POW
OH
おっ
IN… INCREDIBLE.
ASUNA-SAN…
O-
お
OO-
おお
WHAT'S GOING ON?
A MOVIE SHOOT?
SHE REALLY IS INCREDIBLE, ISN'T SHE?
G-G-GAH
SKID
GH…
THAT ATTACK…
WASN'T ONLY THE STEROIDS.

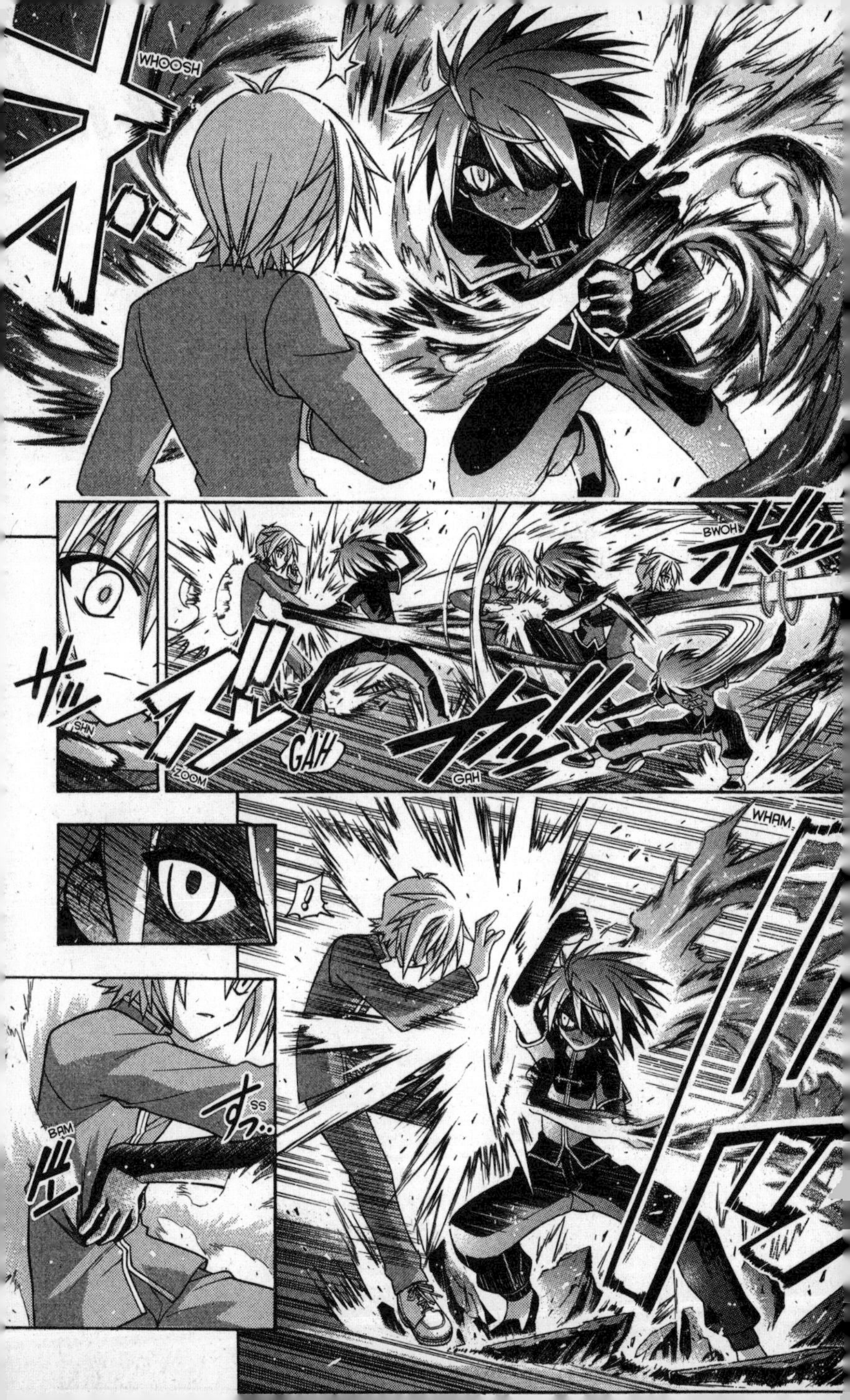
WHOOSH
BWOH
GAH
GAH
ZOOM
SHN
WHAM
!
すっ..
SS
BAM

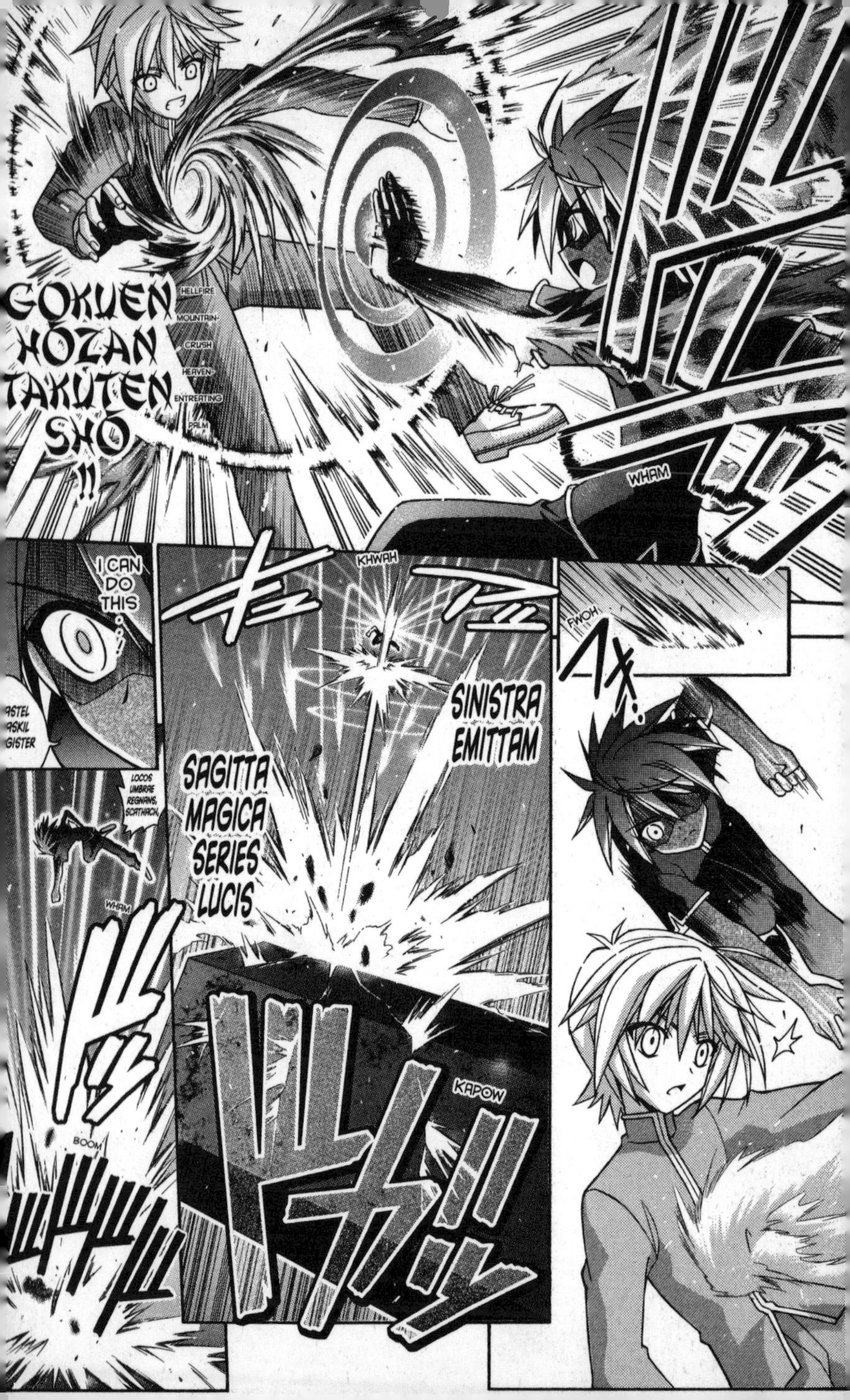
GOKUEN HOZAN TAKUTEN SHO!!
HELLFIRE MOUNTAIN-CRUSH HEAVEN-ENTREATING PALM
WHAM
FWOH
KHWAH
SINISTRA EMITTAM
I CAN DO THIS...!
ASTEL ASKIL AGISTER
LOCOS UMBRAE REGNANS, SCATHACH,
SAGITTA MAGICA SERIES LUCIS
WHAM
KAPOW
BOOM

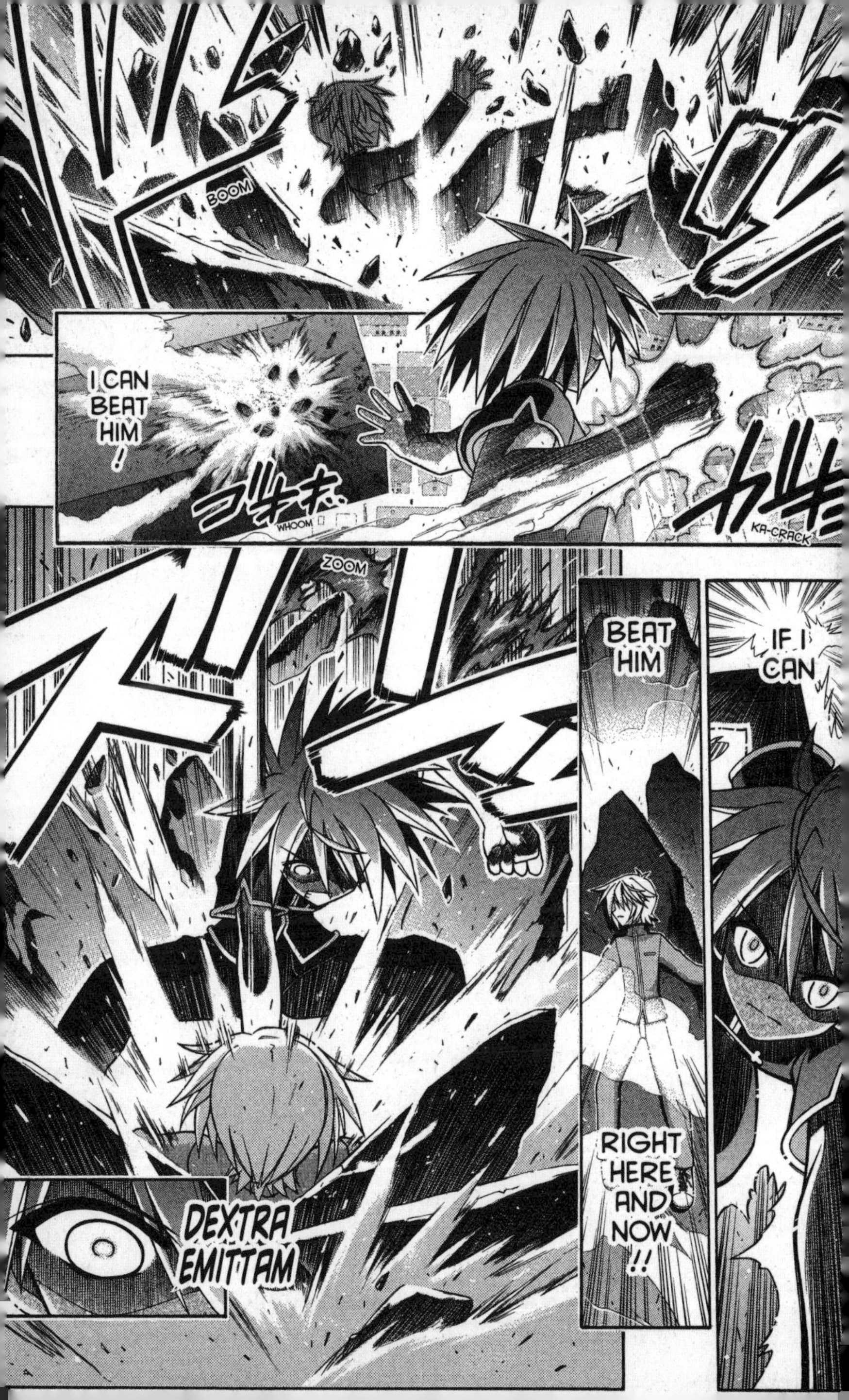
BOOM
KA-CRACK
I CAN BEAT HIM!
WHOOM
IF I CAN
BEAT HIM
RIGHT HERE AND NOW!!
ZOOM
DEXTRA EMITTAM

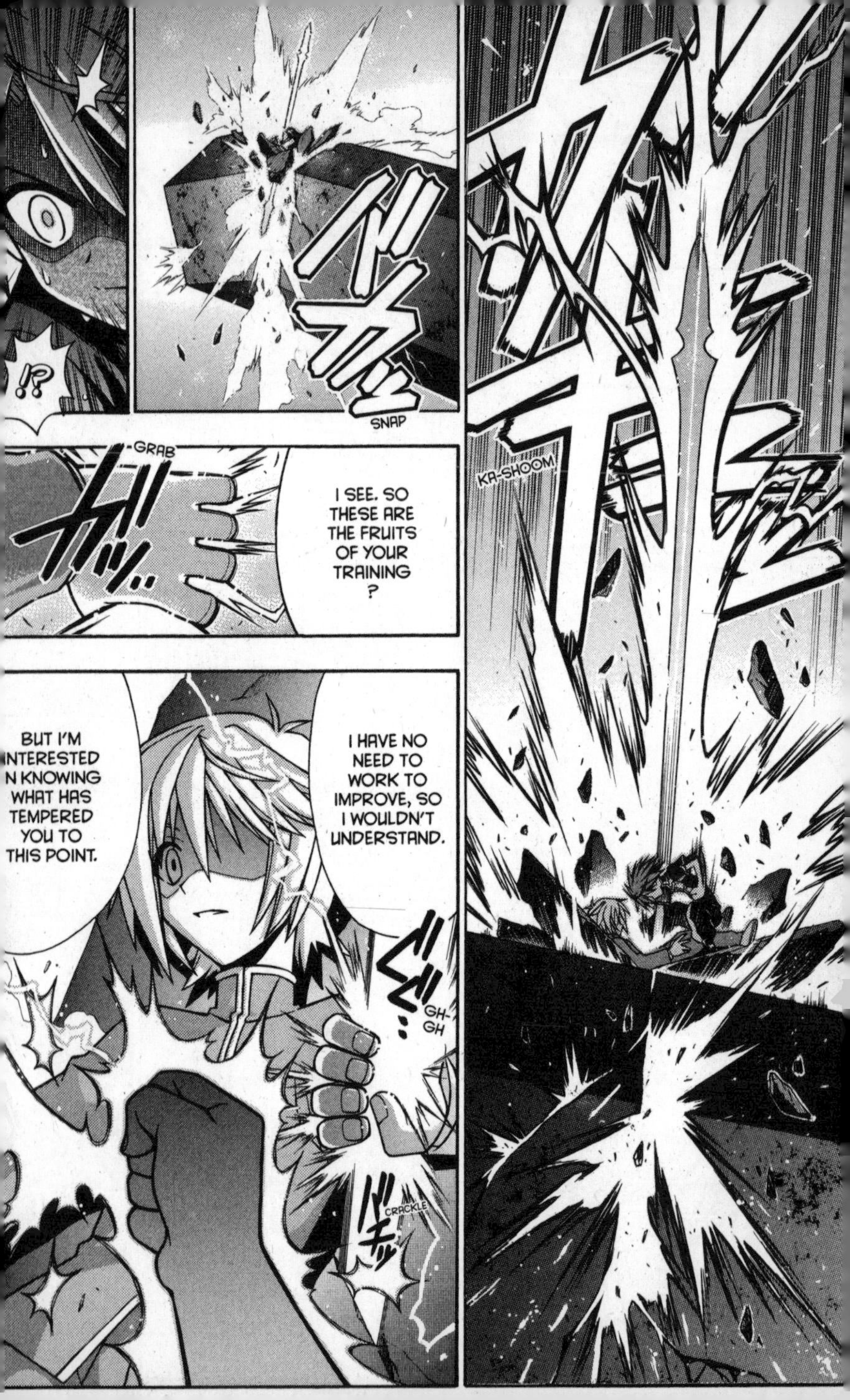
KA-SHOOM
SNAP
!?
-GRAB
I SEE. SO THESE ARE THE FRUITS OF YOUR TRAINING?
I HAVE NO NEED TO WORK TO IMPROVE, SO I WOULDN'T UNDERSTAND.
BUT I'M INTERESTED N KNOWING WHAT HAS TEMPERED YOU TO THIS POINT.
GH-GH
CRACKLE

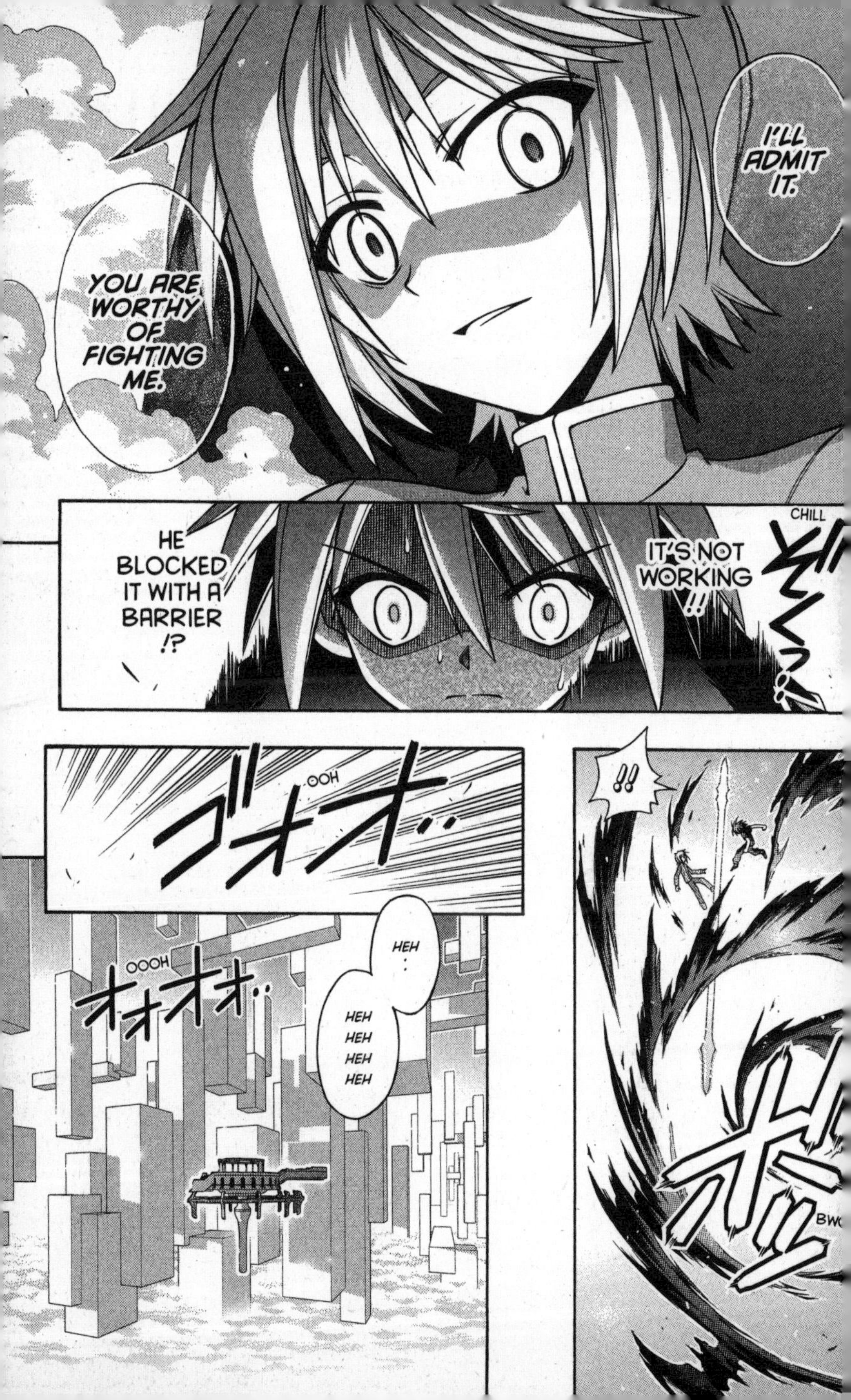
I'LL ADMIT IT.
YOU ARE WORTHY OF FIGHTING ME.
CHILL
IT'S NOT WORKING !!
HE BLOCKED IT WITH A BARRIER !?
!!
BWO
OOH
ゴオオ
HEH... HEH HEH HEH HEH
OOOH
オオオオ

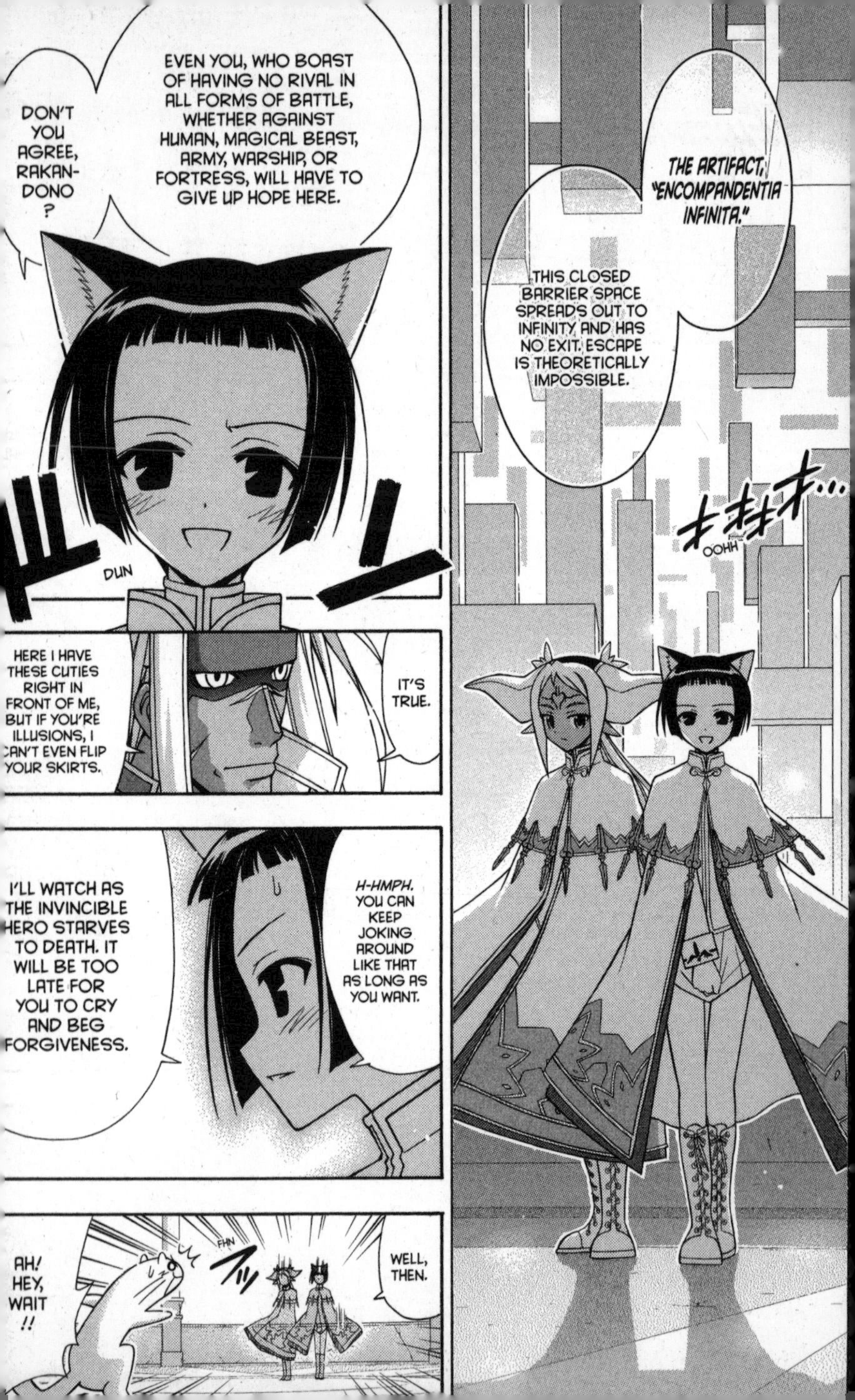
THE ARTIFACT, "ENCOMPANDENTIA INFINITA."
THIS CLOSED BARRIER SPACE SPREADS OUT TO INFINITY AND HAS NO EXIT. ESCAPE IS THEORETICALLY IMPOSSIBLE.
オオオオ…
OOHH
EVEN YOU, WHO BOAST OF HAVING NO RIVAL IN ALL FORMS OF BATTLE, WHETHER AGAINST HUMAN, MAGICAL BEAST, ARMY, WARSHIP, OR FORTRESS, WILL HAVE TO GIVE UP HOPE HERE.
DON'T YOU AGREE, RAKAN-DONO?
DUN
IT'S TRUE.
HERE I HAVE THESE CUTIES RIGHT IN FRONT OF ME, BUT IF YOU'RE ILLUSIONS, I CAN'T EVEN FLIP YOUR SKIRTS.
H-HMPH. YOU CAN KEEP JOKING AROUND LIKE THAT AS LONG AS YOU WANT.
I'LL WATCH AS THE INVINCIBLE HERO STARVES TO DEATH. IT WILL BE TOO LATE FOR YOU TO CRY AND BEG FORGIVENESS.
WELL, THEN.
FHN
AH! HEY, WAIT!!

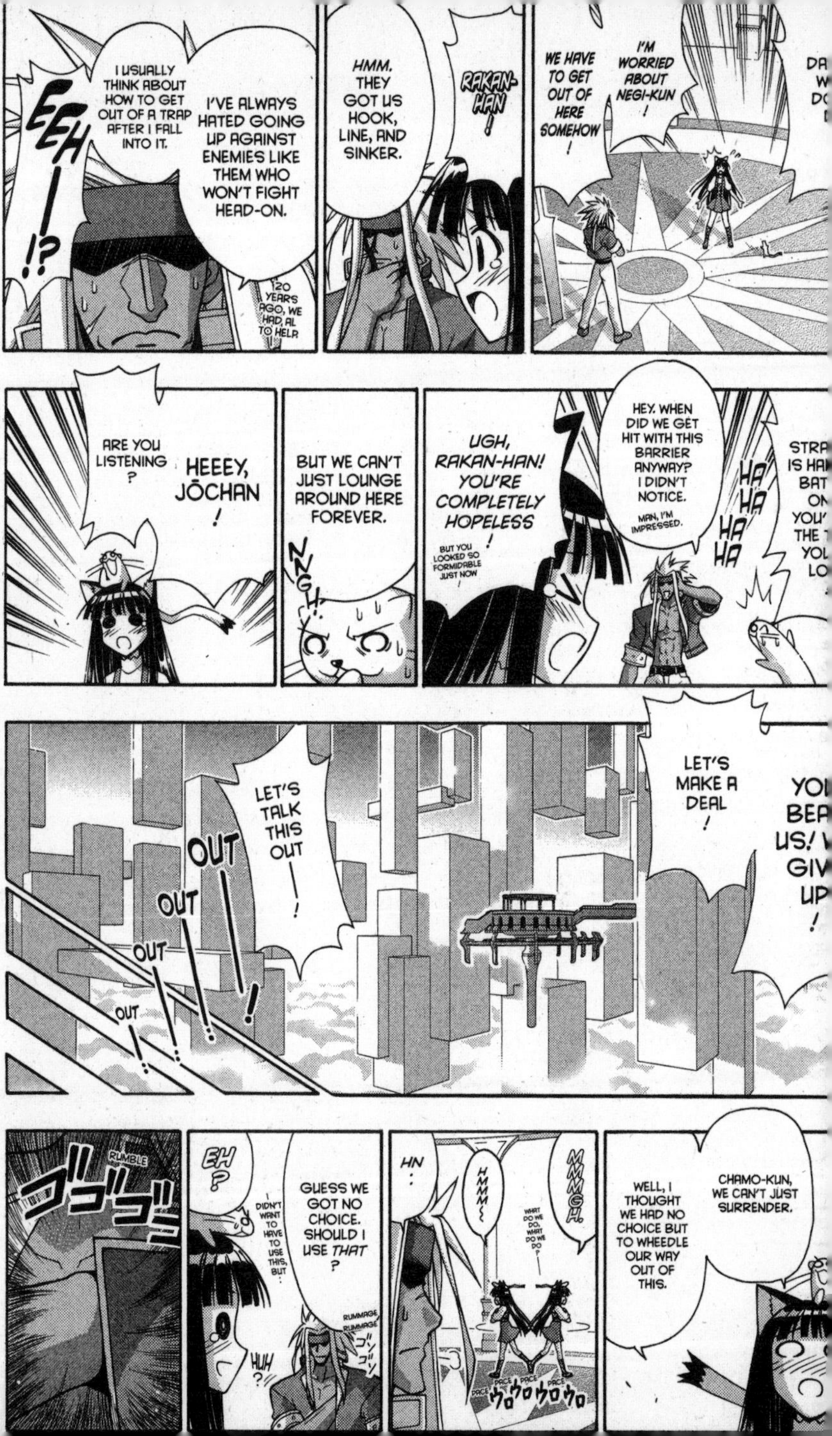
I'M WORRIED ABOUT NEGI-KUN!
WE HAVE TO GET OUT OF HERE SOMEHOW!
RAKAN-HAN!
HMM. THEY GOT US HOOK, LINE, AND SINKER.
I'VE ALWAYS HATED GOING UP AGAINST ENEMIES LIKE THEM WHO WON'T FIGHT HEAD-ON.
I USUALLY THINK ABOUT HOW TO GET OUT OF A TRAP AFTER I FALL INTO IT.
EEH—!?
20 YEARS AGO, WE HAD AL TO HELP.
HEY. WHEN DID WE GET HIT WITH THIS BARRIER ANYWAY? I DIDN'T NOTICE.
MAN, I'M IMPRESSED.
HA HA HA HA
UGH, RAKAN-HAN! YOU'RE COMPLETELY HOPELESS!
BUT YOU LOOKED SO FORMIDABLE JUST NOW!
BUT WE CAN'T JUST LOUNGE AROUND HERE FOREVER.
NNGH!!
HEEEY, JŌCHAN!
ARE YOU LISTENING?
LET'S MAKE A DEAL!
LET'S TALK THIS OUT—!
OUT—!
OUT—!
OUT—!
OUT—!
CHAMO-KUN, WE CAN'T JUST SURRENDER.
WELL, I THOUGHT WE HAD NO CHOICE BUT TO WHEEDLE OUR WAY OUT OF THIS.
MMMGH.
HMMM~
HN...
WHAT DO WE DO, WHAT DO WE DO—
PACE PACE PACE PACE
GUESS WE GOT NO CHOICE. SHOULD I USE THAT?
I DIDN'T WANT TO HAVE TO USE THIS, BUT...
EH?
RUMMAGE RUMMAGE
HUH?
RUMBLE

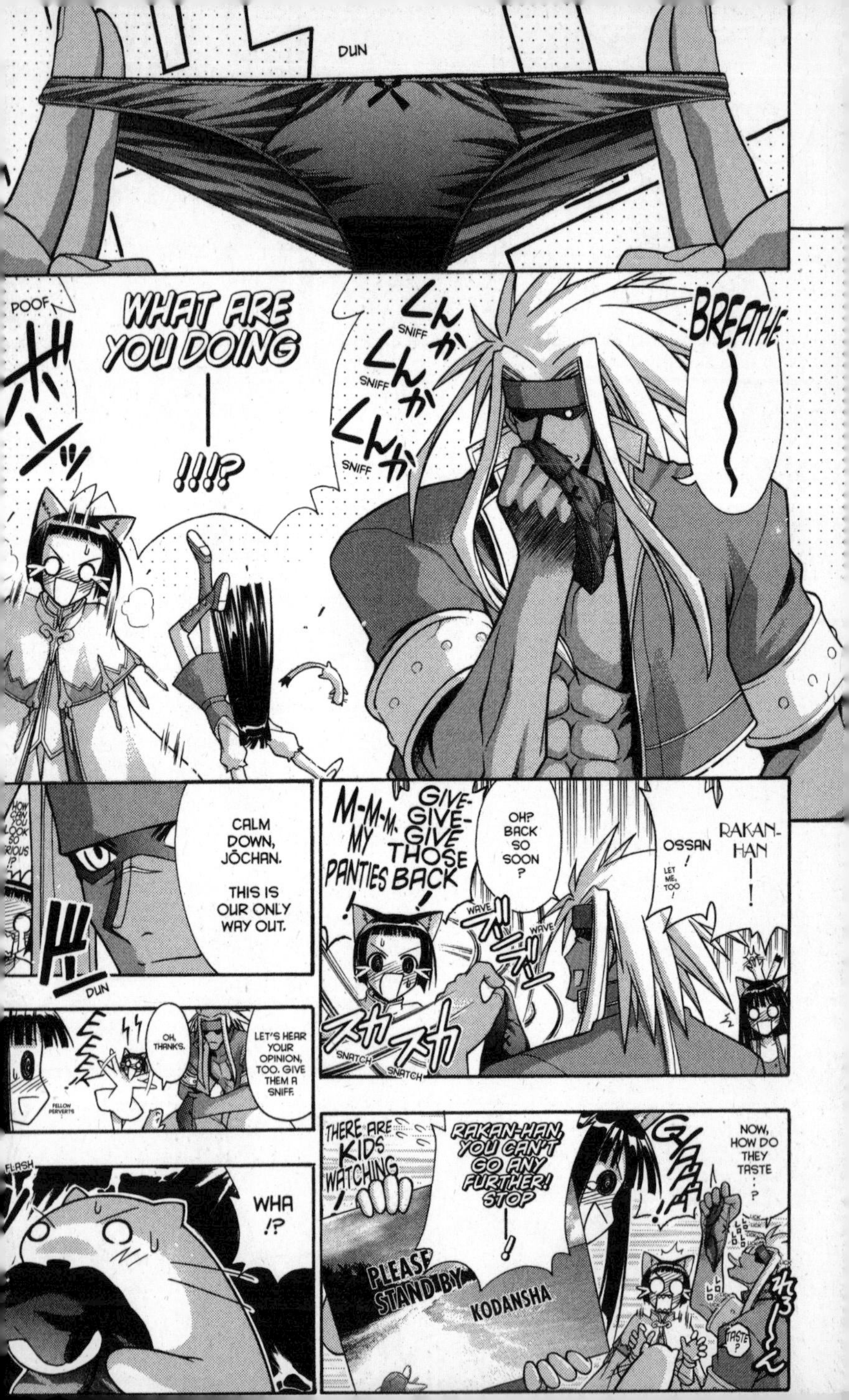
DUN
BREATHE ~~
くんか SNIFF
くんか SNIFF
くんか SNIFF
WHAT ARE YOU DOING —!!!?
POOF
ボンッ
RAKAN-HAN —!!
OSSAN!
LET ME, TOO!
OH? BACK SO SOON?
M-M-M-MY PANTIES!
GIVE-GIVE-GIVE THOSE BACK!
WAVE
WAVE
SNATCH
SNATCH
HOW CAN YOU LOOK SO SERIOUS!?
CALM DOWN, JŌCHAN.
THIS IS OUR ONLY WAY OUT.
DUN
LET'S HEAR YOUR OPINION, TOO. GIVE THEM A SNIFF.
OH, THANKS.
FELLOW PERVERTS
NOW, HOW DO THEY TASTE...?
GYAAA!?
RAKAN-HAN, YOU CAN'T GO ANY FURTHER! STOP —!
THERE ARE KIDS WATCHING!
PLEASE STAND BY
KODANSHA
TASTE?
れろ～ん
FLASH
WHA!?

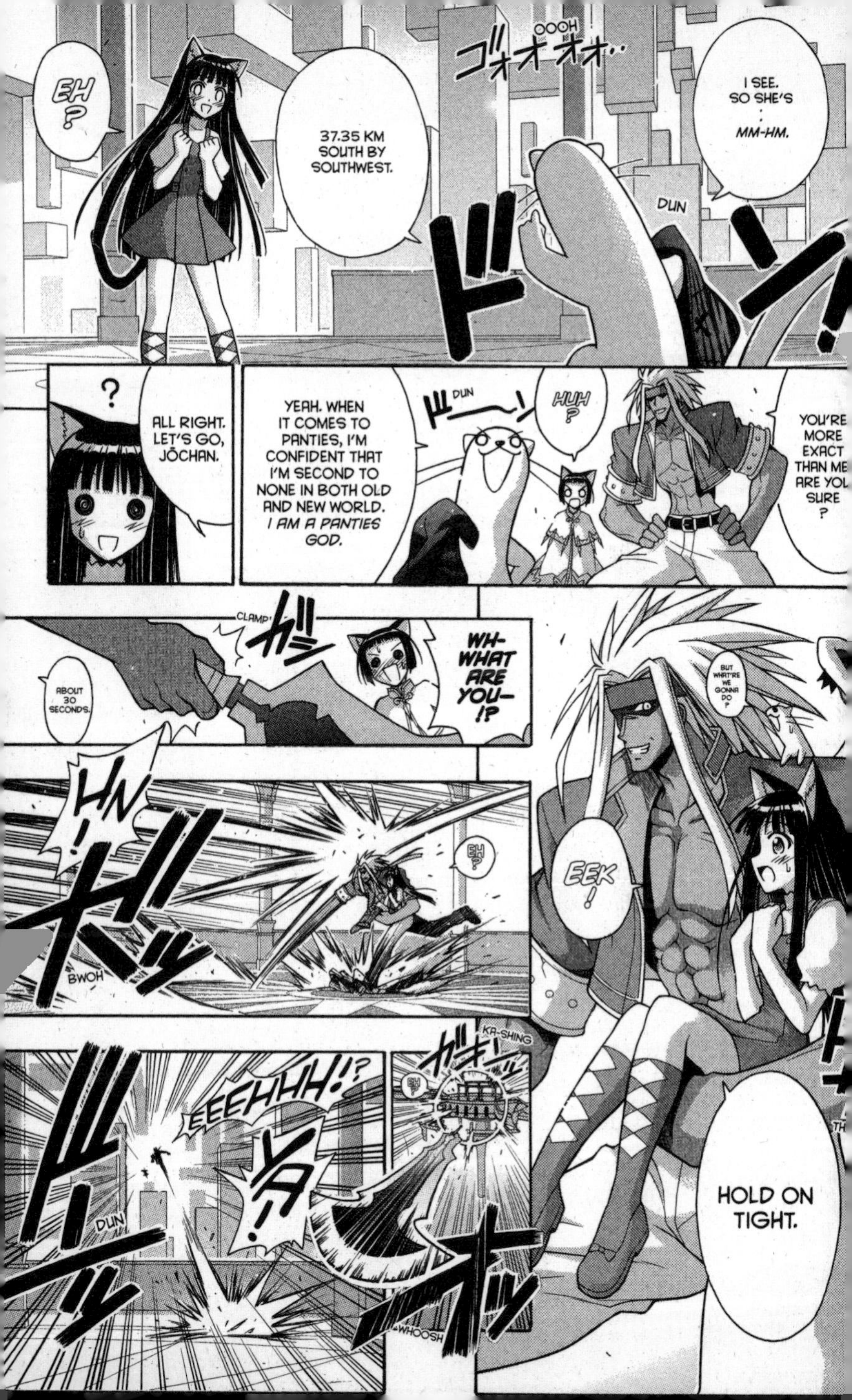
OOOH
I SEE. SO SHE'S
:
MM-HM.
DUN
37.35 KM SOUTH BY SOUTHWEST.
EH ?
YOU'RE MORE EXACT THAN ME ARE YOU SURE ?
HUH ?
DUN
YEAH. WHEN IT COMES TO PANTIES, I'M CONFIDENT THAT I'M SECOND TO NONE IN BOTH OLD AND NEW WORLD. *I AM A PANTIES GOD.*
?
ALL RIGHT. LET'S GO, JŌCHAN.
BUT WHAT'RE WE GONNA DO ?
EEK !
HOLD ON TIGHT.
CLAMP
WH-WHAT ARE YOU-!?
ABOUT 30 SECONDS.
EH ?
HN !
BWOH
KA-SHING
EH ?
EEEHHH!?
YA !
DUN
WHOOSH

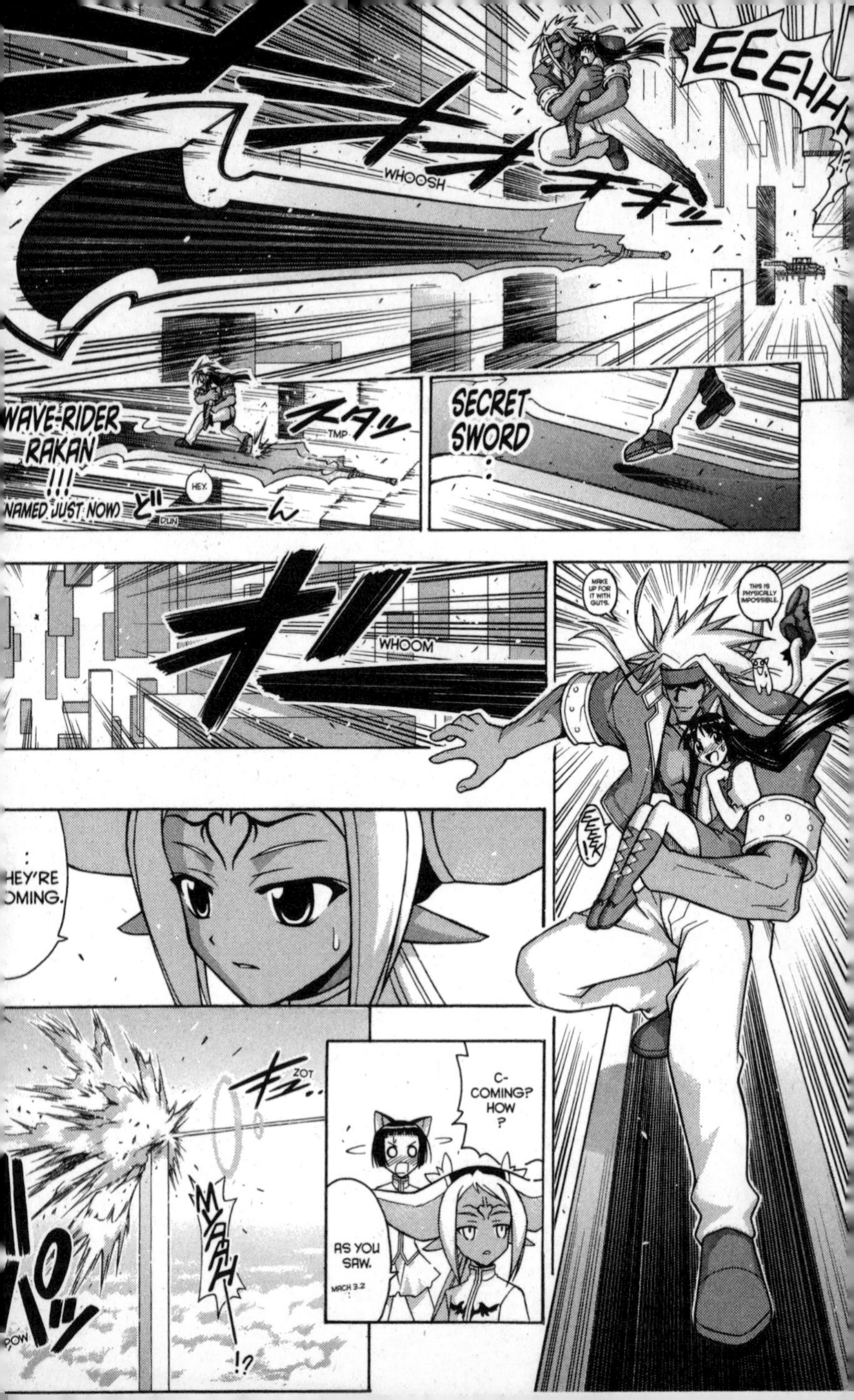
EEEEHHH
!!
WHOOSH
SECRET SWORD
. . .
WAVE-RIDER RAKAN!!!
(NAMED JUST NOW)
TMP
HEY.
DUN
MAKE UP FOR IT WITH GUTS.
THIS IS PHYSICALLY IMPOSSIBLE.
WHOOM
EEEK!
...THEY'RE COMING.
C-COMING? HOW?
AS YOU SAW.
MACH 3.2
ZOT
MYAAH!?
POW

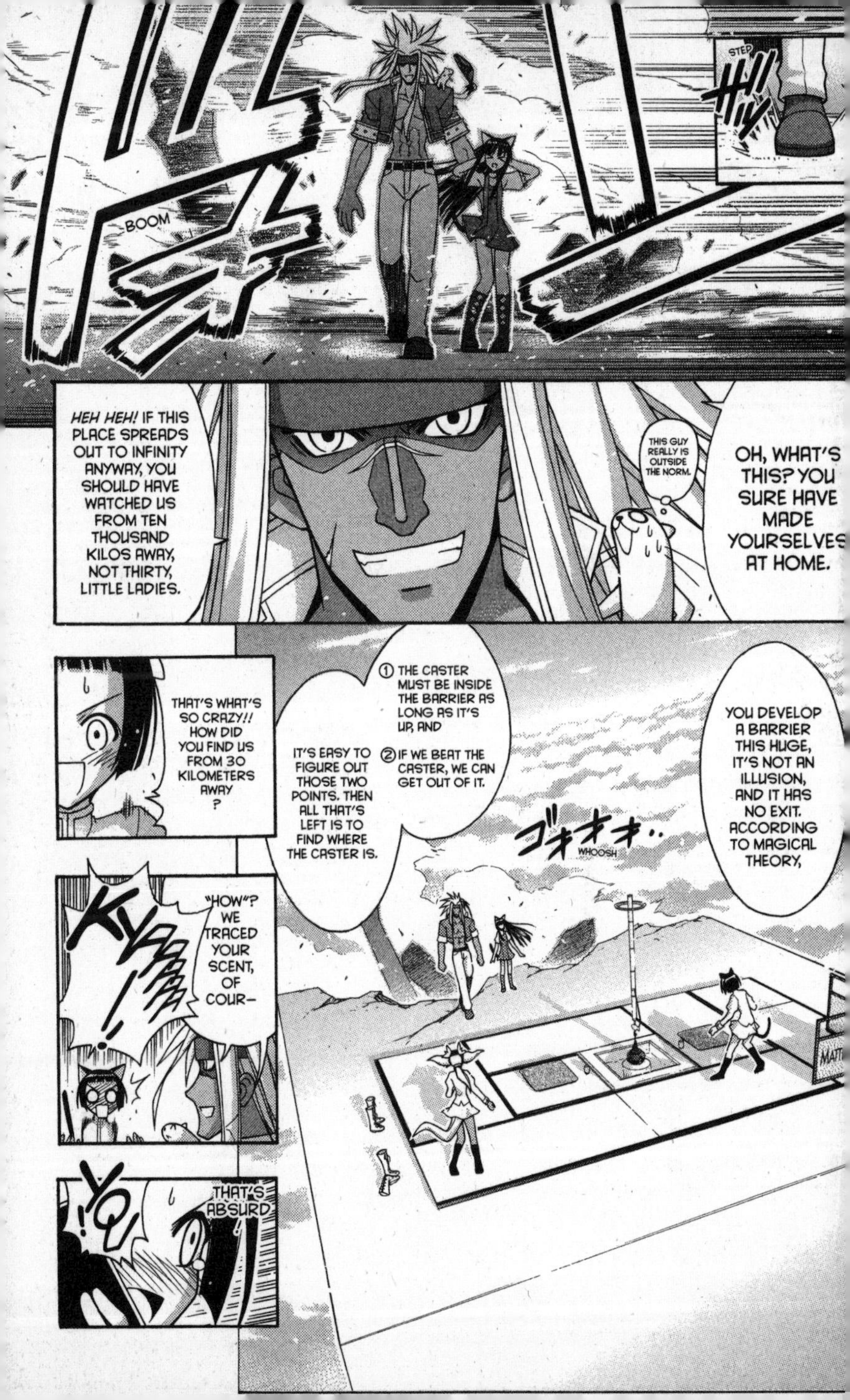
STEP
BOOM
OH, WHAT'S THIS? YOU SURE HAVE MADE YOURSELVES AT HOME.
THIS GUY REALLY IS OUTSIDE THE NORM.
HEH HEH! IF THIS PLACE SPREADS OUT TO INFINITY ANYWAY, YOU SHOULD HAVE WATCHED US FROM TEN THOUSAND KILOS AWAY, NOT THIRTY, LITTLE LADIES.
YOU DEVELOP A BARRIER THIS HUGE, IT'S NOT AN ILLUSION, AND IT HAS NO EXIT. ACCORDING TO MAGICAL THEORY,
① THE CASTER MUST BE INSIDE THE BARRIER AS LONG AS IT'S UP, AND
② IF WE BEAT THE CASTER, WE CAN GET OUT OF IT.
IT'S EASY TO FIGURE OUT THOSE TWO POINTS. THEN ALL THAT'S LEFT IS TO FIND WHERE THE CASTER IS.
WHOOSH
THAT'S WHAT'S SO CRAZY!! HOW DID YOU FIND US FROM 30 KILOMETERS AWAY ?
"HOW"? WE TRACED YOUR SCENT, OF COUR–
KYAAA!!
THAT'S ABSURD
YOU!!

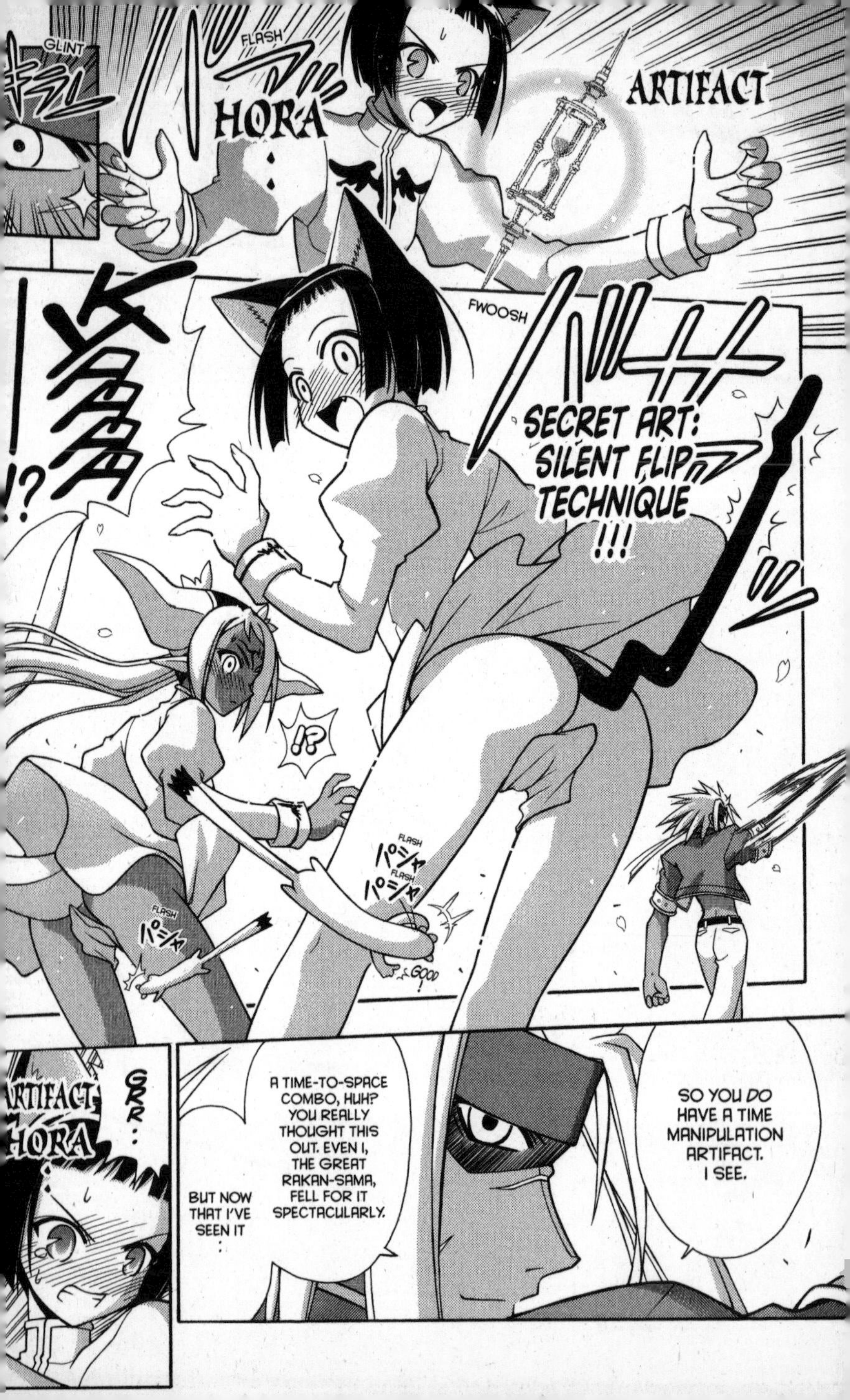
GLINT
FLASH
HORA
ARTIFACT
FWOOSH
SECRET ART: SILENT FLIP TECHNIQUE !!!
!?
!?
FLASH
FLASH
FLASH
GOOD
SO YOU DO HAVE A TIME MANIPULATION ARTIFACT. I SEE.
A TIME-TO-SPACE COMBO, HUH? YOU REALLY THOUGHT THIS OUT. EVEN I, THE GREAT RAKAN-SAMA, FELL FOR IT SPECTACULARLY.
BUT NOW THAT I'VE SEEN IT
GRR...
ARTIFACT HORA

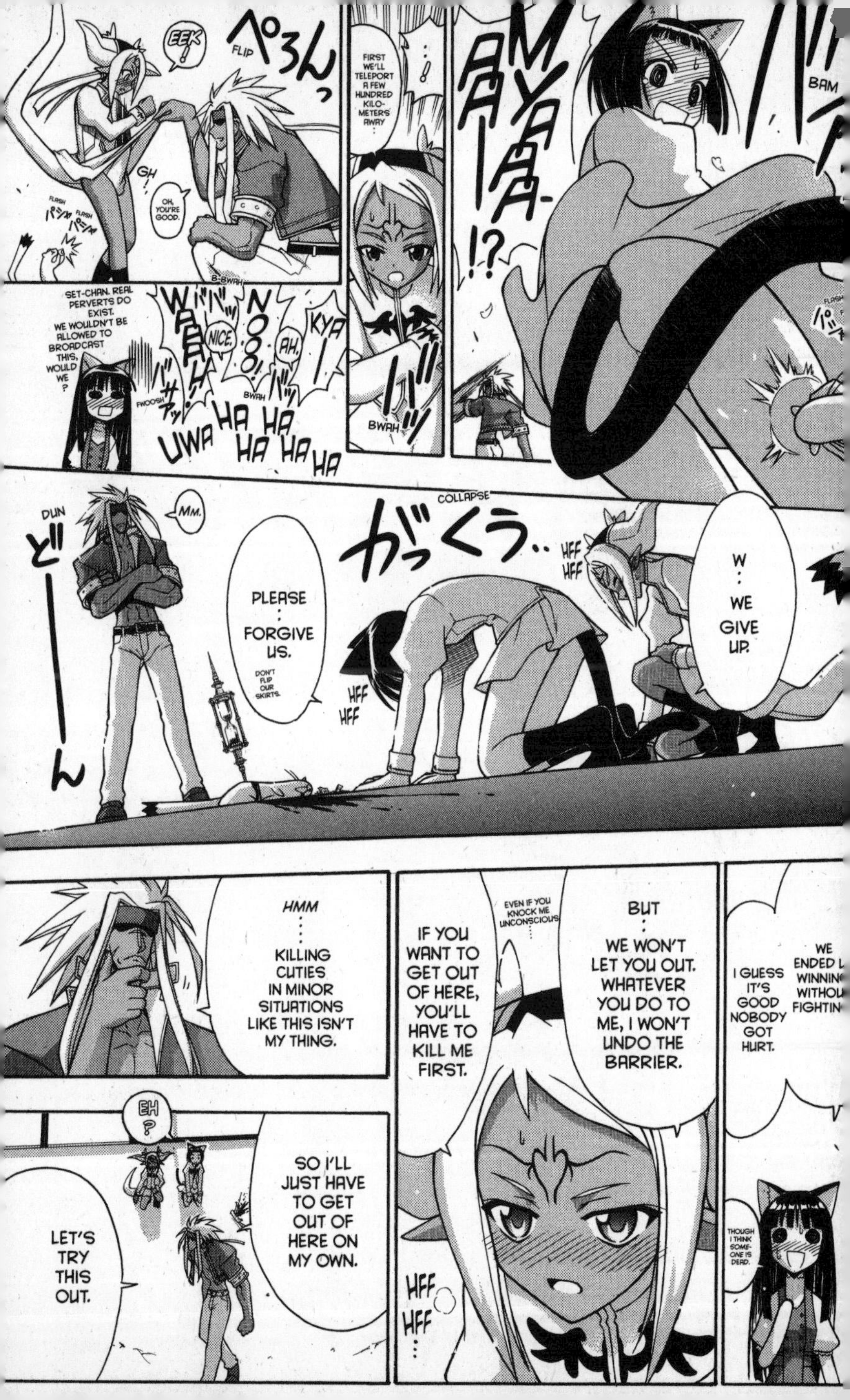

BAM
MYAAAA-!?
FIRST WE'LL TELEPORT A FEW HUNDRED KILOMETERS AWAY...
...!
EEK!
FLIP
OH, YOU'RE GOOD.
GH!
FLASH
FLASH
B-BWAH
BWAH
KYA!
AH.
NOOO!
NICE.
WAAAH!
BWAH
FWOOSH
UWA HA HA HA HA HA
SET-CHAN. REAL PERVERTS DO EXIST. WE WOULDN'T BE ALLOWED TO BROADCAST THIS, WOULD WE?
FLASH
COLLAPSE
HFF HFF
W... WE GIVE UP.
PLEASE... FORGIVE US.
DON'T FLIP OUR SKIRTS.
HFF HFF
MM.
DUN
WE ENDED UP WINNING WITHOUT FIGHTING
I GUESS IT'S GOOD NOBODY GOT HURT.
BUT... WE WON'T LET YOU OUT. WHATEVER YOU DO TO ME, I WON'T UNDO THE BARRIER.
EVEN IF YOU KNOCK ME UNCONSCIOUS...
IF YOU WANT TO GET OUT OF HERE, YOU'LL HAVE TO KILL ME FIRST.
HMM... KILLING CUTIES IN MINOR SITUATIONS LIKE THIS ISN'T MY THING.
THOUGH I THINK SOMEONE IS DEAD.
HFF HFF...
SO I'LL JUST HAVE TO GET OUT OF HERE ON MY OWN.
EH?
LET'S TRY THIS OUT.

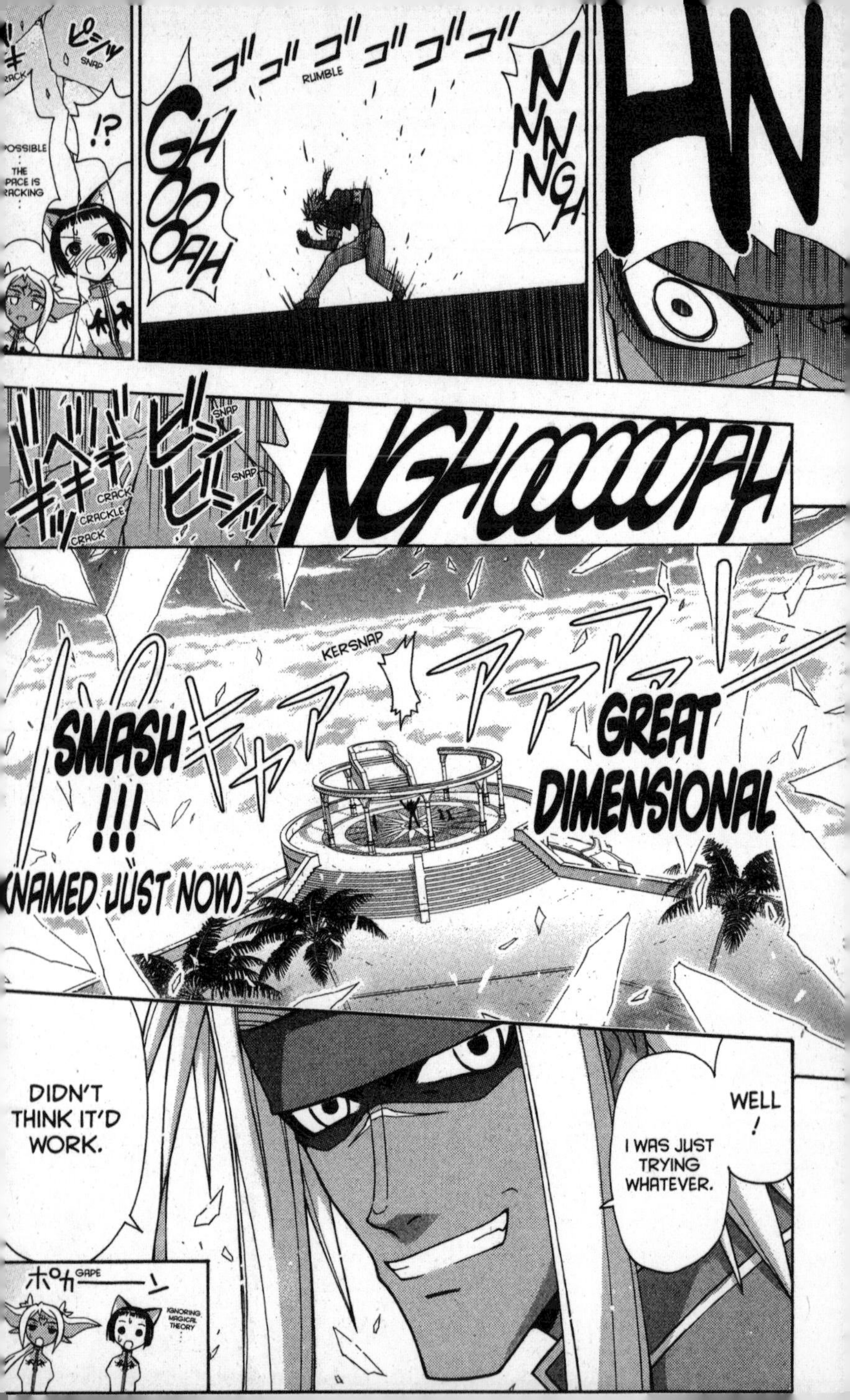
HN
NNNNGH
ゴゴゴゴゴゴ
RUMBLE
GHOOOOAH
ピシッ
SNAP
CRACK
!?
POSSIBLE… THE PACE IS RACKING…
NGHOOOOOAH
SNAP
SNAP
CRACK
CRACKLE
CRACK
KERSNAP
GREAT DIMENSIONAL
SMASH!!!
(NAMED JUST NOW)
WELL! I WAS JUST TRYING WHATEVER.
DIDN'T THINK IT'D WORK.
ポカーン
GAPE
IGNORING MAGICAL THEORY…

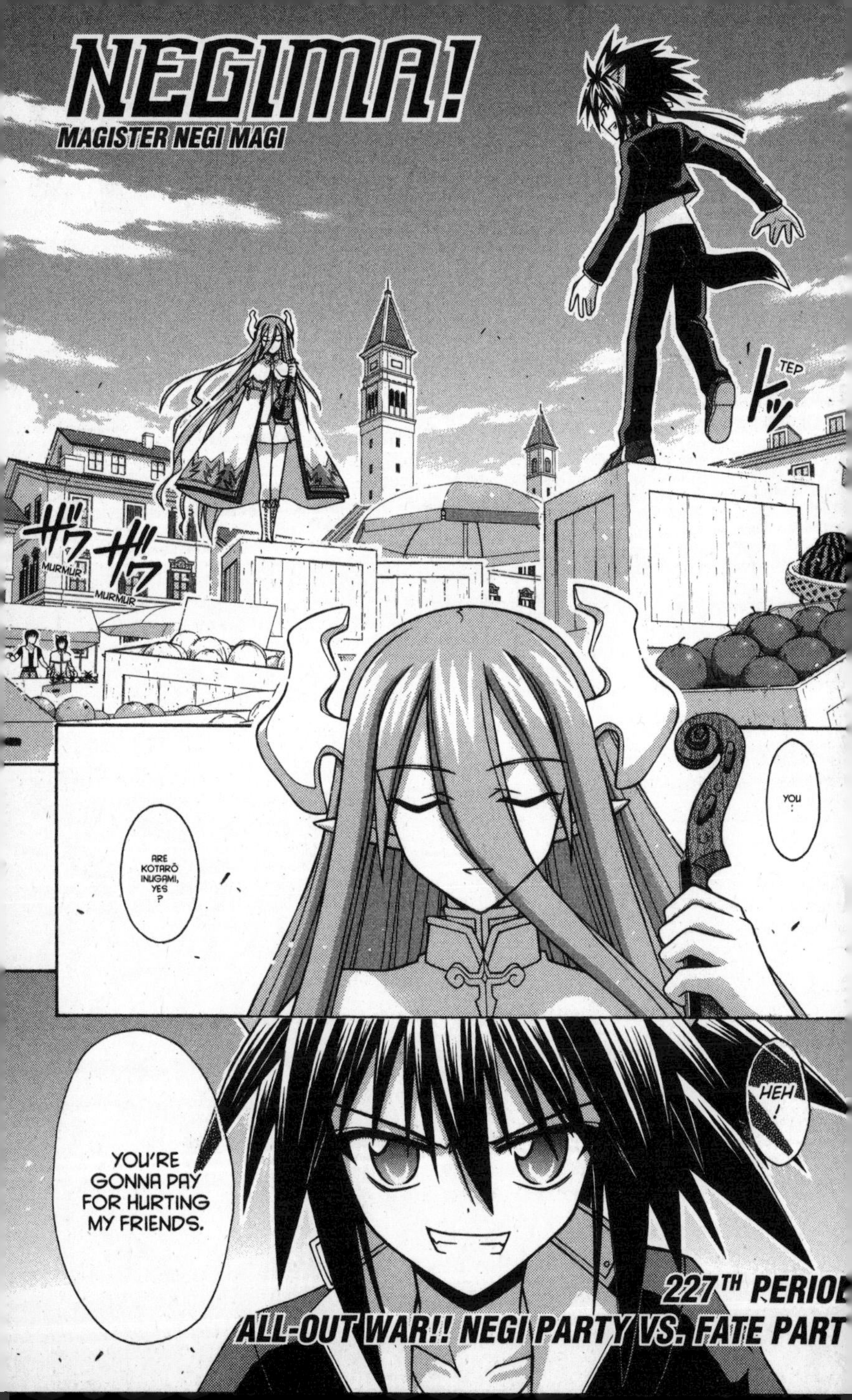

NEGIMA!
MAGISTER NEGI MAGI
TEP
MURMUR
MURMUR
YOU :
ARE KOTARÔ INUGAMI, YES?
HEH!
YOU'RE GONNA PAY FOR HURTING MY FRIENDS.
227TH PERIOD
ALL-OUT WAR!! NEGI PARTY VS. FATE PART

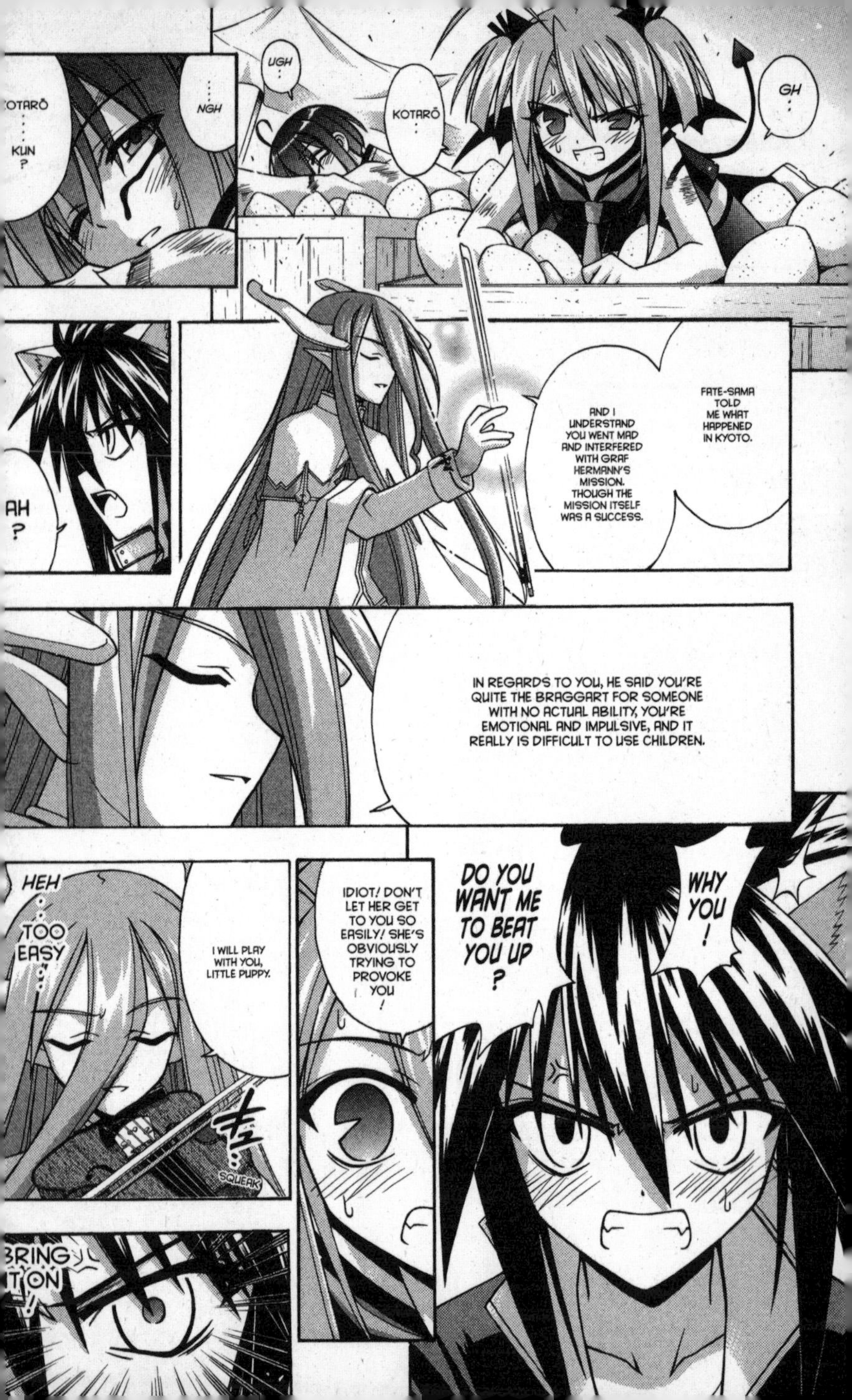
GH...
KOTARŌ...
UGH...
...NGH
KOTARŌ...KUN?
FATE-SAMA TOLD ME WHAT HAPPENED IN KYOTO.
AND I UNDERSTAND YOU WENT MAD AND INTERFERED WITH GRAF HERMANN'S MISSION. THOUGH THE MISSION ITSELF WAS A SUCCESS.
AH?
IN REGARDS TO YOU, HE SAID YOU'RE QUITE THE BRAGGART FOR SOMEONE WITH NO ACTUAL ABILITY, YOU'RE EMOTIONAL AND IMPULSIVE, AND IT REALLY IS DIFFICULT TO USE CHILDREN.
WHY YOU!
DO YOU WANT ME TO BEAT YOU UP?
IDIOT! DON'T LET HER GET TO YOU SO EASILY! SHE'S OBVIOUSLY TRYING TO PROVOKE YOU!
I WILL PLAY WITH YOU, LITTLE PUPPY.
HEH... TOO EASY...
SQUEAK
BRING IT ON!

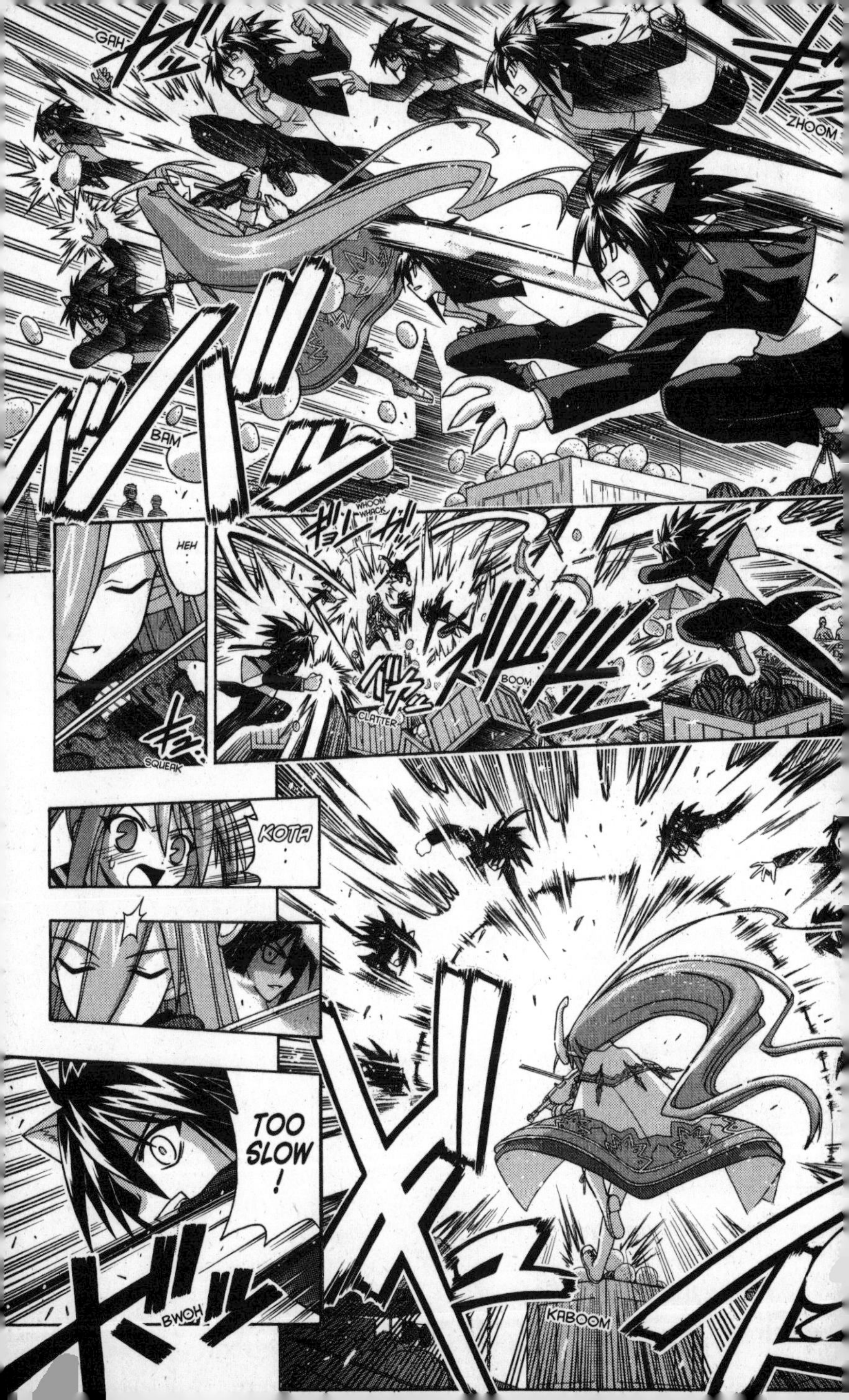
ZHOOM
GAH
BAM
WHOOM
WHACK
BOOM
CLATTER
HEH
SQUEAK
KABOOM
KOTA...
TOO SLOW!
BWOH

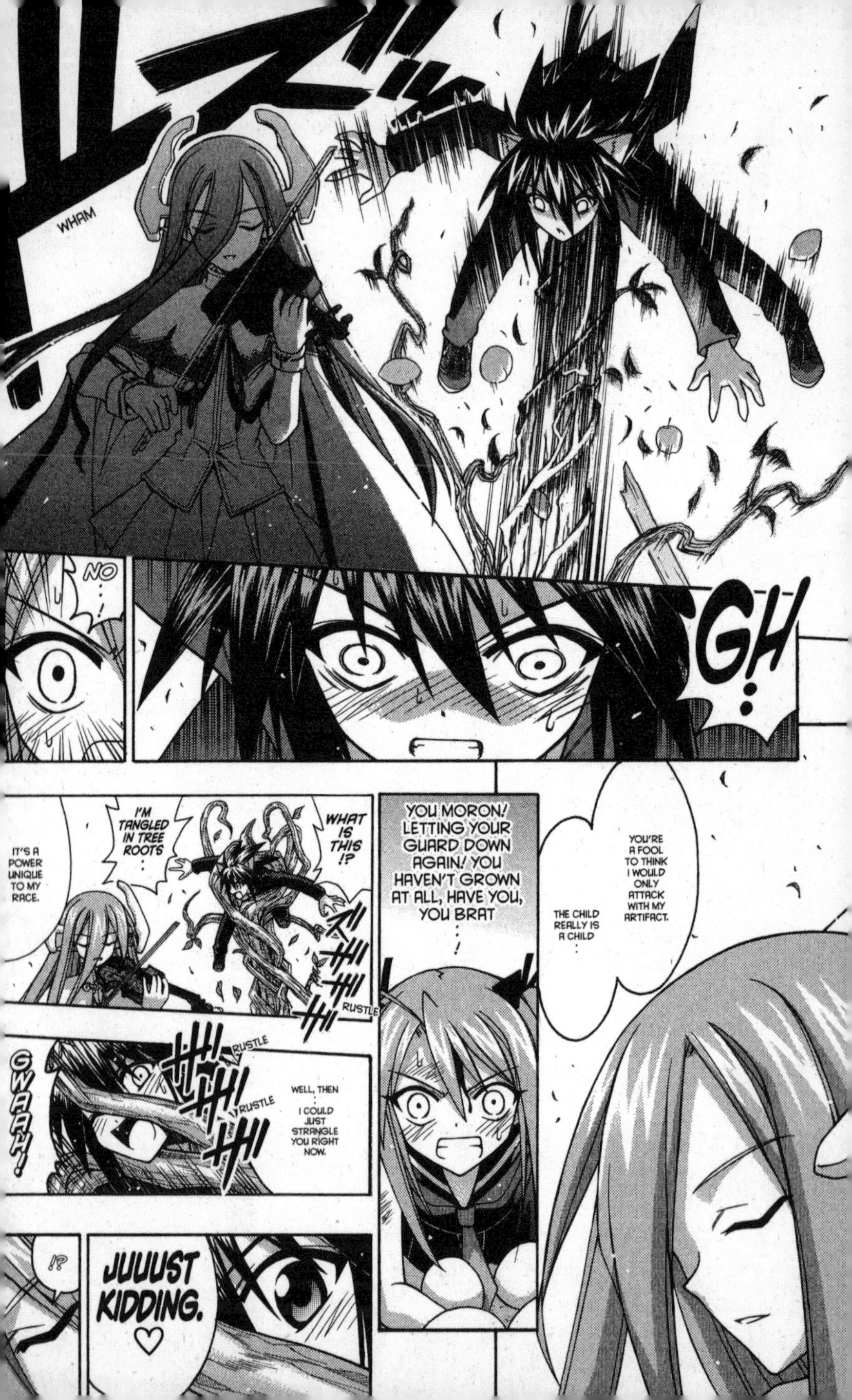
WHAM
GH!
NO...!
YOU'RE A FOOL TO THINK I WOULD ONLY ATTACK WITH MY ARTIFACT.
THE CHILD REALLY IS A CHILD...
YOU MORON! LETTING YOUR GUARD DOWN AGAIN! YOU HAVEN'T GROWN AT ALL, HAVE YOU, YOU BRAT...!
WHAT IS THIS!?
I'M TANGLED IN TREE ROOTS...
IT'S A POWER UNIQUE TO MY RACE.
RUSTLE
RUSTLE
RUSTLE
WELL, THEN... I COULD JUST STRANGLE YOU RIGHT NOW.
GWAAAH!
JUUUST KIDDING. ♥
!?

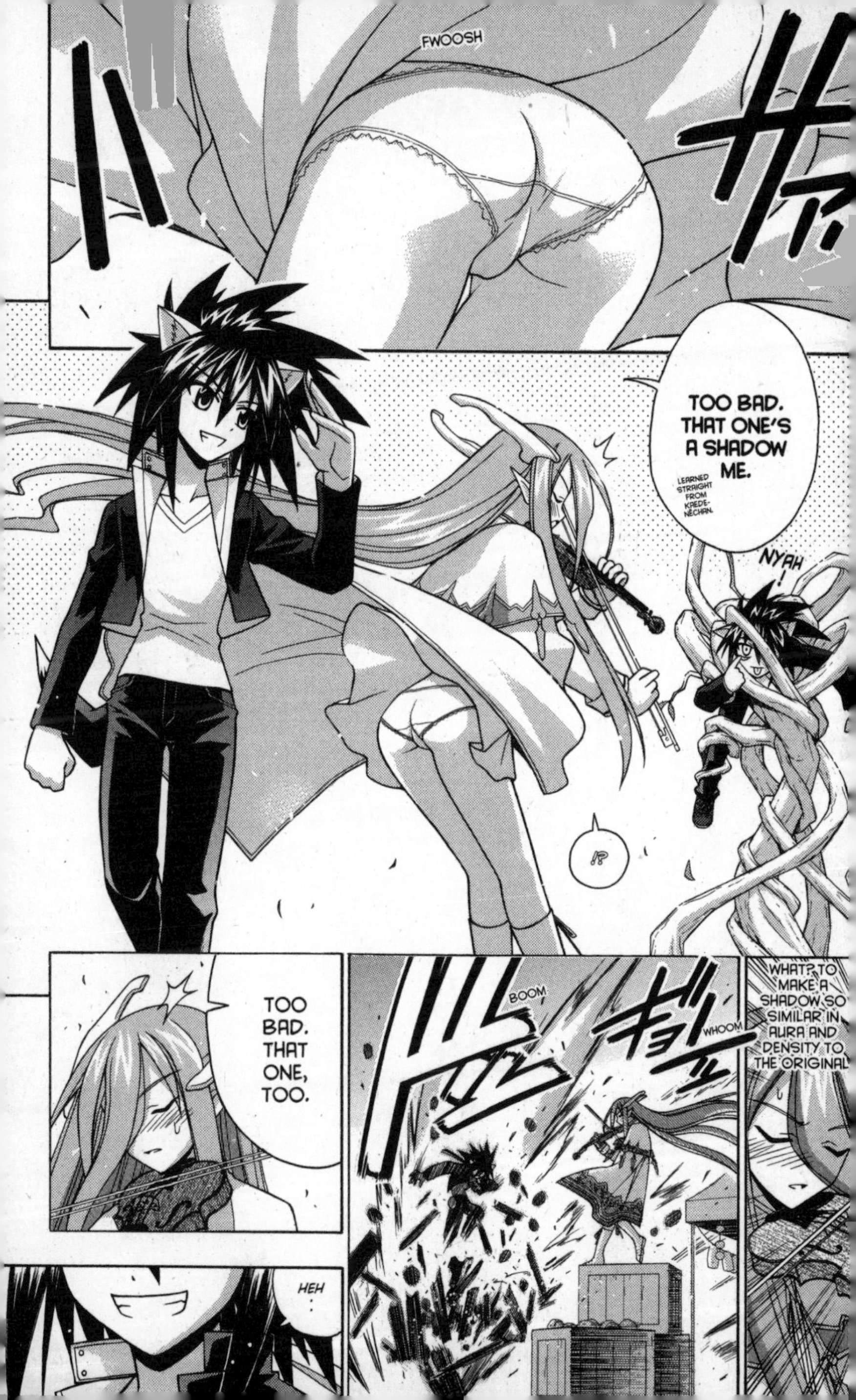
FWOOSH
TOO BAD. THAT ONE'S A SHADOW ME.
LEARNED STRAIGHT FROM KAEDE-NECHAN.
NYAH!
!?
WHAT? TO MAKE A SHADOW SO SIMILAR IN AURA AND DENSITY TO THE ORIGINAL
WHOOM
BOOM
TOO BAD. THAT ONE, TOO.
HEH

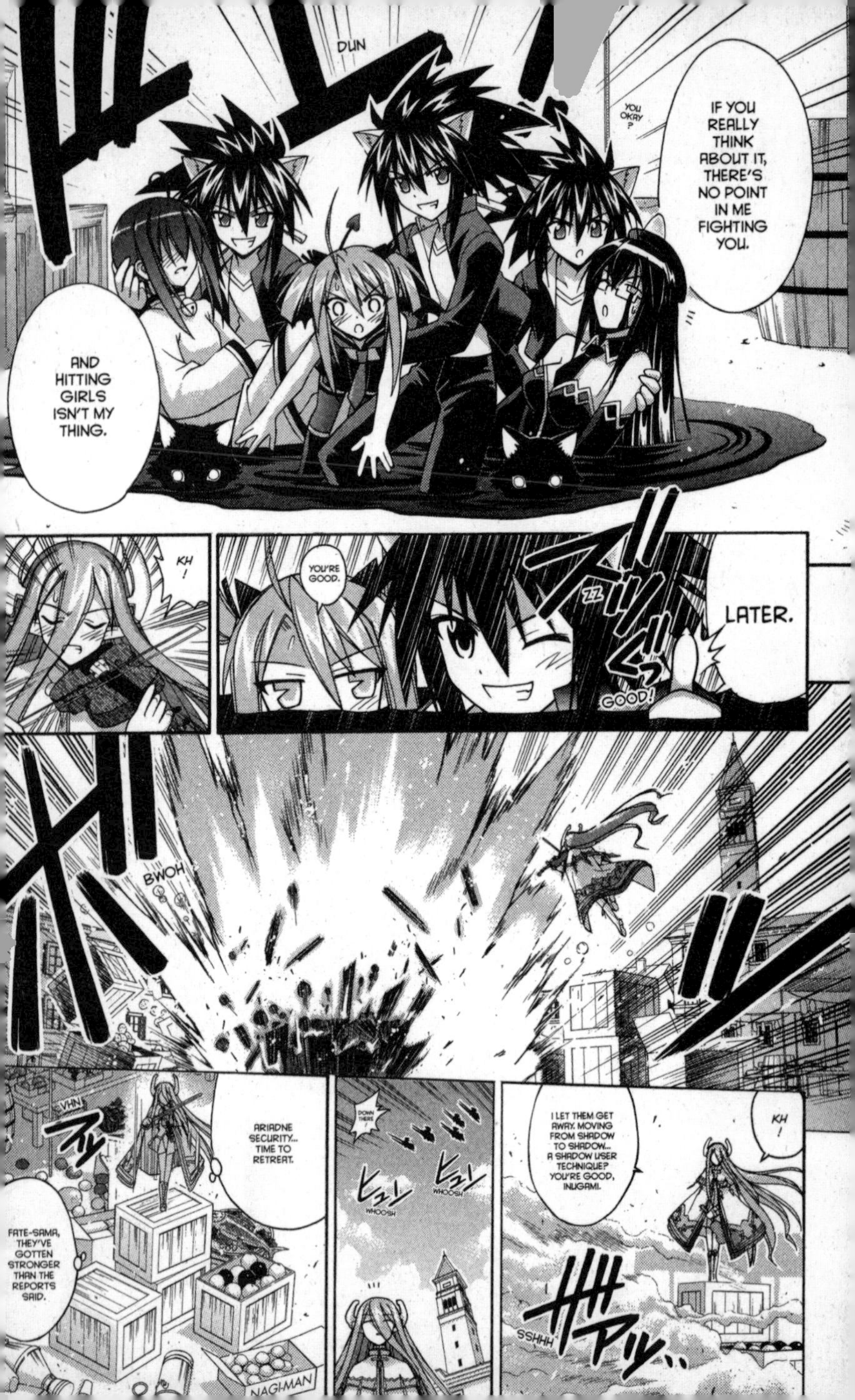
DUN
YOU OKAY?
IF YOU REALLY THINK ABOUT IT, THERE'S NO POINT IN ME FIGHTING YOU.
AND HITTING GIRLS ISN'T MY THING.
YOU'RE GOOD.
LATER.
GOOD!
KH!
BWOH
KH!
I LET THEM GET AWAY. MOVING FROM SHADOW TO SHADOW... A SHADOW USER TECHNIQUE? YOU'RE GOOD, INUGAMI.
SSHHH
DOWN THERE!
WHOOSH
WHOOSH
VHN
ARIADNE SECURITY... TIME TO RETREAT.
FATE-SAMA, THEY'VE GOTTEN STRONGER THAN THE REPORTS SAID.
NAGI-MAN

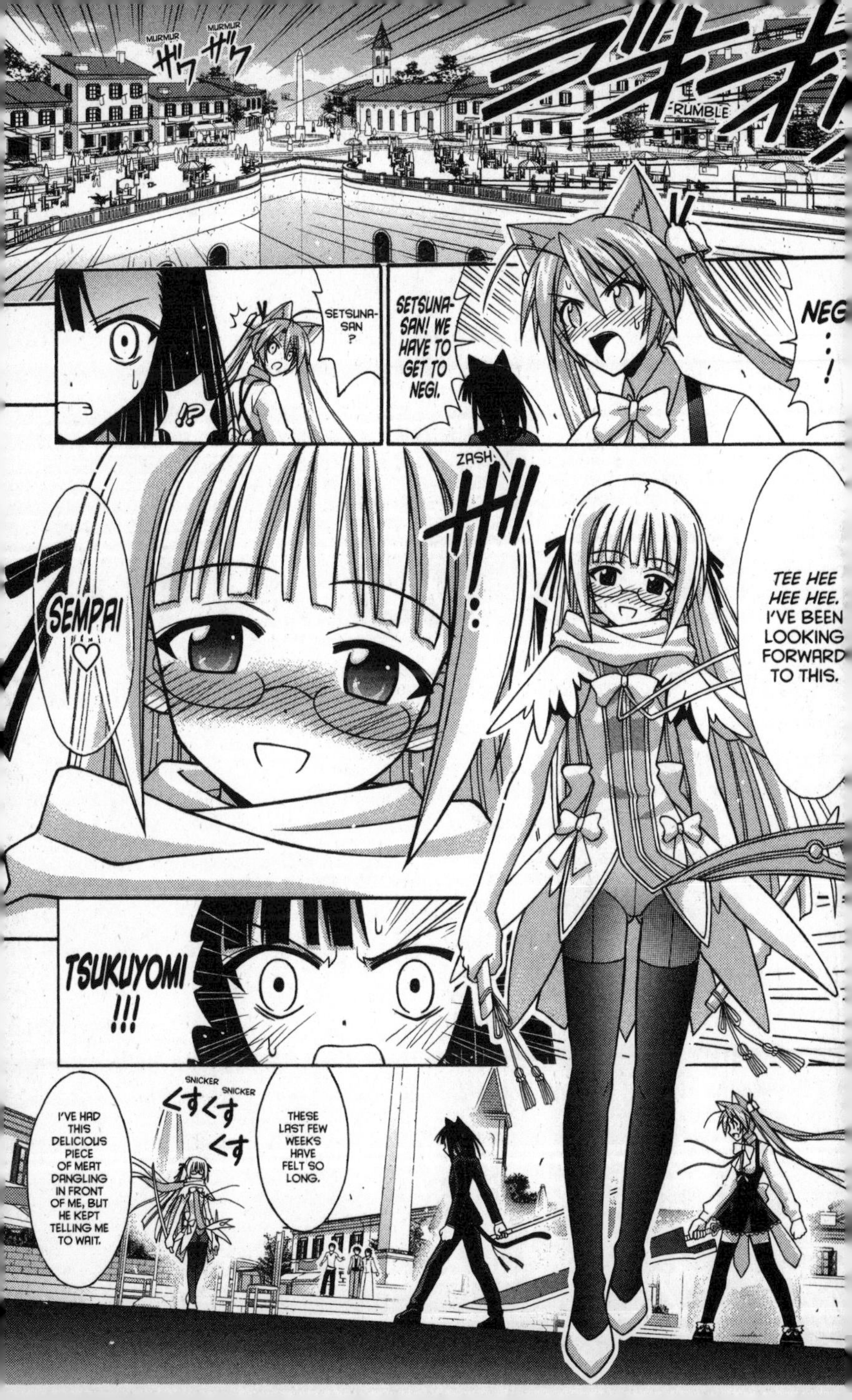
RUMBLE
MURMUR ザワ
MURMUR ザワ
NEG...!
SETSUNA-SAN! WE HAVE TO GET TO NEGI.
SETSUNA-SAN?
!?
ZASH
ザッ
!
TEE HEE HEE HEE. I'VE BEEN LOOKING FORWARD TO THIS.
SEMPAI ♥
TSUKUYOMI!!!
SNICKER くすくす
SNICKER くす
THESE LAST FEW WEEKS HAVE FELT SO LONG.
I'VE HAD THIS DELICIOUS PIECE OF MEAT DANGLING IN FRONT OF ME, BUT HE KEPT TELLING ME TO WAIT.

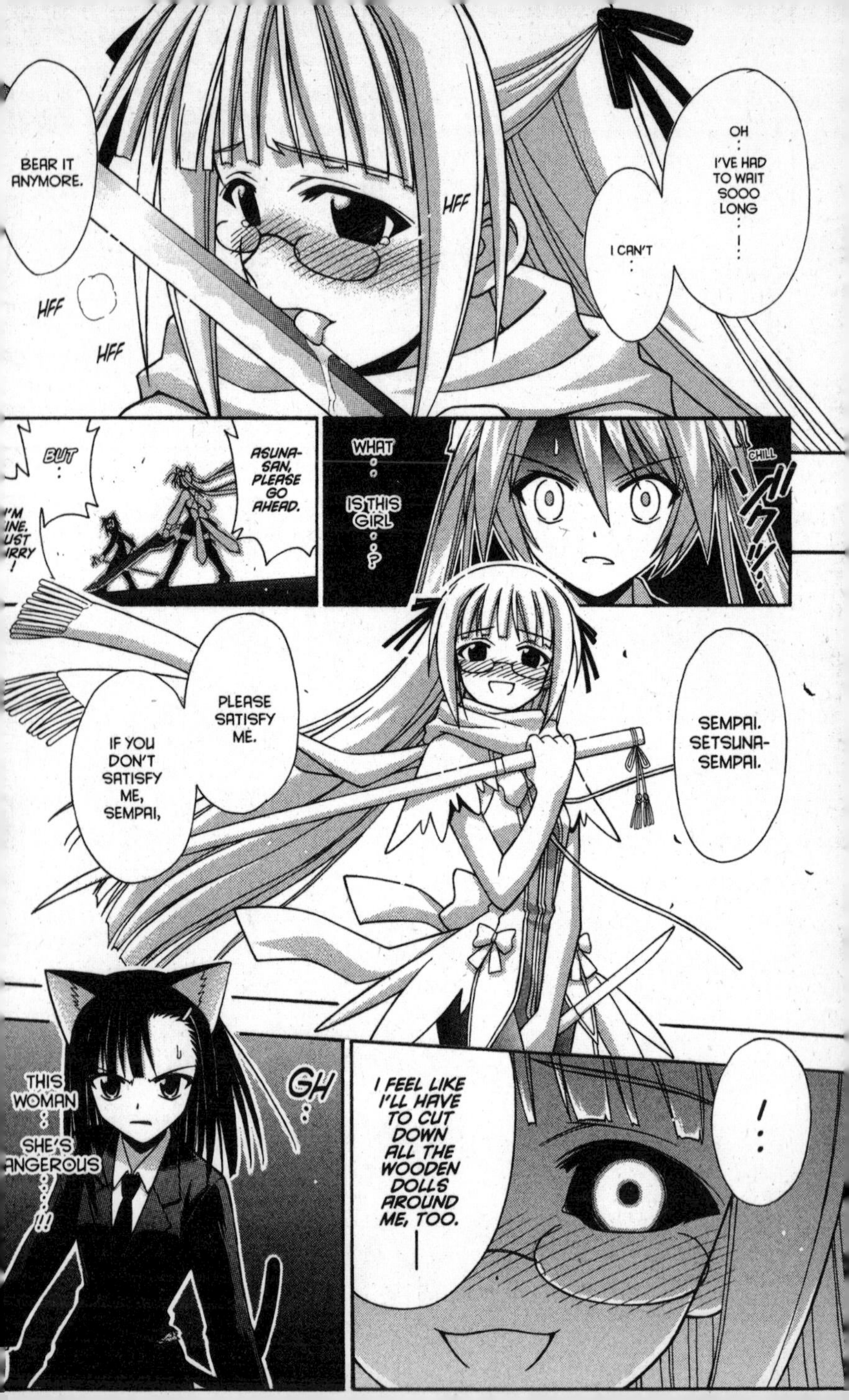
OH... I'VE HAD TO WAIT SOOO LONG...!
I CAN'T...
BEAR IT ANYMORE.
HFF
HFF
HFF
WHAT... IS THIS GIRL...?
CHILL
ASUNA-SAN, PLEASE GO AHEAD.
BUT
'M INE. UST IRRY!
SEMPAI. SETSUNA-SEMPAI.
PLEASE SATISFY ME.
IF YOU DON'T SATISFY ME, SEMPAI,
!...
I FEEL LIKE I'LL HAVE TO CUT DOWN ALL THE WOODEN DOLLS AROUND ME, TOO.
GH...
THIS WOMAN... SHE'S ANGEROUS...!!

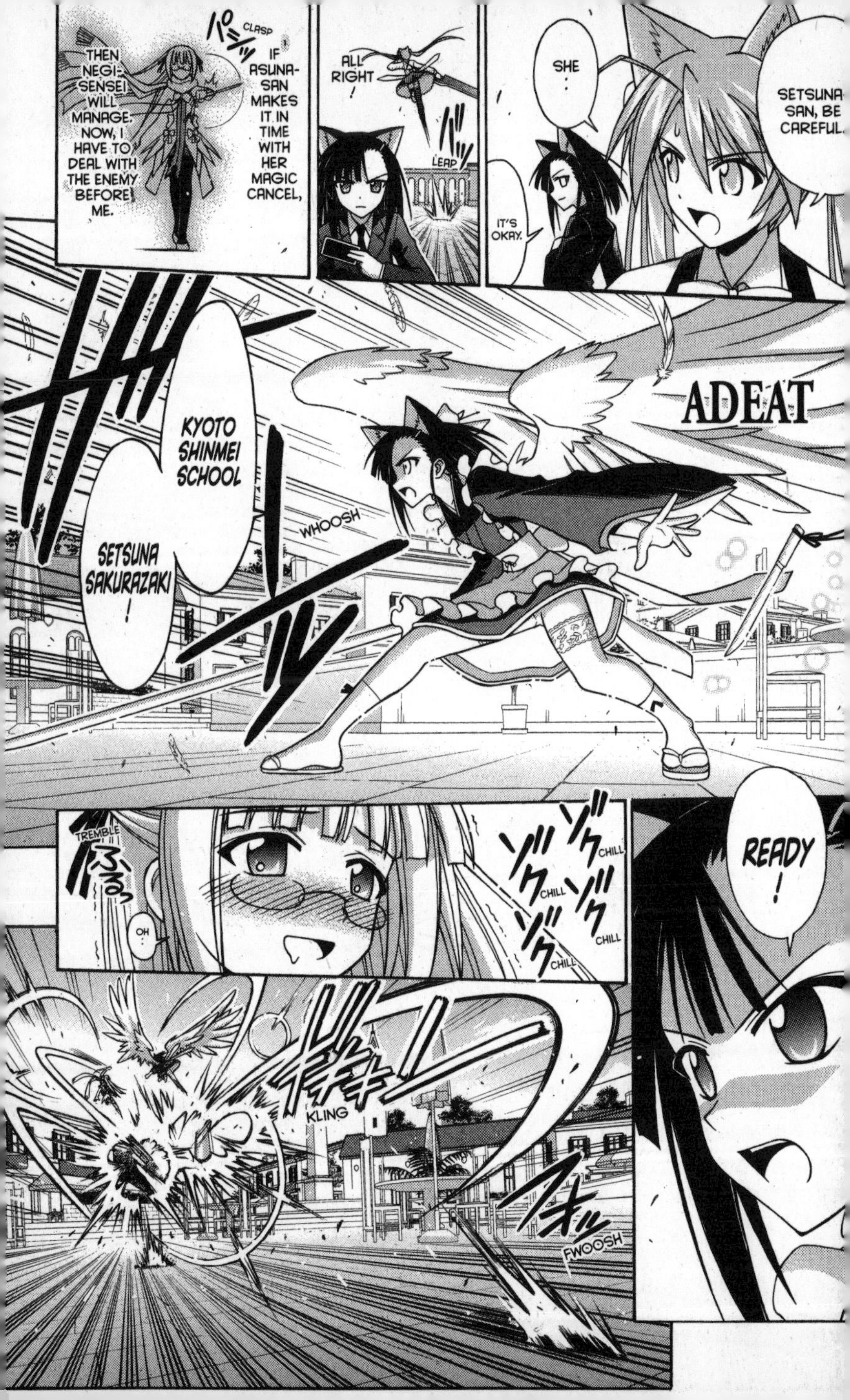

SETSUNA-SAN, BE CAREFUL.
SHE...
IT'S OKAY.
ALL RIGHT!
LEAP
IF ASUNA-SAN MAKES IT IN TIME WITH HER MAGIC CANCEL,
CLASP
THEN NEGI-SENSEI WILL MANAGE. NOW, I HAVE TO DEAL WITH THE ENEMY BEFORE ME.
ADEAT
KYOTO SHINMEI SCHOOL
SETSUNA SAKURAZAKI!
WHOOSH
READY!
CHILL
CHILL
CHILL
CHILL
OH...
TREMBLE
KLING
FWOOSH

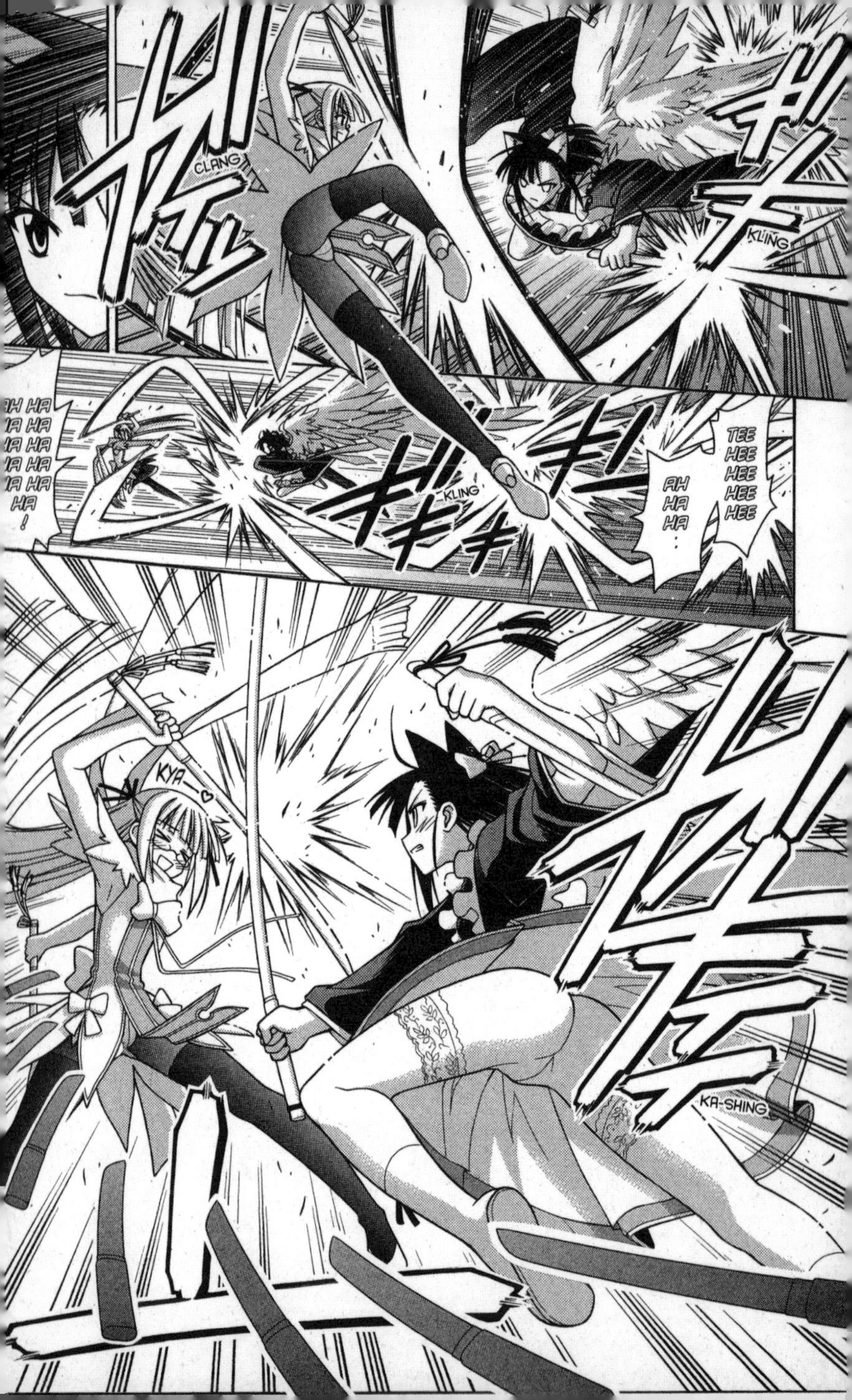
KLING
CLANG
TEE HEE HEE HEE HEE
AH HA HA...
KLING
AH HA HA HA HA HA HA HA HA HA HA!
KA-SHING
KYA—♡

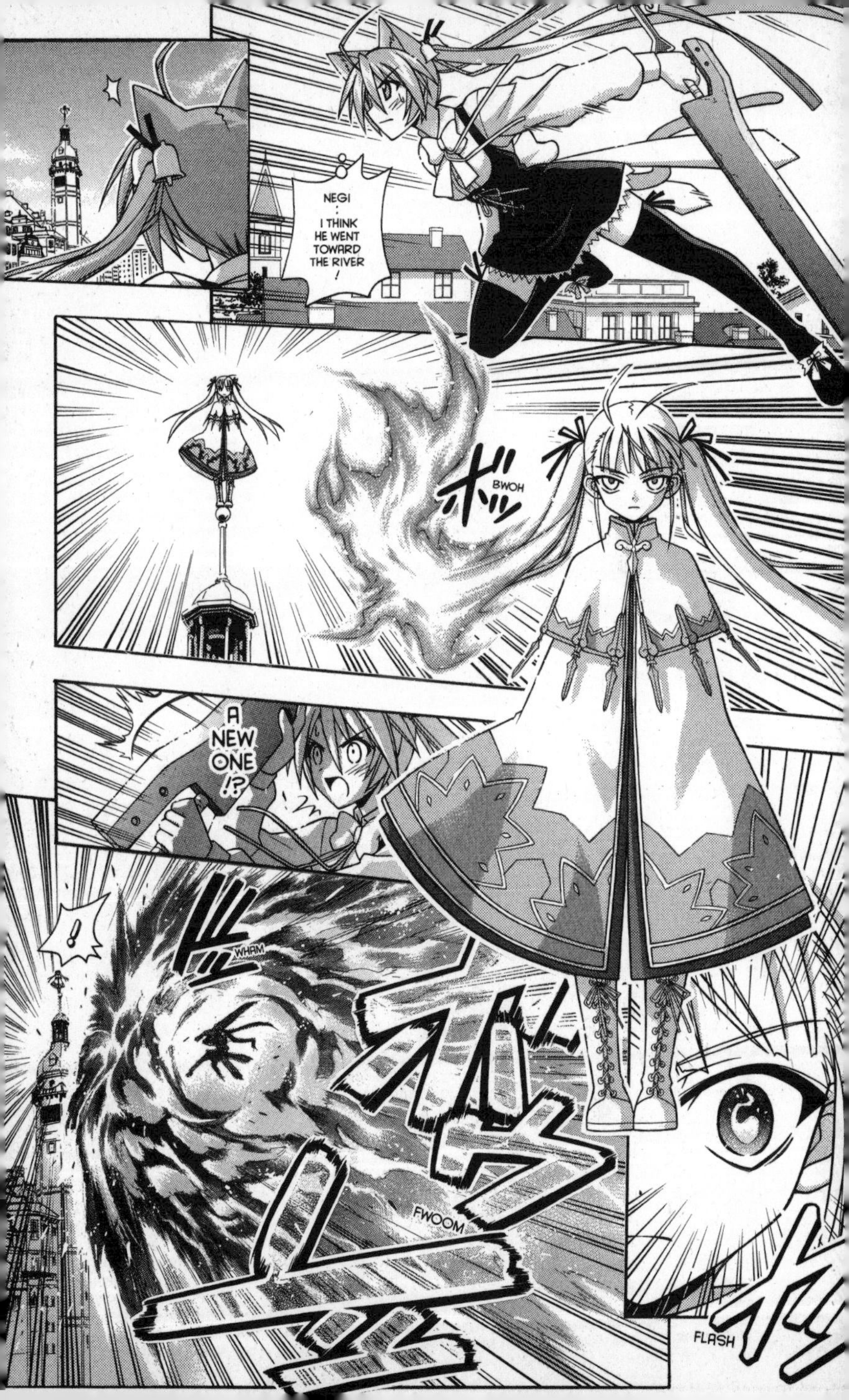
NEGI : I THINK HE WENT TOWARD THE RIVER !
BWOH
A NEW ONE !?
WHAM
FWOOM
FLASH

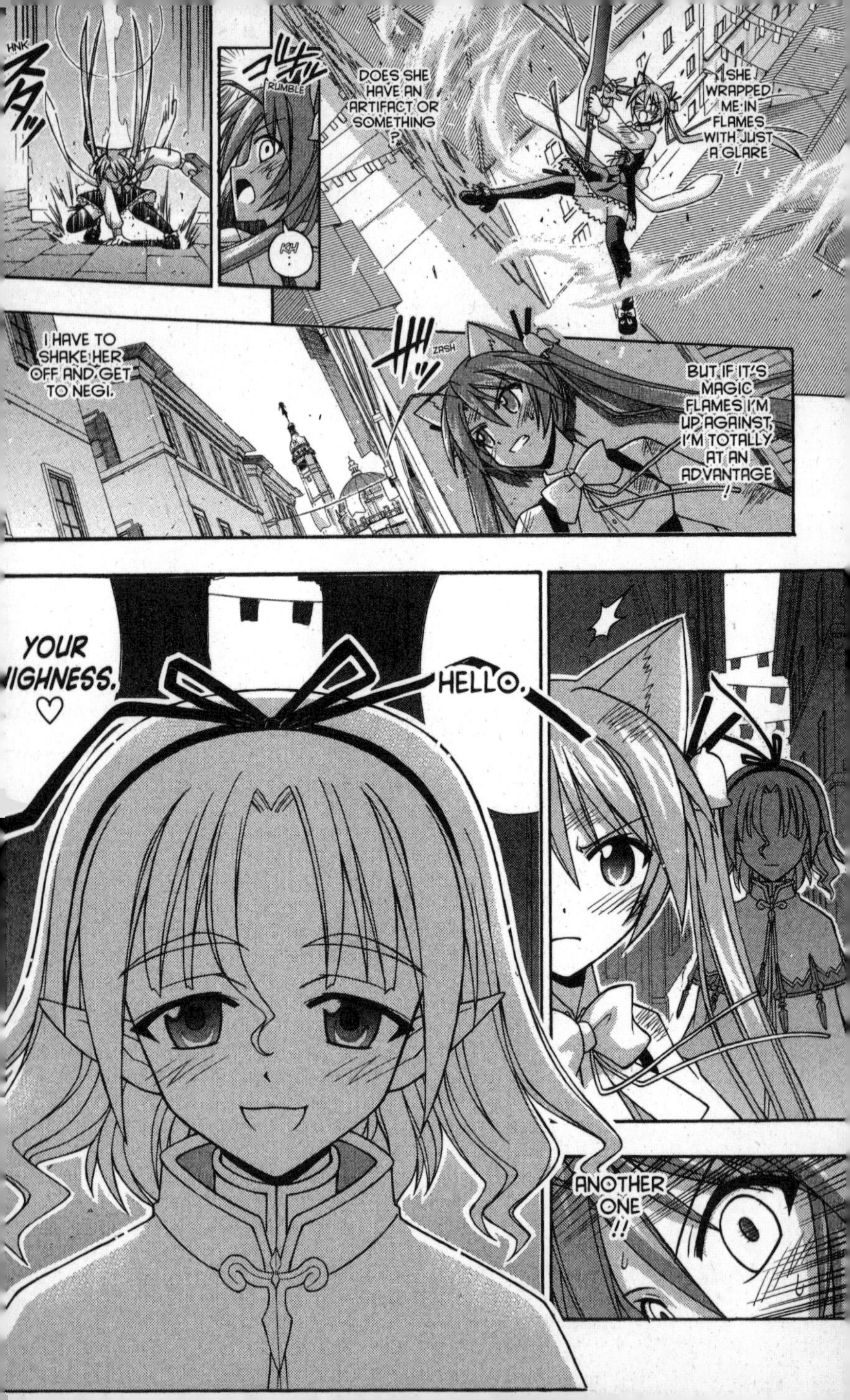

SHE WRAPPED ME IN FLAMES WITH JUST A GLARE!
DOES SHE HAVE AN ARTIFACT OR SOMETHING?
RUMBLE
KH...
HNK
BUT IF IT'S MAGIC FLAMES I'M UP AGAINST, I'M TOTALLY AT AN ADVANTAGE!
ZASH
I HAVE TO SHAKE HER OFF AND GET TO NEGI.
HELLO.
YOUR HIGHNESS. ♡
ANOTHER ONE!!

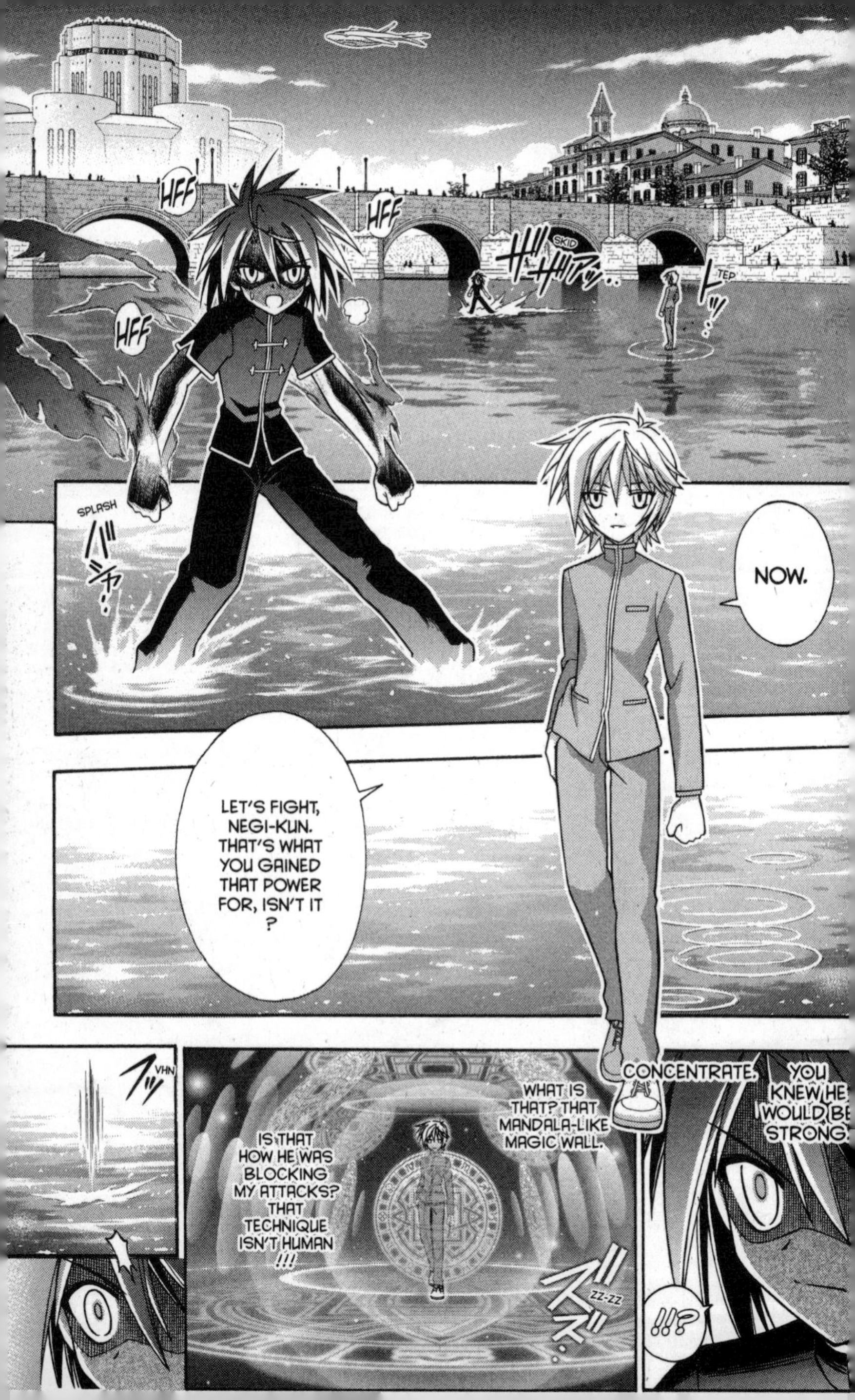
HFF
HFF
HFF
SKID
TEP
SPLASH
NOW.
LET'S FIGHT, NEGI-KUN. THAT'S WHAT YOU GAINED THAT POWER FOR, ISN'T IT ?
VHN
CONCENTRATE.
YOU KNEW HE WOULD BE STRONG.
WHAT IS THAT? THAT MANDALA-LIKE MAGIC WALL.
IS THAT HOW HE WAS BLOCKING MY ATTACKS? THAT TECHNIQUE ISN'T HUMAN !!!
ZZ-ZZ
!!?

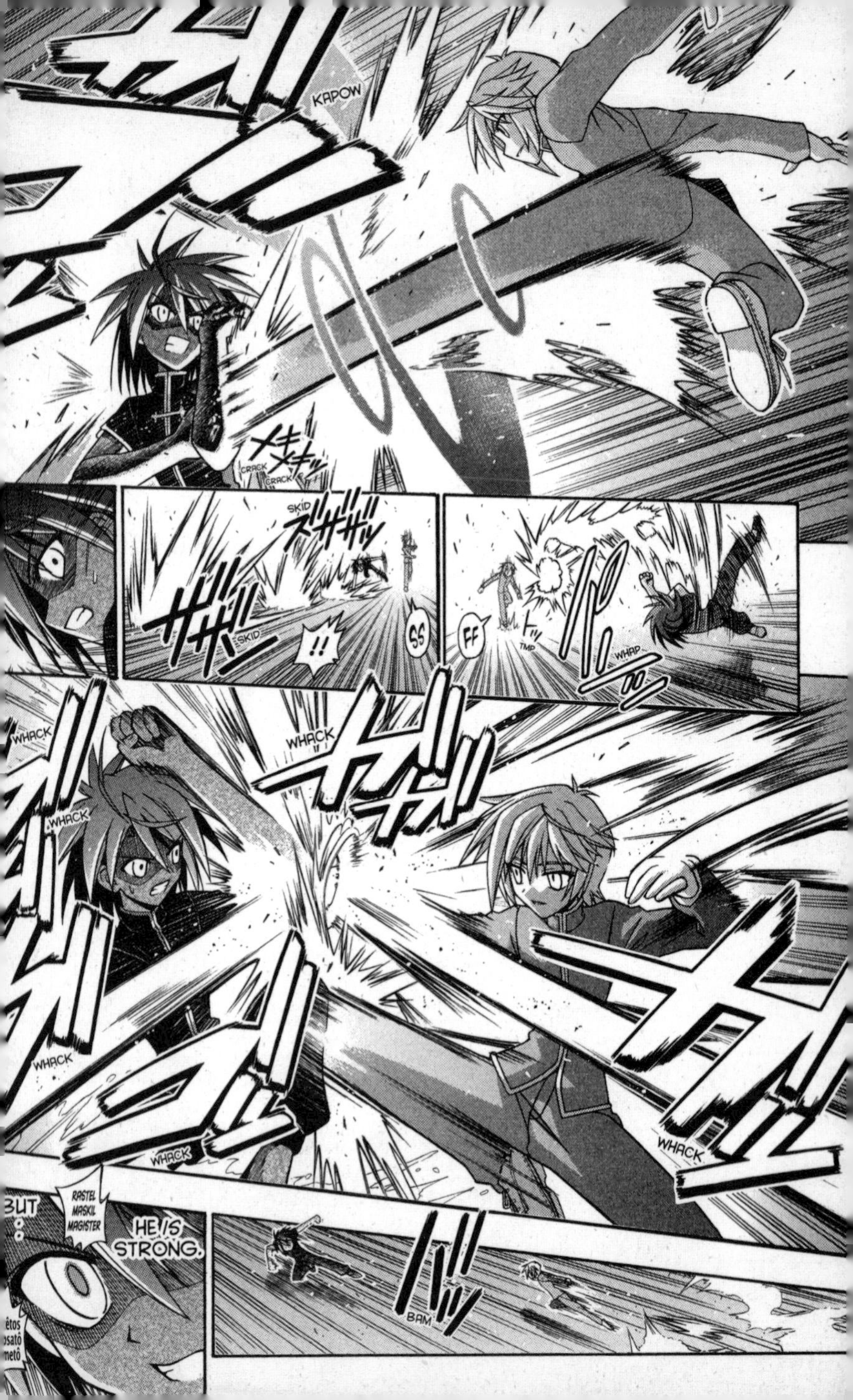
KAPOW
CRACK
CRACK
WHAP
TMP
FF
SKID
SS
!!
SKID
WHACK
WHACK
WHACK
WHACK
WHACK
WHACK
BAM
BUT..
HE IS STRONG.
RASTEL MASKIL MAGISTER

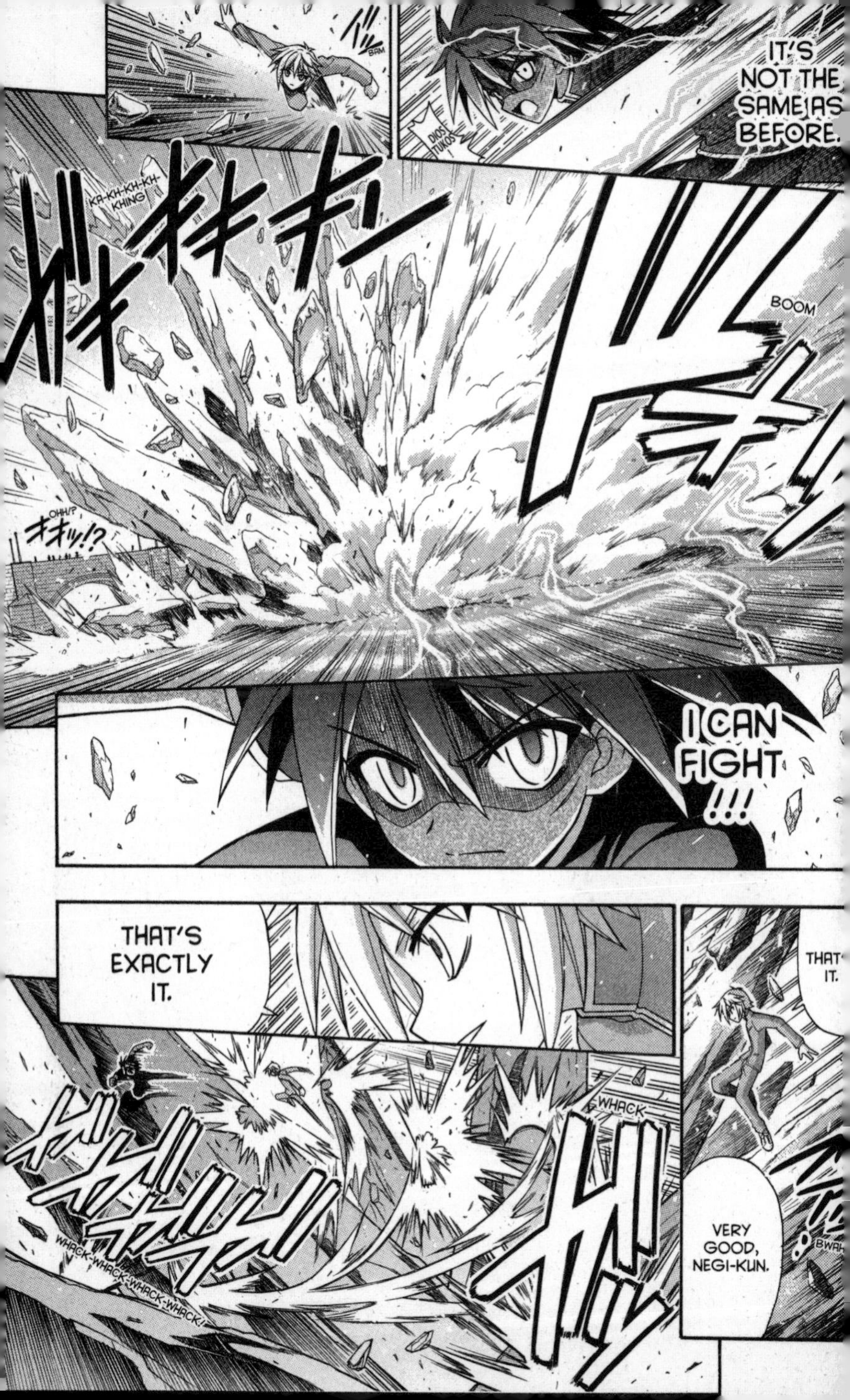
DIOS TUKOS
IT'S NOT THE SAME AS BEFORE.
BAM
BOOM
KA-KH-KH-KH-KHING
OHH!?
I CAN FIGHT!!!
THAT' IT.
VERY GOOD, NEGI-KUN.
BWAH
THAT'S EXACTLY IT.
WHACK
WHACK-WHACK-WHACK-WHACK!

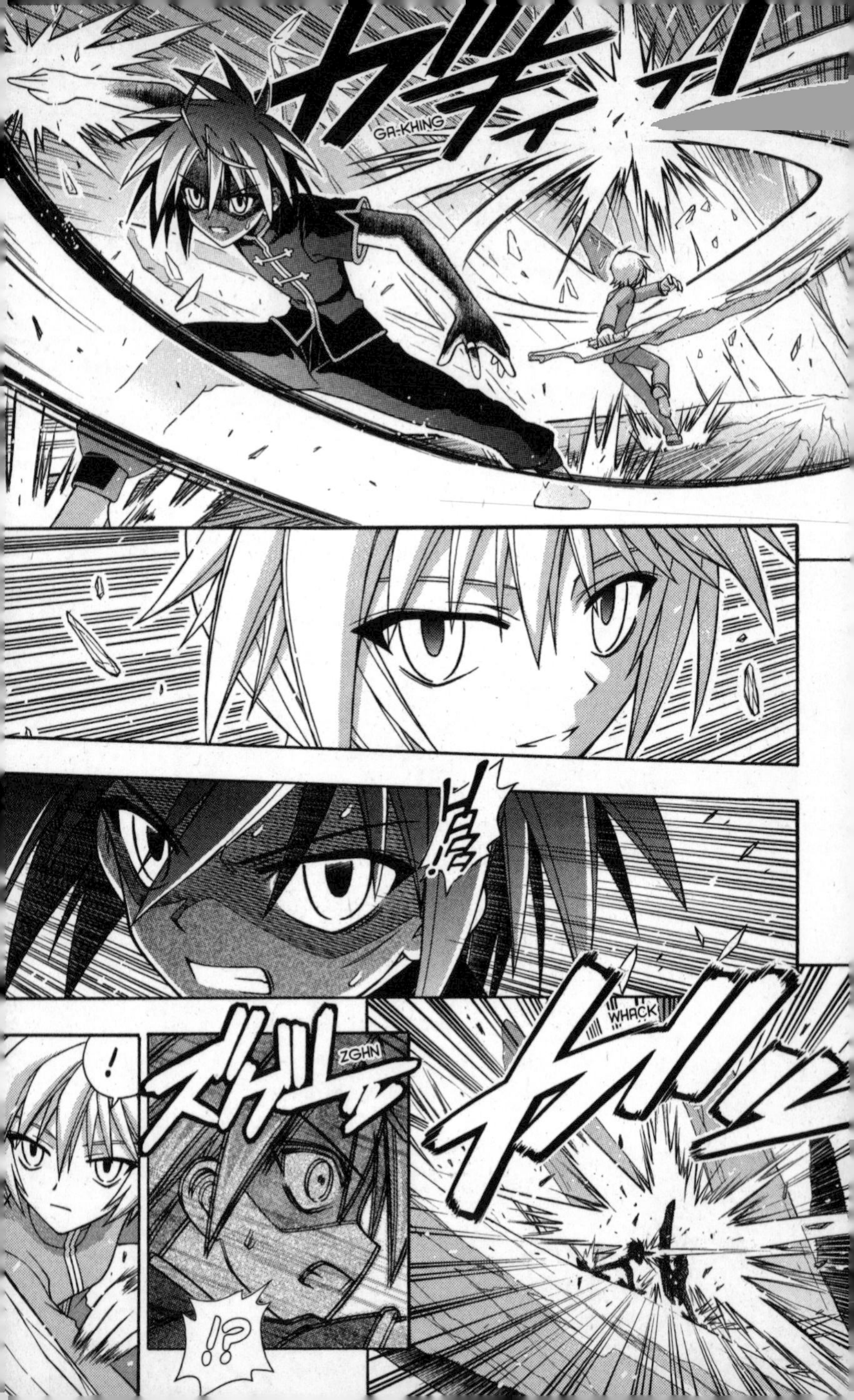
GA-KHING
WHACK
ZGHN
!?
!

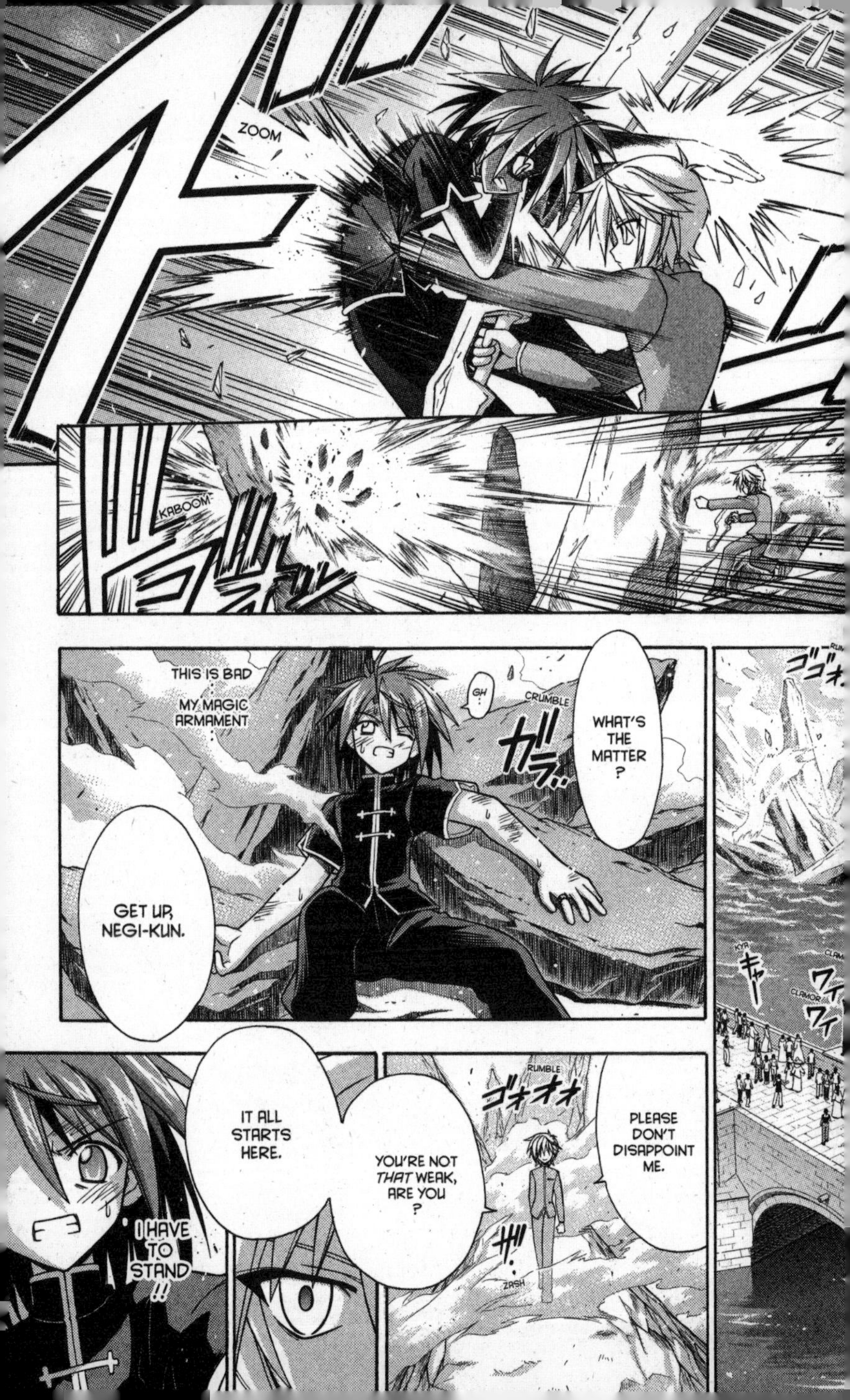
ZOOM
KABOOM
RUMBLE
KYA
CLAMOR
CLAMOR
WHAT'S THE MATTER?
CRUMBLE
GH...
THIS IS BAD... MY MAGIC ARMAMENT...
GET UP, NEGI-KUN.
PLEASE DON'T DISAPPOINT ME.
RUMBLE
ZASH
YOU'RE NOT *THAT* WEAK, ARE YOU?
IT ALL STARTS HERE.
I HAVE TO STAND!!

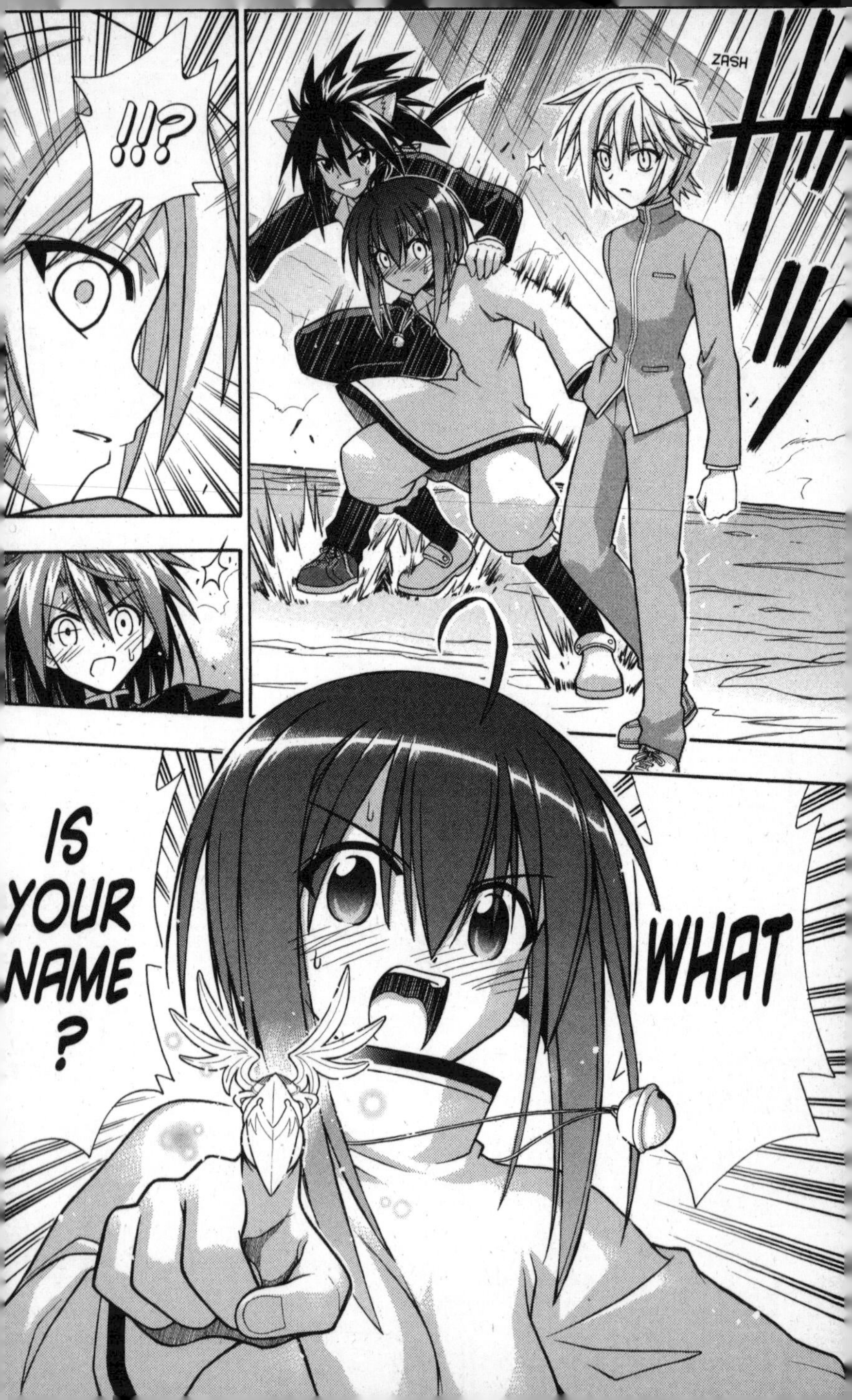
ZASH
!!?
WHAT
IS YOUR NAME ?

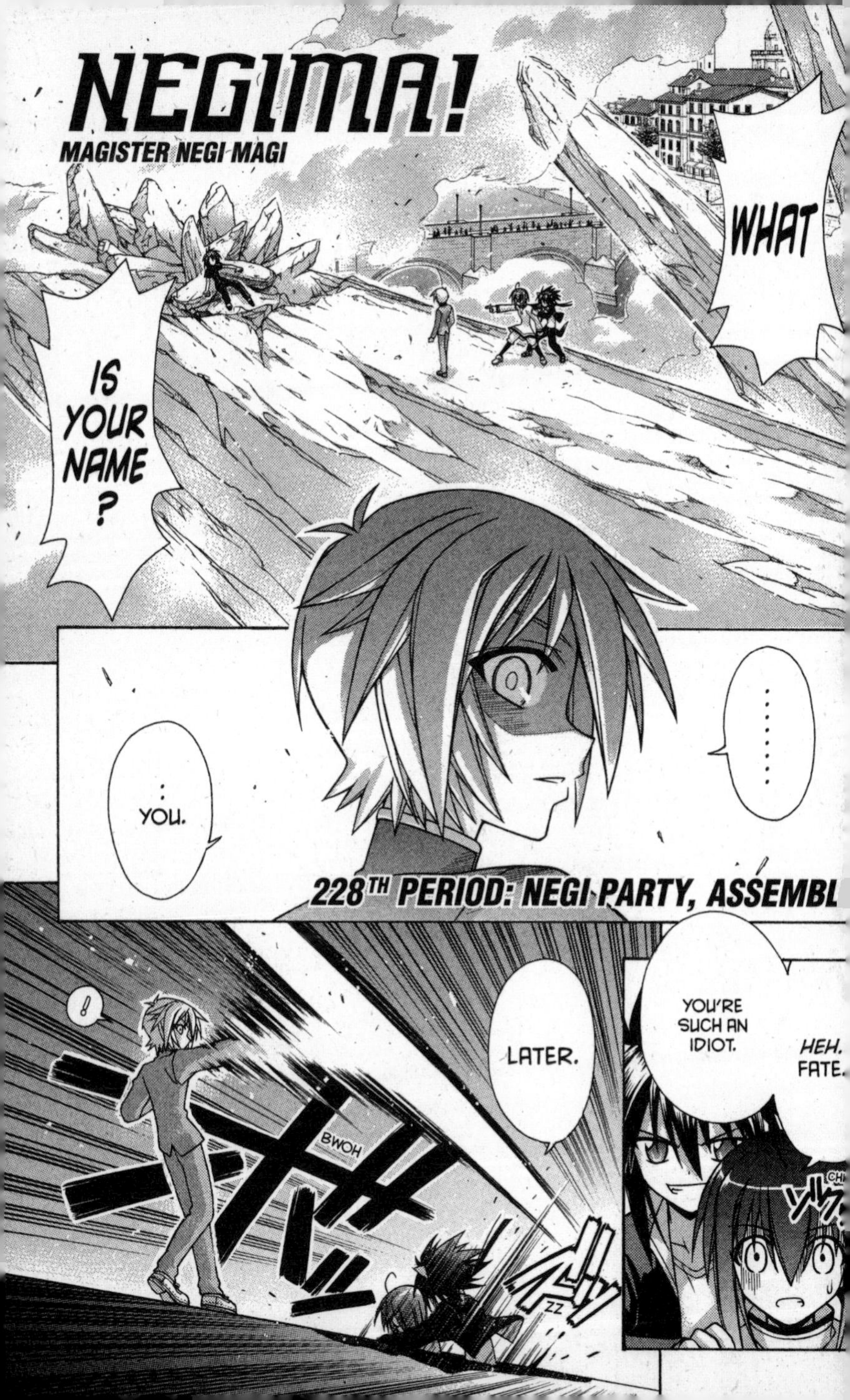
NEGIMA!
MAGISTER NEGI MAGI
WHAT
IS YOUR NAME ?
....
: YOU.
228TH PERIOD: NEGI PARTY, ASSEMBL
HEH. FATE.
YOU'RE SUCH AN IDIOT.
CHI
LATER.
!
BWOH
ZZ

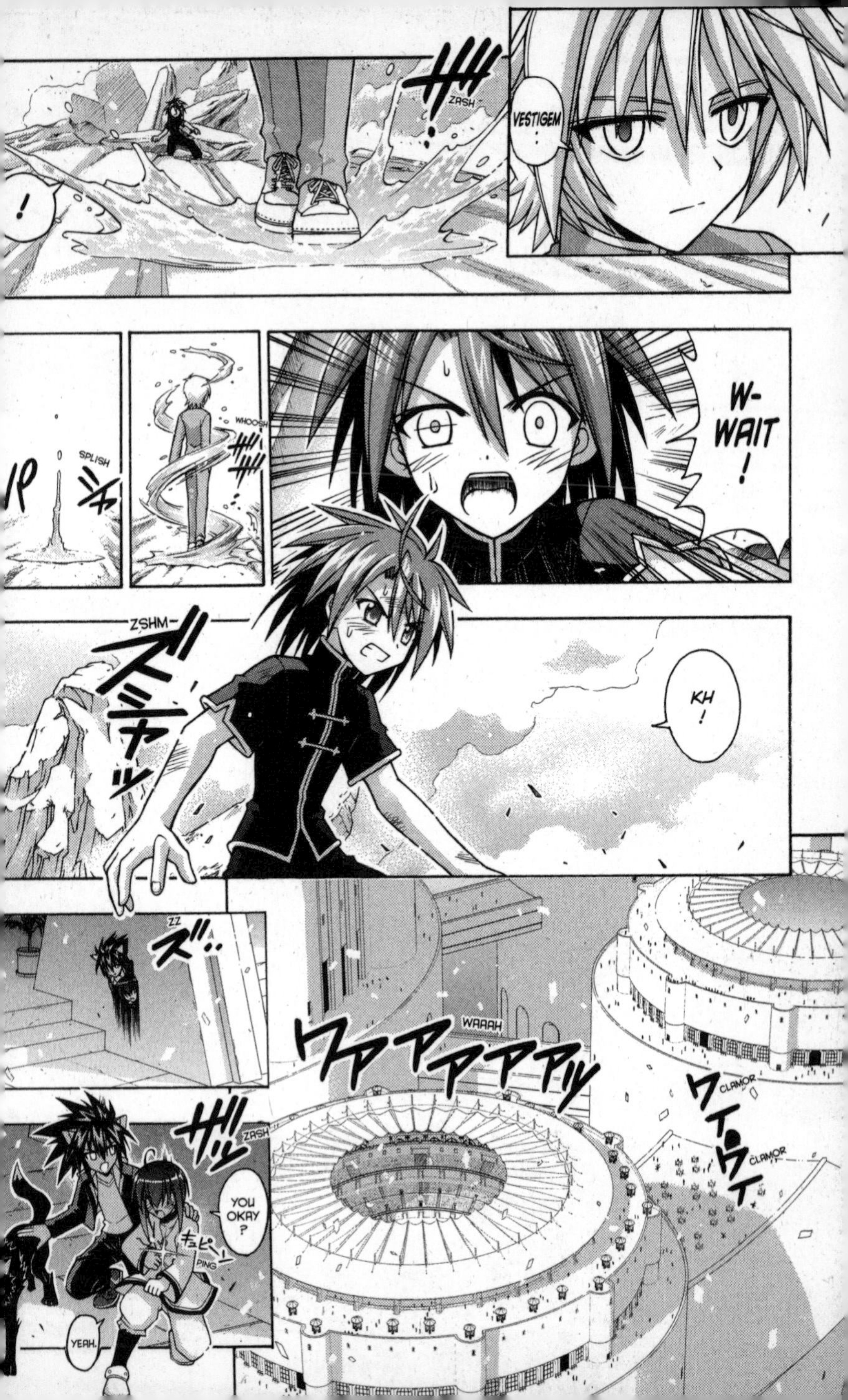
VESTIGEM...
ZASH
!
W-WAIT!
WHOOSH
SPLISH
ZSHM
KH!
WAAAH
CLAMOR
CLAMOR
ZZ
ZASH
YOU OKAY?
PING
YEAH.

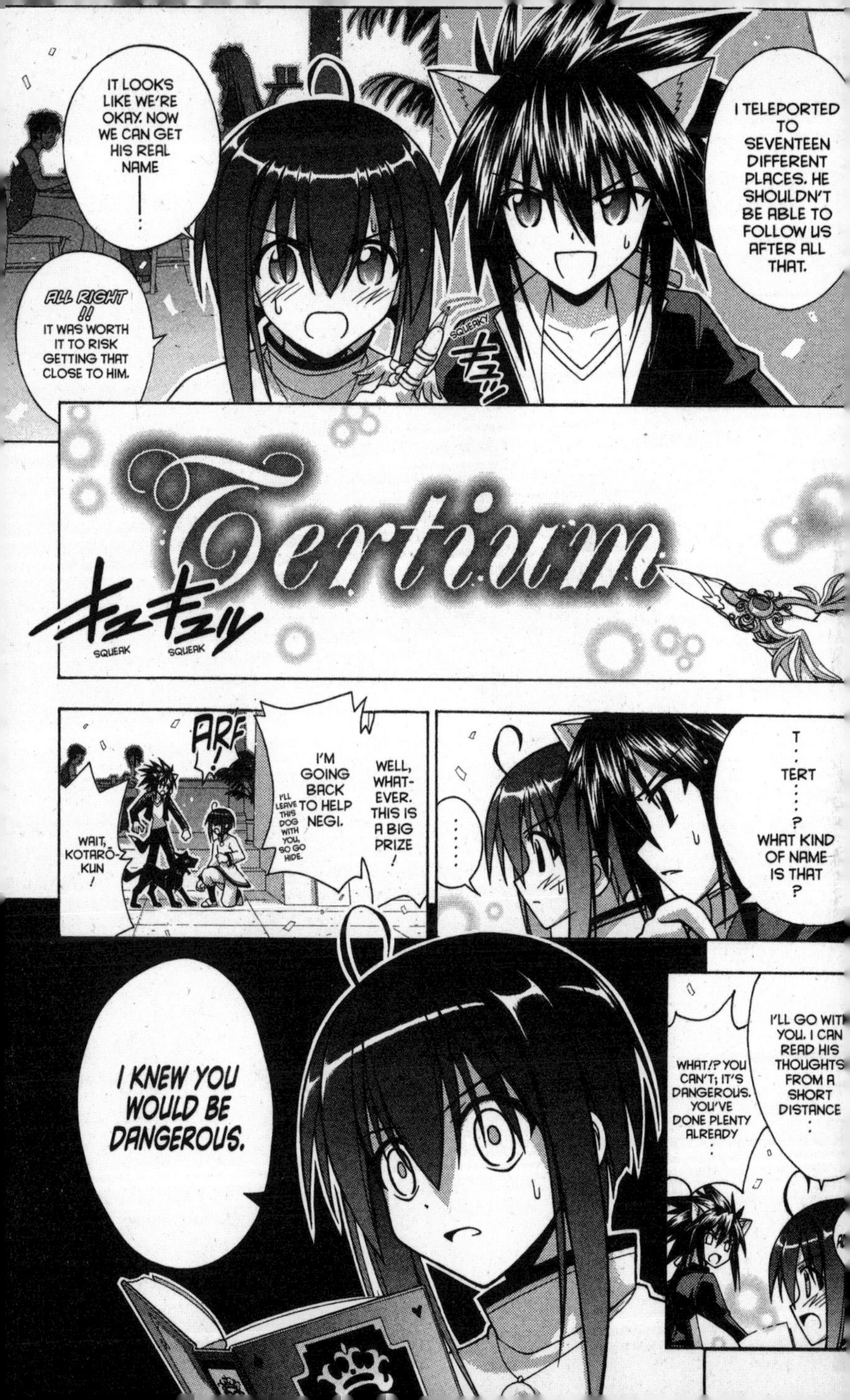
I TELEPORTED TO SEVENTEEN DIFFERENT PLACES. HE SHOULDN'T BE ABLE TO FOLLOW US AFTER ALL THAT.
IT LOOKS LIKE WE'RE OKAY. NOW WE CAN GET HIS REAL NAME...
ALL RIGHT!! IT WAS WORTH IT TO RISK GETTING THAT CLOSE TO HIM.
SQUEAKY
Tertium
SQUEAK SQUEAK
T... TERT.....? WHAT KIND OF NAME IS THAT?
......
WELL, WHATEVER. THIS IS A BIG PRIZE!
I'M GOING BACK TO HELP NEGI.
I'LL LEAVE THIS DOG WITH YOU, SO GO HIDE.
ARF!
WAIT, KOTARŌ-KUN!
I'LL GO WITH YOU. I CAN READ HIS THOUGHTS FROM A SHORT DISTANCE...
WHAT!? YOU CAN'T; IT'S DANGEROUS. YOU'VE DONE PLENTY ALREADY...
I KNEW YOU WOULD BE DANGEROUS.

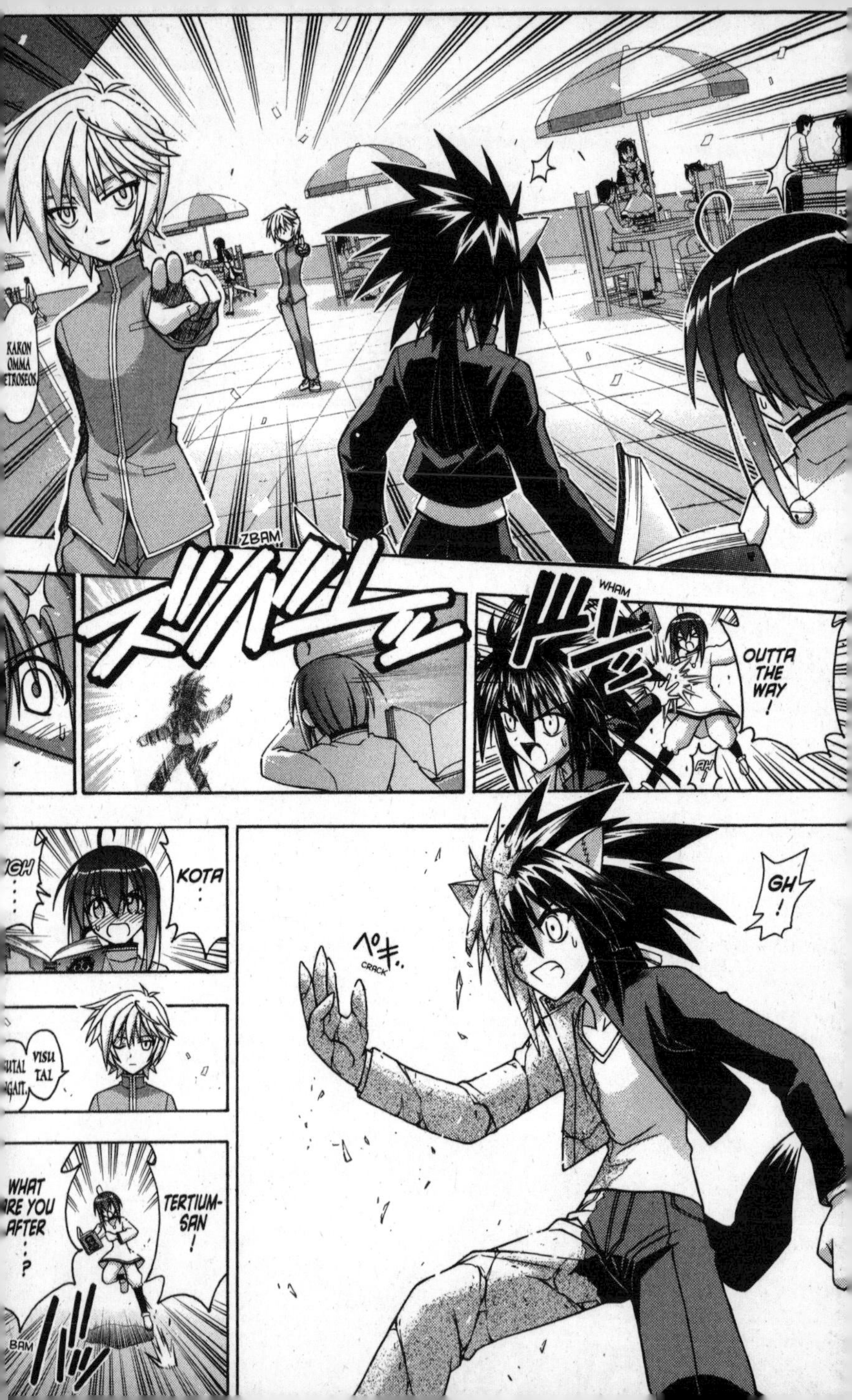
KAKON OMMA ETROSEOS
ZBAM
ズバババ
WHAM
ドッ
OUTTA THE WAY!
AH!
GH!
ペキ
CRACK
KOTA...
GH...
VISU TAL
SUTAL GAIT.
TERTIUM-SAN!
WHAT RE YOU AFTER...?
BAM

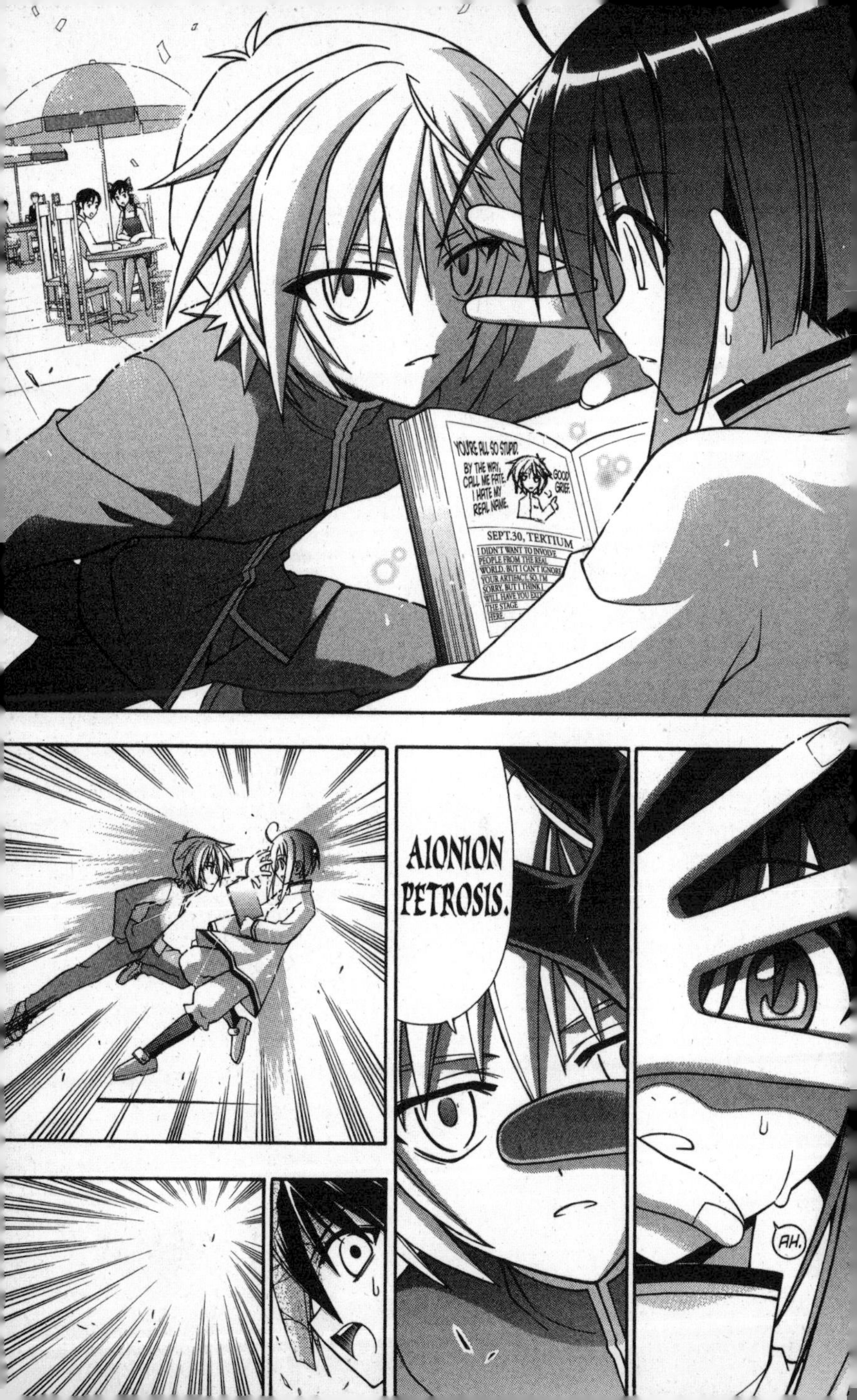
YOU'RE ALL SO STUPID.
BY THE WAY, CALL ME FATE. I HATE MY REAL NAME.
GOOD GRIEF.
SEPT.30, TERTIUM
I DIDN'T WANT TO INVOLVE PEOPLE FROM THE REAL WORLD, BUT I CAN'T IGNORE YOUR ARTIFACT. SO, I'M SORRY, BUT I THINK I WILL HAVE YOU EXI THE STAGE HERE.
AH.
AIONION PETROSIS.

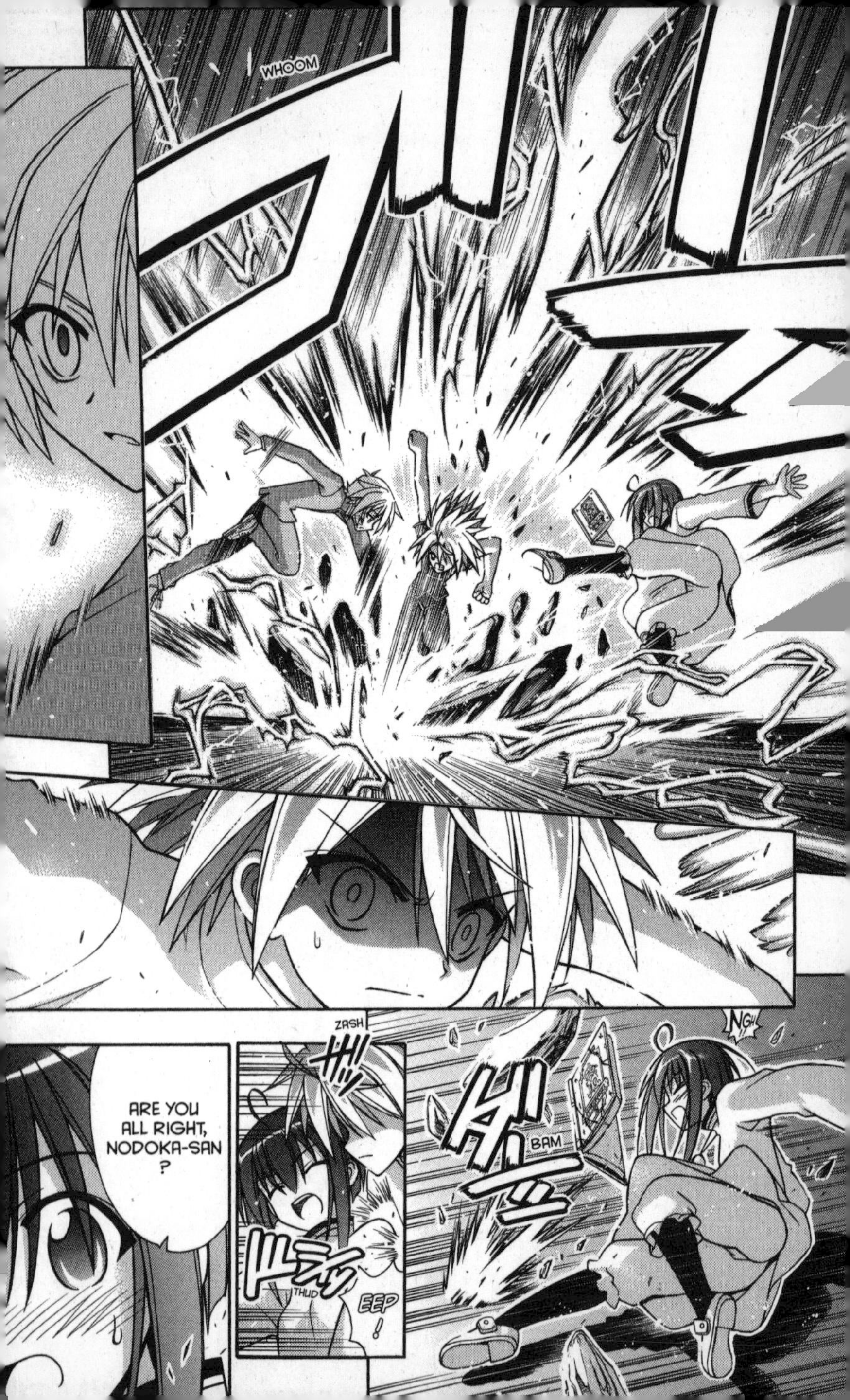
WHOOM
NGH!!
BAM
ZASH
THUD
EEP!
ARE YOU ALL RIGHT, NODOKA-SAN?

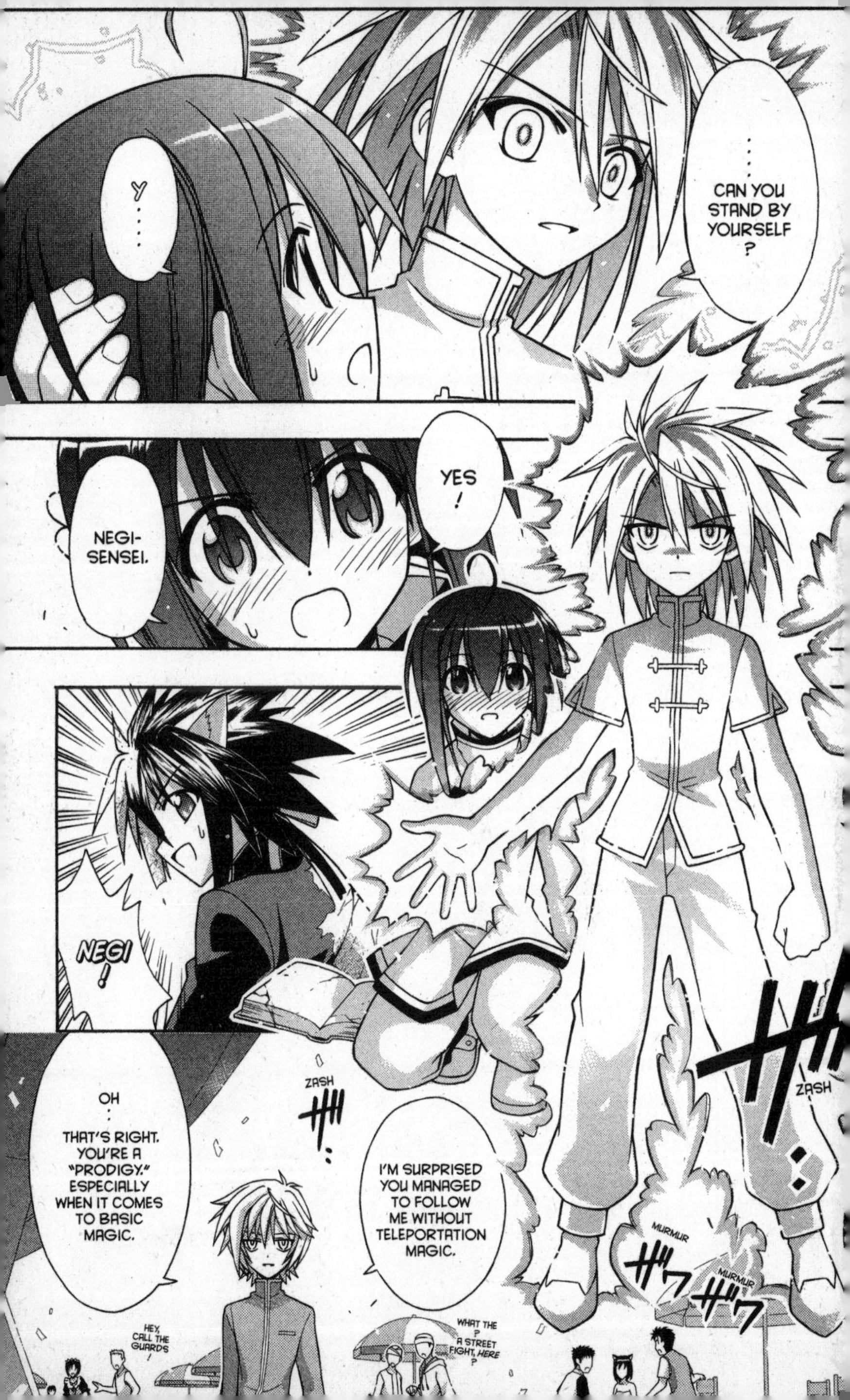

... CAN YOU STAND BY YOURSELF ?
Y....
YES !
NEGI-SENSEI.
NEGI !
ZASH
MURMUR
MURMUR
I'M SURPRISED YOU MANAGED TO FOLLOW ME WITHOUT TELEPORTATION MAGIC.
ZASH
OH : THAT'S RIGHT. YOU'RE A "PRODIGY." ESPECIALLY WHEN IT COMES TO BASIC MAGIC.
WHAT THE ? A STREET FIGHT, *HERE* ?
HEY, CALL THE GUARDS !

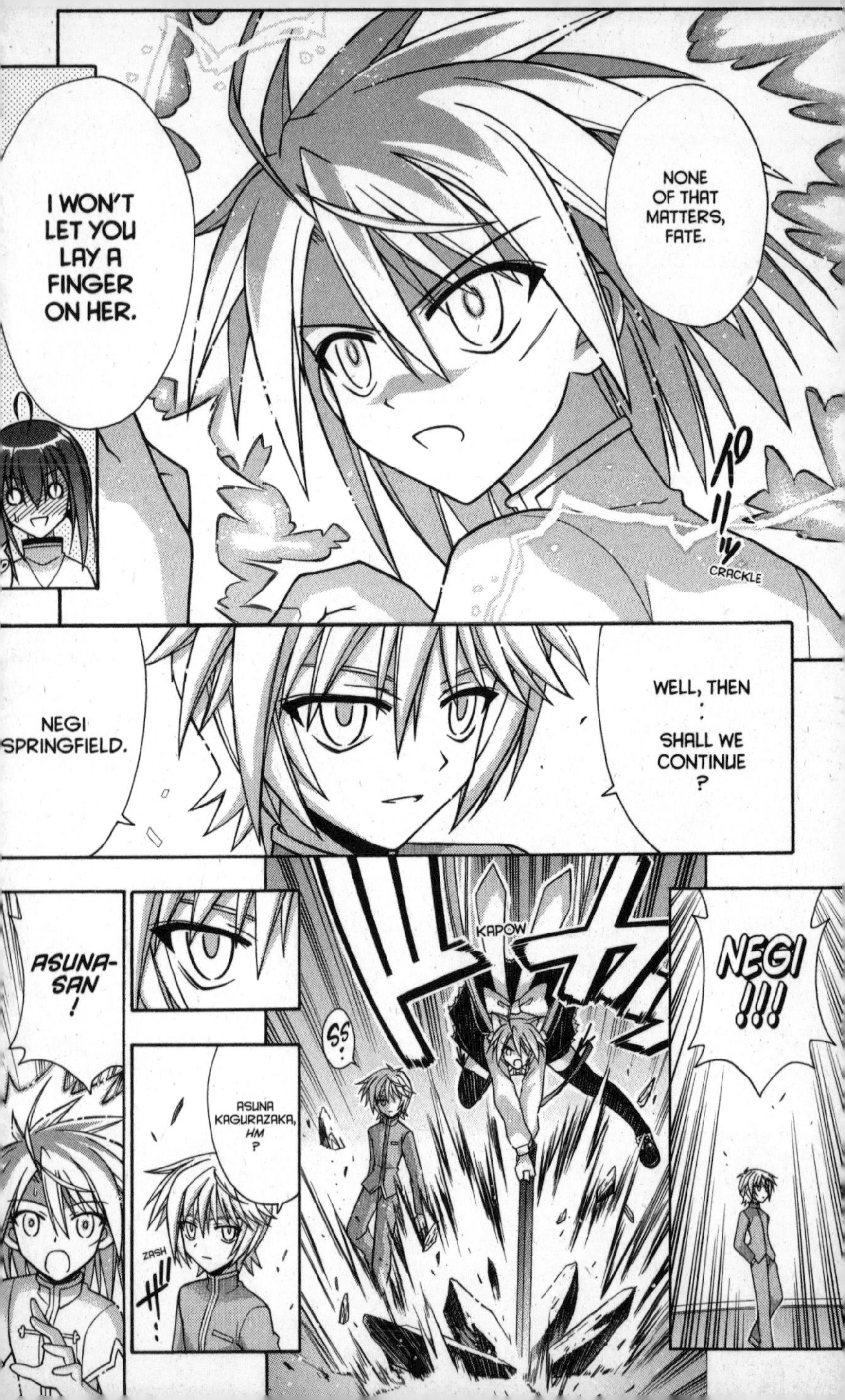
NONE OF THAT MATTERS, FATE.
I WON'T LET YOU LAY A FINGER ON HER.
CRACKLE
WELL, THEN... SHALL WE CONTINUE?
NEGI SPRINGFIELD.
NEGI!!!
KAPOW
SS
ASUNA KAGURAZAKA, HM?
ZASH
ASUNA-SAN!

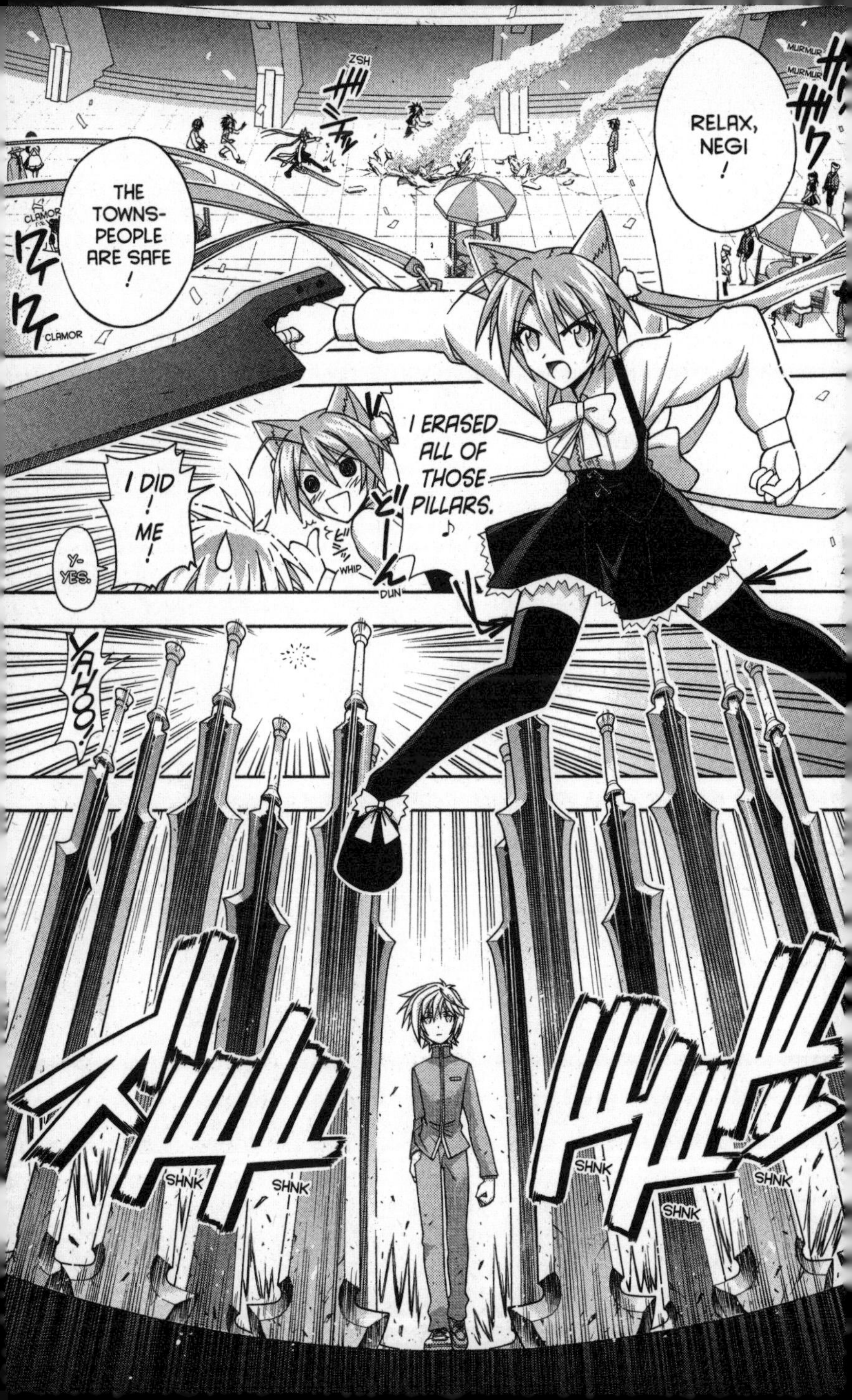
MURMUR
MURMUR
RELAX, NEGI!
ZSH
THE TOWNSPEOPLE ARE SAFE!
CLAMOR
CLAMOR
I ERASED ALL OF THOSE PILLARS. ♪
DUN
WHIP
I DID! ME!
Y-YES.
YAHOO!
SHNK
SHNK
SHNK
SHNK
SHNK
SHNK

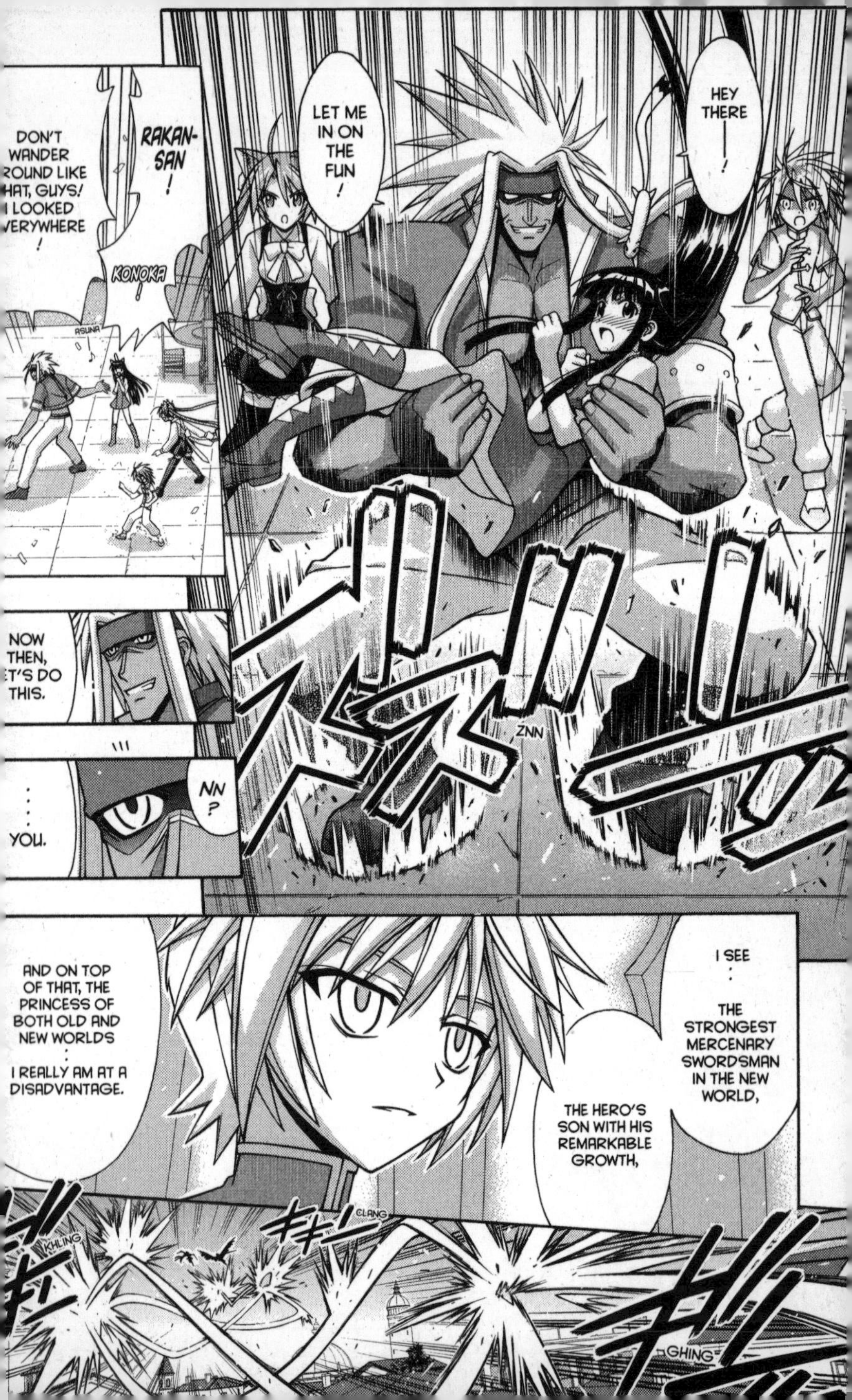
HEY THERE—!
LET ME IN ON THE FUN!
RAKAN-SAN!
DON'T WANDER ROUND LIKE HAT, GUYS! I LOOKED VERYWHERE!
KONOKA!
ASUNA
NOW THEN, T'S DO THIS.
NN?
... YOU.
ZNN
I SEE:
THE STRONGEST MERCENARY SWORDSMAN IN THE NEW WORLD,
THE HERO'S SON WITH HIS REMARKABLE GROWTH,
AND ON TOP OF THAT, THE PRINCESS OF BOTH OLD AND NEW WORLDS: I REALLY AM AT A DISADVANTAGE.
CLANG
KHLING
GHING

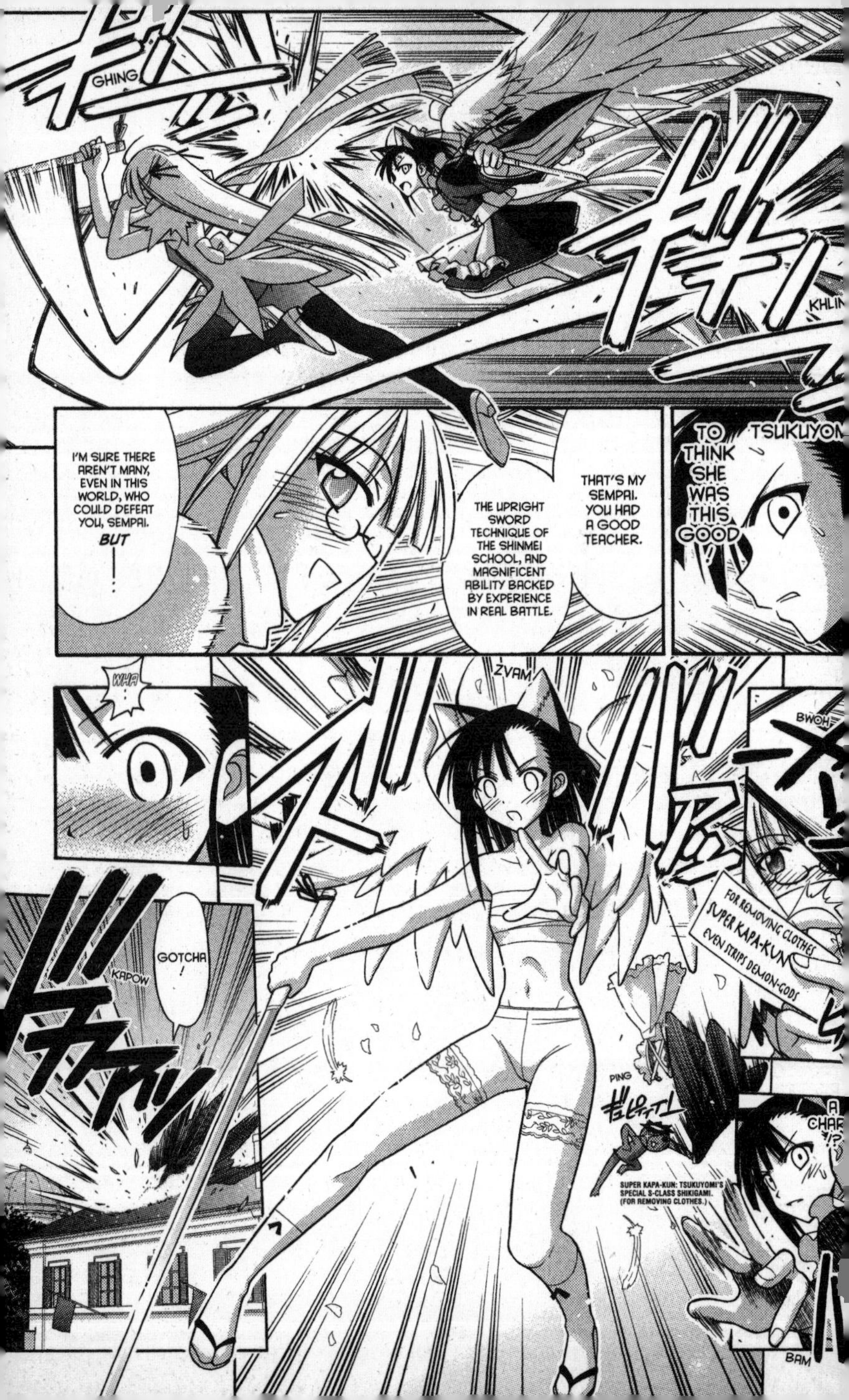
GHING
KHLIN
TSUKUYOM
TO THINK SHE WAS THIS GOOD!
THAT'S MY SEMPAI. YOU HAD A GOOD TEACHER.
THE UPRIGHT SWORD TECHNIQUE OF THE SHINMEI SCHOOL, AND MAGNIFICENT ABILITY BACKED BY EXPERIENCE IN REAL BATTLE.
I'M SURE THERE AREN'T MANY, EVEN IN THIS WORLD, WHO COULD DEFEAT YOU, SEMPAI. BUT!
BWOH
FOR REMOVING CLOTHES
SUPER KAPA-KUN
EVEN STRIPS DEMON-GODS
ZVAM
WHA...!
A CHAR...!?
PING
SUPER KAPA-KUN: TSUKUYOMI'S SPECIAL S-CLASS SHIKIGAMI. (FOR REMOVING CLOTHES.)
BAM
GOTCHA!
KAPOW

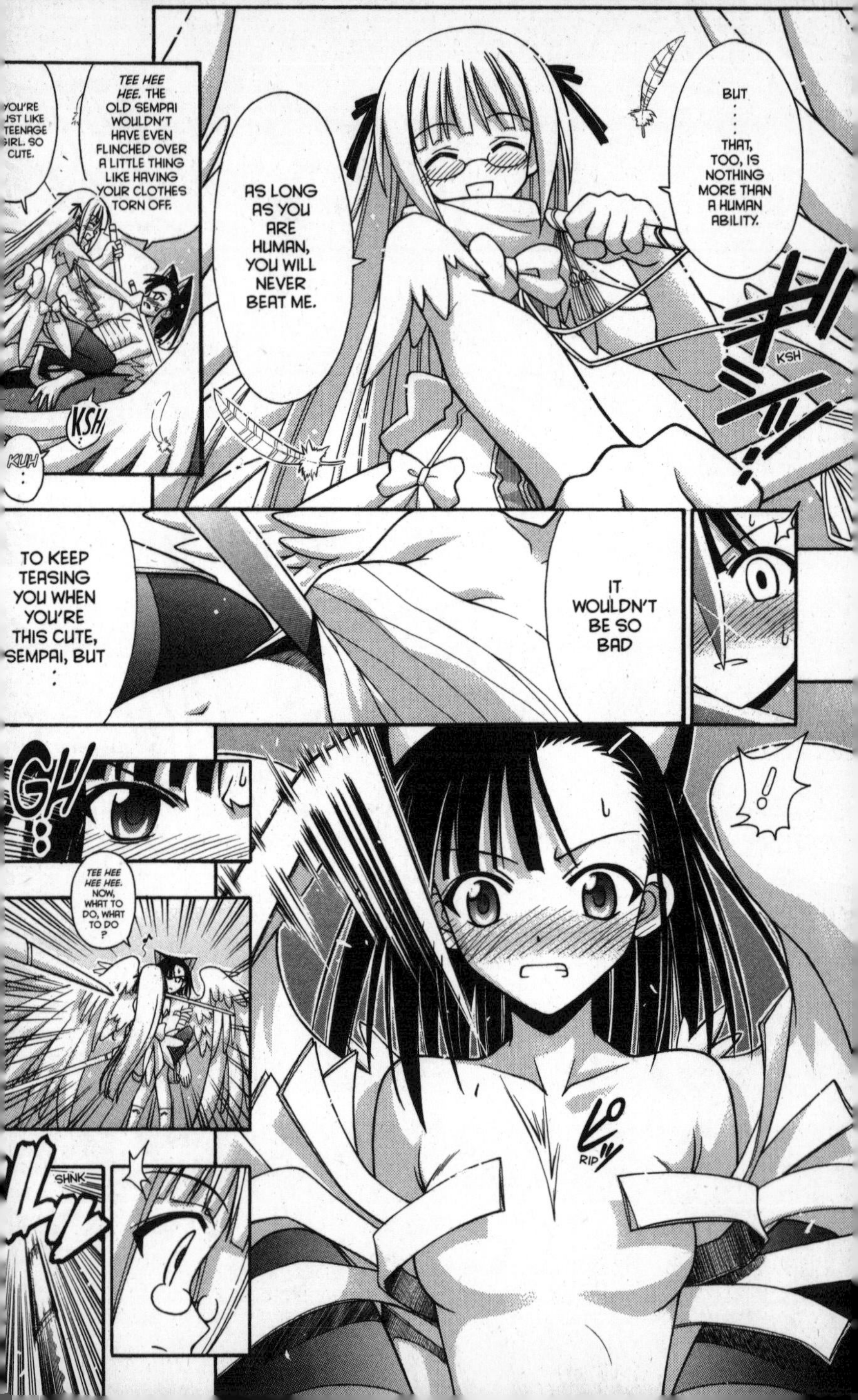
BUT . . . THAT, TOO, IS NOTHING MORE THAN A HUMAN ABILITY.
AS LONG AS YOU ARE HUMAN, YOU WILL NEVER BEAT ME.
KSH
TEE HEE HEE. THE OLD SEMPAI WOULDN'T HAVE EVEN FLINCHED OVER A LITTLE THING LIKE HAVING YOUR CLOTHES TORN OFF.
YOU'RE JUST LIKE TEENAGE GIRL. SO CUTE.
KSH
KUH . . .
IT WOULDN'T BE SO BAD
TO KEEP TEASING YOU WHEN YOU'RE THIS CUTE, SEMPAI, BUT . . .
!
RIP
TEE HEE HEE HEE. NOW, WHAT TO DO, WHAT TO DO?
SHNK

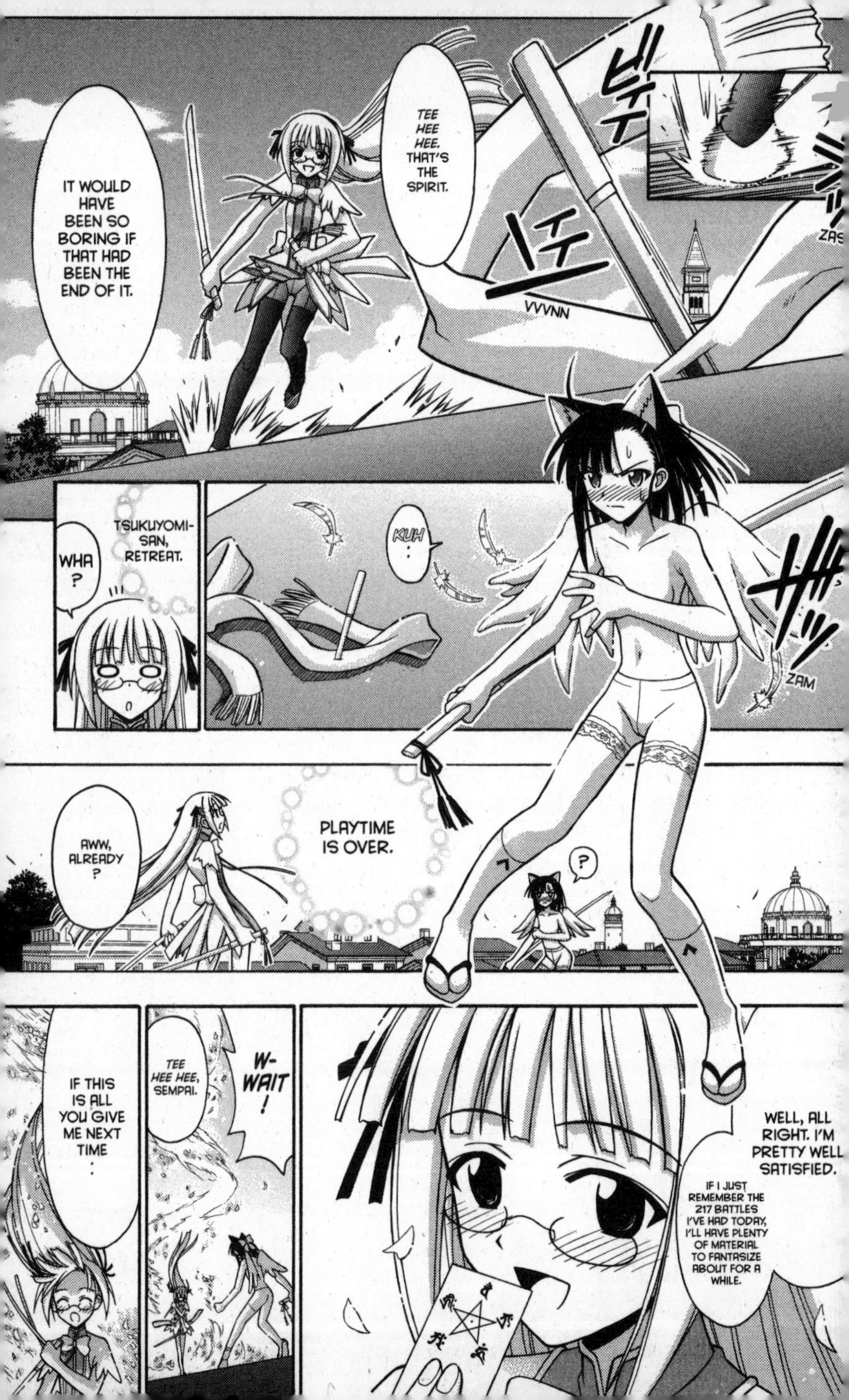
ZAS
VVVNN
TEE HEE HEE. THAT'S THE SPIRIT.
IT WOULD HAVE BEEN SO BORING IF THAT HAD BEEN THE END OF IT.
ZAM
KUH
:
TSUKUYOMI-SAN, RETREAT.
WHA ?
PLAYTIME IS OVER.
?
AWW, ALREADY ?
WELL, ALL RIGHT. I'M PRETTY WELL SATISFIED.
IF I JUST REMEMBER THE 217 BATTLES I'VE HAD TODAY, I'LL HAVE PLENTY OF MATERIAL TO FANTASIZE ABOUT FOR A WHILE.
W-WAIT !
TEE HEE HEE, SEMPAI.
IF THIS IS ALL YOU GIVE ME NEXT TIME
:

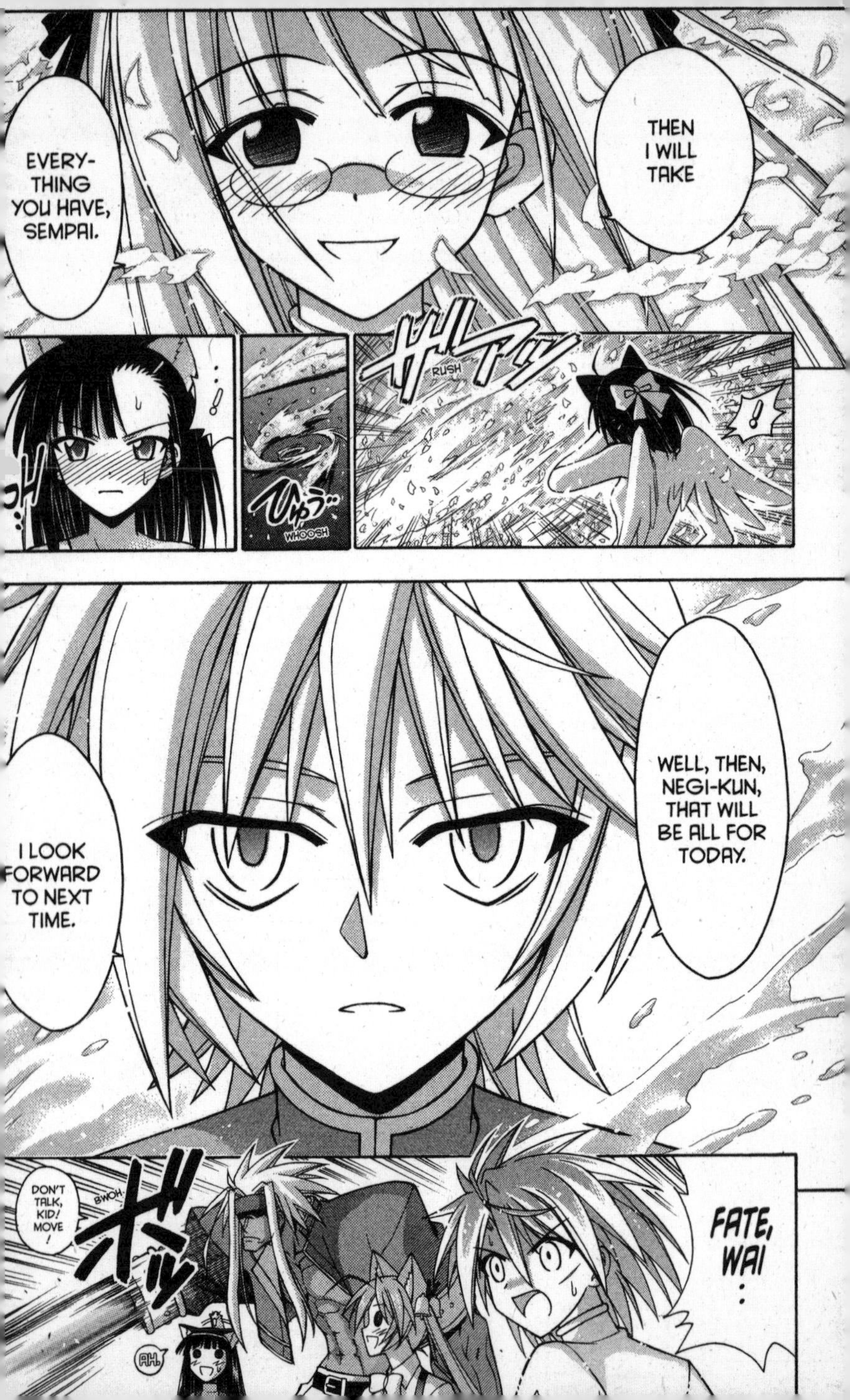
THEN I WILL TAKE
EVERY-THING YOU HAVE, SEMPAI.
RUSH
!
WHOOSH
!
WELL, THEN, NEGI-KUN, THAT WILL BE ALL FOR TODAY.
I LOOK FORWARD TO NEXT TIME.
FATE, WAI...
BWOH
DON'T TALK, KID! MOVE!
AH

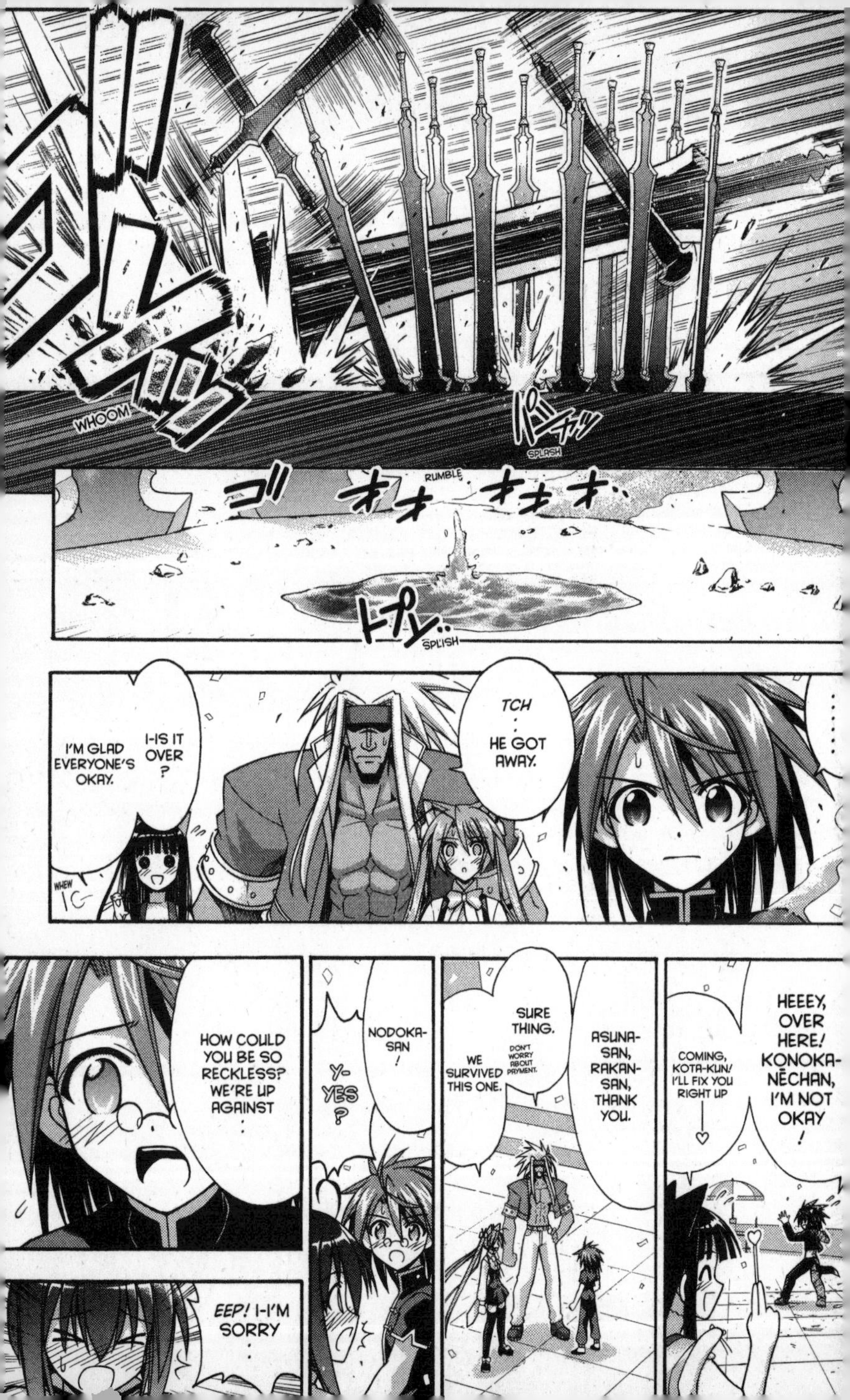
SPLASH
WHOOM
RUMBLE
SPLISH
......
TCH... HE GOT AWAY.
I-IS IT OVER?
I'M GLAD EVERYONE'S OKAY.
WHEW
HEEEY, OVER HERE! KONOKA-NĒCHAN, I'M NOT OKAY!
COMING, KOTA-KUN! I'LL FIX YOU RIGHT UP ♡
ASUNA-SAN, RAKAN-SAN, THANK YOU.
SURE THING.
DON'T WORRY ABOUT PAYMENT.
WE SURVIVED THIS ONE.
NODOKA-SAN!
Y-YES?
HOW COULD YOU BE SO RECKLESS? WE'RE UP AGAINST...
EEP! I-I'M SORRY...

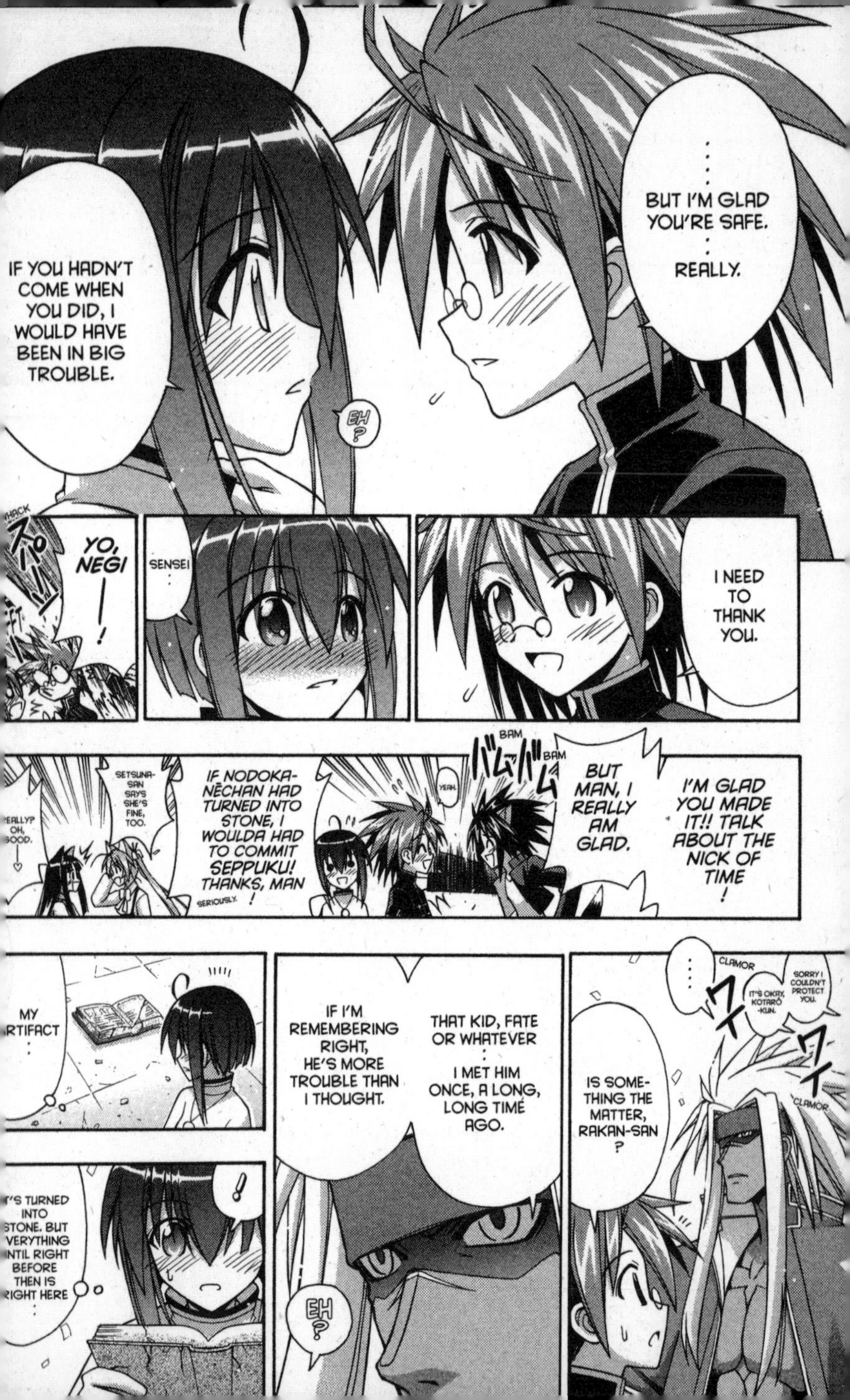

... BUT I'M GLAD YOU'RE SAFE. ... REALLY.
EH?
IF YOU HADN'T COME WHEN YOU DID, I WOULD HAVE BEEN IN BIG TROUBLE.
I NEED TO THANK YOU.
SENSEI...
WHACK
YO, NEGI!
I'M GLAD YOU MADE IT!! TALK ABOUT THE NICK OF TIME!
BAM BAM
BUT MAN, I REALLY AM GLAD.
YEAH.
IF NODOKA-NĒCHAN HAD TURNED INTO STONE, I WOULDA HAD TO COMMIT SEPPUKU! THANKS, MAN!
SERIOUSLY.
SETSUNA-SAN SAYS SHE'S FINE, TOO.
EALLY? OH, OOD.
CLAMOR
SORRY I COULDN'T PROTECT YOU.
IT'S OKAY, KOTARŌ-KUN.
....
IS SOMETHING THE MATTER, RAKAN-SAN?
CLAMOR
THAT KID, FATE OR WHATEVER... I MET HIM ONCE, A LONG, LONG TIME AGO.
IF I'M REMEMBERING RIGHT, HE'S MORE TROUBLE THAN I THOUGHT.
EH?
MY RTIFACT...
!
'S TURNED INTO STONE. BUT VERYTHING NTIL RIGHT BEFORE THEN IS IGHT HERE...

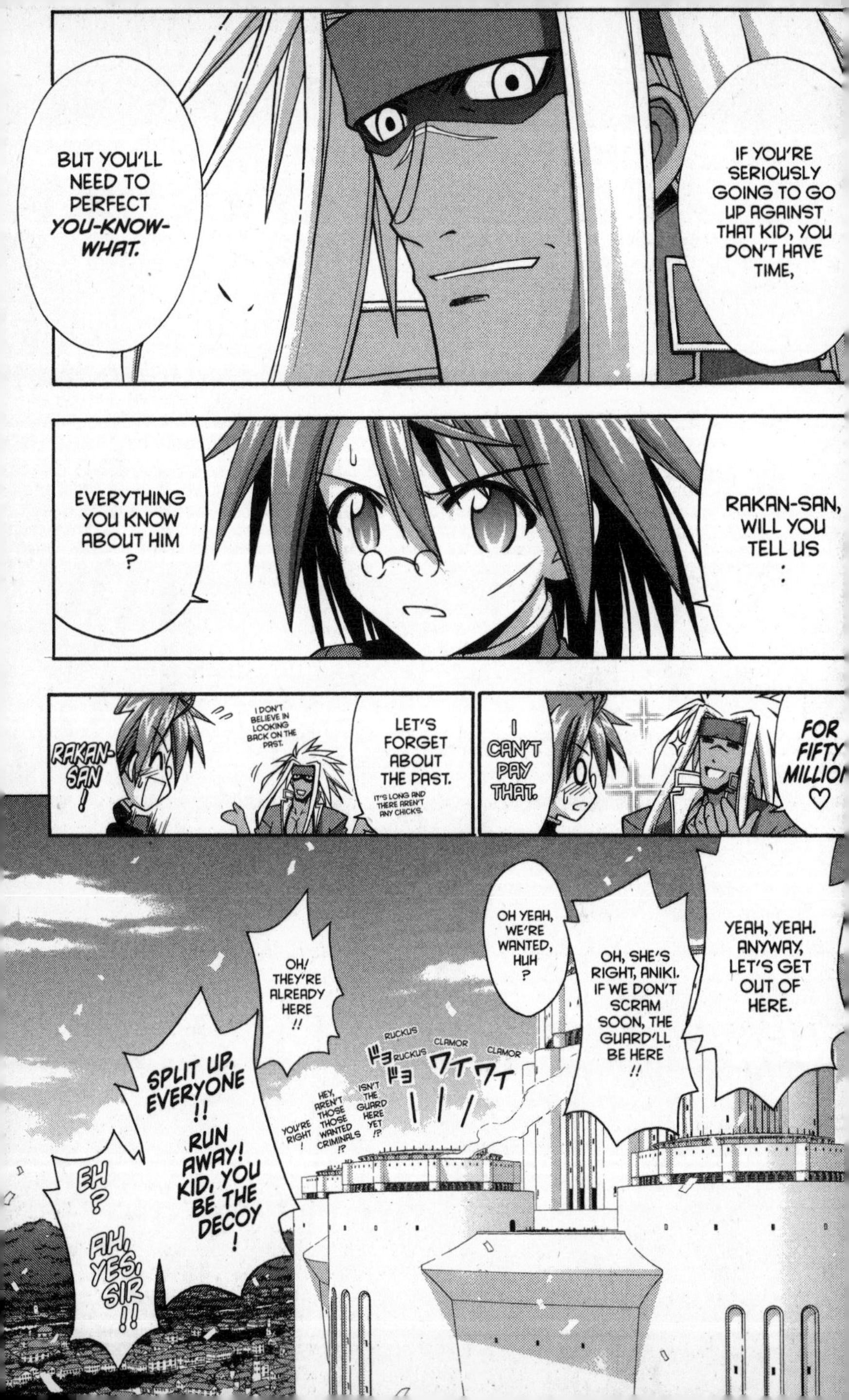
IF YOU'RE SERIOUSLY GOING TO GO UP AGAINST THAT KID, YOU DON'T HAVE TIME,
BUT YOU'LL NEED TO PERFECT *YOU-KNOW-WHAT.*
RAKAN-SAN, WILL YOU TELL US :
EVERYTHING YOU KNOW ABOUT HIM ?
FOR FIFTY MILLIO ♡
I CAN'T PAY THAT.
LET'S FORGET ABOUT THE PAST.
IT'S LONG AND THERE AREN'T ANY CHICKS.
I DON'T BELIEVE IN LOOKING BACK ON THE PAST.
RAKAN-SAN !
YEAH, YEAH. ANYWAY, LET'S GET OUT OF HERE.
OH, SHE'S RIGHT, ANIKI. IF WE DON'T SCRAM SOON, THE GUARD'LL BE HERE !!
OH YEAH, WE'RE WANTED, HUH ?
ワイワイ CLAMOR CLAMOR
ドヨドヨ RUCKUS RUCKUS
ISN'T THE GUARD HERE YET !?
HEY, AREN'T THOSE THOSE WANTED CRIMINALS !?
YOU'RE RIGHT !
OH! THEY'RE ALREADY HERE !!
SPLIT UP, EVERYONE !! RUN AWAY! KID, YOU BE THE DECOY !
EH ? AH, YES, SIR !!

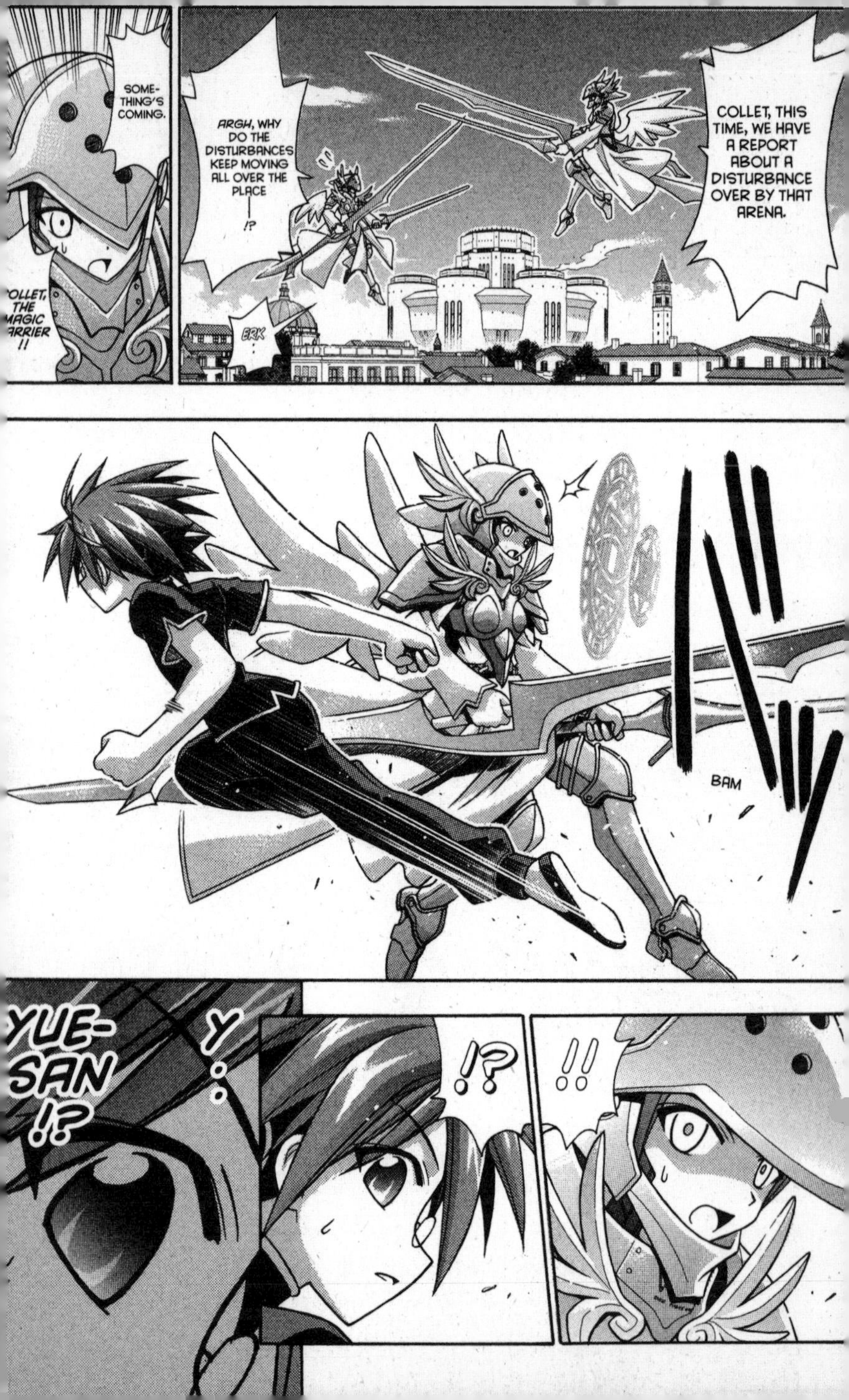
COLLET, THIS TIME, WE HAVE A REPORT ABOUT A DISTURBANCE OVER BY THAT ARENA.
ARGH, WHY DO THE DISTURBANCES KEEP MOVING ALL OVER THE PLACE
!?
ERK
SOME-THING'S COMING.
OLLET, THE AGIC ARRIER !!
BAM
!!
!?
Y...
YUE-SAN !?

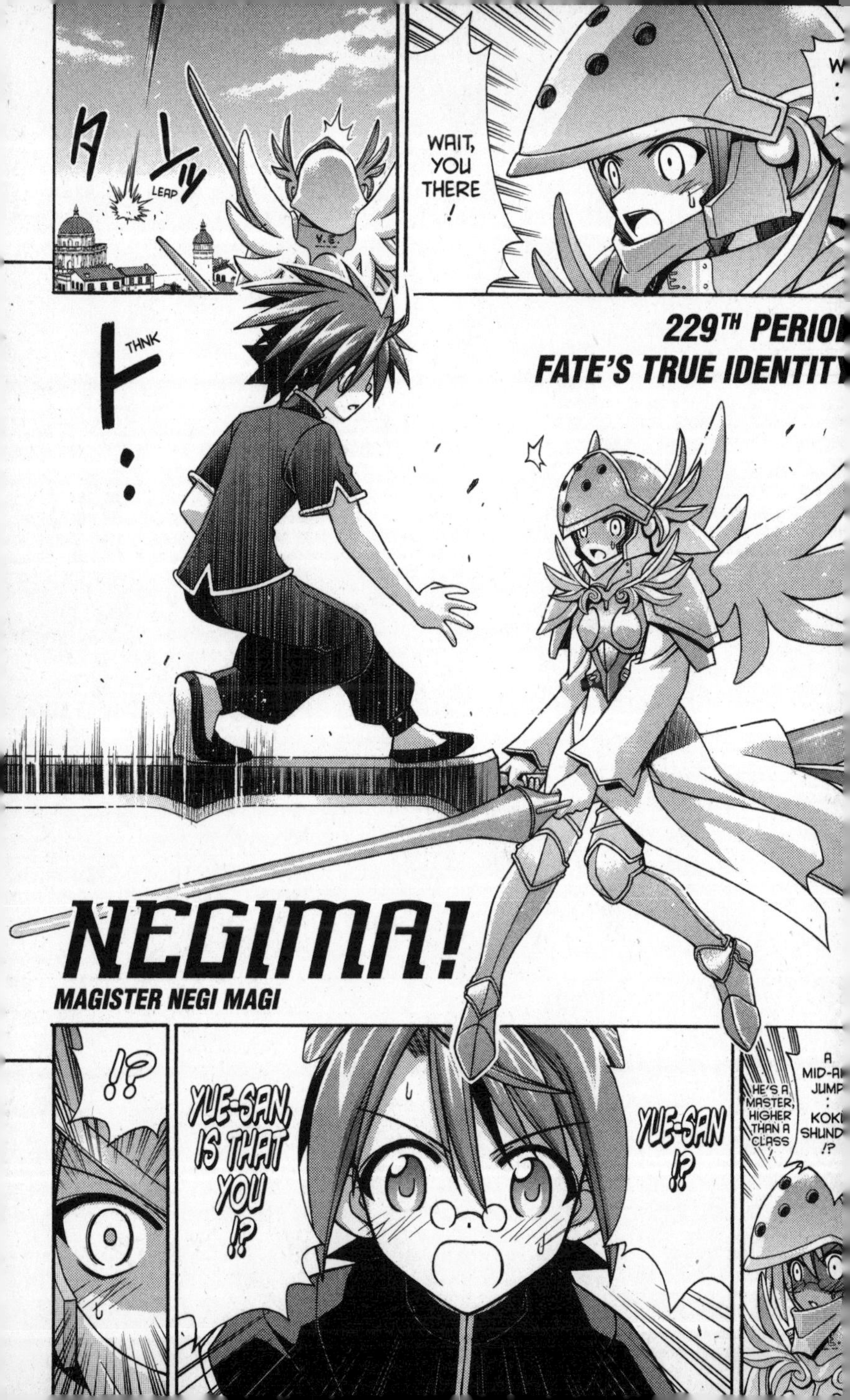
W... : .
WAIT, YOU THERE !
LEAP
THNK
229TH PERIO
FATE'S TRUE IDENTITY
NEGIMA!
MAGISTER NEGI MAGI
A MID-AI JUMP : KOKI SHUND !?
HE'S A MASTER, HIGHER THAN A CLASS !
YUE-SAN !?
YUE-SAN, IS THAT YOU !?
!?

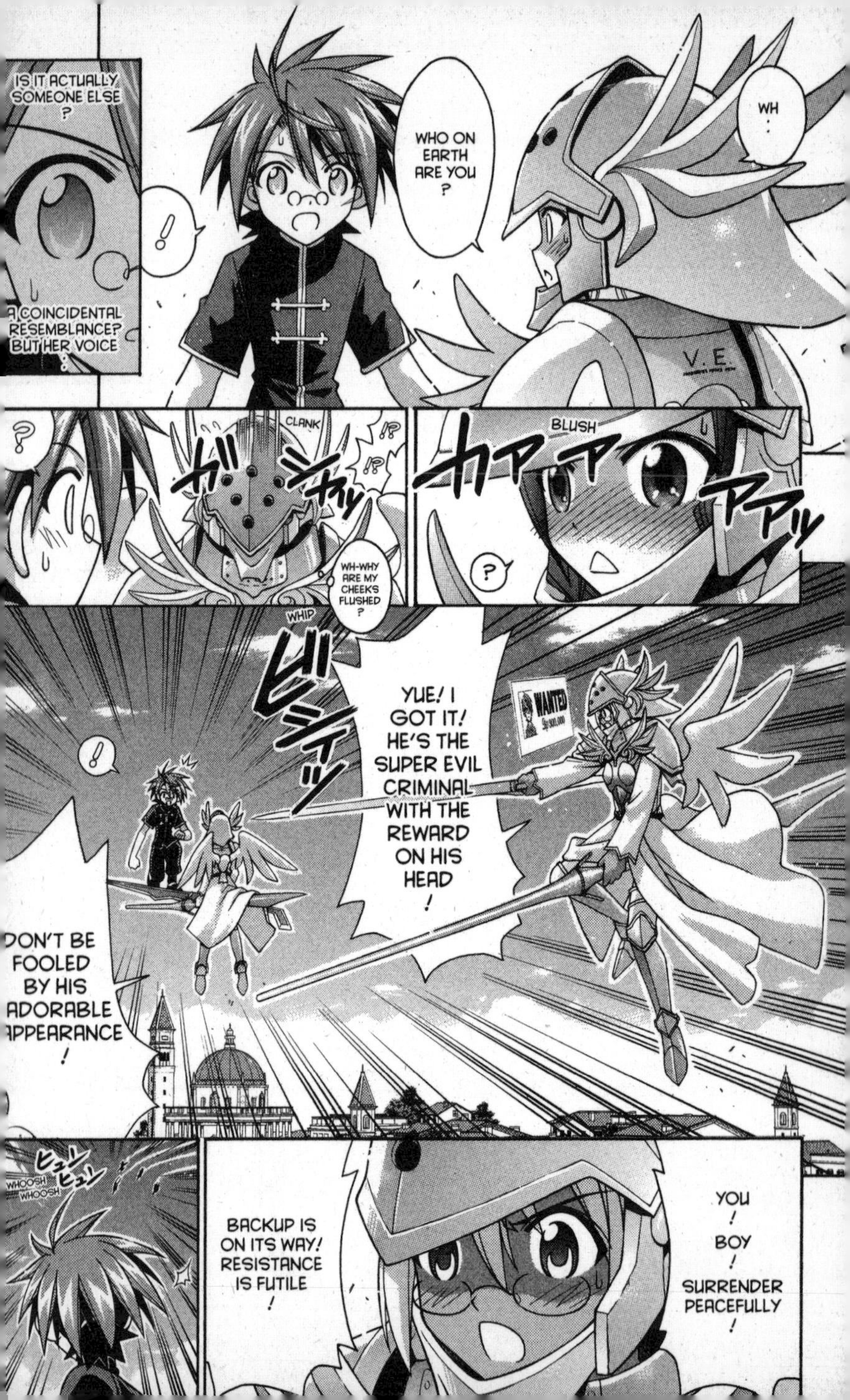
WH...
WHO ON EARTH ARE YOU?
V.E.
!
IS IT ACTUALLY SOMEONE ELSE?
A COINCIDENTAL RESEMBLANCE? BUT HER VOICE...
BLUSH
?
CLANK
!?
!?
?
WH-WHY ARE MY CHEEKS FLUSHED?
WHIP
WANTED
YUE! I GOT IT! HE'S THE SUPER EVIL CRIMINAL WITH THE REWARD ON HIS HEAD!
!
DON'T BE FOOLED BY HIS ADORABLE APPEARANCE!
YOU! BOY! SURRENDER PEACEFULLY!
BACKUP IS ON ITS WAY! RESISTANCE IS FUTILE!
WHOOSH WHOOSH

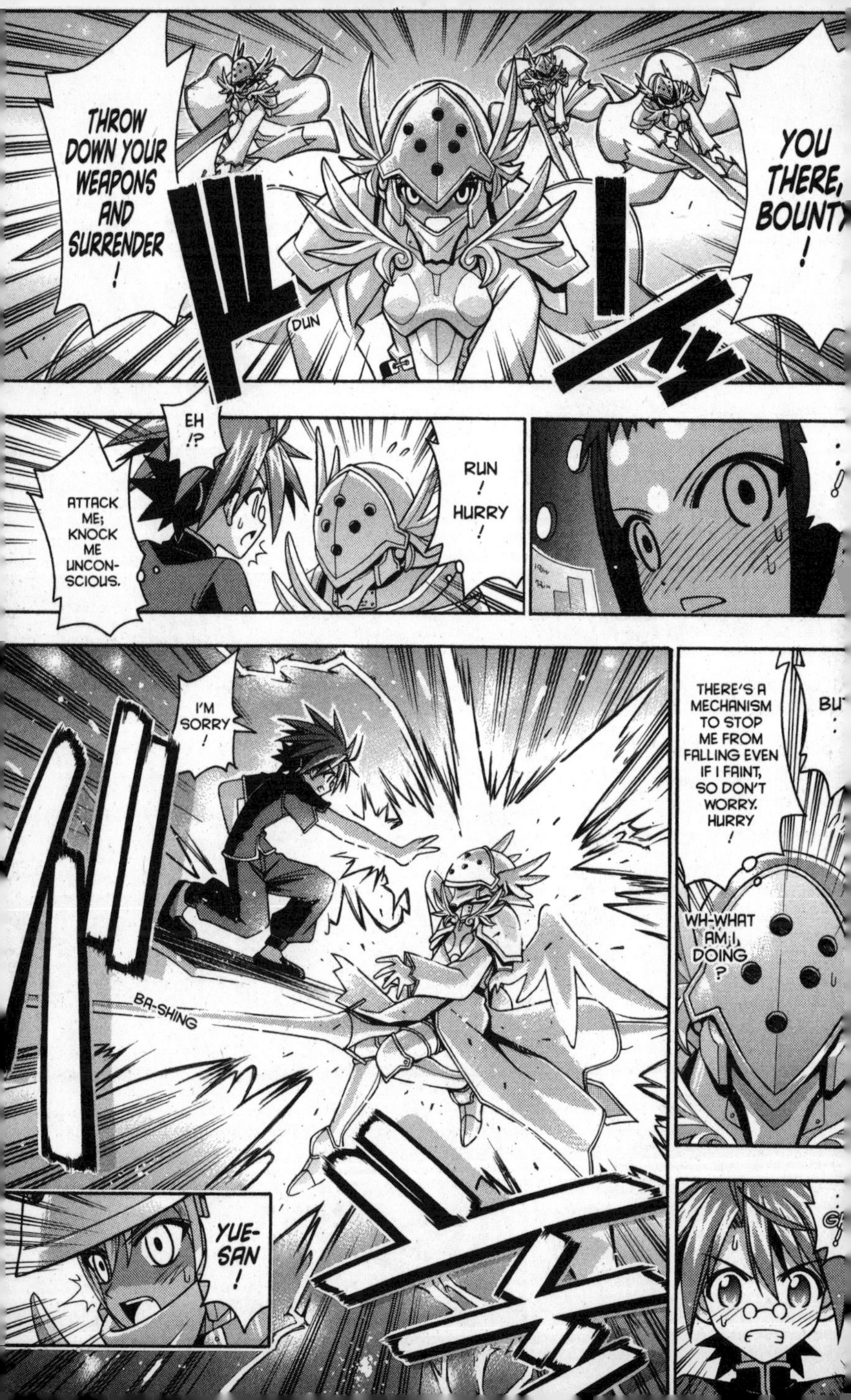
YOU THERE, BOUNTY!
THROW DOWN YOUR WEAPONS AND SURRENDER!
DUN
RUN! HURRY!
EH!?
ATTACK ME; KNOCK ME UNCONSCIOUS.
BUT...
THERE'S A MECHANISM TO STOP ME FROM FALLING EVEN IF I FAINT, SO DON'T WORRY. HURRY!
WH-WHAT AM I DOING?
I'M SORRY!
BA-SHING
YUE-SAN!

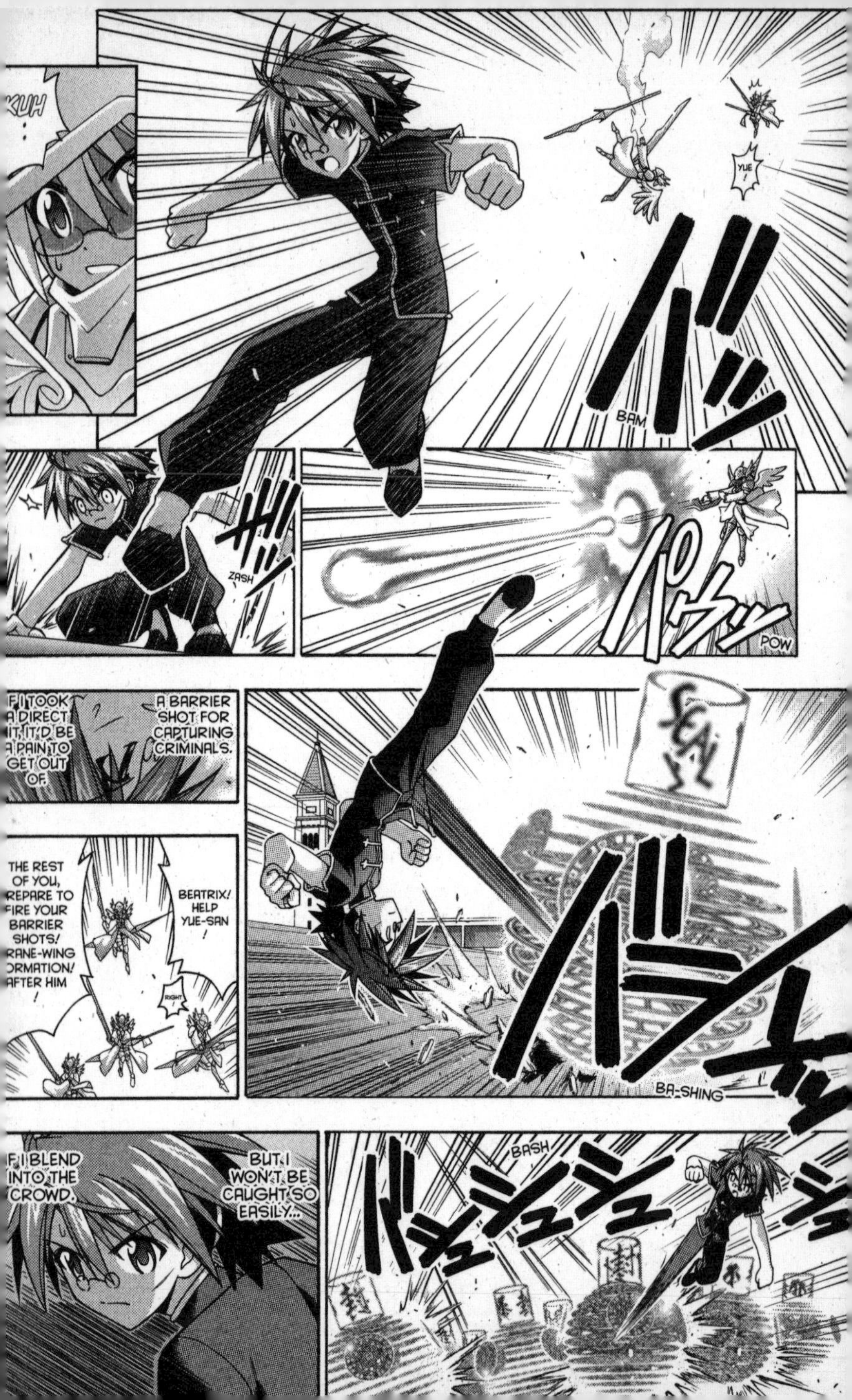
YUE!
KUH...
BAM
ZASH
POW
A BARRIER SHOT FOR CAPTURING CRIMINALS.
IF I TOOK A DIRECT HIT, IT'D BE A PAIN TO GET OUT OF.
BA-SHING
BEATRIX! HELP YUE-SAN!
THE REST OF YOU, PREPARE TO FIRE YOUR BARRIER SHOTS! CRANE-WING FORMATION! AFTER HIM!
RIGHT!
BASH
BUT I WON'T BE CAUGHT SO EASILY...
IF I BLEND INTO THE CROWD.

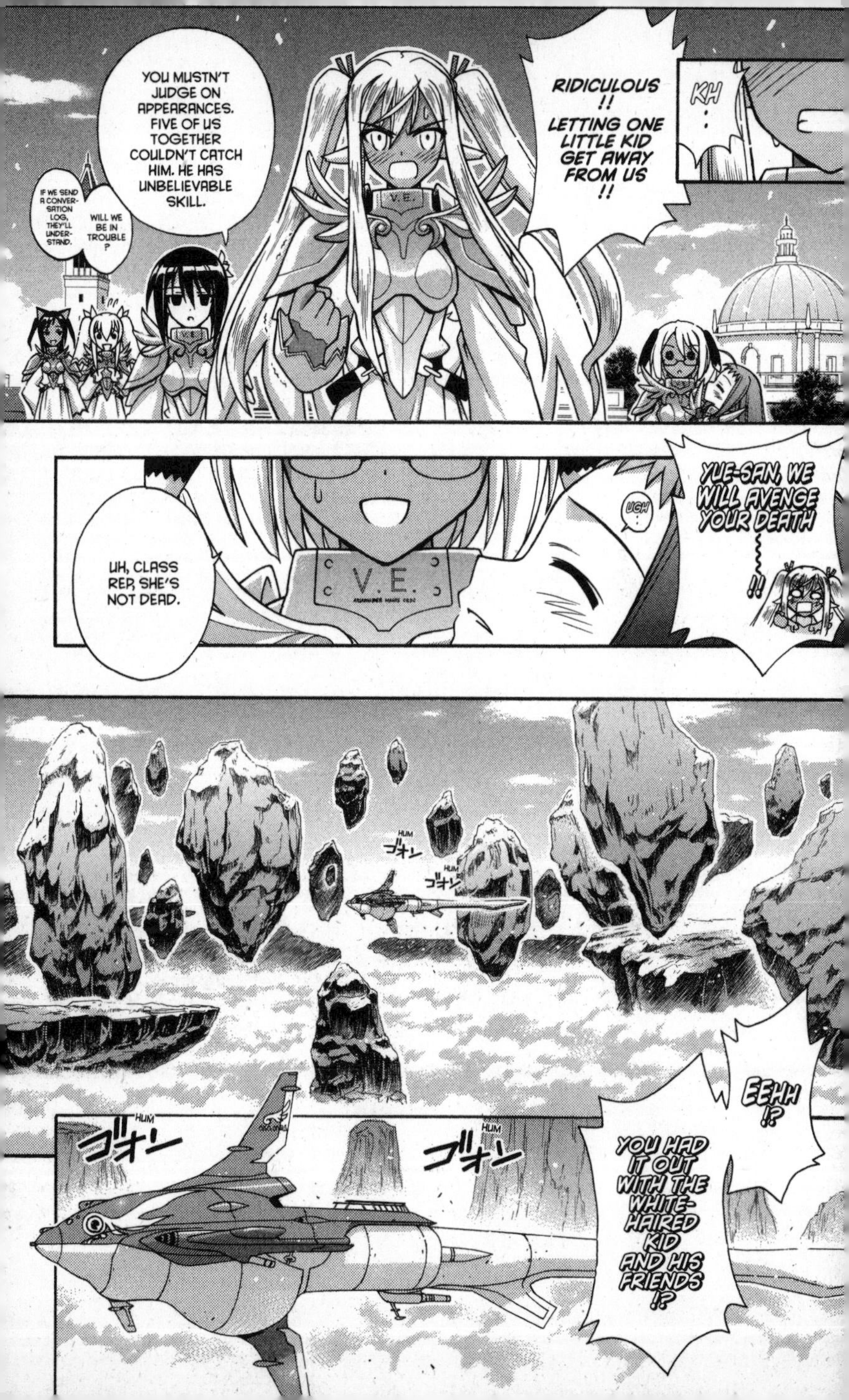
KH...
RIDICULOUS!! LETTING ONE LITTLE KID GET AWAY FROM US!!
YOU MUSTN'T JUDGE ON APPEARANCES. FIVE OF US TOGETHER COULDN'T CATCH HIM. HE HAS UNBELIEVABLE SKILL.
WILL WE BE IN TROUBLE?
IF WE SEND A CONVERSATION LOG, THEY'LL UNDERSTAND.
YUE-SAN, WE WILL AVENGE YOUR DEATH!!
UGH...
UH, CLASS REP, SHE'S NOT DEAD.
HUM ゴオン
HUM ゴオン
EEHH!?
YOU HAD IT OUT WITH THE WHITE-HAIRED KID AND HIS FRIENDS!?
HUM ゴオン
HUM ゴオン

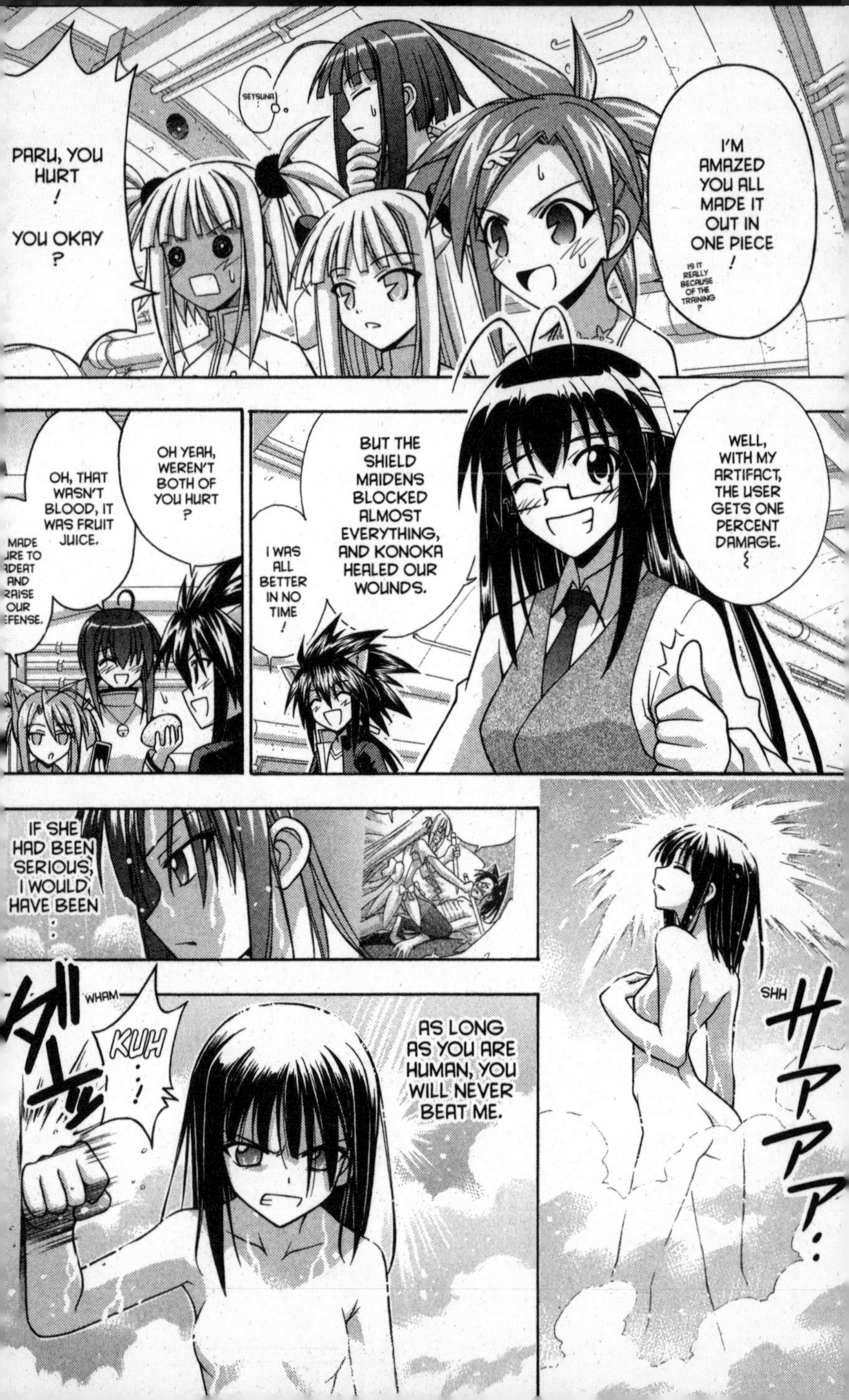
I'M AMAZED YOU ALL MADE IT OUT IN ONE PIECE!
IS IT REALLY BECAUSE OF THE TRAINING?
SETSUNA...
PARU, YOU HURT! YOU OKAY?
WELL, WITH MY ARTIFACT, THE USER GETS ONE PERCENT DAMAGE.
BUT THE SHIELD MAIDENS BLOCKED ALMOST EVERYTHING, AND KONOKA HEALED OUR WOUNDS.
I WAS ALL BETTER IN NO TIME!
OH YEAH, WEREN'T BOTH OF YOU HURT?
OH, THAT WASN'T BLOOD, IT WAS FRUIT JUICE.
MADE URE TO ADEAT AND RAISE OUR EFENSE.
SHH
サァァァ..
IF SHE HAD BEEN SERIOUS, I WOULD HAVE BEEN...
WHAM
ダッ
KUH...!
AS LONG AS YOU ARE HUMAN, YOU WILL NEVER BEAT ME.

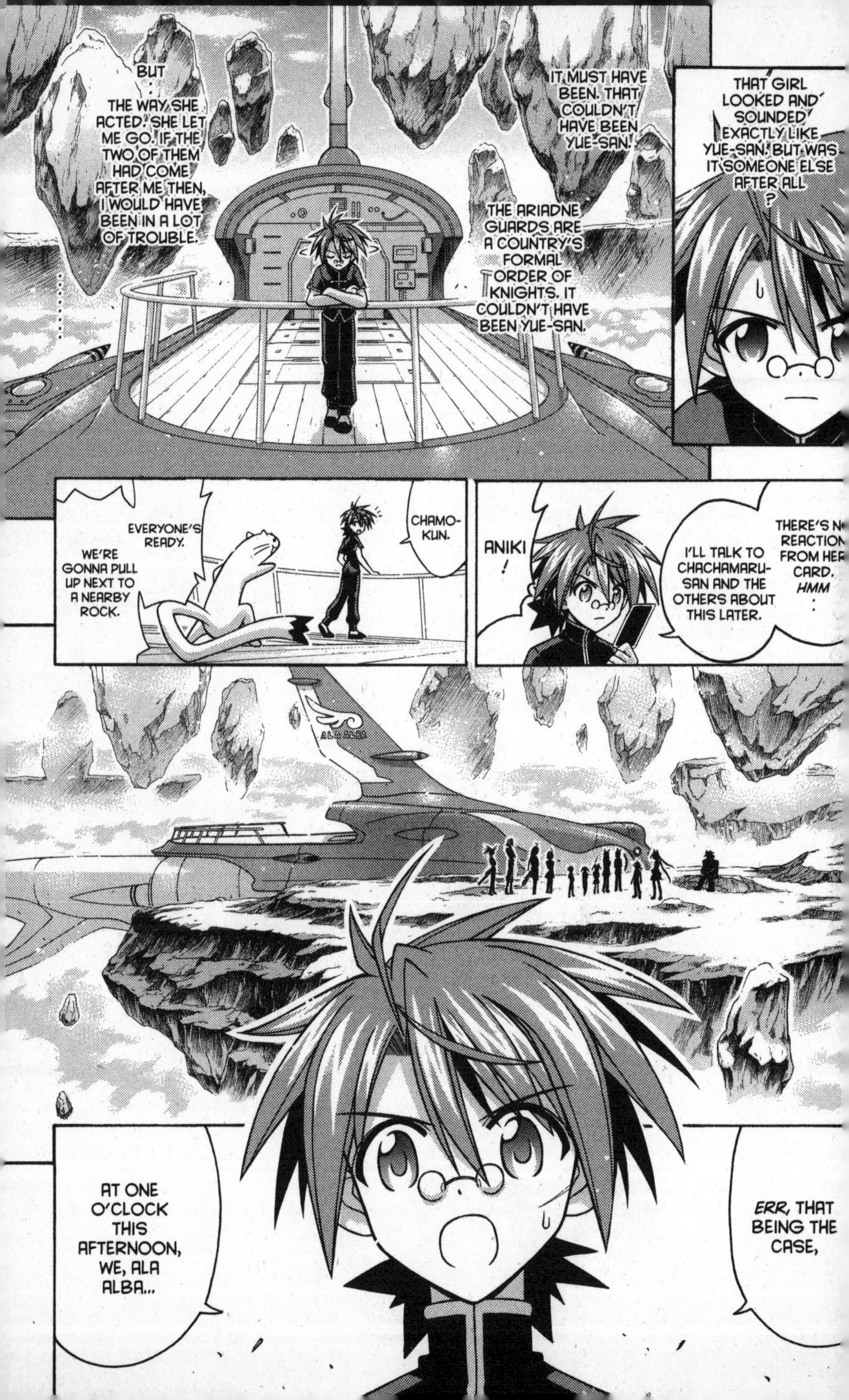
THAT GIRL LOOKED AND SOUNDED EXACTLY LIKE YUE-SAN. BUT WAS IT SOMEONE ELSE AFTER ALL ?
IT MUST HAVE BEEN. THAT COULDN'T HAVE BEEN YUE-SAN!
THE ARIADNE GUARDS ARE A COUNTRY'S FORMAL ORDER OF KNIGHTS. IT COULDN'T HAVE BEEN YUE-SAN.
BUT
THE WAY SHE ACTED. SHE LET ME GO. IF THE TWO OF THEM HAD COME AFTER ME THEN, I WOULD HAVE BEEN IN A LOT OF TROUBLE.
THERE'S NO REACTION FROM HER CARD. *HMM* :
I'LL TALK TO CHACHAMARU-SAN AND THE OTHERS ABOUT THIS LATER.
ANIKI !
CHAMO-KUN.
EVERYONE'S READY.
WE'RE GONNA PULL UP NEXT TO A NEARBY ROCK.
ALA ALBA
ERR, THAT BEING THE CASE,
AT ONE O'CLOCK THIS AFTERNOON, WE, ALA ALBA...

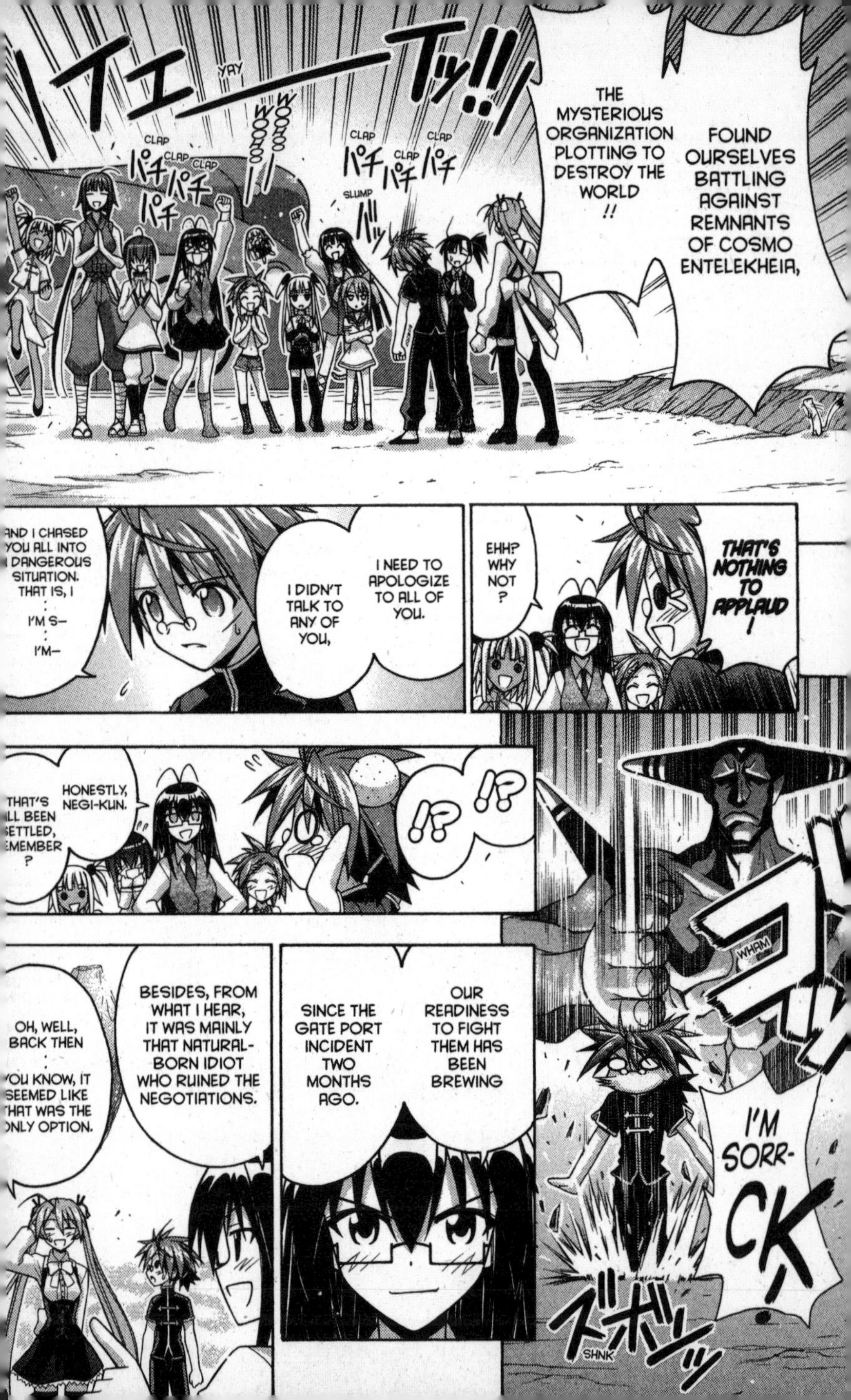
FOUND OURSELVES BATTLING AGAINST REMNANTS OF COSMO ENTELEKHEIA,
THE MYSTERIOUS ORGANIZATION PLOTTING TO DESTROY THE WORLD !!
YAY
WOOHOOOO
CLAP CLAP CLAP
CLAP CLAP CLAP
SLUMP
THAT'S NOTHING TO APPLAUD!
EHH? WHY NOT?
I NEED TO APOLOGIZE TO ALL OF YOU.
I DIDN'T TALK TO ANY OF YOU,
AND I CHASED YOU ALL INTO A DANGEROUS SITUATION. THAT IS, I... I'M S— ... I'M—
WHAM
I'M SORR-CK!
SHNK
!? !?
HONESTLY, NEGI-KUN.
THAT'S ALL BEEN SETTLED, REMEMBER?
OUR READINESS TO FIGHT THEM HAS BEEN BREWING
SINCE THE GATE PORT INCIDENT TWO MONTHS AGO.
BESIDES, FROM WHAT I HEAR, IT WAS MAINLY THAT NATURAL-BORN IDIOT WHO RUINED THE NEGOTIATIONS.
OH, WELL, BACK THEN... YOU KNOW, IT SEEMED LIKE THAT WAS THE ONLY OPTION.

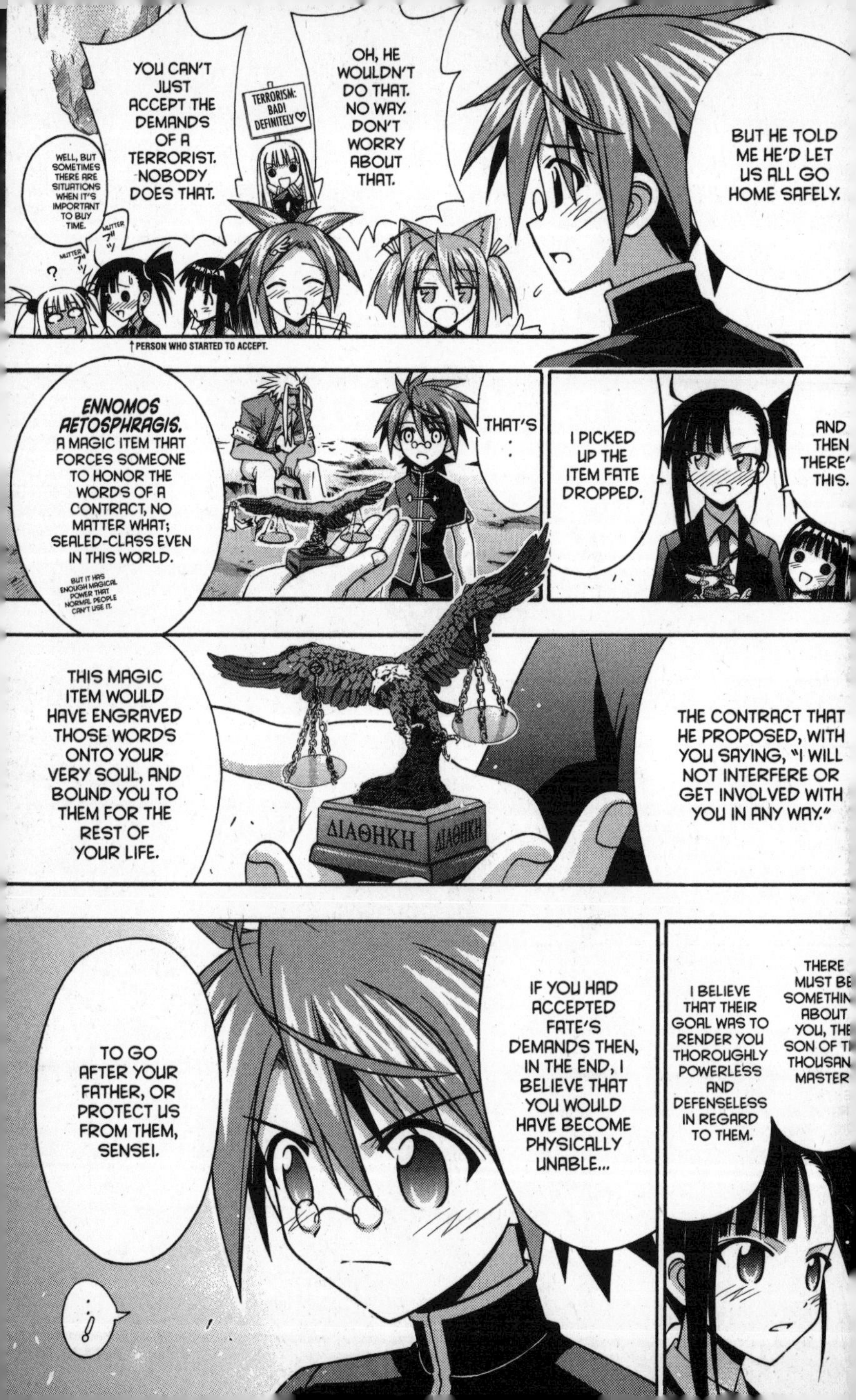
BUT HE TOLD ME HE'D LET US ALL GO HOME SAFELY.
OH, HE WOULDN'T DO THAT. NO WAY. DON'T WORRY ABOUT THAT.
TERRORISM: BAD! DEFINITELY♡
YOU CAN'T JUST ACCEPT THE DEMANDS OF A TERRORIST. NOBODY DOES THAT.
WELL, BUT SOMETIMES THERE ARE SITUATIONS WHEN IT'S IMPORTANT TO BUY TIME.
MUTTER
MUTTER
?
↑PERSON WHO STARTED TO ACCEPT.
AND THEN THERE' THIS.
I PICKED UP THE ITEM FATE DROPPED.
THAT'S :
ENNOMOS AETOSPHRAGIS. A MAGIC ITEM THAT FORCES SOMEONE TO HONOR THE WORDS OF A CONTRACT, NO MATTER WHAT; SEALED-CLASS EVEN IN THIS WORLD.
BUT IT HAS ENOUGH MAGICAL POWER THAT NORMAL PEOPLE CAN'T USE IT.
THE CONTRACT THAT HE PROPOSED, WITH YOU SAYING, "I WILL NOT INTERFERE OR GET INVOLVED WITH YOU IN ANY WAY."
THIS MAGIC ITEM WOULD HAVE ENGRAVED THOSE WORDS ONTO YOUR VERY SOUL, AND BOUND YOU TO THEM FOR THE REST OF YOUR LIFE.
ΔΙΑΘΗΚΗ ΔΙΑΘΗΚΗ
THERE MUST BE SOMETHIN ABOUT YOU, THE SON OF T THOUSAN MASTER
I BELIEVE THAT THEIR GOAL WAS TO RENDER YOU THOROUGHLY POWERLESS AND DEFENSELESS IN REGARD TO THEM.
IF YOU HAD ACCEPTED FATE'S DEMANDS THEN, IN THE END, I BELIEVE THAT YOU WOULD HAVE BECOME PHYSICALLY UNABLE...
TO GO AFTER YOUR FATHER, OR PROTECT US FROM THEM, SENSEI.
...!

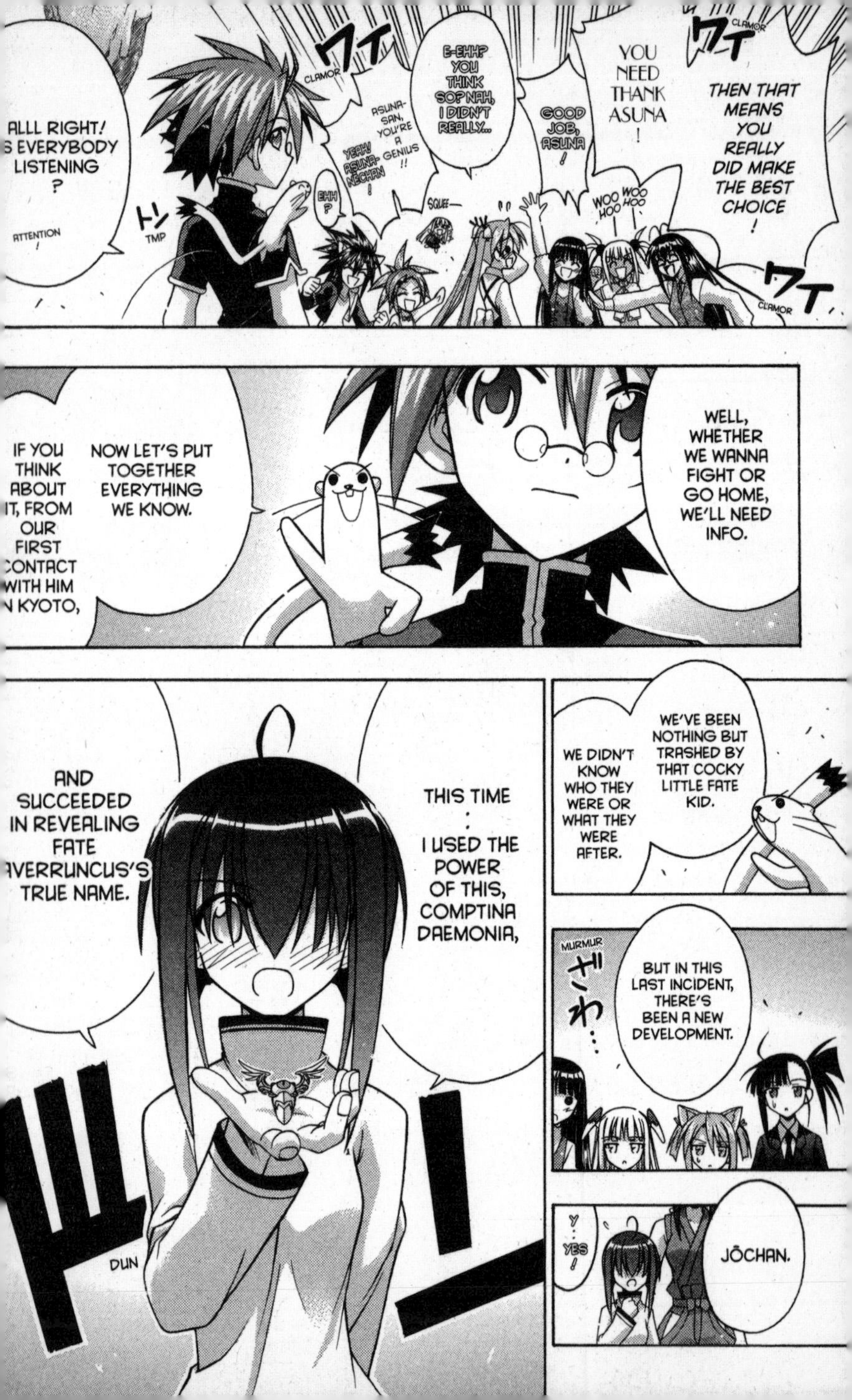
CLAMOR
THEN THAT MEANS YOU REALLY DID MAKE THE BEST CHOICE!
YOU NEED THANK ASUNA!
GOOD JOB, ASUNA!
WOO HOO WOO HOO
E-EHH? YOU THINK SO? NAH, I DIDN'T REALLY...
ASUNA-SAN, YOU'RE A GENIUS!!
YEAH! ASUNA-NECHAN!
SQUEE—
EHH?
CLAMOR
CLAMOR
ALLL RIGHT! IS EVERYBODY LISTENING?
TMP
ATTENTION!
WELL, WHETHER WE WANNA FIGHT OR GO HOME, WE'LL NEED INFO.
NOW LET'S PUT TOGETHER EVERYTHING WE KNOW.
IF YOU THINK ABOUT IT, FROM OUR FIRST CONTACT WITH HIM IN KYOTO,
WE'VE BEEN NOTHING BUT TRASHED BY THAT COCKY LITTLE FATE KID.
WE DIDN'T KNOW WHO THEY WERE OR WHAT THEY WERE AFTER.
MURMUR
BUT IN THIS LAST INCIDENT, THERE'S BEEN A NEW DEVELOPMENT.
JŌCHAN.
Y... YES!
THIS TIME: I USED THE POWER OF THIS, COMPTINA DAEMONIA,
AND SUCCEEDED IN REVEALING FATE AVERRUNCUS'S TRUE NAME.
DUN

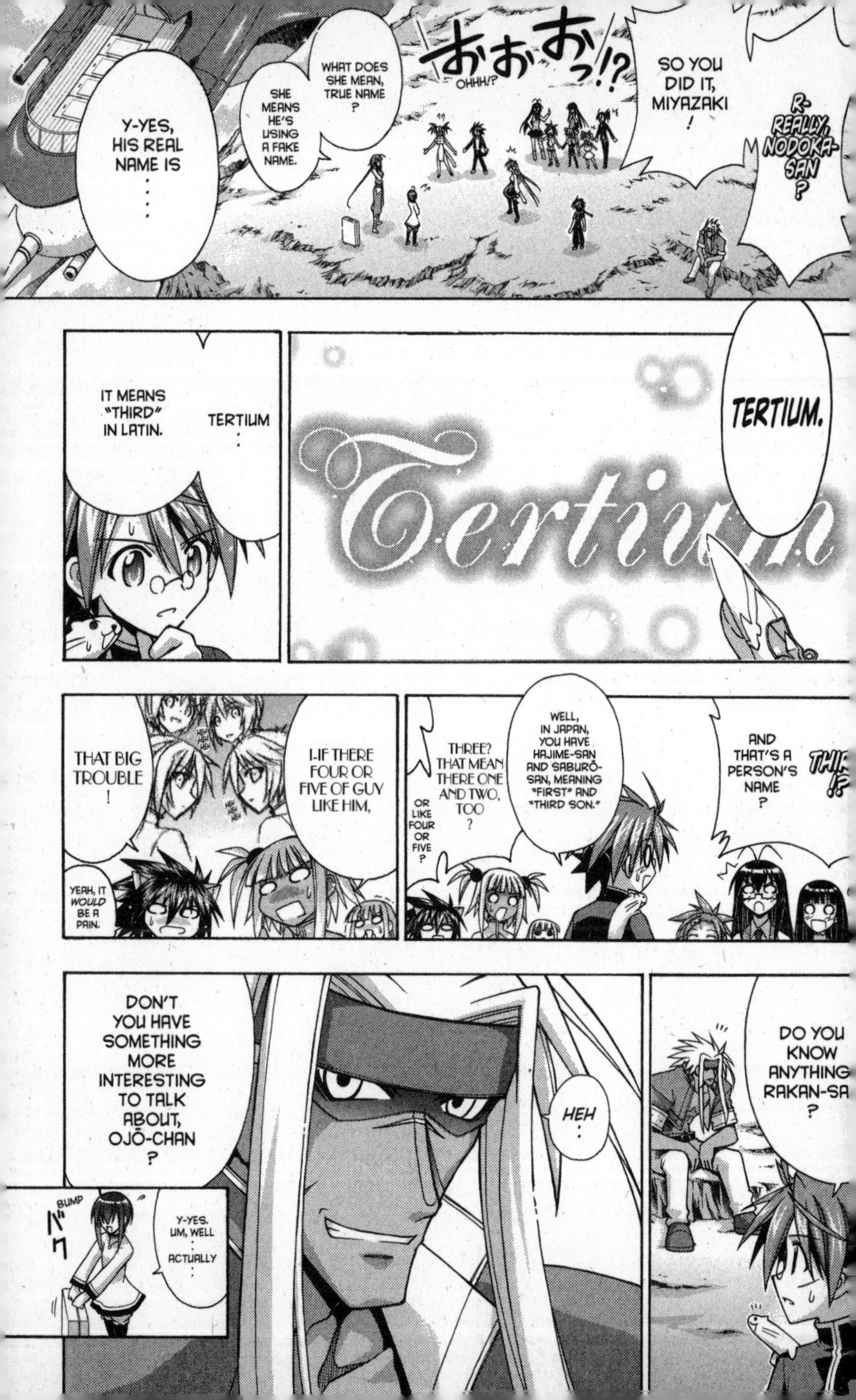
R-REALLY, NODOKA-SAN?
SO YOU DID IT, MIYAZAKI!
おぉおっ!!?
OHHH!?
WHAT DOES SHE MEAN, TRUE NAME?
SHE MEANS HE'S USING A FAKE NAME.
Y-YES, HIS REAL NAME IS ......
TERTIUM.
Tertium
TERTIUM...
IT MEANS "THIRD" IN LATIN.
THIRD!?
AND THAT'S A PERSON'S NAME?
WELL, IN JAPAN, YOU HAVE HAJIME-SAN AND SABURŌ-SAN, MEANING "FIRST" AND "THIRD SON."
THREE? THAT MEAN THERE ONE AND TWO, TOO?
OR LIKE FOUR OR FIVE?
I-IF THERE FOUR OR FIVE OF GUY LIKE HIM,
THAT BIG TROUBLE!
YEAH, IT WOULD BE A PAIN.
DO YOU KNOW ANYTHING RAKAN-SA?
HEH...
DON'T YOU HAVE SOMETHING MORE INTERESTING TO TALK ABOUT, OJŌ-CHAN?
バク
BUMP
Y-YES. UM, WELL... ACTUALLY

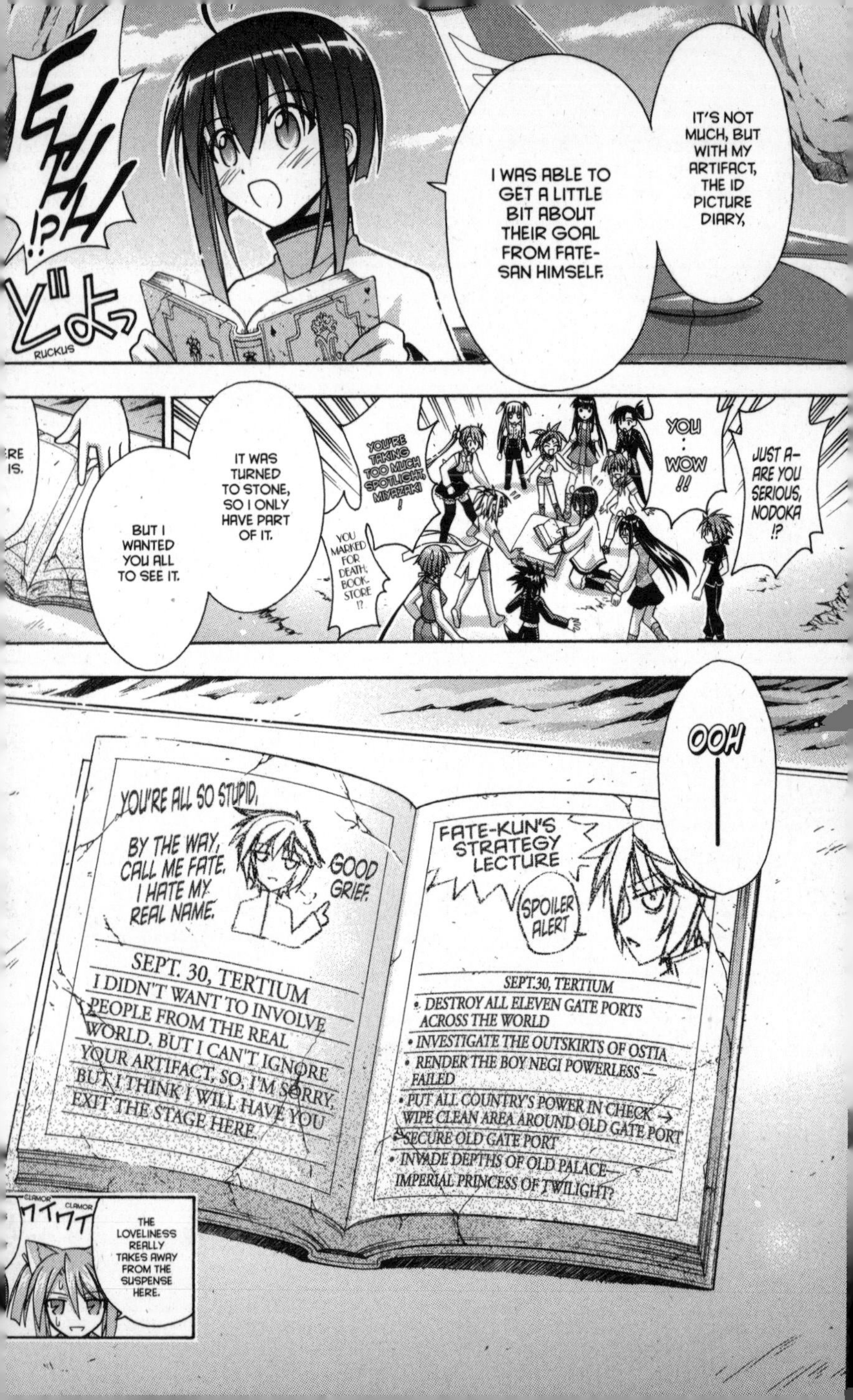
IT'S NOT MUCH, BUT WITH MY ARTIFACT, THE ID PICTURE DIARY,
I WAS ABLE TO GET A LITTLE BIT ABOUT THEIR GOAL FROM FATE-SAN HIMSELF.
EHHH!?
RUCKUS
JUST A-ARE YOU SERIOUS, NODOKA!?
YOU... WOW!!
YOU'RE TAKING TOO MUCH SPOTLIGHT, MIYAZAKI!
YOU MARKED FOR DEATH, BOOKSTORE!?
IT WAS TURNED TO STONE, SO I ONLY HAVE PART OF IT.
BUT I WANTED YOU ALL TO SEE IT.
OOH—
FATE-KUN'S STRATEGY LECTURE
SPOILER ALERT
SEPT.30, TERTIUM
• DESTROY ALL ELEVEN GATE PORTS ACROSS THE WORLD
• INVESTIGATE THE OUTSKIRTS OF OSTIA
• RENDER THE BOY NEGI POWERLESS — FAILED
• PUT ALL COUNTRY'S POWER IN CHECK → WIPE CLEAN AREA AROUND OLD GATE PORT
• SECURE OLD GATE PORT
• INVADE DEPTHS OF OLD PALACE— IMPERIAL PRINCESS OF TWILIGHT?
YOU'RE ALL SO STUPID.
BY THE WAY, CALL ME FATE. I HATE MY REAL NAME.
GOOD GRIEF.
SEPT. 30, TERTIUM
I DIDN'T WANT TO INVOLVE PEOPLE FROM THE REAL WORLD. BUT I CAN'T IGNORE YOUR ARTIFACT, SO, I'M SORRY, BUT I THINK I WILL HAVE YOU EXIT THE STAGE HERE.
CLAMOR CLAMOR
THE LOVELINESS REALLY TAKES AWAY FROM THE SUSPENSE HERE.

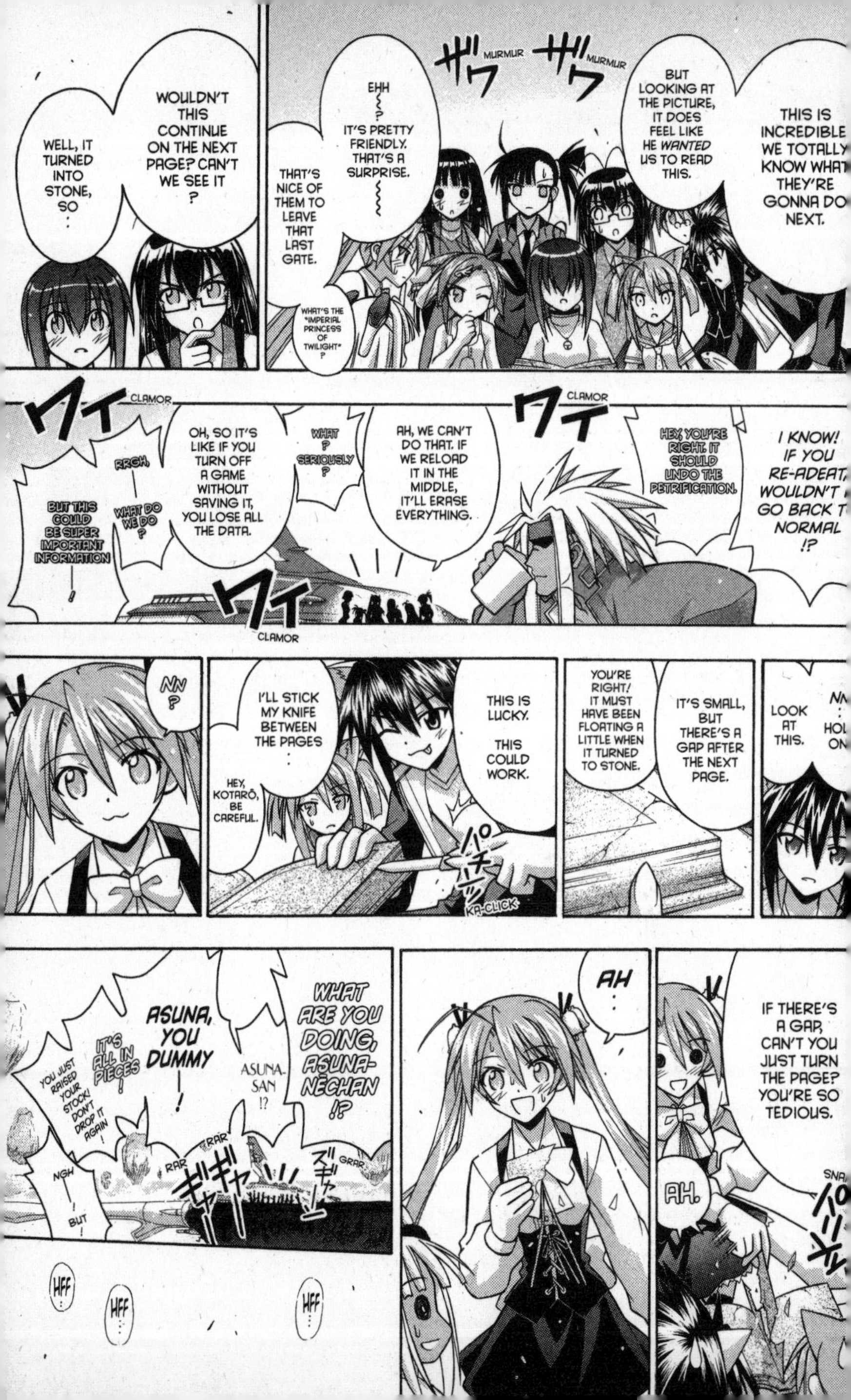
MURMUR
MURMUR
THIS IS INCREDIBLE WE TOTALLY KNOW WHAT THEY'RE GONNA DO NEXT.
BUT LOOKING AT THE PICTURE, IT DOES FEEL LIKE HE WANTED US TO READ THIS.
EHH ~~~? IT'S PRETTY FRIENDLY. THAT'S A SURPRISE. ~~~
THAT'S NICE OF THEM TO LEAVE THAT LAST GATE.
WHAT'S THE "IMPERIAL PRINCESS OF TWILIGHT"?
WOULDN'T THIS CONTINUE ON THE NEXT PAGE? CAN'T WE SEE IT?
WELL, IT TURNED INTO STONE, SO...
I KNOW! IF YOU RE-ADEAT, WOULDN'T GO BACK T NORMAL!?
HEY, YOU'RE RIGHT. IT SHOULD UNDO THE PETRIFICATION.
CLAMOR
AH, WE CAN'T DO THAT. IF WE RELOAD IT IN THE MIDDLE, IT'LL ERASE EVERYTHING.
WHAT? SERIOUSLY?
OH, SO IT'S LIKE IF YOU TURN OFF A GAME WITHOUT SAVING IT, YOU LOSE ALL THE DATA.
RRGH, WHAT DO WE DO?
BUT THIS COULD BE SUPER IMPORTANT INFORMATION!
CLAMOR
CLAMOR
LOOK AT THIS.
IT'S SMALL, BUT THERE'S A GAP AFTER THE NEXT PAGE.
YOU'RE RIGHT! IT MUST HAVE BEEN FLOATING A LITTLE WHEN IT TURNED TO STONE.
THIS IS LUCKY. THIS COULD WORK.
I'LL STICK MY KNIFE BETWEEN THE PAGES...
HEY, KOTARŌ, BE CAREFUL.
KA-CLICK
NN?
IF THERE'S A GAP, CAN'T YOU JUST TURN THE PAGE? YOU'RE SO TEDIOUS.
AH.
AH...
WHAT ARE YOU DOING, ASUNA-NĒCHAN!?
ASUNA-SAN!?
ASUNA, YOU DUMMY!
IT'S ALL IN PIECES!
YOU JUST RAISED YOUR STOCK! DON'T DROP IT AGAIN!
GRAR
RAR
RAR
NGH! BUT!
HFF...
HFF...
HFF...

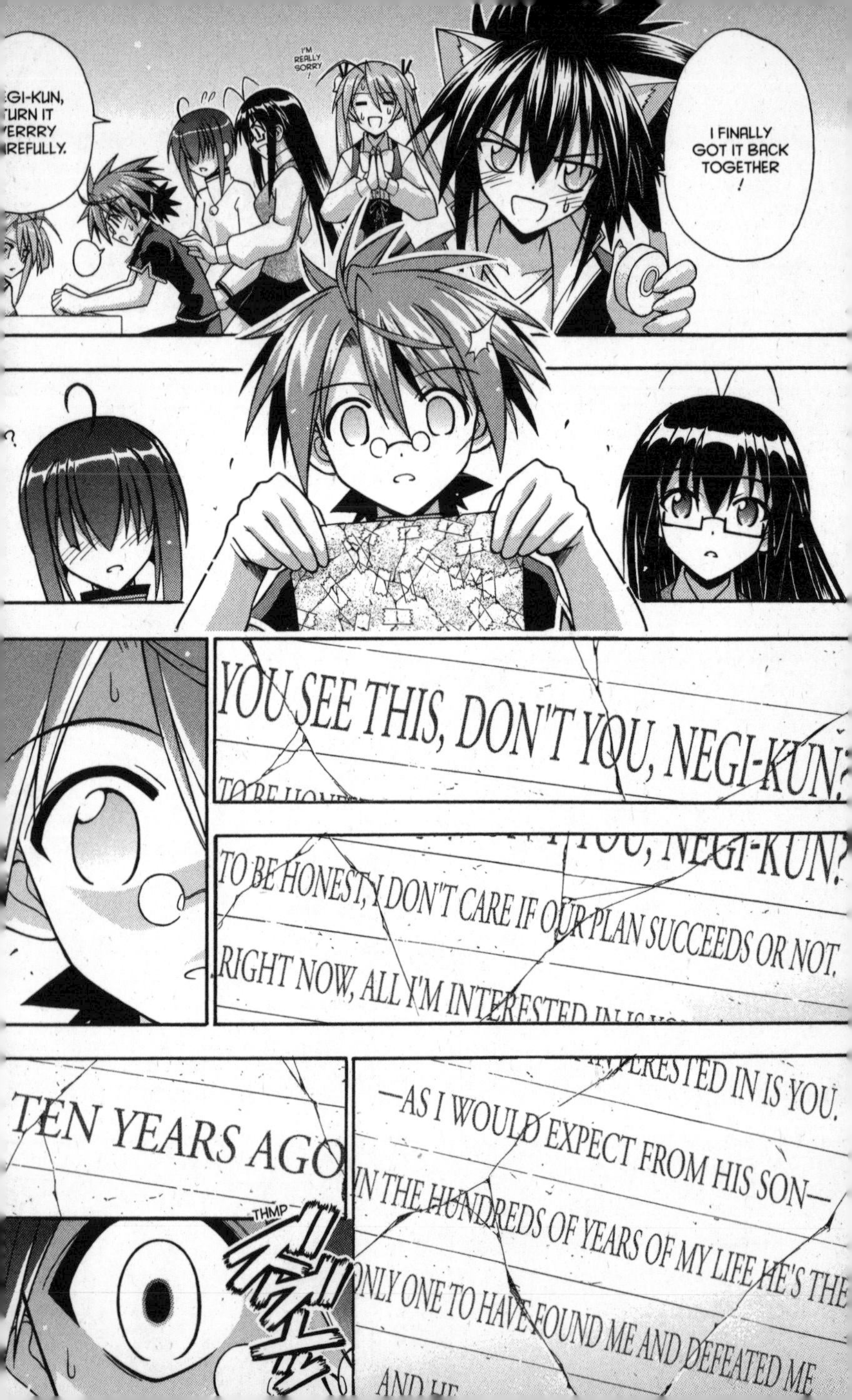
I FINALLY GOT IT BACK TOGETHER!
I'M REALLY SORRY!
EGI-KUN, TURN IT ERRRY REFULLY.
YOU SEE THIS, DON'T YOU, NEGI-KUN?
YOU, NEGI-KUN?
TO BE HONEST, I DON'T CARE IF OUR PLAN SUCCEEDS OR NOT.
RIGHT NOW, ALL I'M INTERESTED IN IS
ERESTED IN IS YOU.
—AS I WOULD EXPECT FROM HIS SON—
IN THE HUNDREDS OF YEARS OF MY LIFE HE'S THE ONLY ONE TO HAVE FOUND ME AND DEFEATED ME
TEN YEARS AGO
THMP

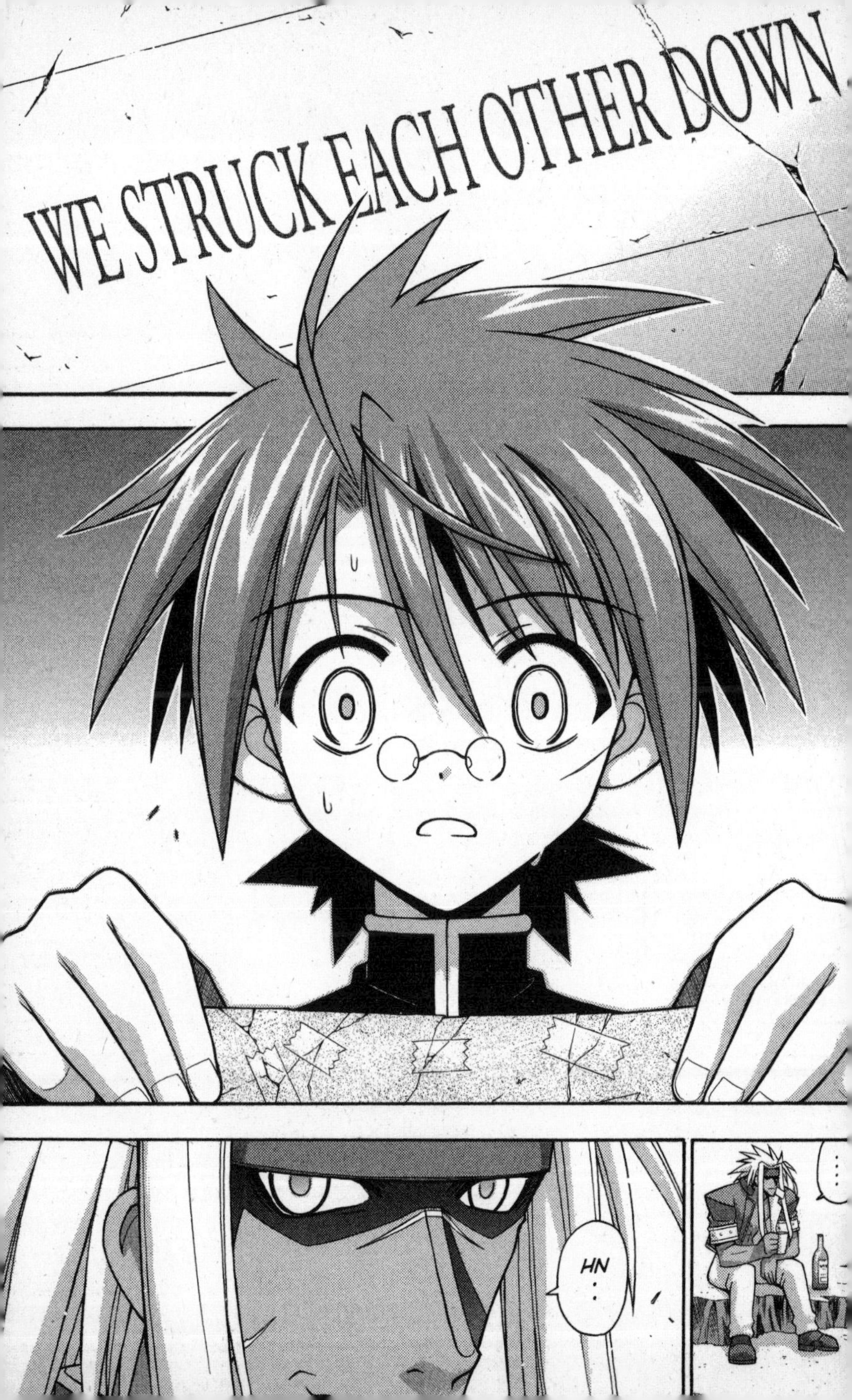
WE STRUCK EACH OTHER DOWN
...
HN..

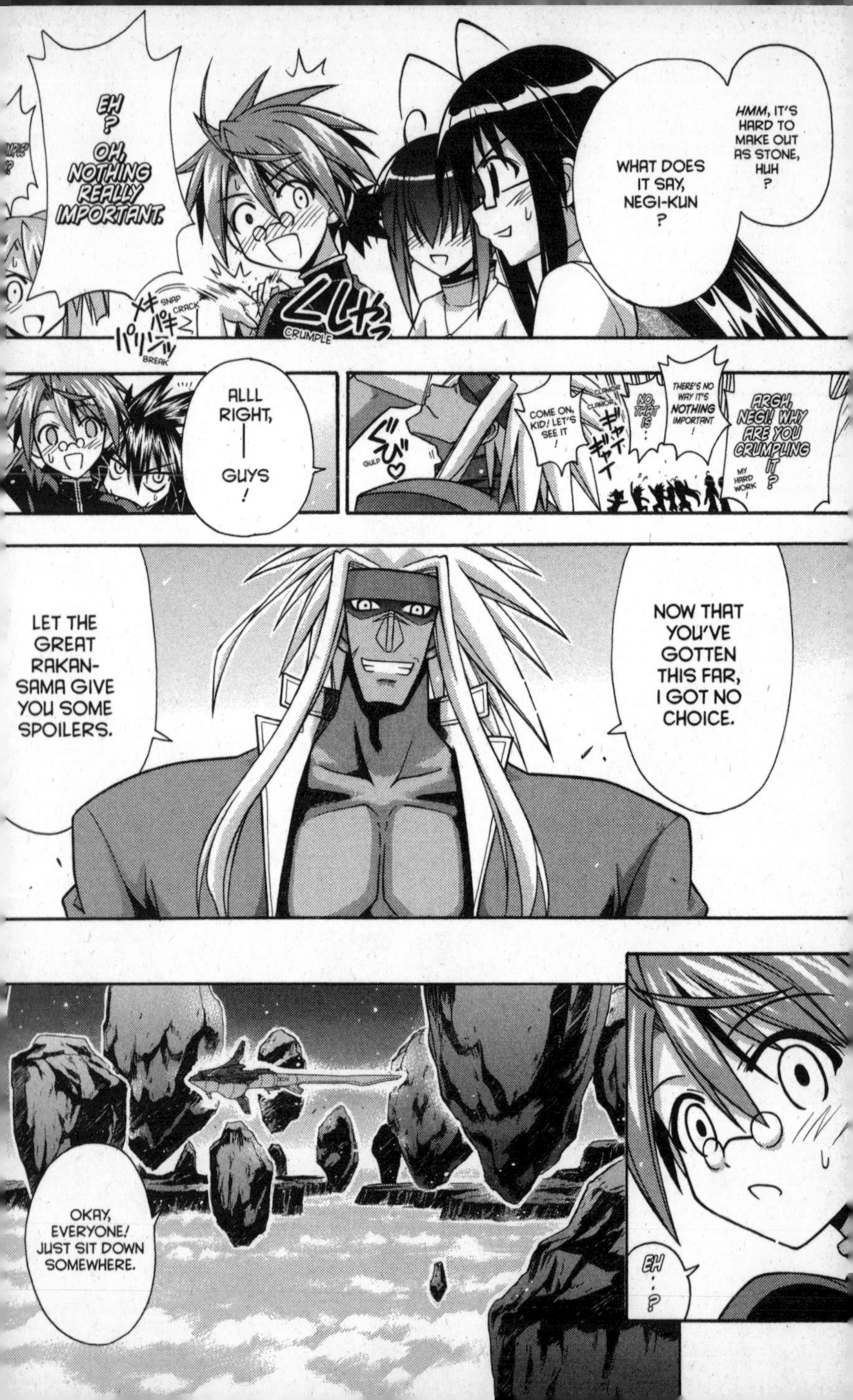
HMM, IT'S HARD TO MAKE OUT AS STONE, HUH?
WHAT DOES IT SAY, NEGI-KUN?
EH? OH, NOTHING REALLY IMPORTANT.
CRUMPLE
SNAP CRACK
BREAK
ARGH, NEGI!! WHY ARE YOU CRUMPLING IT?
MY HARD WORK!
THERE'S NO WAY IT'S NOTHING IMPORTANT!
NO, THAT IS...
CLAMOR CLAMOR
COME ON, KID! LET'S SEE IT!
GULP
ALLL RIGHT, — GUYS!
NOW THAT YOU'VE GOTTEN THIS FAR, I GOT NO CHOICE.
LET THE GREAT RAKAN-SAMA GIVE YOU SOME SPOILERS.
EH..?
OKAY, EVERYONE! JUST SIT DOWN SOMEWHERE.

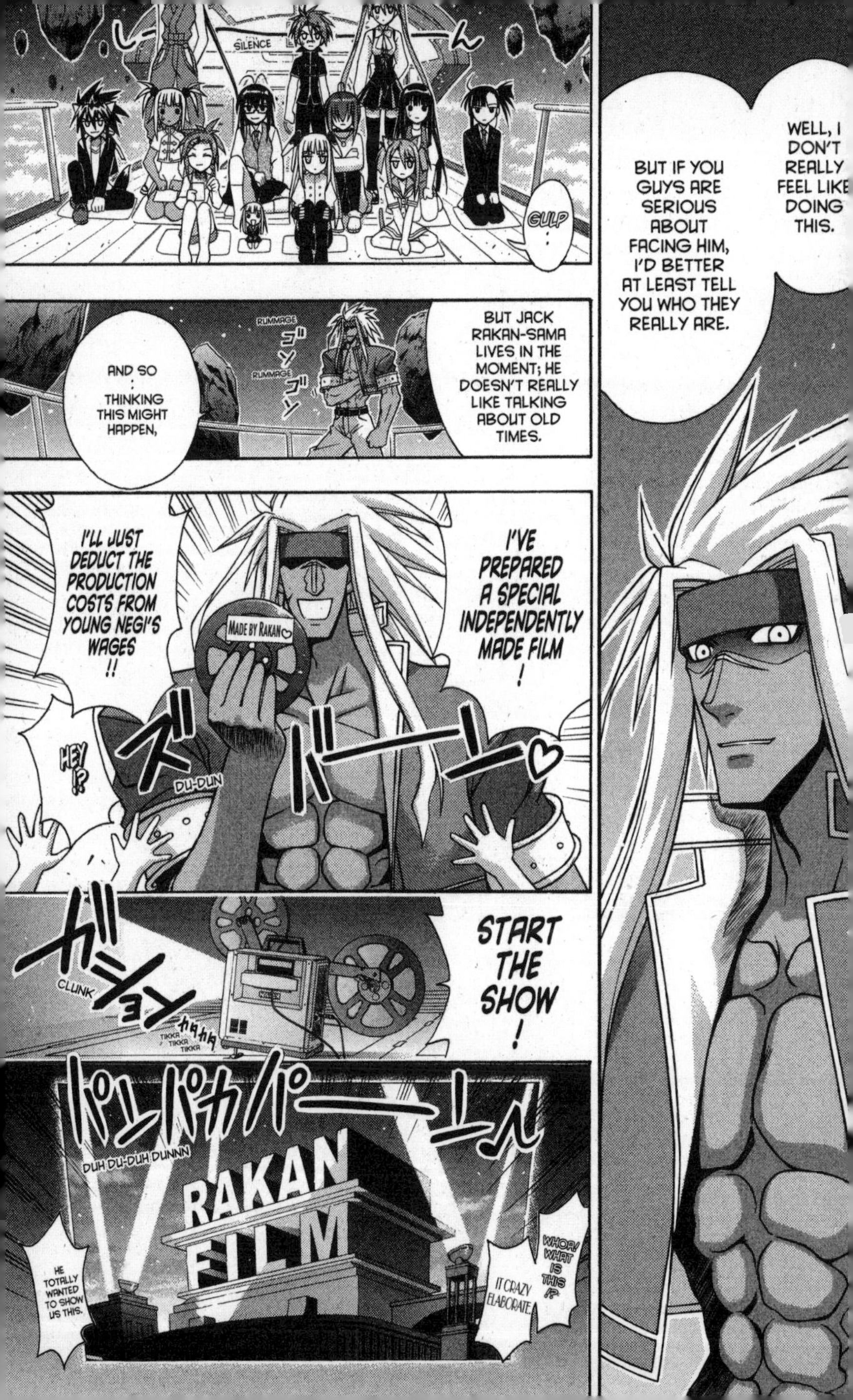
WELL, I DON'T REALLY FEEL LIKE DOING THIS.
BUT IF YOU GUYS ARE SERIOUS ABOUT FACING HIM, I'D BETTER AT LEAST TELL YOU WHO THEY REALLY ARE.
SILENCE
GULP
:
BUT JACK RAKAN-SAMA LIVES IN THE MOMENT; HE DOESN'T REALLY LIKE TALKING ABOUT OLD TIMES.
RUMMAGE
RUMMAGE
AND SO
:
THINKING THIS MIGHT HAPPEN,
I'VE PREPARED A SPECIAL INDEPENDENTLY MADE FILM
!
MADE BY RAKAN♡
I'LL JUST DEDUCT THE PRODUCTION COSTS FROM YOUNG NEGI'S WAGES
!!
HEY!?
DU-DUN
START THE SHOW
!
CLUNK
TIKKA TIKKA TIKKA
DUH DU-DUH DUNNN
RAKAN FILM
WHOA! WHAT IS THIS!?
IT CRAZY ELABORATE.
HE TOTALLY WANTED TO SHOW US THIS.

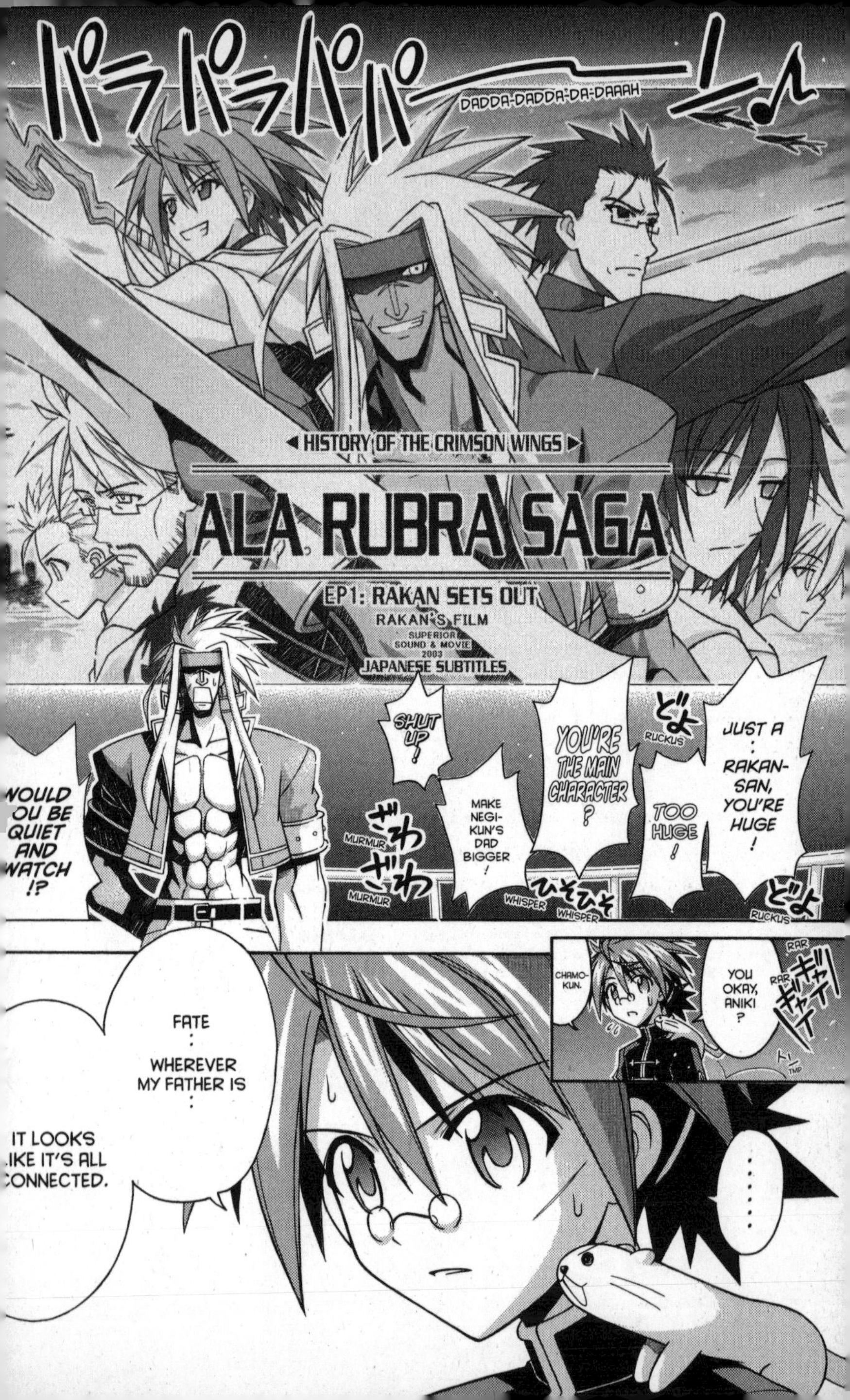
パラパラパーーーン♪
DADDA-DADDA-DA-DAAAH
HISTORY OF THE CRIMSON WINGS
ALA RUBRA SAGA
EP1: RAKAN SETS OUT
RAKAN'S FILM
SUPERIOR SOUND & MOVIE 2003
JAPANESE SUBTITLES
JUST A : RAKAN-SAN, YOU'RE HUGE!
どよ
RUCKUS
どよ
RUCKUS
TOO HUGE!
YOU'RE THE MAIN CHARACTER?
ひそひそ
WHISPER WHISPER
SHUT UP!
MAKE NEGI-KUN'S DAD BIGGER!
ざわざわ
MURMUR MURMUR
WOULD OU BE QUIET AND WATCH!?
ギャイギャイ
RAR RAR
YOU OKAY, ANIKI?
CHAMO-KUN.
TMP
FATE : WHEREVER MY FATHER IS :
IT LOOKS IKE IT'S ALL CONNECTED.
......

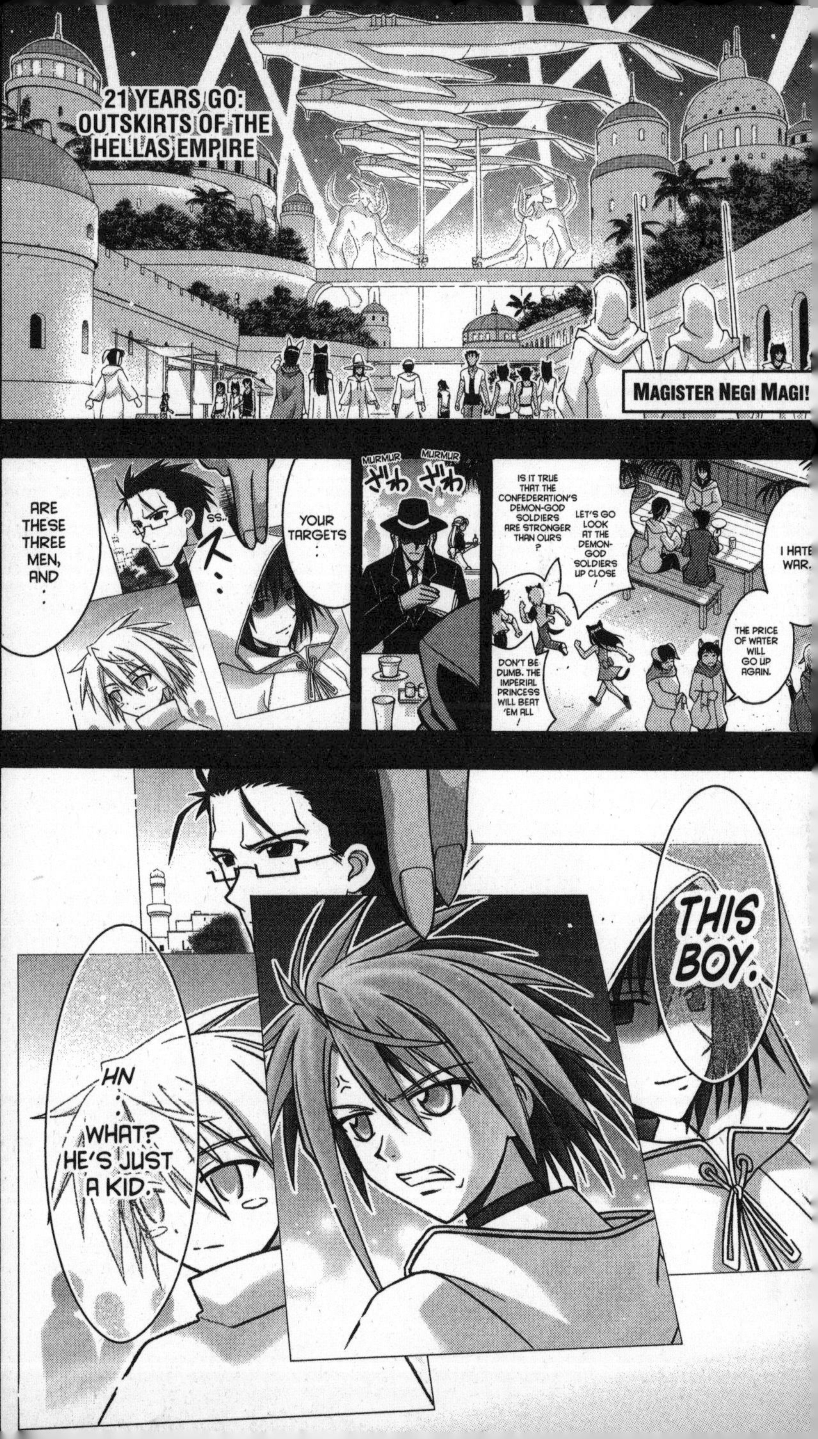
21 YEARS GO: OUTSKIRTS OF THE HELLAS EMPIRE
MAGISTER NEGI MAGI!
I HATE WAR.
THE PRICE OF WATER WILL GO UP AGAIN.
IS IT TRUE THAT THE CONFEDERATION'S DEMON-GOD SOLDIERS ARE STRONGER THAN OURS?
LET'S GO LOOK AT THE DEMON-GOD SOLDIERS UP CLOSE!
DON'T BE DUMB. THE IMPERIAL PRINCESS WILL BEAT 'EM ALL!
MURMUR MURMUR
ざわ ざわ
YOUR TARGETS...
SS..
ス...
ARE THESE THREE MEN, AND...
THIS BOY.
HN... WHAT? HE'S JUST A KID.

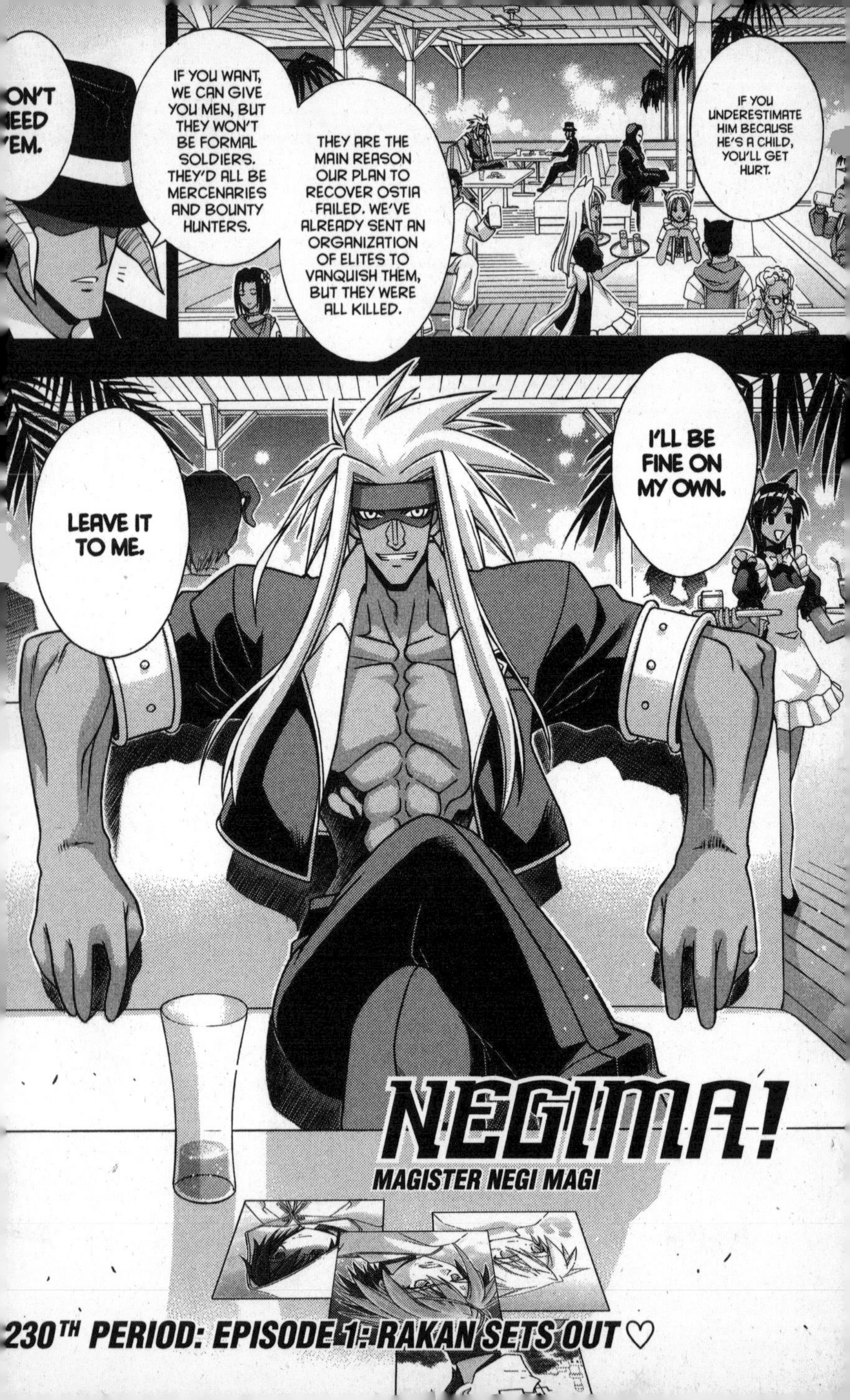
IF YOU UNDERESTIMATE HIM BECAUSE HE'S A CHILD, YOU'LL GET HURT.
THEY ARE THE MAIN REASON OUR PLAN TO RECOVER OSTIA FAILED. WE'VE ALREADY SENT AN ORGANIZATION OF ELITES TO VANQUISH THEM, BUT THEY WERE ALL KILLED.
IF YOU WANT, WE CAN GIVE YOU MEN, BUT THEY WON'T BE FORMAL SOLDIERS. THEY'D ALL BE MERCENARIES AND BOUNTY HUNTERS.
ON'T EED 'EM.
I'LL BE FINE ON MY OWN.
LEAVE IT TO ME.
NEGIMA!
MAGISTER NEGI MAGI
230TH PERIOD: EPISODE 1: RAKAN SETS OUT ♡

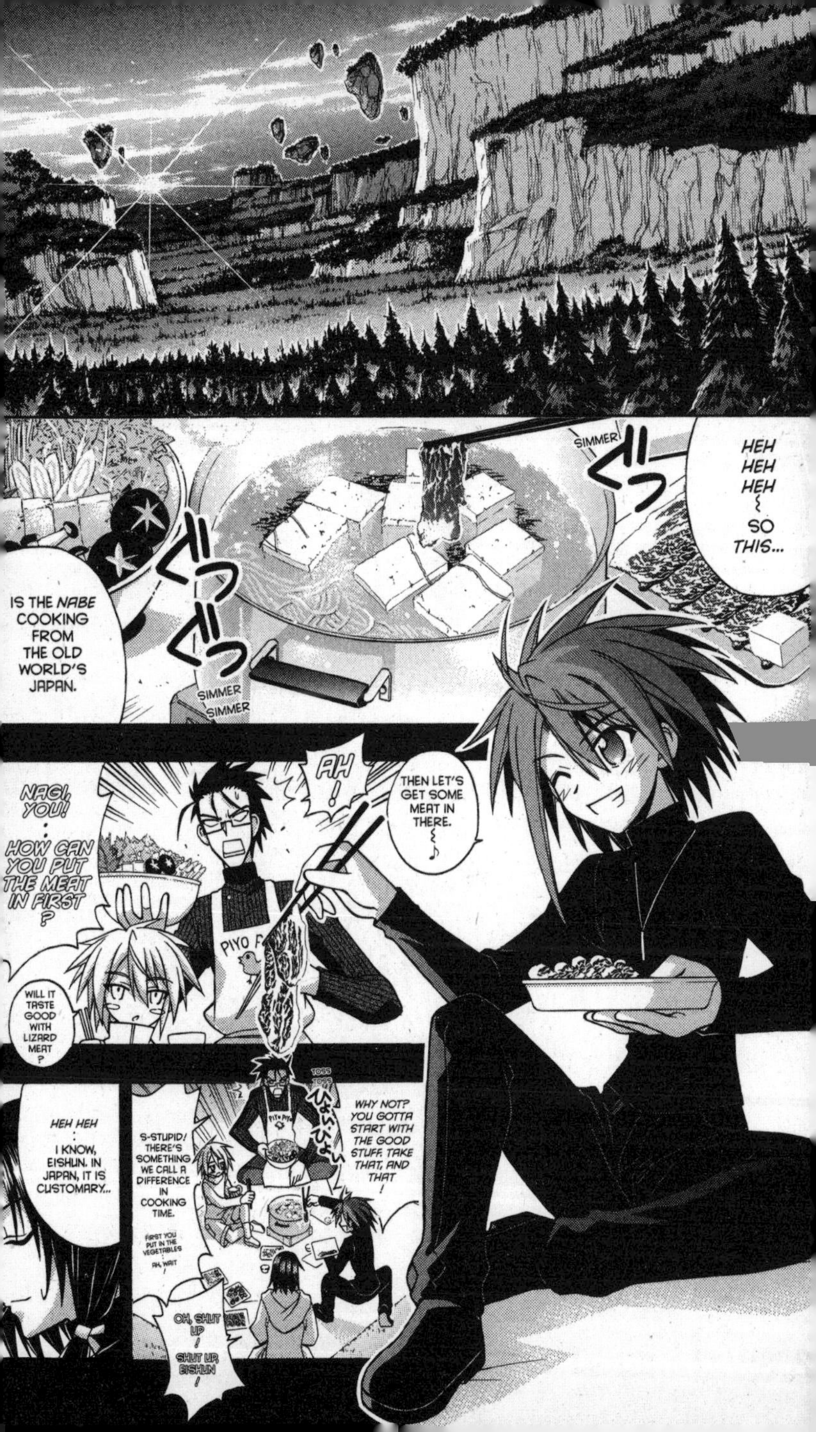
SIMMER
HEH HEH HEH~ SO THIS...
IS THE NABE COOKING FROM THE OLD WORLD'S JAPAN.
SIMMER
SIMMER
AH!
THEN LET'S GET SOME MEAT IN THERE.~♪
NAGI, YOU!
HOW CAN YOU PUT THE MEAT IN FIRST?
PIYO P
WILL IT TASTE GOOD WITH LIZARD MEAT?
TOSS TOSS
WHY NOT? YOU GOTTA START WITH THE GOOD STUFF. TAKE THAT, AND THAT!
S-STUPID! THERE'S SOMETHING WE CALL A DIFFERENCE IN COOKING TIME.
FIRST YOU PUT IN THE VEGETABLES
AH, WAIT
HEH HEH
I KNOW, EISHUN. IN JAPAN, IT IS CUSTOMARY...
OH, SHUT UP!
SHUT UP, EISHUN!

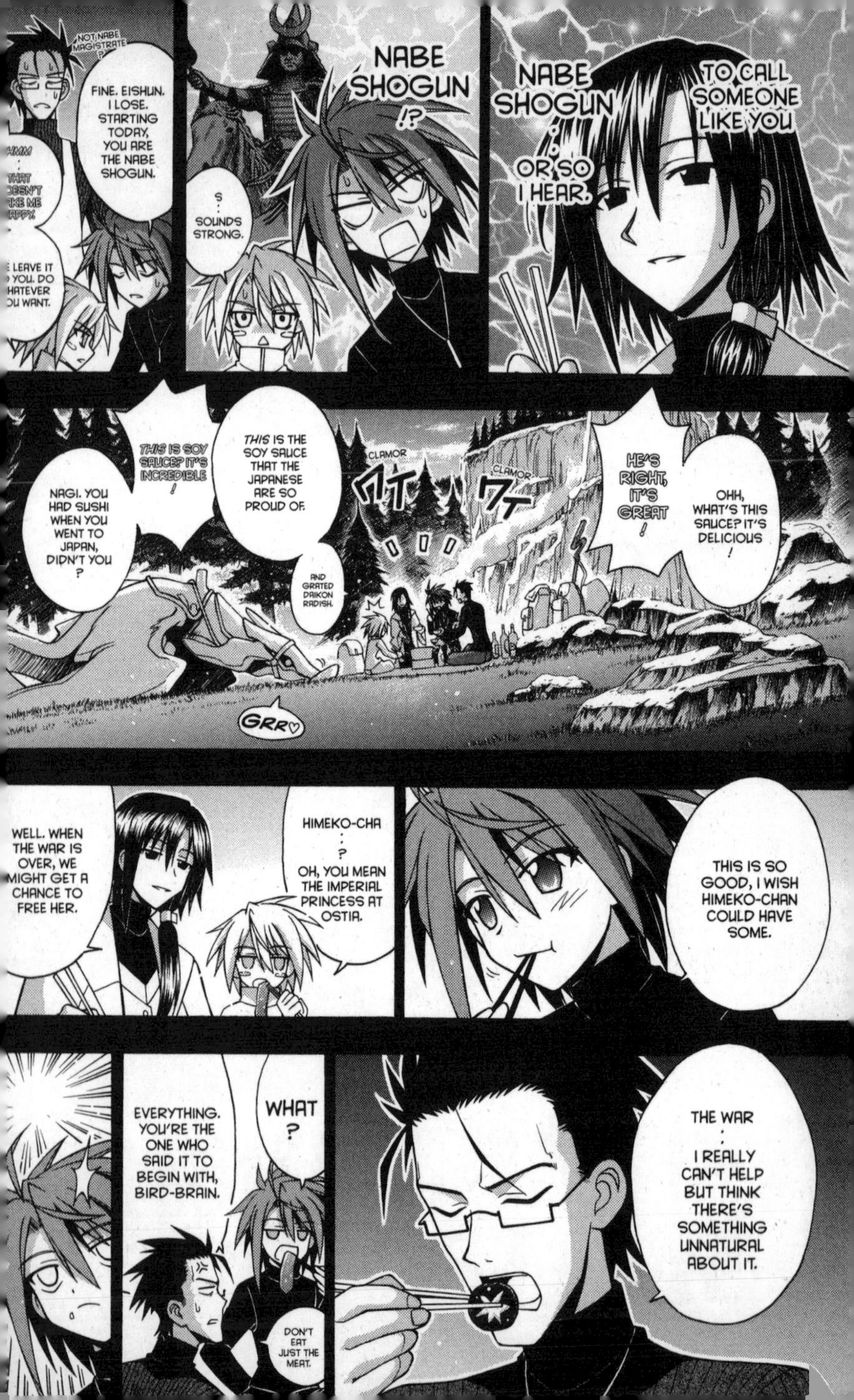
TO CALL SOMEONE LIKE YOU
NABE SHOGUN . . . OR SO I HEAR.
NABE SHOGUN !?
S . . . SOUNDS STRONG.
NOT NABE MAGISTRATE ?
FINE. EISHUN. I LOSE. STARTING TODAY, YOU ARE THE NABE SHOGUN.
HMM . . . THAT OESN'T AKE ME APPY.
E LEAVE IT O YOU. DO HATEVER OU WANT.
OHH, WHAT'S THIS SAUCE? IT'S DELICIOUS !
HE'S RIGHT, IT'S GREAT !
CLAMOR
CLAMOR
THIS IS THE SOY SAUCE THAT THE JAPANESE ARE SO PROUD OF.
AND GRATED DAIKON RADISH.
THIS IS SOY SAUCE? IT'S INCREDIBLE !
NAGI. YOU HAD SUSHI WHEN YOU WENT TO JAPAN, DIDN'T YOU ?
GRR♡
THIS IS SO GOOD, I WISH HIMEKO-CHAN COULD HAVE SOME.
HIMEKO-CHA . . ? OH, YOU MEAN THE IMPERIAL PRINCESS AT OSTIA.
WELL. WHEN THE WAR IS OVER, WE MIGHT GET A CHANCE TO FREE HER.
THE WAR . I REALLY CAN'T HELP BUT THINK THERE'S SOMETHING UNNATURAL ABOUT IT.
WHAT ?
EVERYTHING. YOU'RE THE ONE WHO SAID IT TO BEGIN WITH, BIRD-BRAIN.
DON'T EAT JUST THE MEAT.

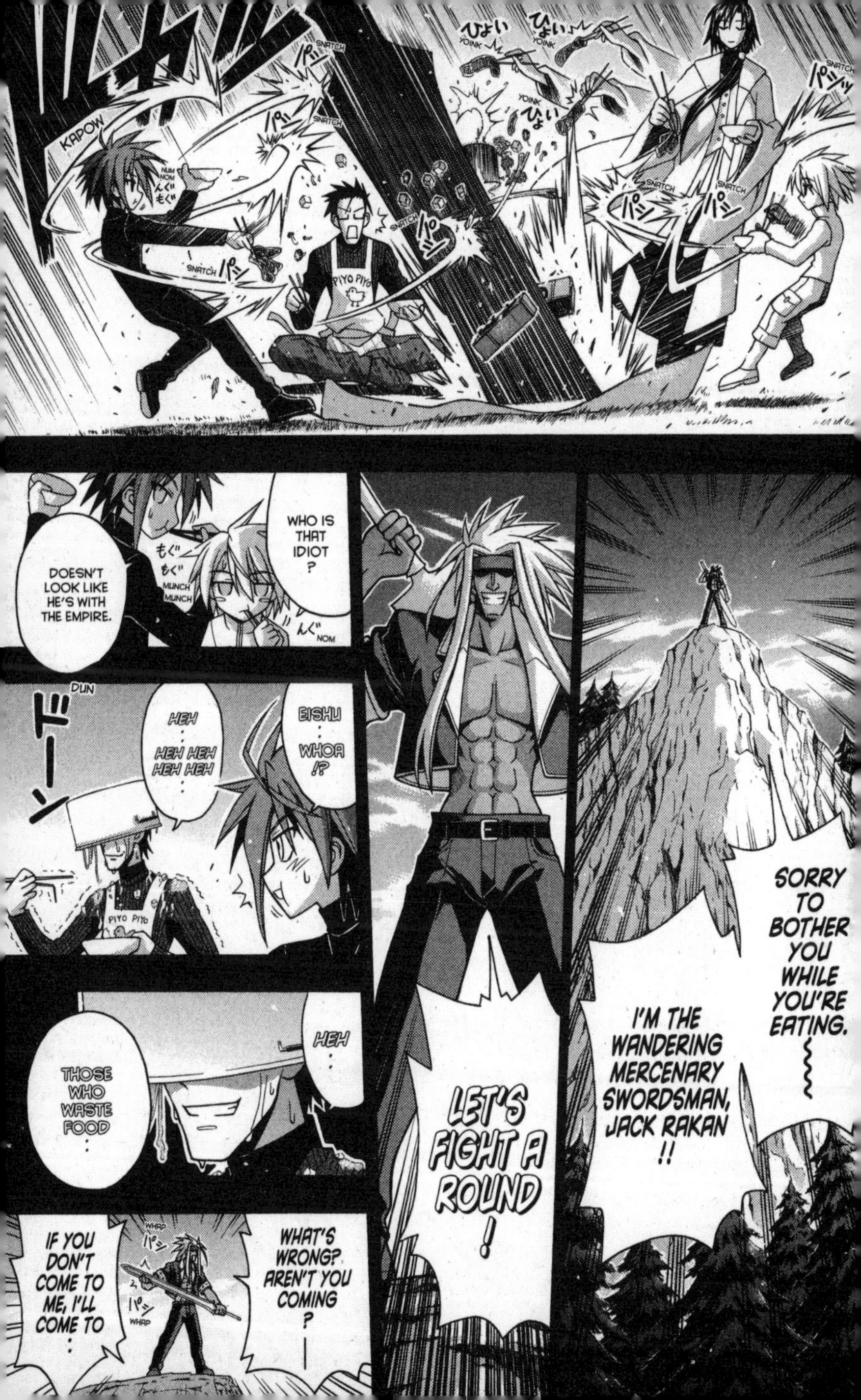
パシッ
SNATCH
ひょい
YOINK
ひょい
YOINK
ひょい
YOINK
パシ
SNATCH
パシ
SNATCH
パシ
SNATCH
パシ
SNATCH
KAPOW
NUM NOM
んぐもぐ
パシ
SNATCH
SORRY TO BOTHER YOU WHILE YOU'RE EATING.
I'M THE WANDERING MERCENARY SWORDSMAN, JACK RAKAN!!
LET'S FIGHT A ROUND!
WHO IS THAT IDIOT?
DOESN'T LOOK LIKE HE'S WITH THE EMPIRE.
もぐもぐ
MUNCH MUNCH
んぐ
NOM
EISHU... WHOA!?
HEH... HEH HEH HEH HEH...
ドーン
DUN
HEH...
THOSE WHO WASTE FOOD...
WHAT'S WRONG? AREN'T YOU COMING?
IF YOU DON'T COME TO ME, I'LL COME TO...
パシ
WHAP
パシ
WHAP

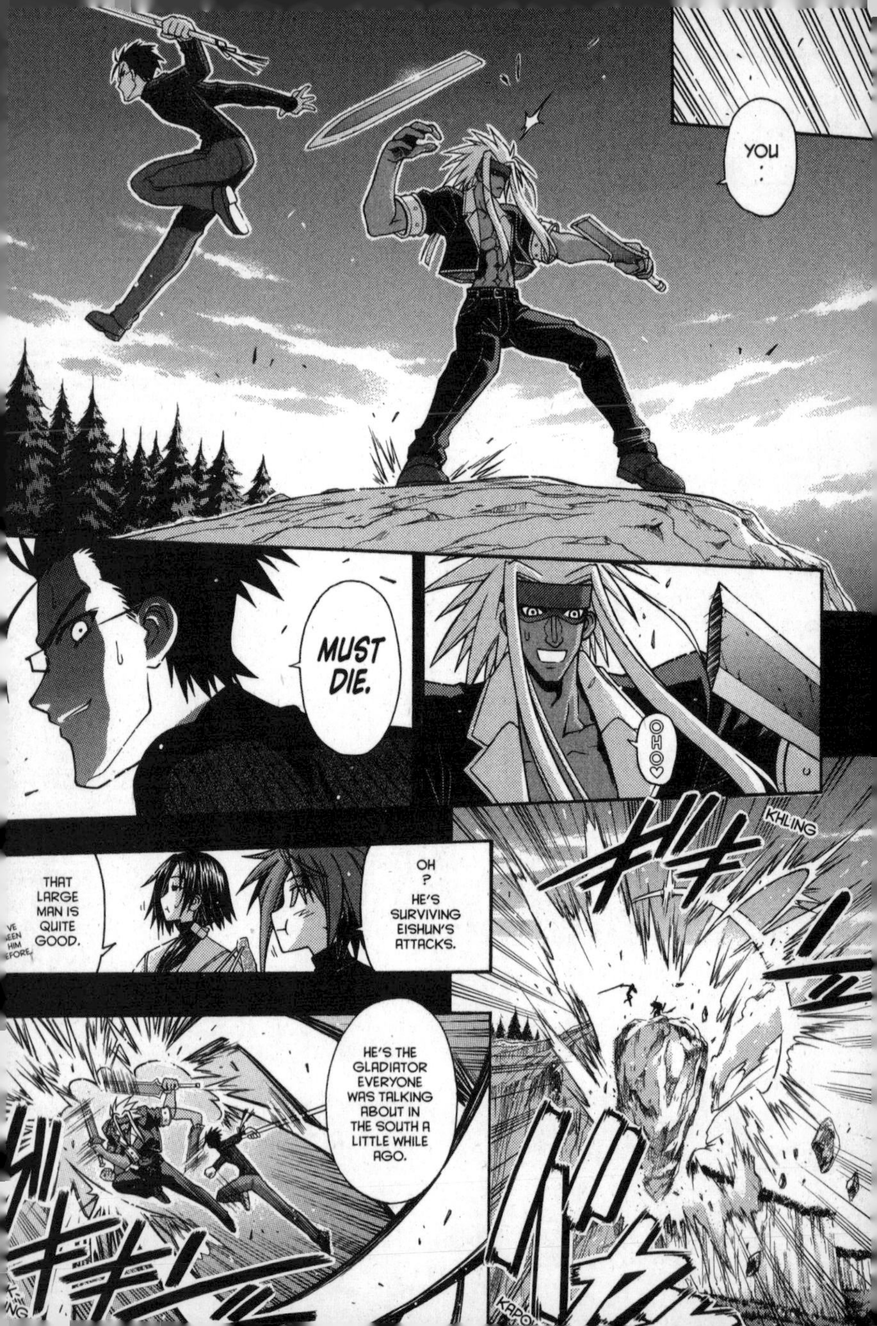
YOU
:
MUST DIE.
OHO♥
KHLING
OH? HE'S SURVIVING EISHUN'S ATTACKS.
THAT LARGE MAN IS QUITE GOOD.
HE'S THE GLADIATOR EVERYONE WAS TALKING ABOUT IN THE SOUTH A LITTLE WHILE AGO.

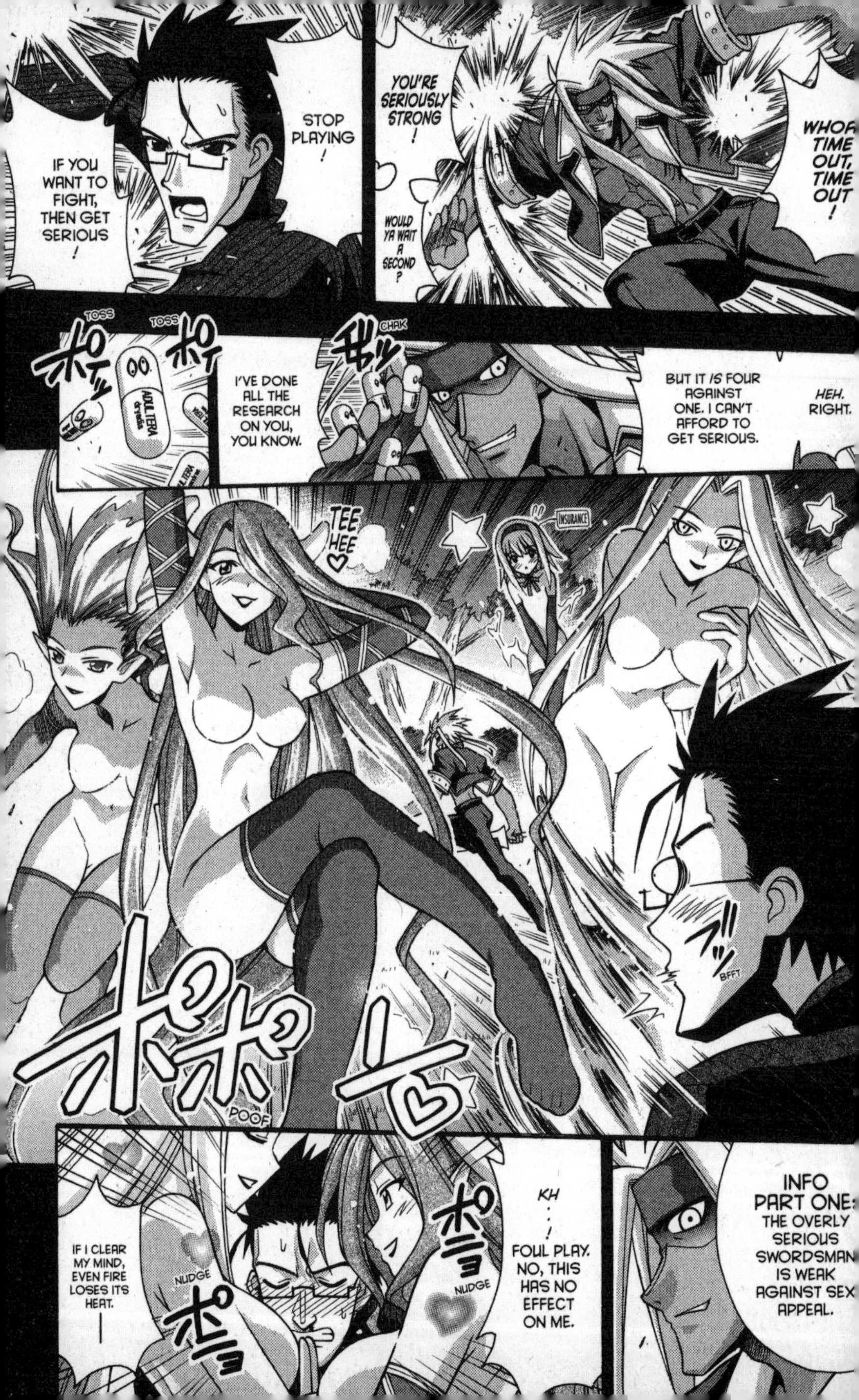
WHOA TIME OUT, TIME OUT!
YOU'RE SERIOUSLY STRONG!
WOULD YA WAIT A SECOND?
STOP PLAYING!
IF YOU WANT TO FIGHT, THEN GET SERIOUS!
HEH. RIGHT.
BUT IT IS FOUR AGAINST ONE. I CAN'T AFFORD TO GET SERIOUS.
CHAK
I'VE DONE ALL THE RESEARCH ON YOU, YOU KNOW.
TOSS
TOSS
ADULTERA
INSURANCE
TEE HEE
BFFT
POOF
INFO PART ONE: THE OVERLY SERIOUS SWORDSMAN IS WEAK AGAINST SEX APPEAL.
KH...!
FOUL PLAY. NO, THIS HAS NO EFFECT ON ME.
NUDGE
NUDGE
IF I CLEAR MY MIND, EVEN FIRE LOSES ITS HEAT.

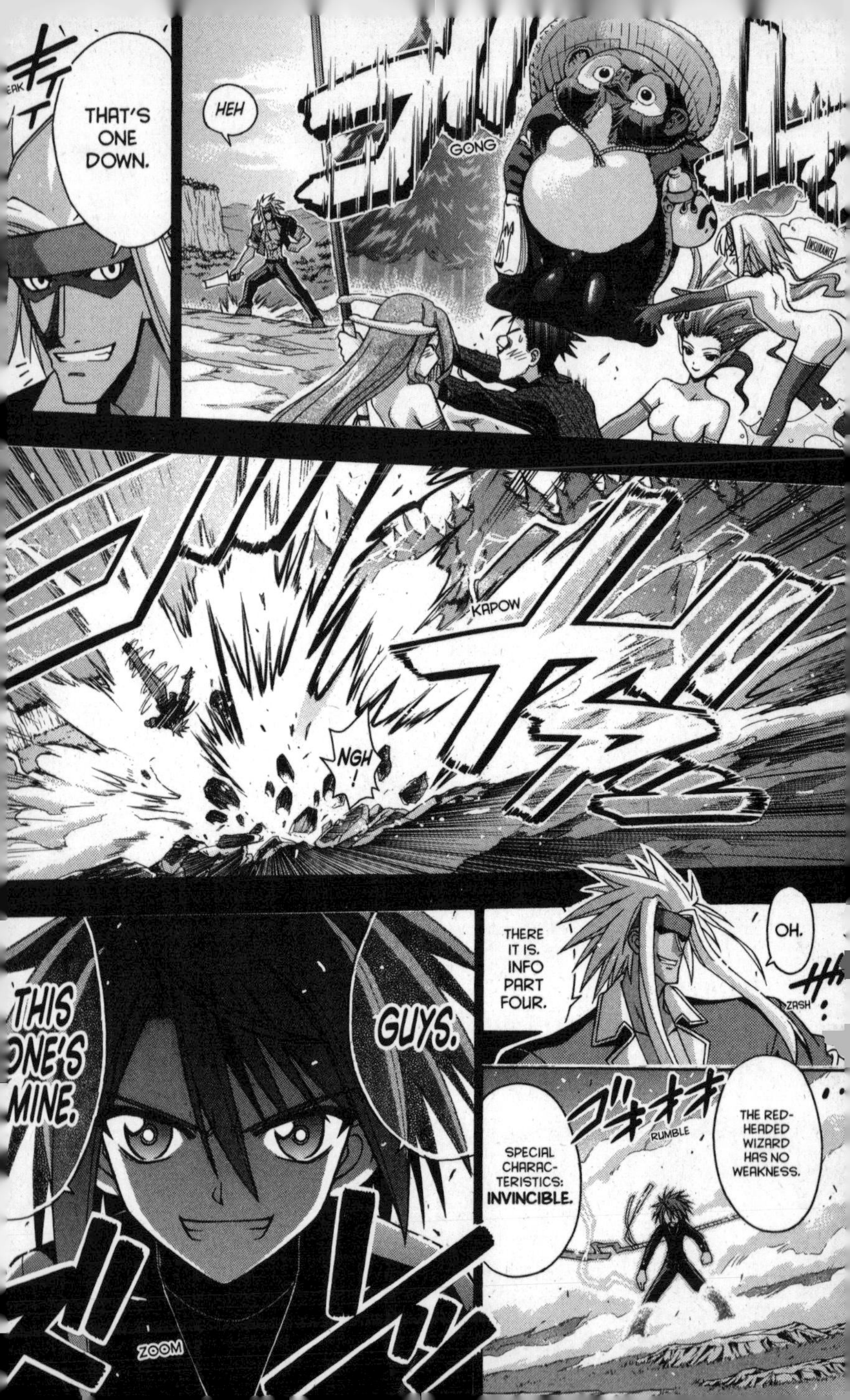
HEH
GONG
INSURANCE
THAT'S ONE DOWN.
KAPOW
NGH!
OH.
THERE IT IS. INFO PART FOUR.
ZASH
THE RED-HEADED WIZARD HAS NO WEAKNESS.
RUMBLE
SPECIAL CHARAC-TERISTICS: **INVINCIBLE.**
GUYS.
THIS ONE'S MINE.
ZOOM

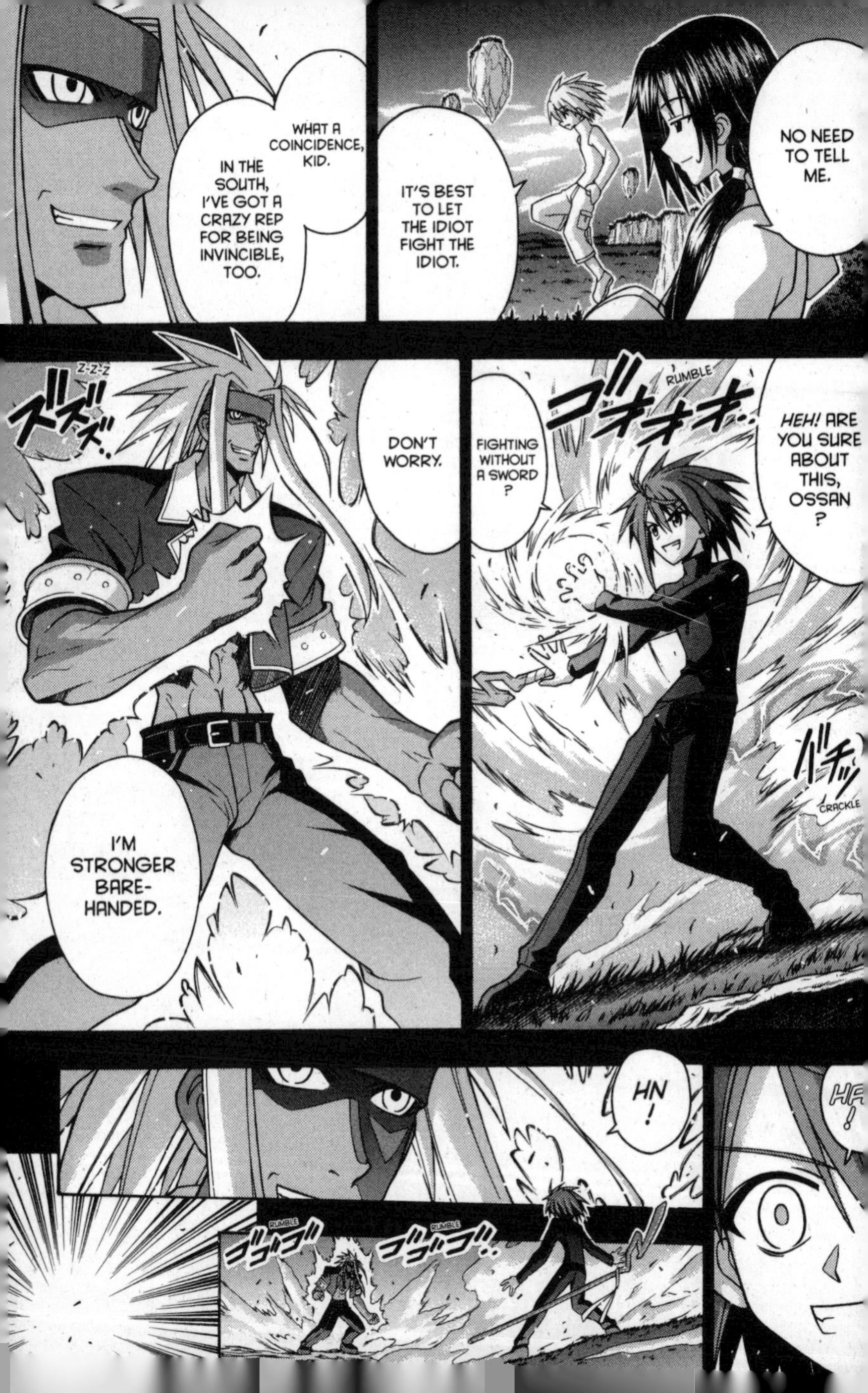
IT'S BEST TO LET THE IDIOT FIGHT THE IDIOT.
NO NEED TO TELL ME.
WHAT A COINCIDENCE, KID.
IN THE SOUTH, I'VE GOT A CRAZY REP FOR BEING INVINCIBLE, TOO.
HEH! ARE YOU SURE ABOUT THIS, OSSAN?
RUMBLE
FIGHTING WITHOUT A SWORD?
CRACKLE
Z-Z-Z
DON'T WORRY.
I'M STRONGER BARE-HANDED.
HA!
HN!
RUMBLE
RUMBLE

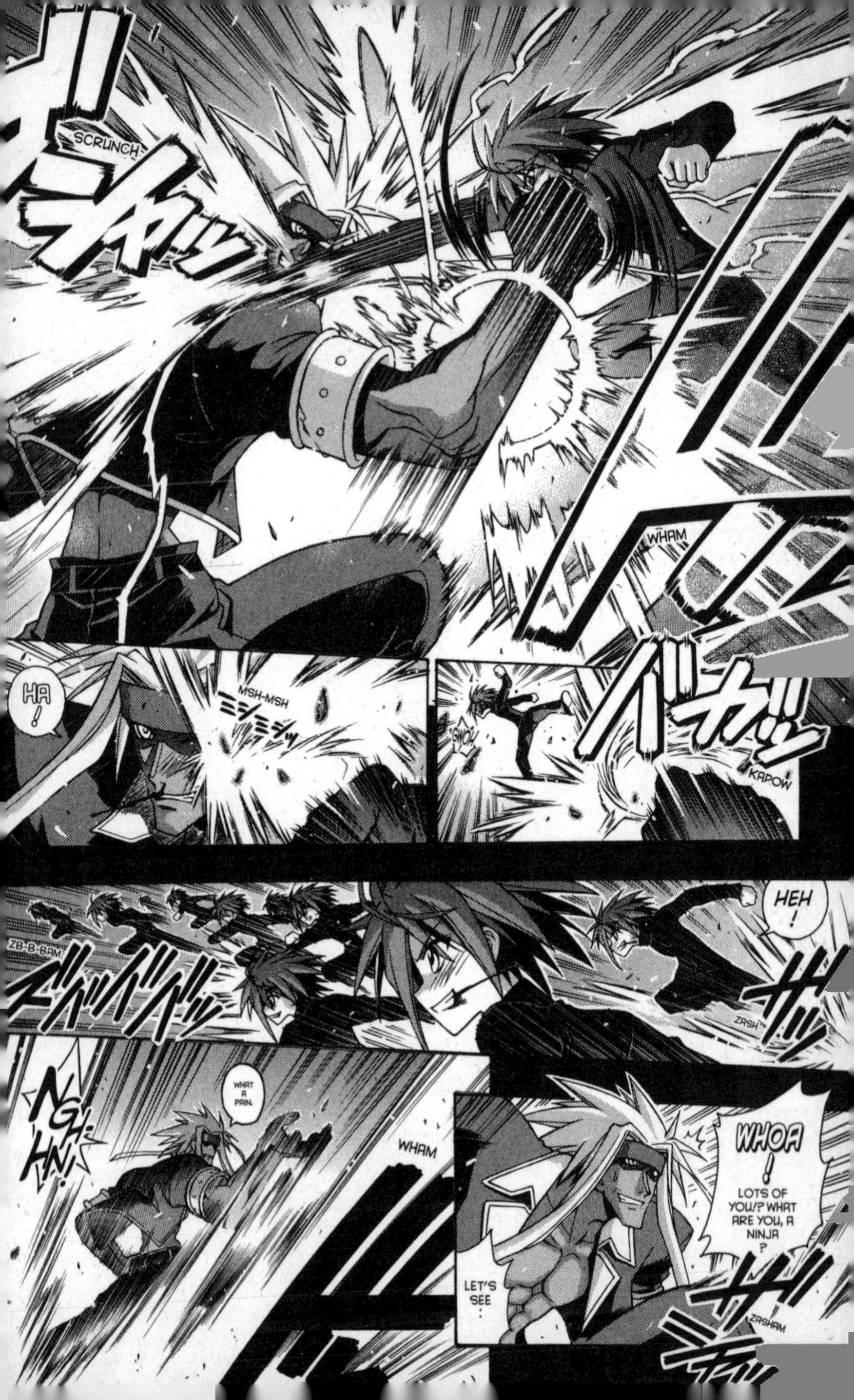
SCRUNCH
WHAM
KAPOW
GWOH
HA!
MSH-MSH
HEH!
ZASH
ZB-B-BAM
WHOA! LOTS OF YOU!? WHAT ARE YOU, A NINJA?
LET'S SEE...
ZASHAM
WHAM
WHAT A PAIN.
NGH-HN!

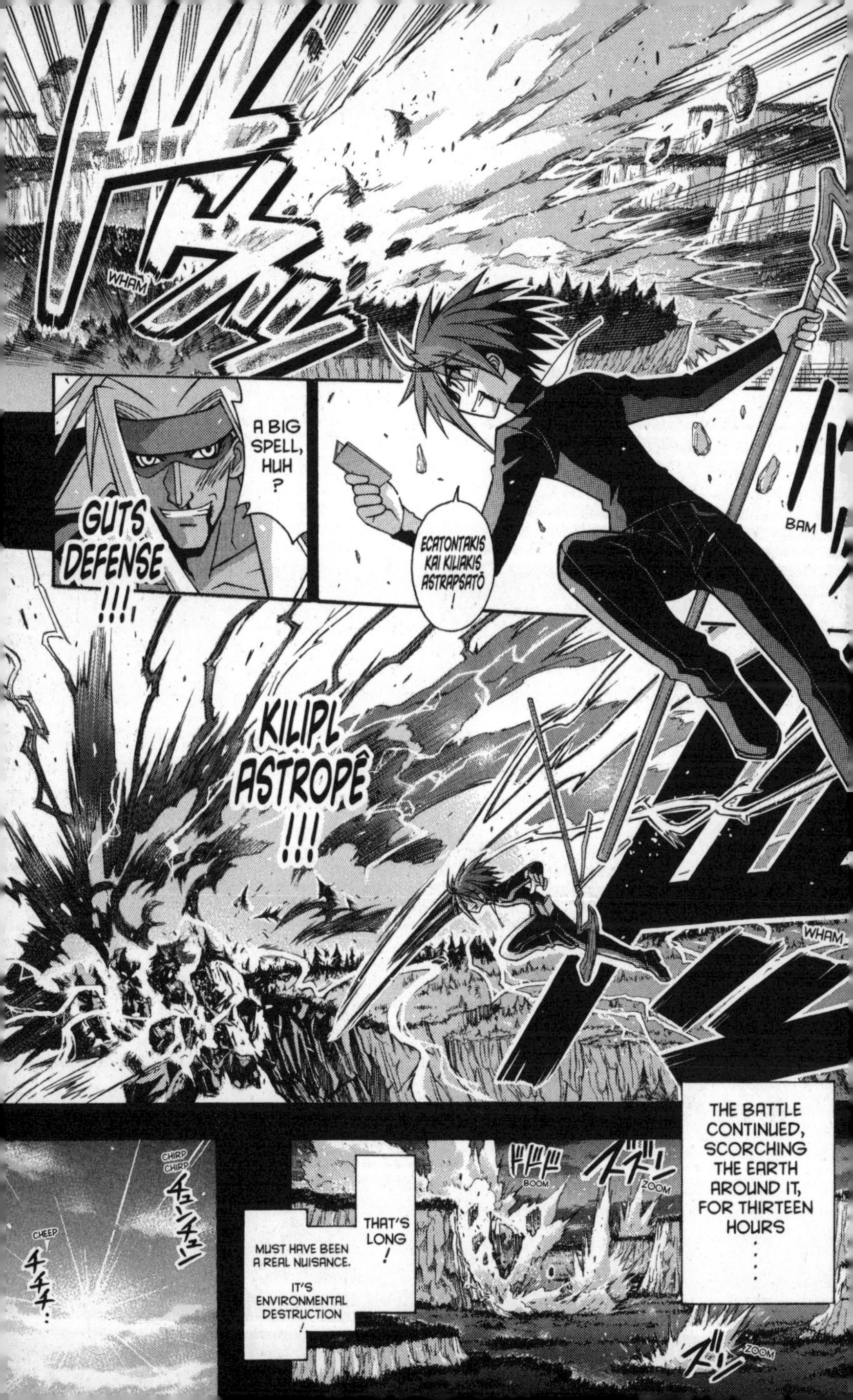
WHAM
A BIG SPELL, HUH?
GUTS DEFENSE!!!
ECATONTAKIS KAI KILIAKIS ASTRAPSATÔ!
BAM
KILIPL ASTROPÊ!!!
WHAM
THE BATTLE CONTINUED, SCORCHING THE EARTH AROUND IT, FOR THIRTEEN HOURS....
ZOOM
BOOM
THAT'S LONG!
MUST HAVE BEEN A REAL NUISANCE.
IT'S ENVIRONMENTAL DESTRUCTION!
ZOOM
CHIRP CHIRP
チュンチュン
CHEEP
チチチ...

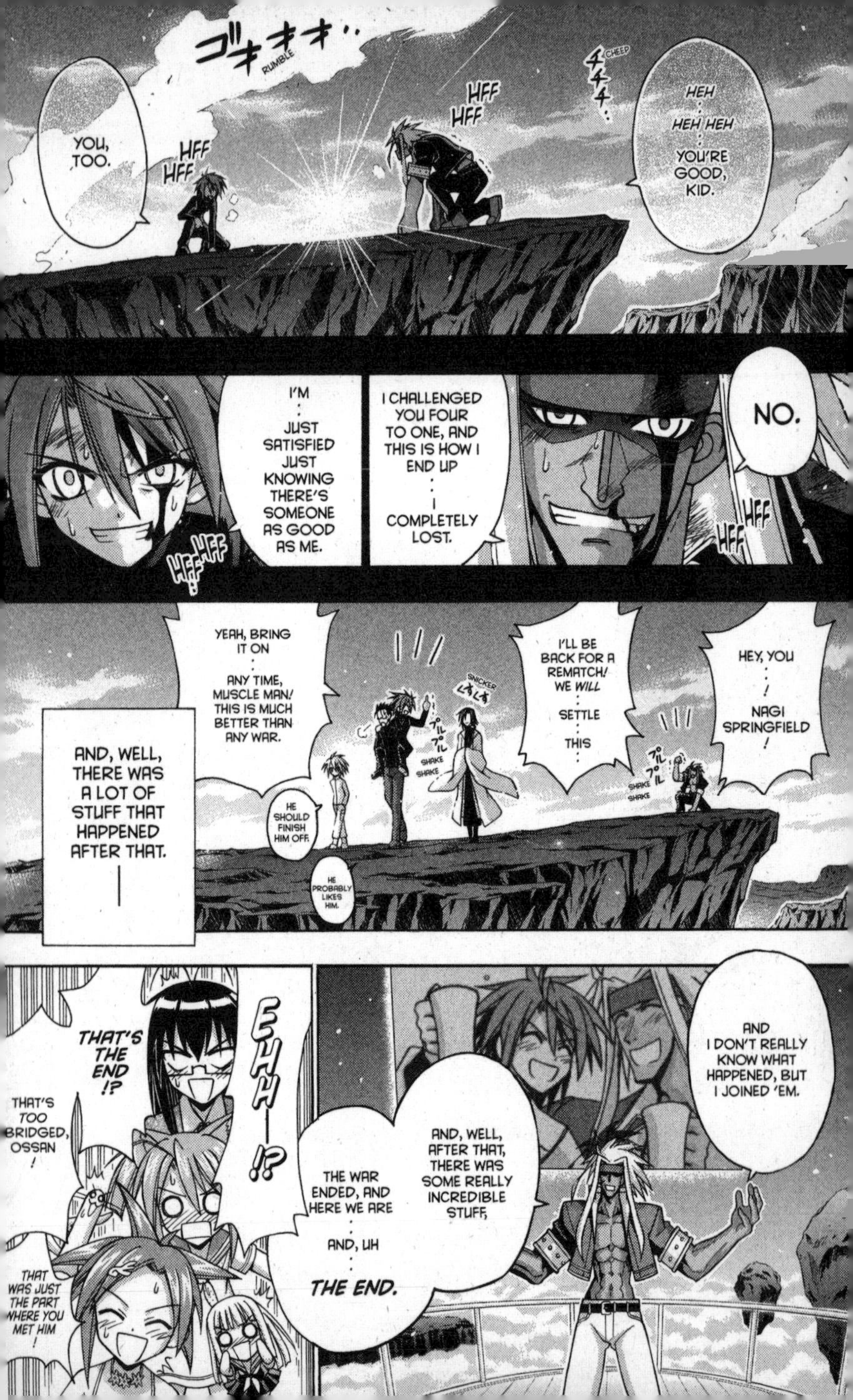
HEH... HEH HEH... YOU'RE GOOD, KID.
CHEEP
HFF HFF
RUMBLE
YOU, TOO.
HFF HFF
NO.
HFF HFF
I CHALLENGED YOU FOUR TO ONE, AND THIS IS HOW I END UP... I COMPLETELY LOST.
I'M... JUST SATISFIED JUST KNOWING THERE'S SOMEONE AS GOOD AS ME.
HFF HFF
HEY, YOU...! NAGI SPRINGFIELD!
SHAKE SHAKE
I'LL BE BACK FOR A REMATCH! WE *WILL*... SETTLE... THIS...
SNICKER
SHAKE SHAKE
YEAH, BRING IT ON... ANY TIME, MUSCLE MAN! THIS IS MUCH BETTER THAN ANY WAR.
HE SHOULD FINISH HIM OFF.
HE PROBABLY LIKES HIM.
AND, WELL, THERE WAS A LOT OF STUFF THAT HAPPENED AFTER THAT.
AND I DON'T REALLY KNOW WHAT HAPPENED, BUT I JOINED 'EM.
AND, WELL, AFTER THAT, THERE WAS SOME REALLY INCREDIBLE STUFF,
THE WAR ENDED, AND HERE WE ARE... AND, UH... *THE END.*
EHH—!?
THAT'S THE END!?
THAT'S *TOO* BRIDGED, OSSAN!
THAT WAS JUST THE PART WHERE YOU MET HIM!

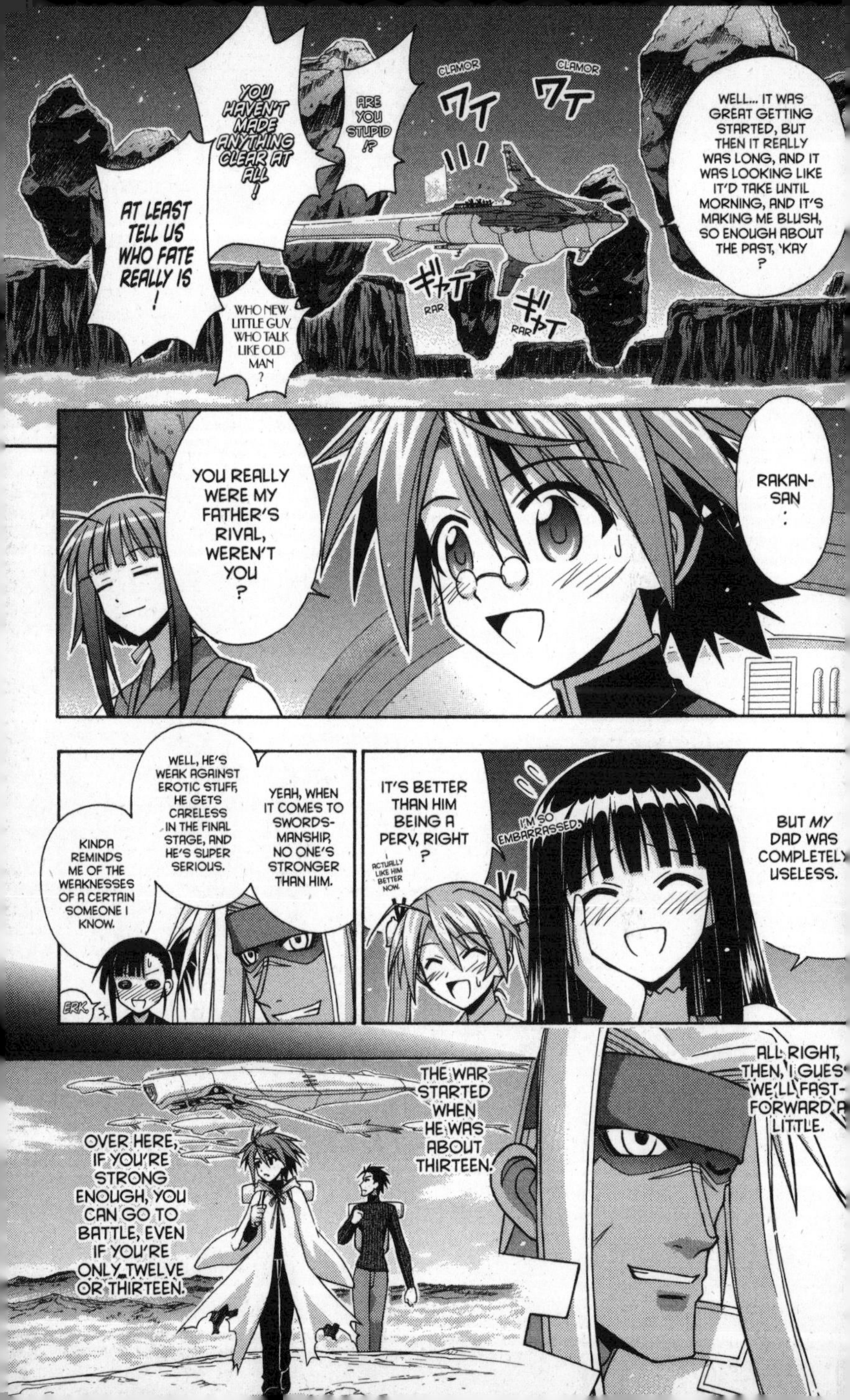

WELL... IT WAS GREAT GETTING STARTED, BUT THEN IT REALLY WAS LONG, AND IT WAS LOOKING LIKE IT'D TAKE UNTIL MORNING, AND IT'S MAKING ME BLUSH, SO ENOUGH ABOUT THE PAST, 'KAY?
ワァ CLAMOR
ワイ CLAMOR
ARE YOU STUPID!?
YOU HAVEN'T MADE ANYTHING CLEAR AT ALL!
AT LEAST TELL US WHO FATE REALLY IS!
ギャア RAR
ギャア RAR
WHO NEW LITTLE GUY WHO TALK LIKE OLD MAN?
RAKAN-SAN...
YOU REALLY WERE MY FATHER'S RIVAL, WEREN'T YOU?
BUT MY DAD WAS COMPLETEL USELESS.
I'M SO EMBARRASSED.
IT'S BETTER THAN HIM BEING A PERV, RIGHT?
I ACTUALLY LIKE HIM BETTER NOW.
YEAH, WHEN IT COMES TO SWORDS-MANSHIP, NO ONE'S STRONGER THAN HIM.
WELL, HE'S WEAK AGAINST EROTIC STUFF, HE GETS CARELESS IN THE FINAL STAGE, AND HE'S SUPER SERIOUS.
KINDA REMINDS ME OF THE WEAKNESSES OF A CERTAIN SOMEONE I KNOW.
ERK.
ALL RIGHT, THEN, I GUES WE'LL FAST-FORWARD A LITTLE.
THE WAR STARTED WHEN HE WAS ABOUT THIRTEEN.
OVER HERE, IF YOU'RE STRONG ENOUGH, YOU CAN GO TO BATTLE, EVEN IF YOU'RE ONLY TWELVE OR THIRTEEN.

HELLAS EMPIRE
IMPERIUM HELLADIS

IMPERIAL CAPITAL HELLAS

ARGYRE PLAINS

Argyre

Hellas

Hellas

Noachis

NYANDOMA

VULCAN

Bosporus

MESEMBRINA CONFEDERATION

MEGALO-MESEMBRIA
Megalomesembria

ARIADNE

EOS

SIRENIUM

ZEPHYRIA

GREAT BRIDGE

TRISTAN

Noctis

VESPERTATIA KINGDOM
Regnum Vespertatiae

SYRTIS SUBCONTINENT
Syrtis subconti.

ROYAL CAPITAL OSTIA
Ostia

ORESTES

CLYTAMNESTRA

Cerberus

MESEMBRINA CONFEDERATION
CONFEDERATIO MESEMBRINA

Tempe Terra

Elysium conti.

ELFANHAFT

AL JAMIRA

VAIROCANA

Boreslis dom.

TŌGEN

Lóngshán Mon.

ANTIGONE

0   1000   2000km

IT STARTED
OUT WITH
A MINOR
DISPUTE
ON THE
FRONTIER,
BUT
EVENTUALLY
THE EMPIRE
STARTED
INVADING
WITH REAL
INTENT.

BUT THEIR
TRUE AIM
WAS TO
RETAKE THE
HOLY LAND,
THE CRADLE
OF THE OLD
CULTURE,
OSTIA.

THEY INVADED
THE ARGYRE
SYRTIS
SUBCONTINENT

■	CONTROLLED BY HELLAS EMPIRE'S ARMY

THEY FAILED
TWICE TO
CAPTURE OSTIA,
BUT THROUGH
THE USE OF AN
IMPOSSIBLY
LARGE-SCALE
METASTASIS
SPELL...

THE INVASIVE
FORCE OF
THE HELLAS
EMPIRE, WITH ITS
STRONG MAGIC
POWER, WAS
OVERWHELMING.

WE IN ALA
RUBRA
HAD BEEN
TEMPORARILY
DRIVEN
BACK TO THE
OUTSKIRTS
OF ARGYRE.

THAT
WAS
WHERE
WE
CAME
IN !!

THE MOVE
AMOUNTED TO
A CHECKMATE,
AND EVERYONE
THOUGHT THE
FATE OF THE
CONFEDERATION
HUNG BY
A THREAD,
HOWEVER...

VULCAN

WARP ATTACK

EOS

TRISTAN

IBRIA

THE EMPIRE
FINALLY
BROUGHT
ABOUT THE FALL
OF THE GIANT
STRONGHOLD
AT THE THROAT
OF THE
CONFEDERATION,
THE GREAT
BRIDGE THAT
SPANNED AN
ENTIRE 300
KILOMETERS.

↑
GREAT BRIDGE

VESPERTATIA KINGDOM
Regnum Vespertatiae

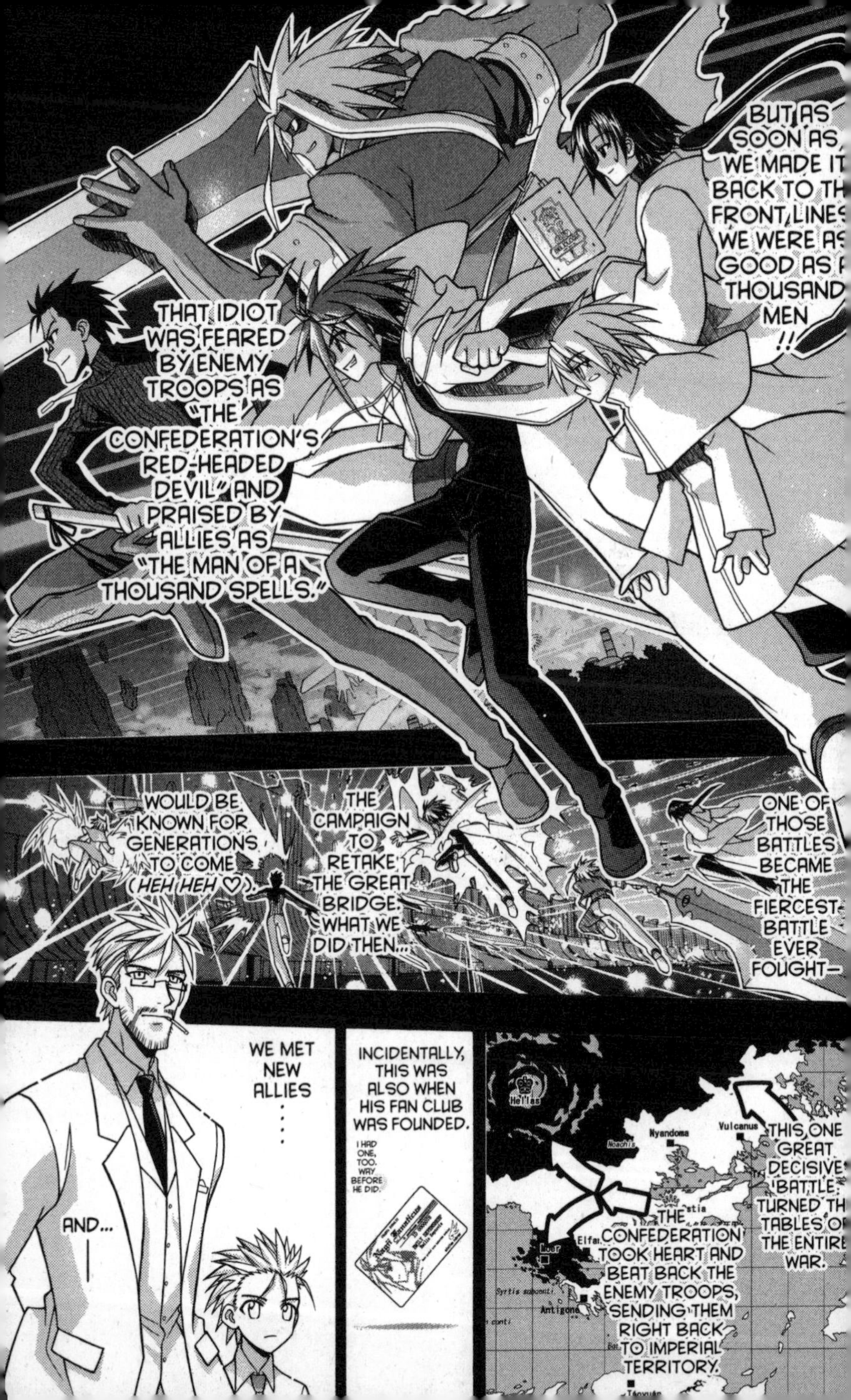
BUT AS SOON AS WE MADE IT BACK TO TH FRONT LINES WE WERE AS GOOD AS THOUSAND MEN!!
THAT IDIOT WAS FEARED BY ENEMY TROOPS AS "THE CONFEDERATION'S RED-HEADED DEVIL" AND PRAISED BY ALLIES AS "THE MAN OF A THOUSAND SPELLS."
ONE OF THOSE BATTLES BECAME THE FIERCEST BATTLE EVER FOUGHT—
THE CAMPAIGN TO RETAKE THE GREAT BRIDGE. WHAT WE DID THEN...
WOULD BE KNOWN FOR GENERATIONS TO COME (*HEH HEH* ♡).
THIS ONE GREAT DECISIVE BATTLE TURNED TH TABLES O THE ENTIR WAR.
Hellas
Nyandoma
Vulcanus
Noachis
Elfa
Syrtis
Antigone
THE CONFEDERATION TOOK HEART AND BEAT BACK THE ENEMY TROOPS, SENDING THEM RIGHT BACK TO IMPERIAL TERRITORY.
INCIDENTALLY, THIS WAS ALSO WHEN HIS FAN CLUB WAS FOUNDED.
I HAD ONE, TOO. WAY BEFORE HE DID.
WE MET NEW ALLIES...
AND...

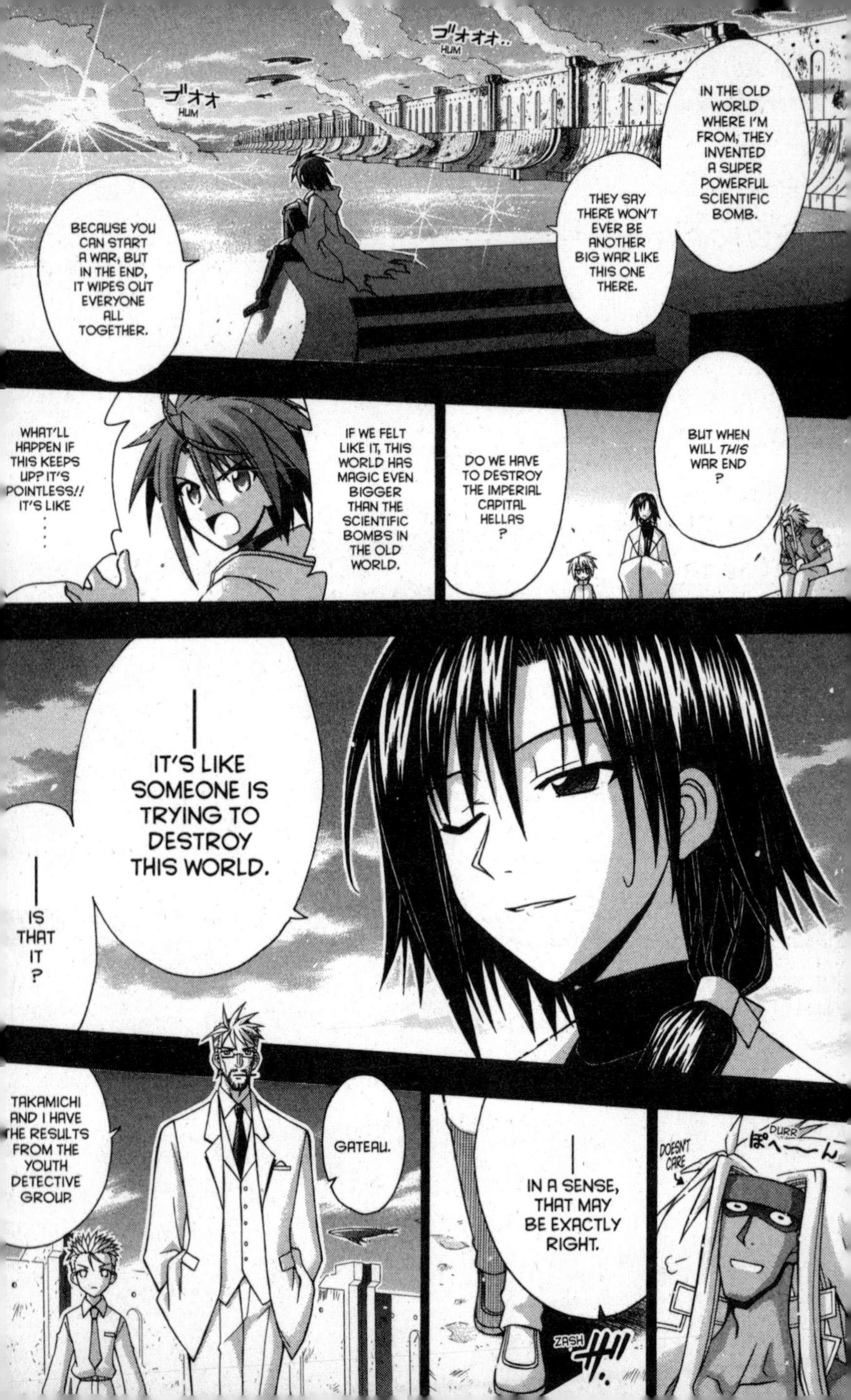
ゴオオオ..
HUM
ゴオオ
HUM
IN THE OLD WORLD WHERE I'M FROM, THEY INVENTED A SUPER POWERFUL SCIENTIFIC BOMB.
THEY SAY THERE WON'T EVER BE ANOTHER BIG WAR LIKE THIS ONE THERE.
BECAUSE YOU CAN START A WAR, BUT IN THE END, IT WIPES OUT EVERYONE ALL TOGETHER.
BUT WHEN WILL *THIS* WAR END?
DO WE HAVE TO DESTROY THE IMPERIAL CAPITAL HELLAS?
IF WE FELT LIKE IT, THIS WORLD HAS MAGIC EVEN BIGGER THAN THE SCIENTIFIC BOMBS IN THE OLD WORLD.
WHAT'LL HAPPEN IF THIS KEEPS UP? IT'S POINTLESS!! IT'S LIKE ......
—IT'S LIKE SOMEONE IS TRYING TO DESTROY THIS WORLD.
—IS THAT IT?
ぽへ〜ん
DURR
DOESN'T CARE
—IN A SENSE, THAT MAY BE EXACTLY RIGHT.
ZASH
GATEAU.
TAKAMICHI AND I HAVE THE RESULTS FROM THE YOUTH DETECTIVE GROUP.

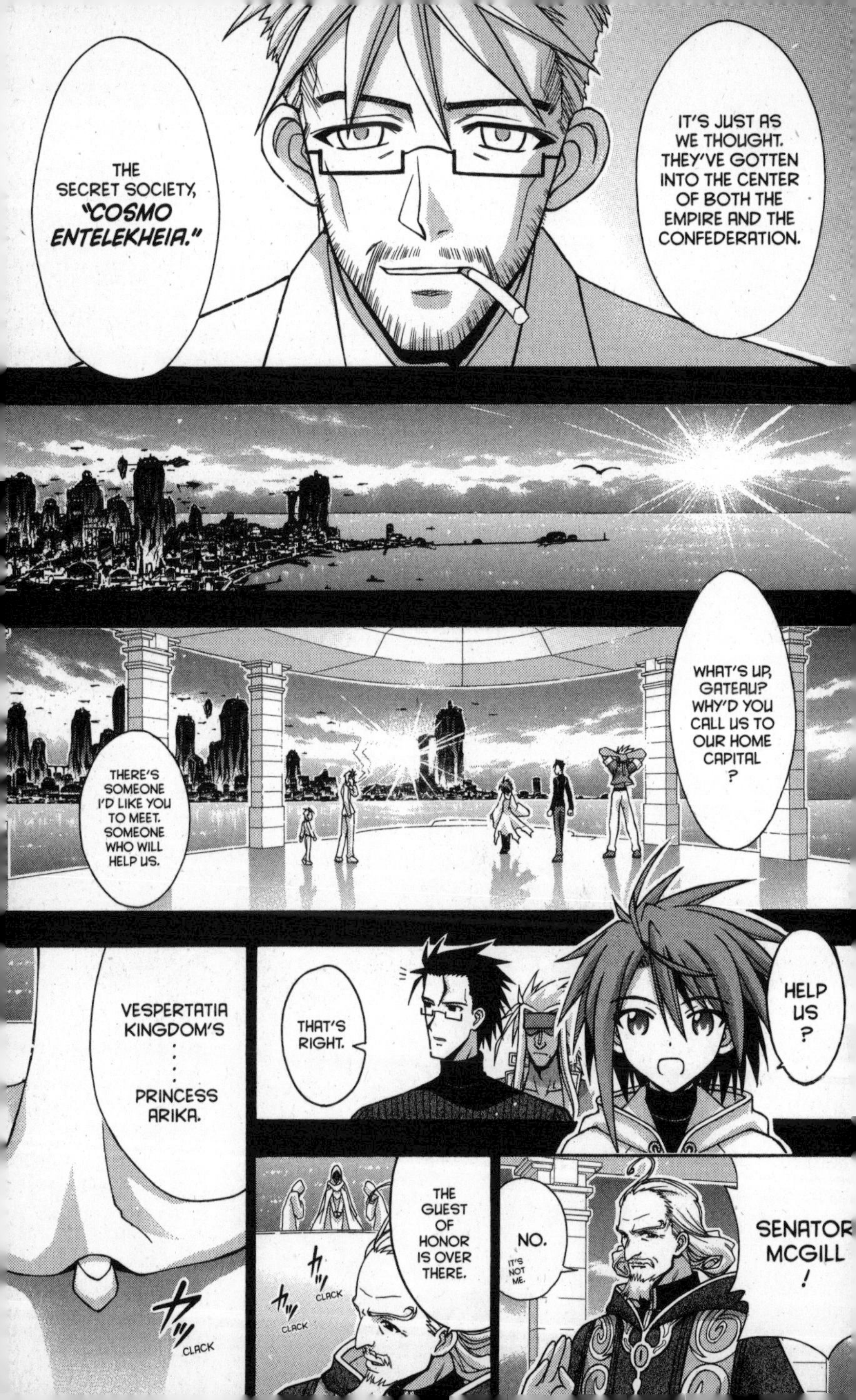
IT'S JUST AS WE THOUGHT. THEY'VE GOTTEN INTO THE CENTER OF BOTH THE EMPIRE AND THE CONFEDERATION.
THE SECRET SOCIETY, "COSMO ENTELEKHEIA."
WHAT'S UP, GATEAU? WHY'D YOU CALL US TO OUR HOME CAPITAL?
THERE'S SOMEONE I'D LIKE YOU TO MEET. SOMEONE WHO WILL HELP US.
HELP US?
THAT'S RIGHT.
SENATOR MCGILL!
NO.
IT'S NOT ME.
THE GUEST OF HONOR IS OVER THERE.
CLACK
CLACK
VESPERTATIA KINGDOM'S . . . PRINCESS ARIKA.
CLACK

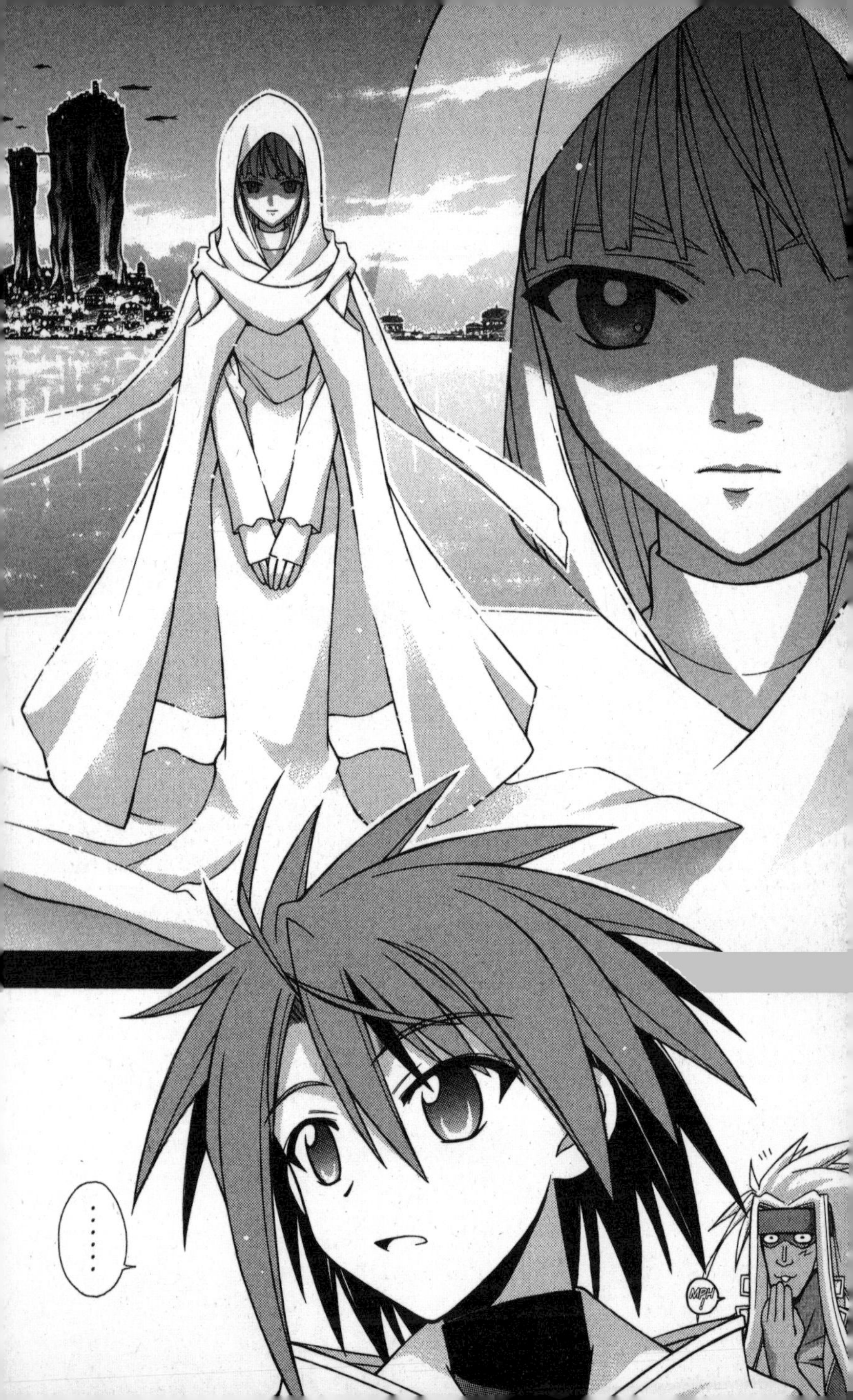
……
MPH!

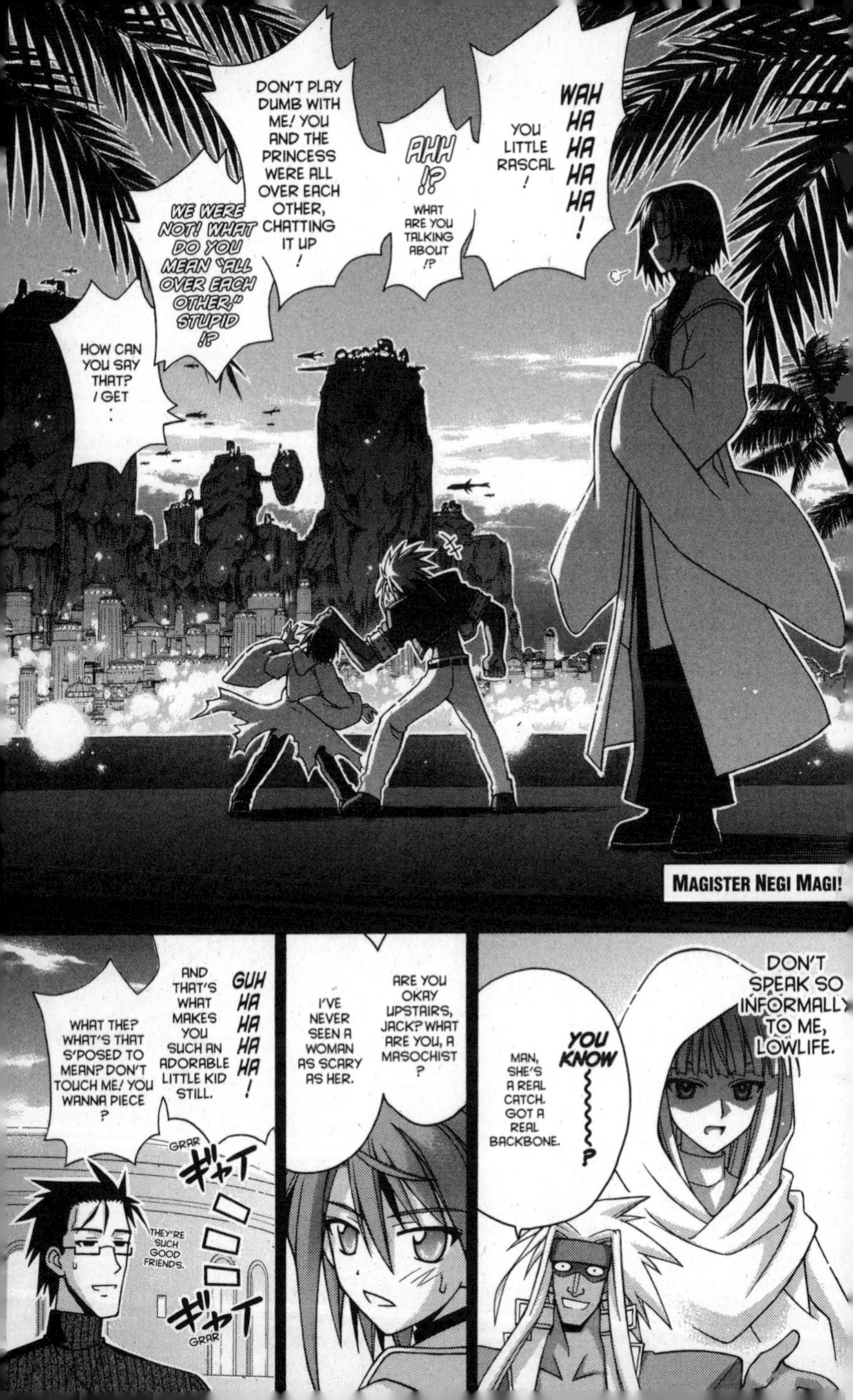
WAH HA HA HA HA!
YOU LITTLE RASCAL!
AHH!?
WHAT ARE YOU TALKING ABOUT!?
DON'T PLAY DUMB WITH ME! YOU AND THE PRINCESS WERE ALL OVER EACH OTHER, CHATTING IT UP!
WE WERE NOT! WHAT DO YOU MEAN "ALL OVER EACH OTHER," STUPID!?
HOW CAN YOU SAY THAT? I GET!
MAGISTER NEGI MAGI!
DON'T SPEAK SO INFORMALLY TO ME, LOWLIFE.
YOU KNOW~~~?
MAN, SHE'S A REAL CATCH. GOT A REAL BACKBONE.
ARE YOU OKAY UPSTAIRS, JACK? WHAT ARE YOU, A MASOCHIST?
I'VE NEVER SEEN A WOMAN AS SCARY AS HER.
GUH HA HA HA HA!
AND THAT'S WHAT MAKES YOU SUCH AN ADORABLE LITTLE KID STILL.
WHAT THE? WHAT'S THAT S'POSED TO MEAN? DON'T TOUCH ME! YOU WANNA PIECE?
GRAR
ギャイ
THEY'RE SUCH GOOD FRIENDS.
ギャイ
GRAR

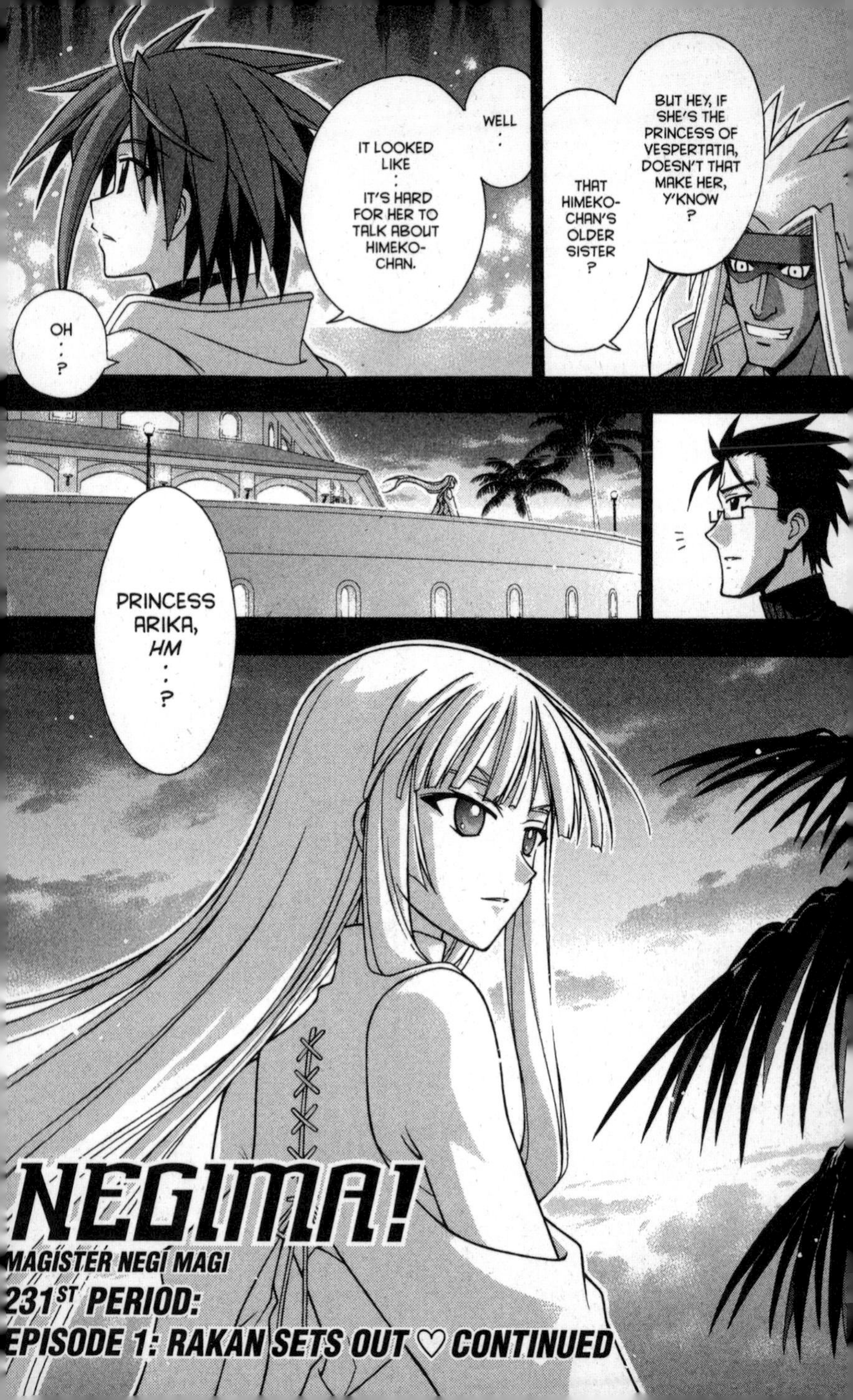
BUT HEY, IF SHE'S THE PRINCESS OF VESPERTATIA, DOESN'T THAT MAKE HER, Y'KNOW ?
THAT HIMEKO-CHAN'S OLDER SISTER ?
WELL . .
IT LOOKED LIKE . . . IT'S HARD FOR HER TO TALK ABOUT HIMEKO-CHAN.
OH . . ?
PRINCESS ARIKA, HM . . ?
NEGIMA!
MAGISTER NEGI MAGI
231ST PERIOD:
EPISODE 1: RAKAN SETS OUT ♡ CONTINUED

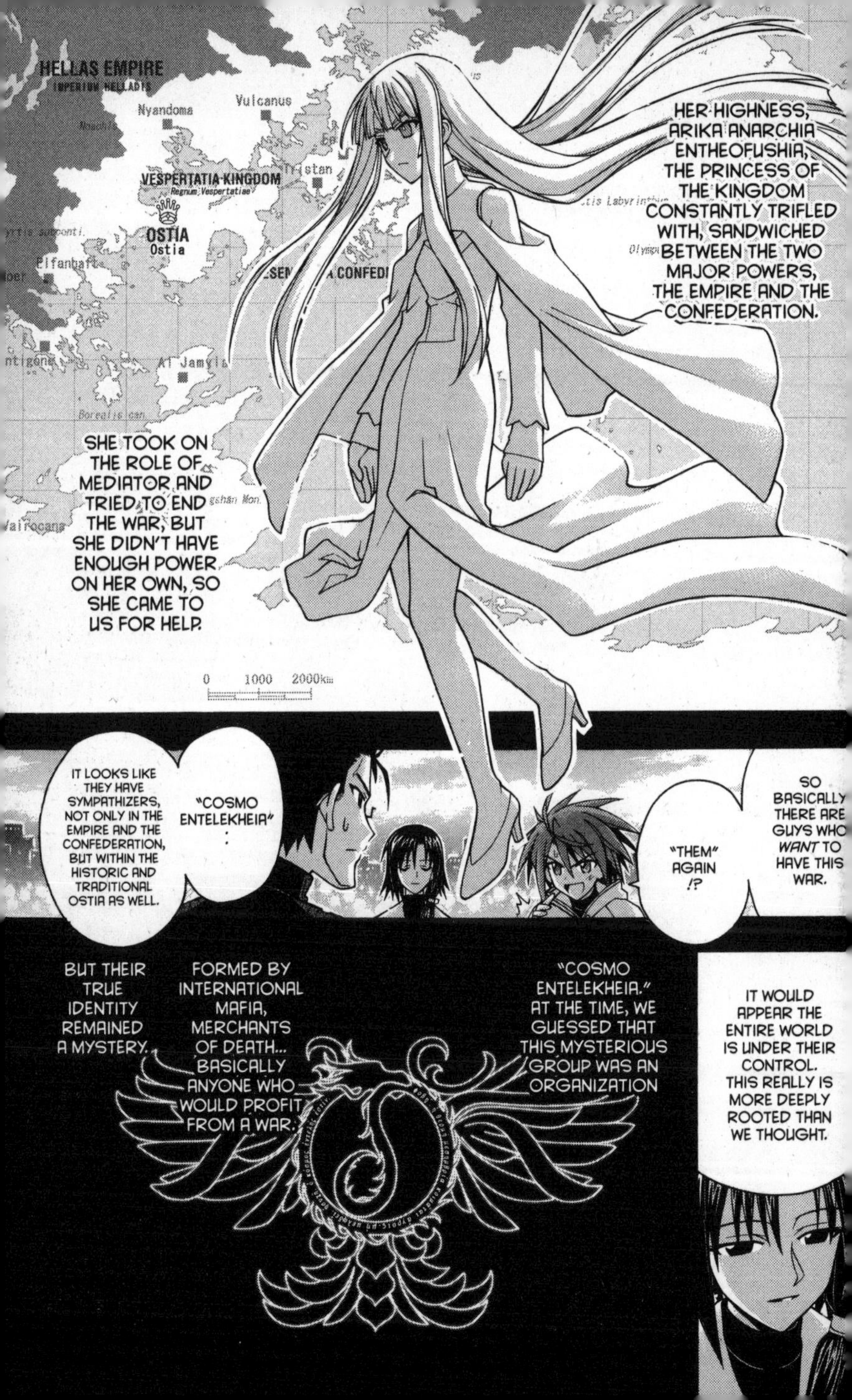
HELLAS EMPIRE
IMPERIUM HELLADIS
Nyandoma
Vulcanus
VESPERTATIA KINGDOM
Regnum Vespertatiae
OSTIA
Ostia
Tristan
Al Jamyis
0 1000 2000km
HER HIGHNESS, ARIKA ANARCHIA ENTHEOFUSHIA, THE PRINCESS OF THE KINGDOM CONSTANTLY TRIFLED WITH, SANDWICHED BETWEEN THE TWO MAJOR POWERS, THE EMPIRE AND THE CONFEDERATION.
SHE TOOK ON THE ROLE OF MEDIATOR AND TRIED TO END THE WAR, BUT SHE DIDN'T HAVE ENOUGH POWER ON HER OWN, SO SHE CAME TO US FOR HELP.
SO BASICALLY THERE ARE GUYS WHO *WANT* TO HAVE THIS WAR.
"THEM" AGAIN !?
"COSMO ENTELEKHEIA" :
IT LOOKS LIKE THEY HAVE SYMPATHIZERS, NOT ONLY IN THE EMPIRE AND THE CONFEDERATION, BUT WITHIN THE HISTORIC AND TRADITIONAL OSTIA AS WELL.
IT WOULD APPEAR THE ENTIRE WORLD IS UNDER THEIR CONTROL. THIS REALLY IS MORE DEEPLY ROOTED THAN WE THOUGHT.
"COSMO ENTELEKHEIA." AT THE TIME, WE GUESSED THAT THIS MYSTERIOUS GROUP WAS AN ORGANIZATION
FORMED BY INTERNATIONAL MAFIA, MERCHANTS OF DEATH... BASICALLY ANYONE WHO WOULD PROFIT FROM A WAR.
BUT THEIR TRUE IDENTITY REMAINED A MYSTERY.

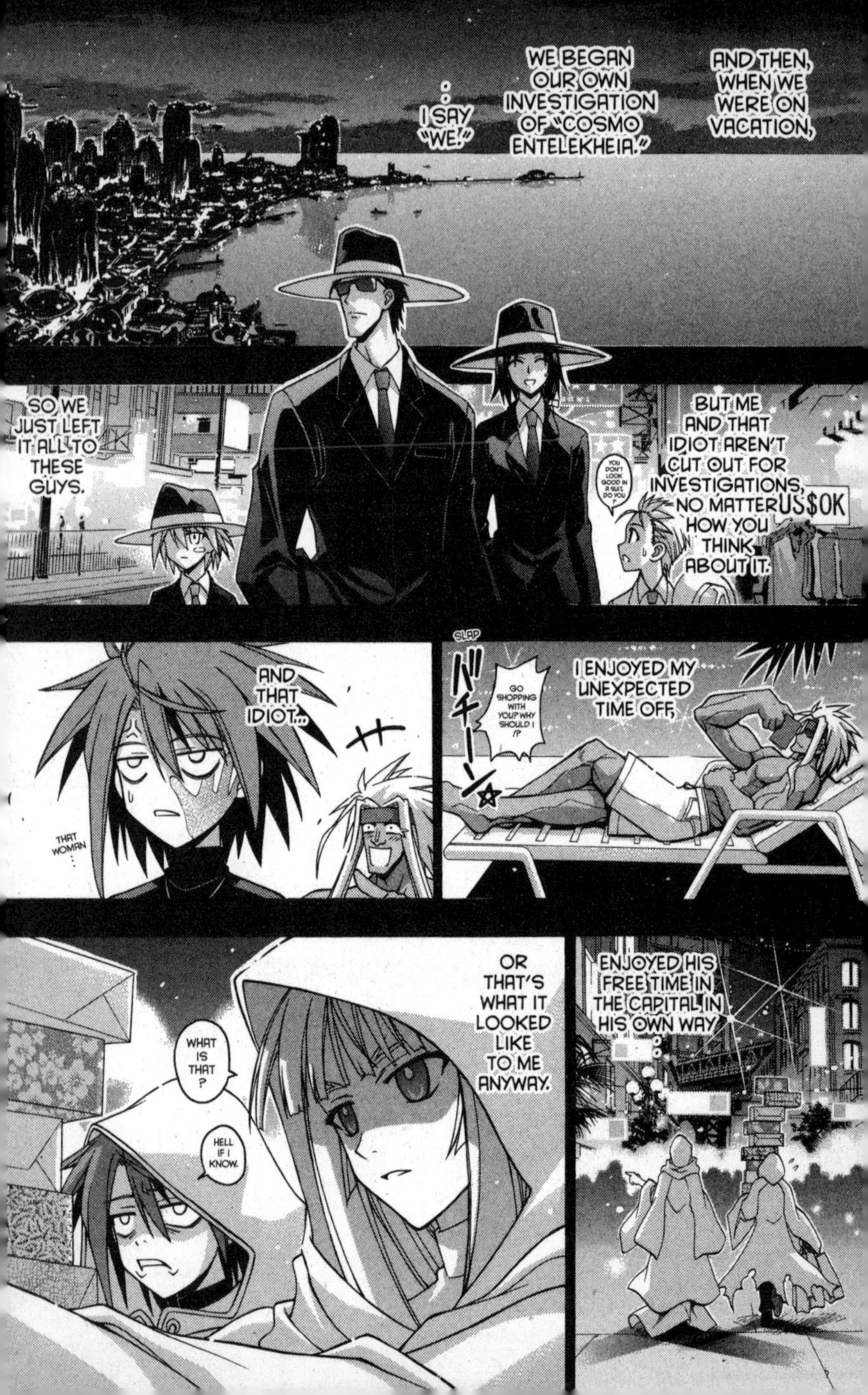
AND THEN, WHEN WE WERE ON VACATION,
WE BEGAN OUR OWN INVESTIGATION OF "COSMO ENTELEKHEIA."
...I SAY "WE."
BUT ME AND THAT IDIOT AREN'T CUT OUT FOR INVESTIGATIONS, NO MATTER HOW YOU THINK ABOUT IT.
US$0K
YOU DON'T LOOK GOOD IN A SUIT, DO YOU!?
SO WE JUST LEFT IT ALL TO THESE GUYS.
I ENJOYED MY UNEXPECTED TIME OFF,
SLAP
GO SHOPPING WITH YOU? WHY SHOULD I!?
AND THAT IDIOT...
THAT WOMAN...
ENJOYED HIS FREE TIME IN THE CAPITAL IN HIS OWN WAY...
OR THAT'S WHAT IT LOOKED LIKE TO ME ANYWAY.
WHAT IS THAT?
HELL IF I KNOW.

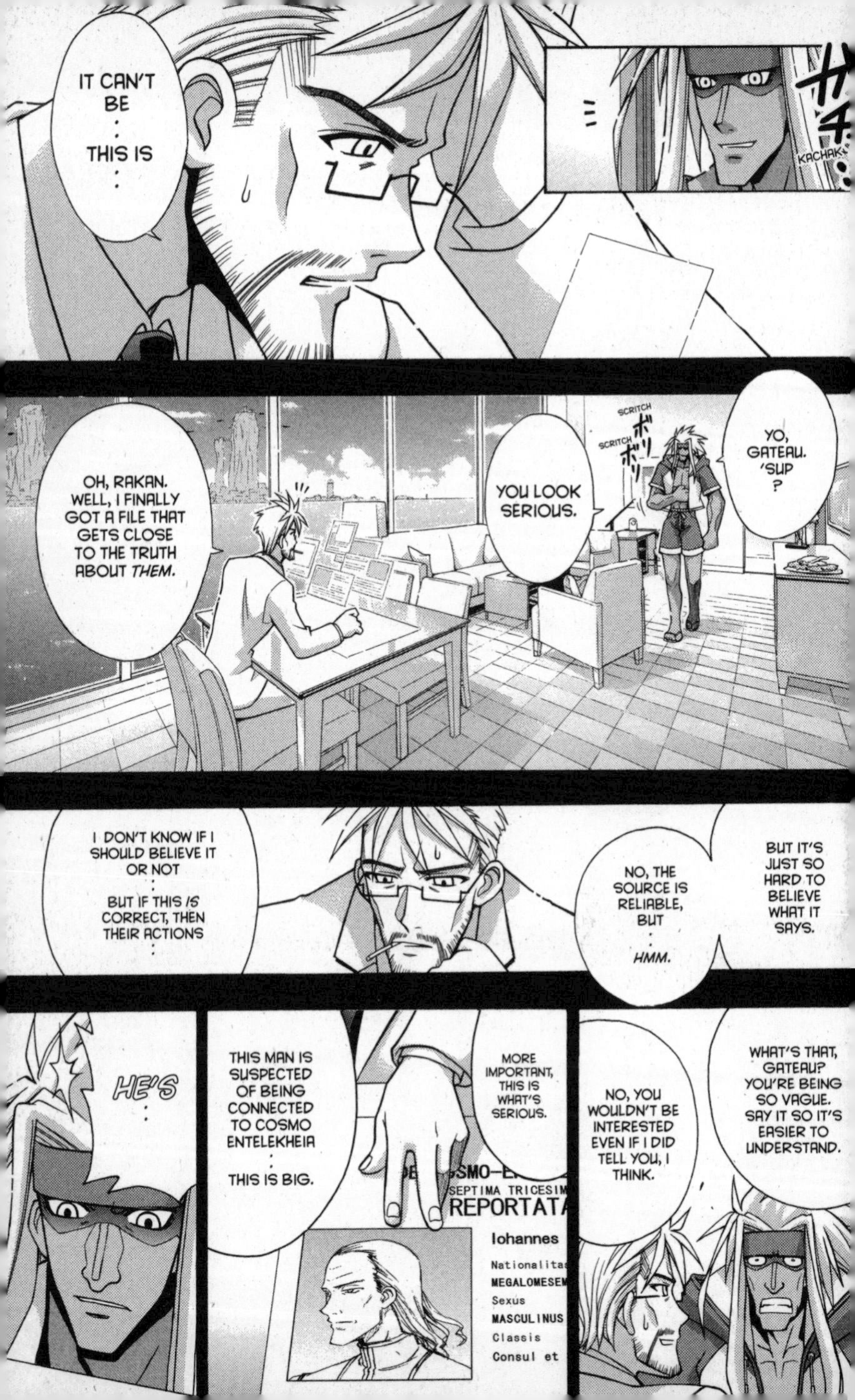

...
KACHAK
IT CAN'T BE : THIS IS :
SCRITCH SCRITCH
YO, GATEAU. 'SUP?
YOU LOOK SERIOUS.
OH, RAKAN. WELL, I FINALLY GOT A FILE THAT GETS CLOSE TO THE TRUTH ABOUT *THEM*.
BUT IT'S JUST SO HARD TO BELIEVE WHAT IT SAYS.
NO, THE SOURCE IS RELIABLE, BUT : *HMM.*
I DON'T KNOW IF I SHOULD BELIEVE IT OR NOT : BUT IF THIS *IS* CORRECT, THEN THEIR ACTIONS :
WHAT'S THAT, GATEAU? YOU'RE BEING SO VAGUE. SAY IT SO IT'S EASIER TO UNDERSTAND.
NO, YOU WOULDN'T BE INTERESTED EVEN IF I DID TELL YOU, I THINK.
MORE IMPORTANT, THIS IS WHAT'S SERIOUS.
THIS MAN IS SUSPECTED OF BEING CONNECTED TO COSMO ENTELEKHEIA : THIS IS BIG.
SEPTIMA TRICESIM
REPORTATA
Iohannes
Nationalitas
MEGALOMESEM
Sexus
MASCULINUS
Classis
Consul et
HE'S :

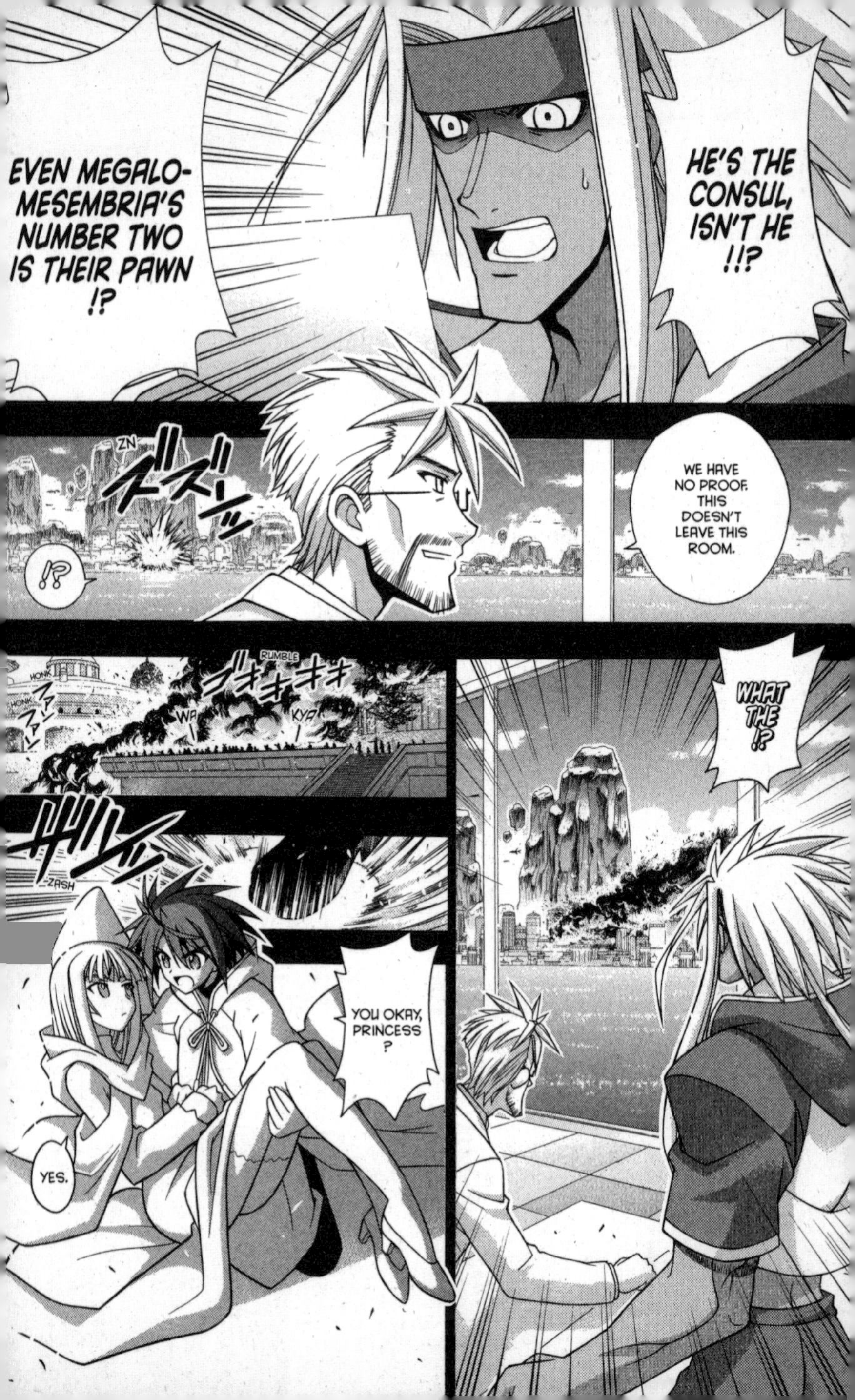
HE'S THE CONSUL, ISN'T HE !!?
EVEN MEGALO-MESEMBRIA'S NUMBER TWO IS THEIR PAWN !?
WE HAVE NO PROOF. THIS DOESN'T LEAVE THIS ROOM.
ZN
!?
WHAT THE !?
RUMBLE
HONK
HONK
WA
KYA
ZASH
YOU OKAY, PRINCESS ?
YES.

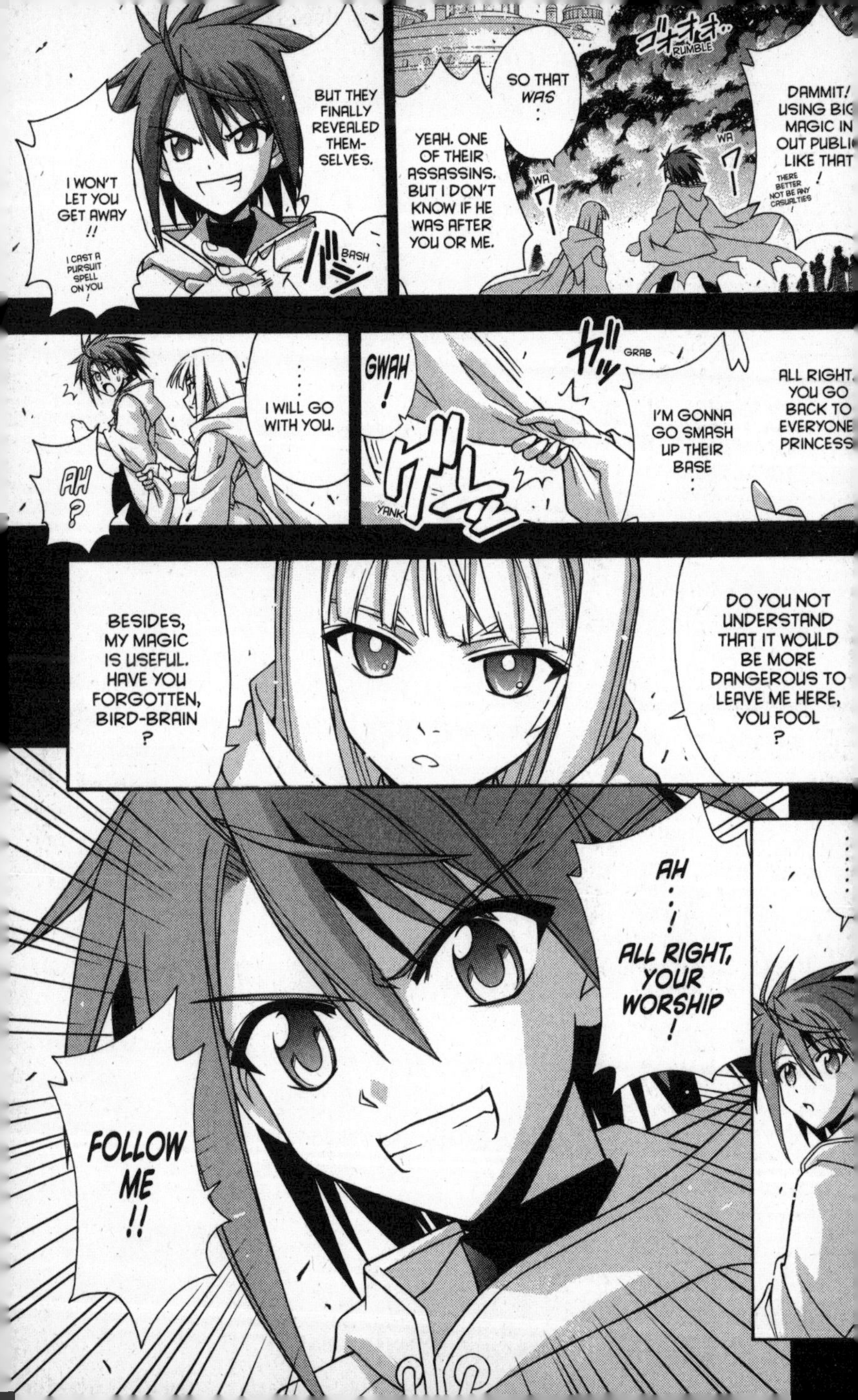
RUMBLE
DAMMIT! USING BIG MAGIC IN OUT PUBLIC LIKE THAT
THERE BETTER NOT BE ANY CASUALTIES!
WA
WA
SO THAT WAS...
YEAH. ONE OF THEIR ASSASSINS. BUT I DON'T KNOW IF HE WAS AFTER YOU OR ME.
BUT THEY FINALLY REVEALED THEM-SELVES.
BASH
I WON'T LET YOU GET AWAY!!
I CAST A PURSUIT SPELL ON YOU!
ALL RIGHT. YOU GO BACK TO EVERYONE PRINCESS
I'M GONNA GO SMASH UP THEIR BASE...
GRAB
GWAH!
YANK
...I WILL GO WITH YOU.
AH?
DO YOU NOT UNDERSTAND THAT IT WOULD BE MORE DANGEROUS TO LEAVE ME HERE, YOU FOOL?
BESIDES, MY MAGIC IS USEFUL. HAVE YOU FORGOTTEN, BIRD-BRAIN?
AH...! ALL RIGHT, YOUR WORSHIP!
FOLLOW ME!!

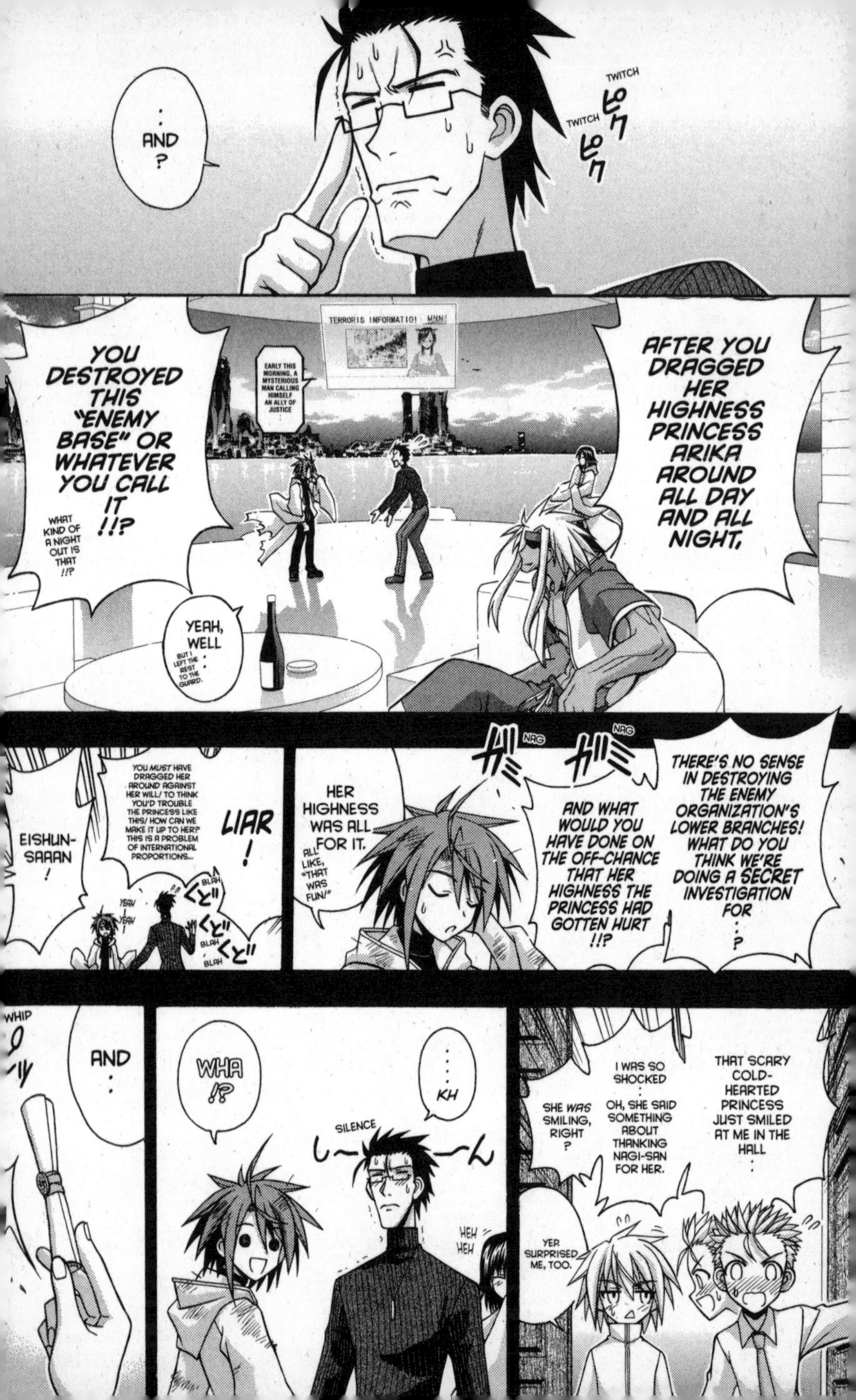

...AND?
TWITCH ピク
TWITCH ピク
AFTER YOU DRAGGED HER HIGHNESS PRINCESS ARIKA AROUND ALL DAY AND ALL NIGHT,
TERRORIS INFORMATIO! MNN!
EARLY THIS MORNING, A MYSTERIOUS MAN CALLING HIMSELF AN ALLY OF JUSTICE...
YOU DESTROYED THIS "ENEMY BASE" OR WHATEVER YOU CALL IT!!?
WHAT KIND OF A NIGHT OUT IS THAT!!?
YEAH, WELL...
BUT I LEFT THE REST TO THE GUARD.
NAG ガミ
NAG ガミ
THERE'S NO SENSE IN DESTROYING THE ENEMY ORGANIZATION'S LOWER BRANCHES! WHAT DO YOU THINK WE'RE DOING A SECRET INVESTIGATION FOR...?
AND WHAT WOULD YOU HAVE DONE ON THE OFF-CHANCE THAT HER HIGHNESS THE PRINCESS HAD GOTTEN HURT!!?
HER HIGHNESS WAS ALL FOR IT.
ALL LIKE, "THAT WAS FUN!"
LIAR!
YOU MUST HAVE DRAGGED HER AROUND AGAINST HER WILL! TO THINK YOU'D TROUBLE THE PRINCESS LIKE THIS! HOW CAN WE MAKE IT UP TO HER? THIS IS A PROBLEM OF INTERNATIONAL PROPORTIONS...
EISHUN-SAAAN!
YEAH YEAH
BLAH くど
BLAH くど
BLAH くど
THAT SCARY COLD-HEARTED PRINCESS JUST SMILED AT ME IN THE HALL...
I WAS SO SHOCKED...
OH, SHE SAID SOMETHING ABOUT THANKING NAGI-SAN FOR HER.
SHE WAS SMILING, RIGHT?
YER SURPRISED ME, TOO.
......KH
WHA!?
SILENCE しーーん
HEH HEH
AND...
WHIP

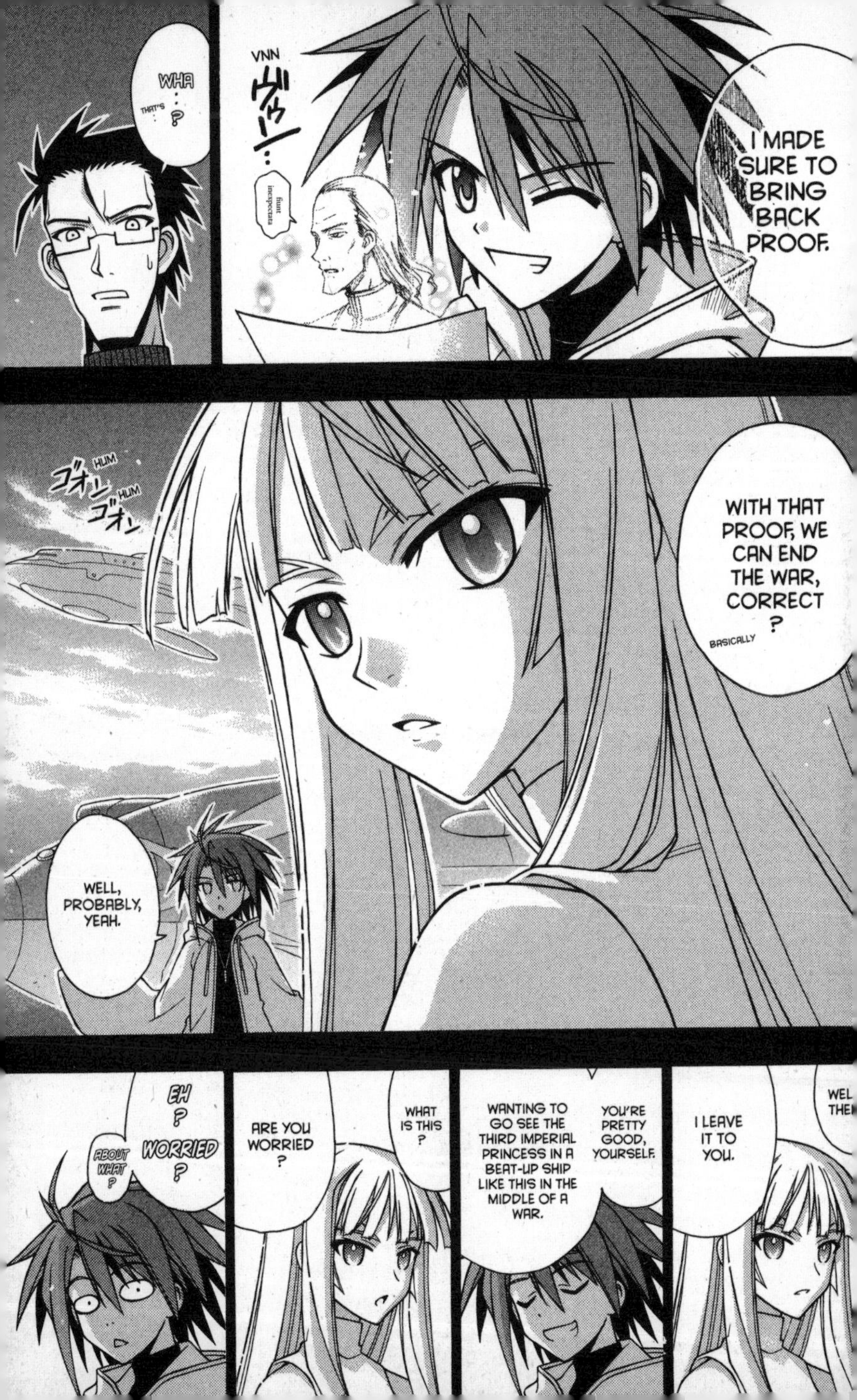
I MADE SURE TO BRING BACK PROOF.
VNN
ヴゥン…
fiunt inexpectata
WHA... THAT'S ...?
WITH THAT PROOF, WE CAN END THE WAR, CORRECT?
BASICALLY
HUM
ゴオン
HUM
ゴオン
WELL, PROBABLY, YEAH.
WEL THE
I LEAVE IT TO YOU.
YOU'RE PRETTY GOOD, YOURSELF.
WANTING TO GO SEE THE THIRD IMPERIAL PRINCESS IN A BEAT-UP SHIP LIKE THIS IN THE MIDDLE OF A WAR.
WHAT IS THIS?
ARE YOU WORRIED?
EH? WORRIED?
ABOUT WHAT?

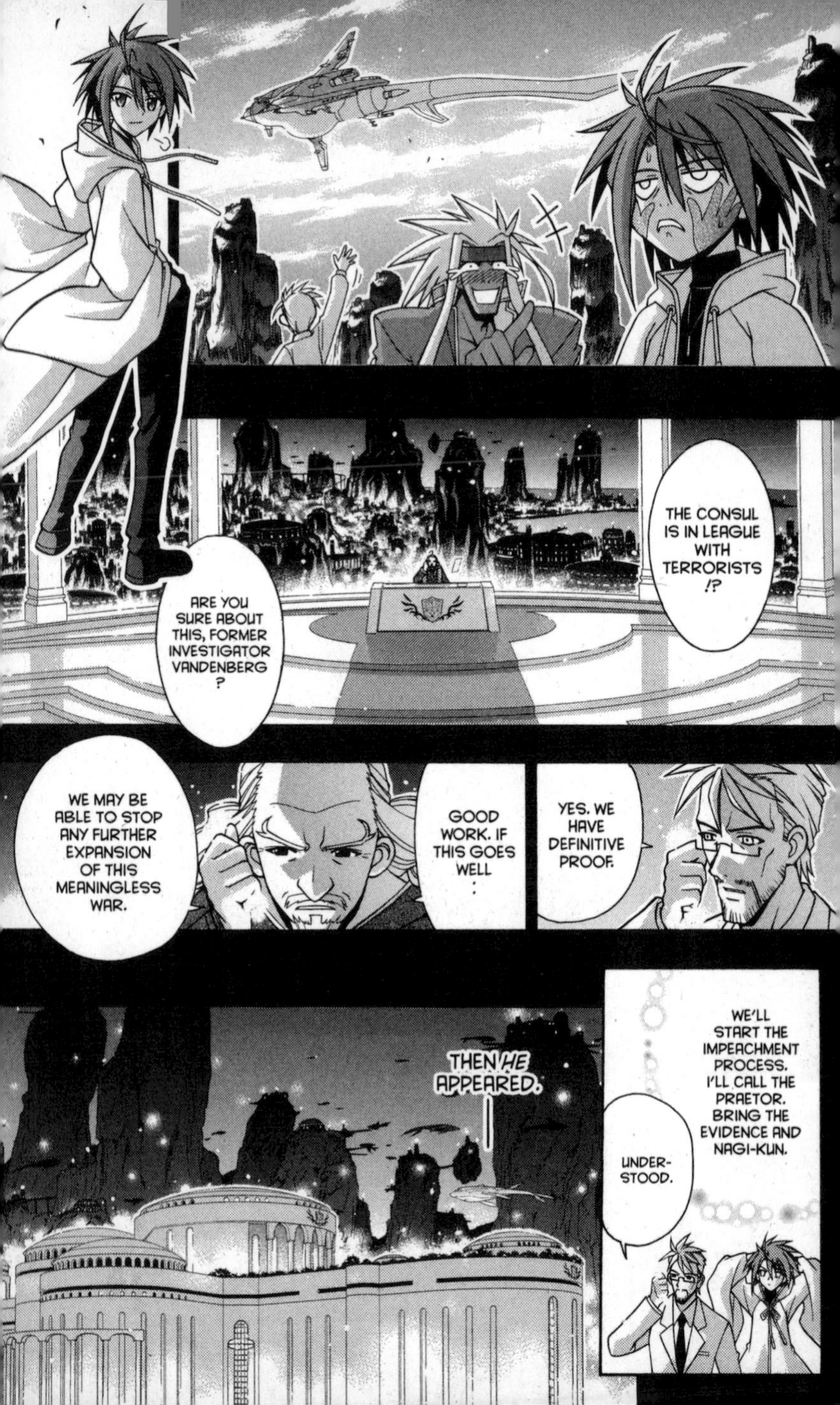
THE CONSUL IS IN LEAGUE WITH TERRORISTS!?
ARE YOU SURE ABOUT THIS, FORMER INVESTIGATOR VANDENBERG?
YES. WE HAVE DEFINITIVE PROOF.
GOOD WORK. IF THIS GOES WELL…
WE MAY BE ABLE TO STOP ANY FURTHER EXPANSION OF THIS MEANINGLESS WAR.
WE'LL START THE IMPEACHMENT PROCESS. I'LL CALL THE PRAETOR. BRING THE EVIDENCE AND NAGI-KUN.
UNDER-STOOD.
THEN *HE* APPEARED.

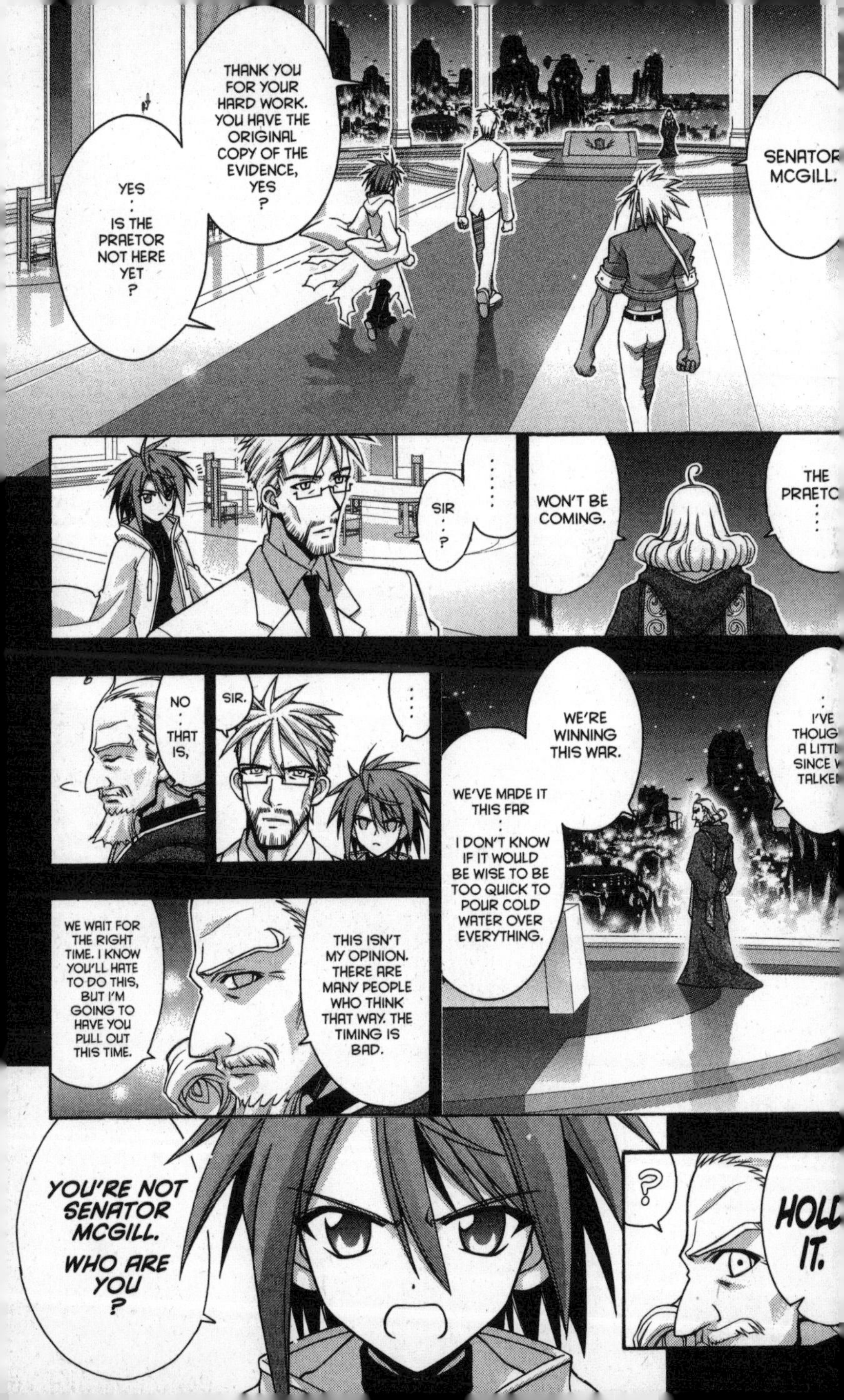
SENATOR MCGILL.
THANK YOU FOR YOUR HARD WORK. YOU HAVE THE ORIGINAL COPY OF THE EVIDENCE, YES ?
YES . . . IS THE PRAETOR NOT HERE YET ?
THE PRAETO . . .
WON'T BE COMING.
. . . . .
SIR . . . ?
I'VE THOUG A LITTL SINCE W TALKE
WE'RE WINNING THIS WAR.
WE'VE MADE IT THIS FAR : I DON'T KNOW IF IT WOULD BE WISE TO BE TOO QUICK TO POUR COLD WATER OVER EVERYTHING.
. . . .
SIR.
NO . . THAT IS,
THIS ISN'T MY OPINION. THERE ARE MANY PEOPLE WHO THINK THAT WAY. THE TIMING IS BAD.
WE WAIT FOR THE RIGHT TIME. I KNOW YOU'LL HATE TO DO THIS, BUT I'M GOING TO HAVE YOU PULL OUT THIS TIME.
HOLD IT.
?
YOU'RE NOT SENATOR MCGILL. WHO ARE YOU ?

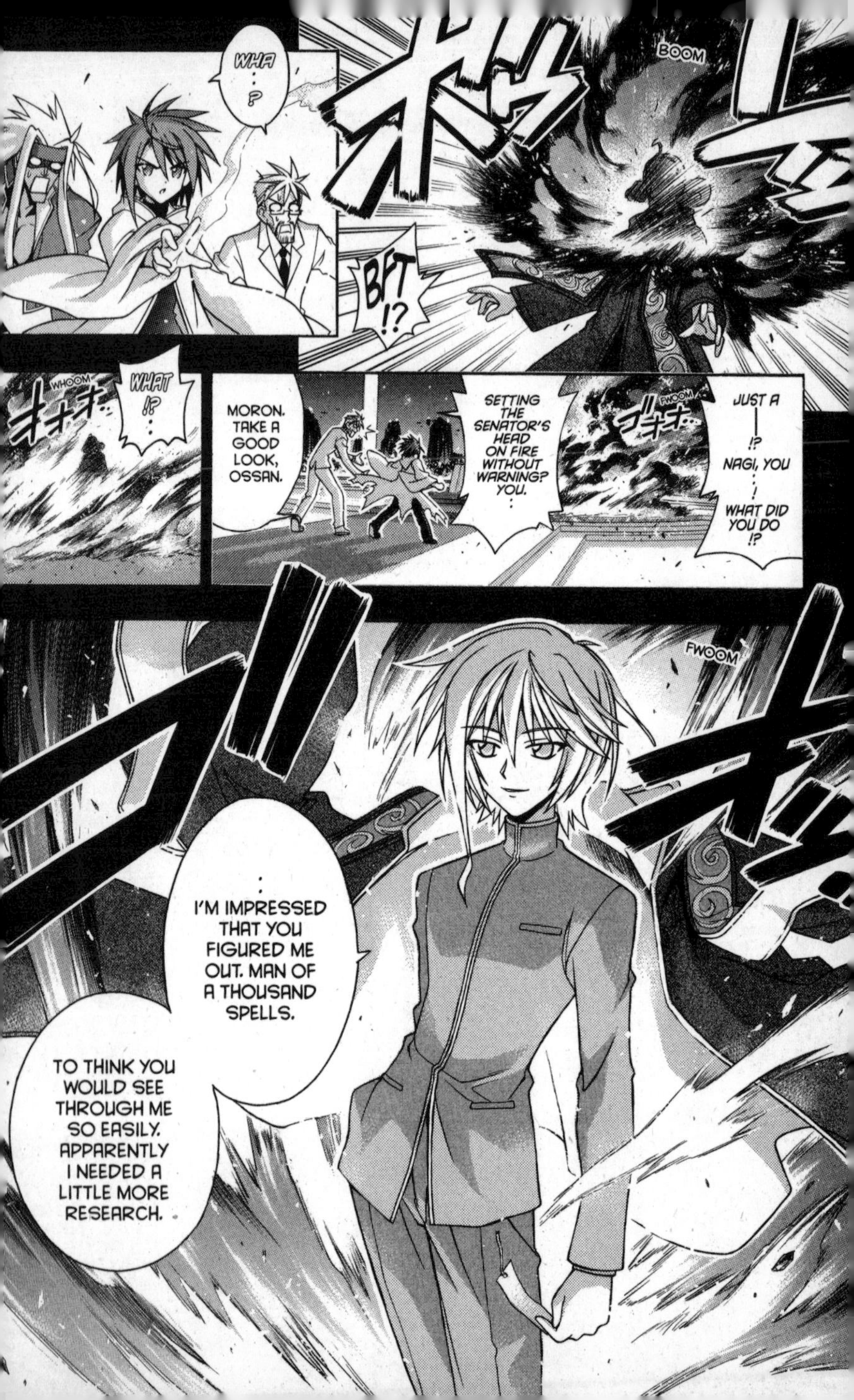
BOOM
BFT !?
WHA...?
JUST A—!? NAGI, YOU...! WHAT DID YOU DO!?
FWOOM
SETTING THE SENATOR'S HEAD ON FIRE WITHOUT WARNING? YOU...
MORON. TAKE A GOOD LOOK, OSSAN.
WHAT!?...
WHOOM
FWOOM
...I'M IMPRESSED THAT YOU FIGURED ME OUT. MAN OF A THOUSAND SPELLS.
TO THINK YOU WOULD SEE THROUGH ME SO EASILY. APPARENTLY I NEEDED A LITTLE MORE RESEARCH.

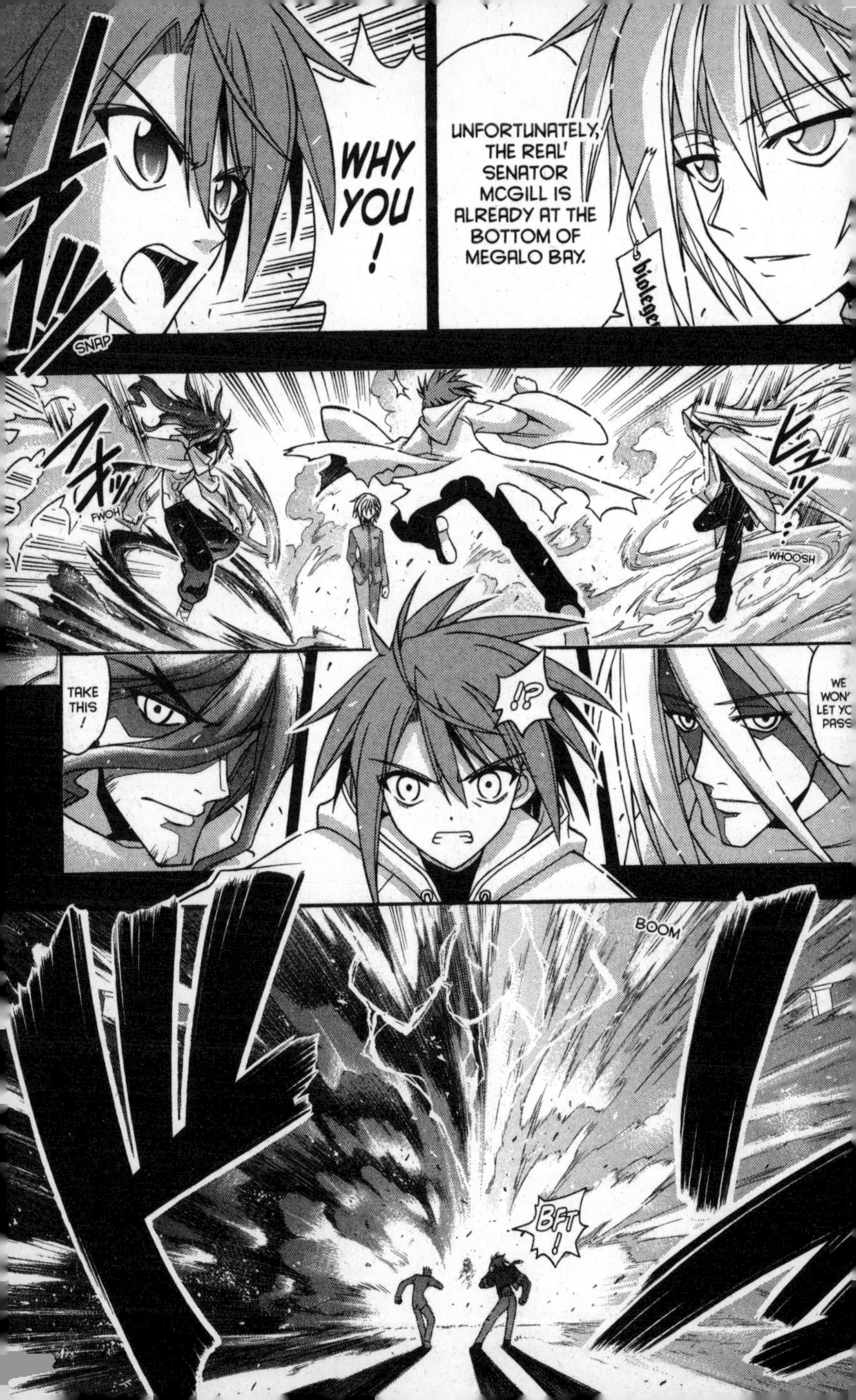
UNFORTUNATELY, THE REAL SENATOR MCGILL IS ALREADY AT THE BOTTOM OF MEGALO BAY.
bioleger
WHY YOU!
SNAP
WHOOSH
FWOH
WE WON' LET YO PASS
!?
TAKE THIS!
BOOM
BFT!

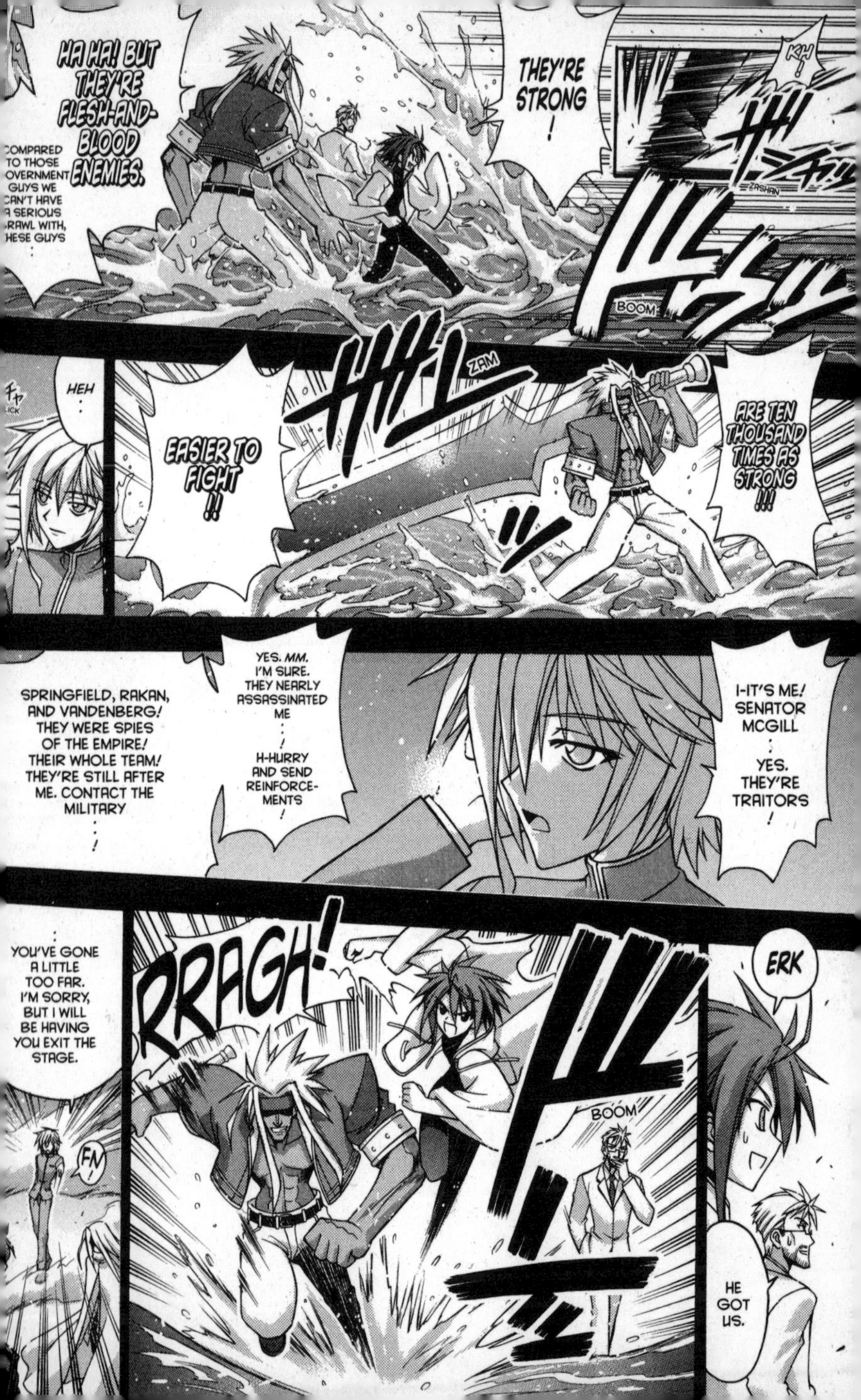
KH!
ZASHAN
BOOM
THEY'RE STRONG!
HA HA! BUT THEY'RE FLESH-AND-BLOOD ENEMIES.
COMPARED TO THOSE GOVERNMENT GUYS WE CAN'T HAVE A SERIOUS BRAWL WITH, THESE GUYS...
ARE TEN THOUSAND TIMES AS STRONG!!!
ZAM
EASIER TO FIGHT!!
HEH...
CLICK
I-IT'S ME! SENATOR MCGILL... YES. THEY'RE TRAITORS!
YES. MM. I'M SURE. THEY NEARLY ASSASSINATED ME...!
H-HURRY AND SEND REINFORCEMENTS!
SPRINGFIELD, RAKAN, AND VANDENBERG! THEY WERE SPIES OF THE EMPIRE! THEIR WHOLE TEAM! THEY'RE STILL AFTER ME. CONTACT THE MILITARY...!
ERK
HE GOT US.
BOOM
RRAGH!
FN!
...YOU'VE GONE A LITTLE TOO FAR. I'M SORRY, BUT I WILL BE HAVING YOU EXIT THE STAGE.

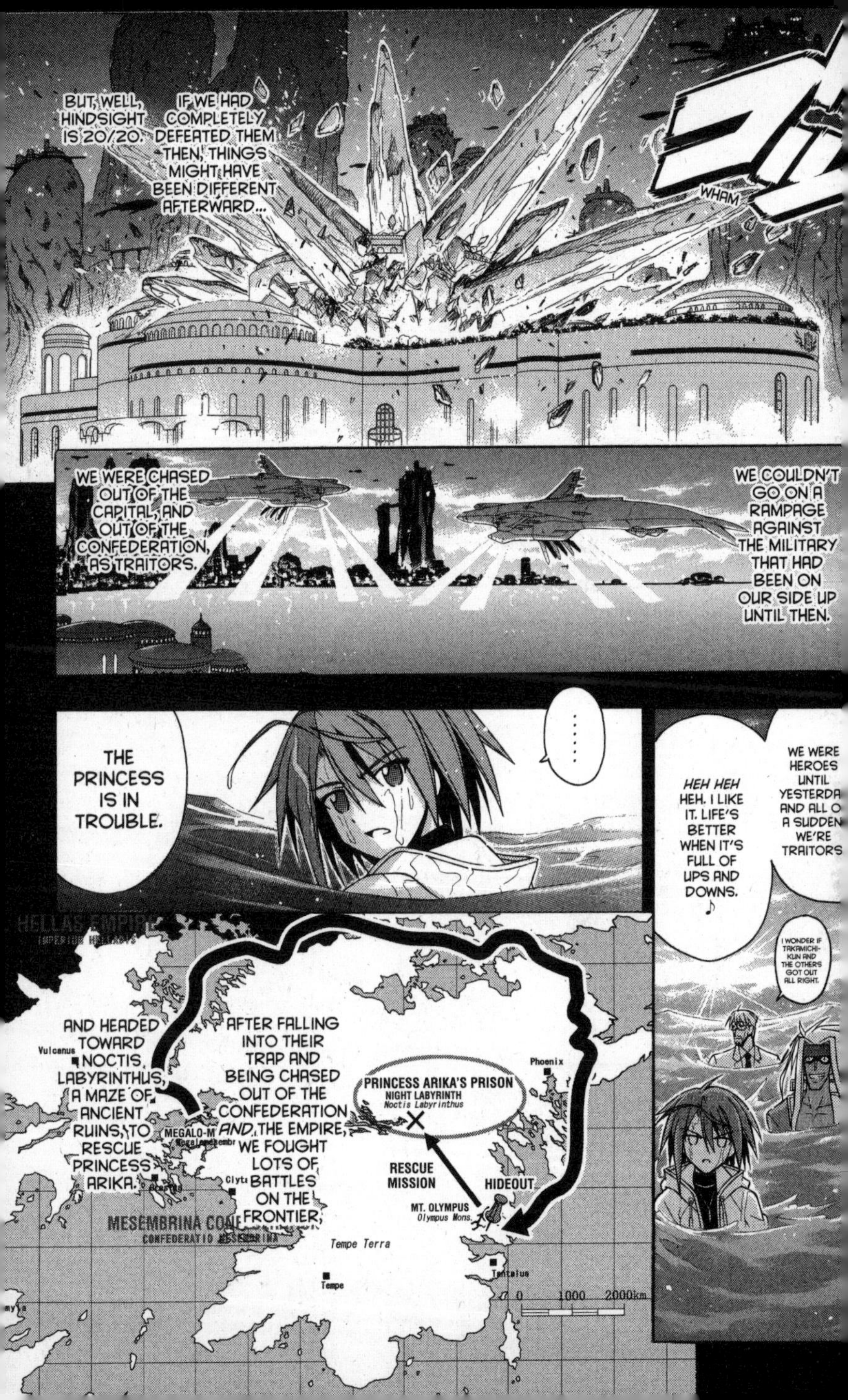
WHAM
IF WE HAD COMPLETELY DEFEATED THEM THEN, THINGS MIGHT HAVE BEEN DIFFERENT AFTERWARD...
BUT, WELL, HINDSIGHT IS 20/20.
WE COULDN'T GO ON A RAMPAGE AGAINST THE MILITARY THAT HAD BEEN ON OUR SIDE UP UNTIL THEN.
WE WERE CHASED OUT OF THE CAPITAL, AND OUT OF THE CONFEDERATION, AS TRAITORS.
WE WERE HEROES UNTIL YESTERDA AND ALL O A SUDDEN WE'RE TRAITORS
HEH HEH HEH. I LIKE IT. LIFE'S BETTER WHEN IT'S FULL OF UPS AND DOWNS. ♪
I WONDER IF TAKAMICHI-KUN AND THE OTHERS GOT OUT ALL RIGHT.
......
THE PRINCESS IS IN TROUBLE.
AFTER FALLING INTO THEIR TRAP AND BEING CHASED OUT OF THE CONFEDERATION AND THE EMPIRE, WE FOUGHT LOTS OF BATTLES ON THE FRONTIER,
AND HEADED TOWARD NOCTIS LABYRINTHUS, A MAZE OF ANCIENT RUINS, TO RESCUE PRINCESS ARIKA.
PRINCESS ARIKA'S PRISON
NIGHT LABYRINTH
Noctis Labyrinthus
RESCUE MISSION
HIDEOUT
MT. OLYMPUS
Olympus Mons.
Phoenix
Vulcanus
MEGALO-M
Tempe Terra
Tempe
0 1000 2000km

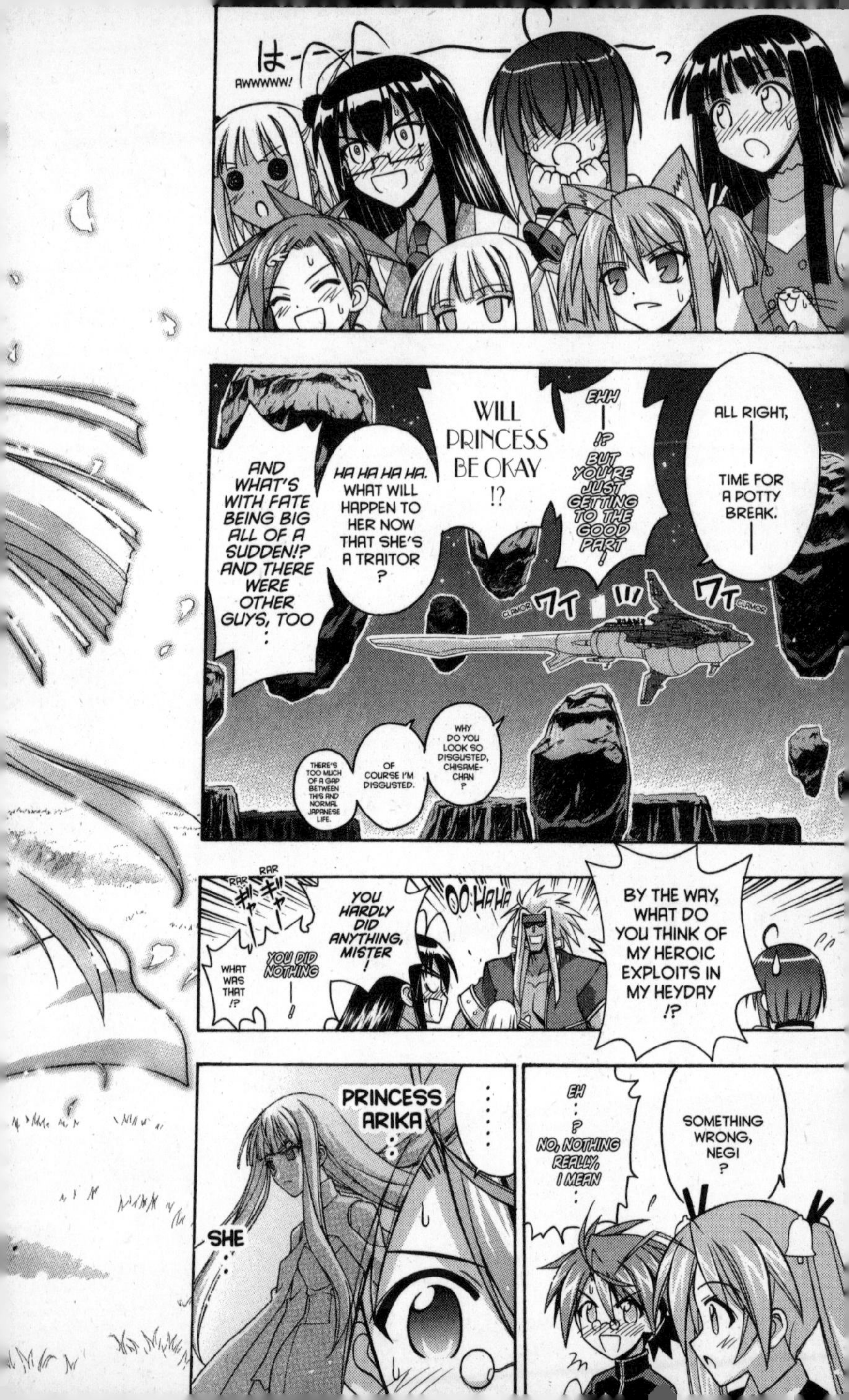

は──っ
AWWWWWW!
ALL RIGHT, — TIME FOR A POTTY BREAK. —
EHH —!? BUT YOU'RE JUST GETTING TO THE GOOD PART!
WILL PRINCESS BE OKAY !?
HA HA HA HA. WHAT WILL HAPPEN TO HER NOW THAT SHE'S A TRAITOR?
AND WHAT'S WITH FATE BEING BIG ALL OF A SUDDEN!? AND THERE WERE OTHER GUYS, TOO...
ワイ CLAMOR
ワイ CLAMOR
WHY DO YOU LOOK SO DISGUSTED, CHISAME-CHAN?
OF COURSE I'M DISGUSTED.
THERE'S TOO MUCH OF A GAP BETWEEN THIS AND NORMAL JAPANESE LIFE.
BY THE WAY, WHAT DO YOU THINK OF MY HEROIC EXPLOITS IN MY HEYDAY !?
HAHA
YOU HARDLY DID ANYTHING, MISTER!
YOU DID NOTHING —!
WHAT WAS THAT !?
ギャー RAR
ギャー RAR
SOMETHING WRONG, NEGI?
EH...? NO, NOTHING REALLY, I MEAN...
......
PRINCESS ARIKA...
SHE...

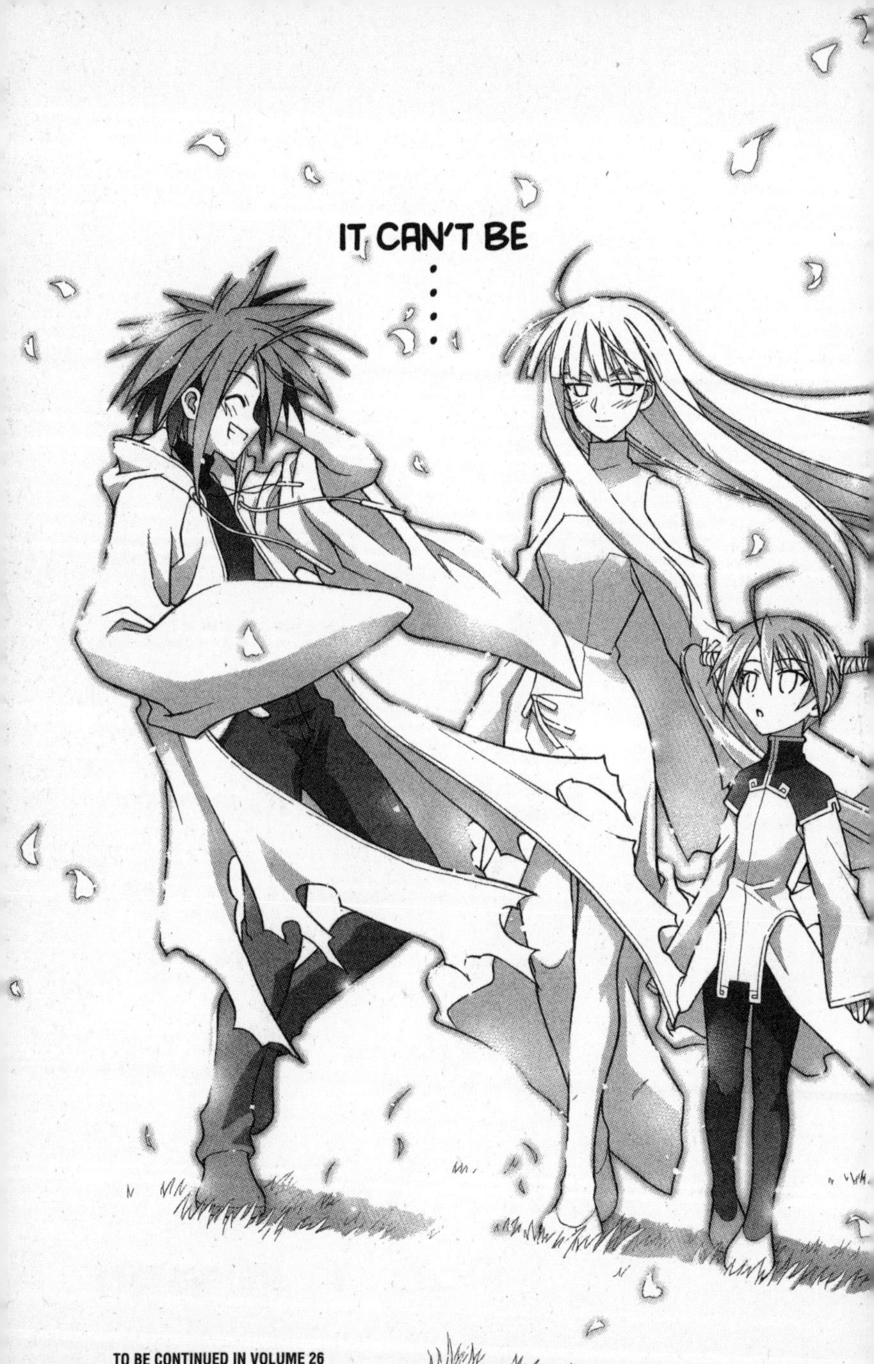
IT CAN'T BE
....

TO BE CONTINUED IN VOLUME 26

-STAFF-

Ken Akamatsu

Takashi Takemoto

Kenichi Nakamura

Masaki Ohyama

Keiichi Yamashita

Tadashi Maki

Tohru Mitsuhashi

Yuichi Yoshida

Thanks to

Ran Ayanaga

LEXICON NEGIMARIUM

[*Negima!* 223rd Period Lexicon Negimarium]

■ Lunatic Fiddle

(fidicula lunatica)

The girl known as Shirabe is awarded this item for her use by the power of the pactio with the white-haired boy. "Fidicula" is Latin for a small, stringed instruments, and, in this case, refers to a violin. In the Middle Ages, stringed instruments played with bows were all called violas ("viola" in Latin, also). For small violas, they attached the diminutive "-ina" to "viola," and called them "violina," and thus the modern name "violin" was born.

Objects showered in the strong sound waves emitted from Fidicula Lunatica are blasted into dust. But because these sound waves have directivity, merely listening to the sound will not expose one to its destructive powers. Otherwise, we would be mincemeat before we could comment on the poor quality of Shirabe's playing, and more than anything, Shirabe herself would fall victim to her own performance.

[*Negima!* 224th Period Lexicon Negimarium]

■ Song of Saving Mercy

(cantus elemosynes)

An omnidirectional attack using the sound waves of Fidicula Lunatica. How waves sent from a single source can become an omnidirectional attack remains a mystery. "Cantus" is Latin for "song," and "elemosynes" is the genitive case of "elemosyne." "Elemosyne" is a Latinized version of ἐλημοσύνη (elêmosynê), Ancient Greek for "mercy."

■ Infinite Embrace

(encompandentia infinita)

The girl known as Tamaki is awarded this item for her use by the power of the pactio with the white-haired boy. She uses a finite amount of magic power to develop and control a barrier space of infinite expanse around herself.

■ Randgrid

(Randgríð)

The flying patrol ship of the Ariadne Magic Knights. It is equipped with a long cruising range and superior ability to search out enemies. However, its firepower is minimal, and its ability to bombard other ships in battle is low. Patrol ships of the same model are widely used in the Mesembrina Confederation city-states.

Randgríð is the name of a page in Odin's hall, who appears in "The Ballad of Grimnir," recorded in the *Elder Edda*. The name means "shield hall" in Old Norse. According to later-written *Snorri's Edda*, Randgríð was counted as one of the Valkyries, but this is no more than Snorri Sturluson's (1178-1241) interpretation, and it is not made clear in the *Elder Edda* whether or not she was a Valkyrie.

[*Negima!* 225th Period Lexicon Negimarium]

■ "Hell's Refining Fire"

(sim fabricatus ab incendio)

One of the practical uses of dark magic, it takes the magic power from "Flames of Hell (Incendium Gehennae)" into one's flesh and fuses it with the spirit. In doing so, the caster's flesh gains powerful hardness and resistance to heat, and is imbued with a sinister spiritual power that steals magical power from any living thing it touches. But if it fails, not only is there a danger that the blaze of "Flames of Hell" will damage the caster's flesh, but there are also cases when the fire spirits (spritus) violate the caster's mind (spiritus) and make him go mad.

[*Negima!* 226th Period Lexicon Negimarium]

■ Left Arm Release

(sinistra emittam)

"Sinistra" is a Latin ablative meaning "left hand." An "ablative" indicates a place or a method. *"Emittam"* is in the first person singular present active subjunctive mood. Therefore, this phrase means "may I release from my left hand." This spell is incanted in order to release delayed magic and the like from the left hand.

■ Time Corridor

(horaria porticus)

The girl known as Koyomi is awarded this item for her use by the power of the pactio with the white-haired boy. It creates a sphere of effect in which physical phenomena and mental phenomena are delayed. The user can determine the extent of the phenomena's delay at her pleasure, and can cancel the delay whenever she likes.

To persons outside the sphere of effect created by the Horaria Porticus, phenomena inside the sphere become abnormally slow, while to those inside the sphere, phenomena outside become abnormally fast. For that reason, once captured inside the sphere of effect, even relatively quick actions will be no more than lagging movements as long as they are viewed from outside. Even the artifact's user is not exempt from this.

That being the case, even an attack with projectiles from outside the sphere, whether they be arrows or bullets, will lag once it enters the sphere, so it is not effective for direct offensive battle. If she is to use it in battle, it would be most suitable for such uses as setting traps outside the sphere, as depicted in the story, or moving to places where it would be easier to fight.

■ Great Dimensional Smash (named just now)

(magna confractio dimensionis [modo nomino])

Using gravity magic learned by watching others, it warps four-dimensional worlds and destroys them.

In a vacuum, when light (electromagnetic waves, to be precise) moves from one point to another, the course the light follows is the shortest distance between those two points. To put it in classical physics terms, light "moves linearly." However, when gravity is at work (no matter how small), the course the light follows becomes a "curved line." This is because in space (space-time to be precise) where gravity is at work, the shortest distance between two points is not a straight line. This is the "warping of space-time."

The curvature of space-time doesn't only *look* bent; it actually is bent. For that reason, space-time warping regulates not only the behavior of light, but also of matter. The reason gravity attracts matter is precisely that space-time is warped. Therefore, it can be said that space-time warping generates gravity, and it can also be said that gravity generates warping of space-time.

Objects with mass or energy (especially heavenly bodies) pull the matter and electromagnetic waves around them toward their gravitational center. In most cases, these objects do not cause any special phenomena. However, special cases do occur when the object is contained within the radius r_g created by this equation,

$$r_g = 2GM \div c^2$$

where M is the mass of the object, G is the gravitational constant, and c is the speed of light. The r_g created in the above formula is called the "Schwarzschild radius." In this Schwarzschild radius, because the force of gravity is so strong, and therefore space-time is curved so greatly, the course light takes is not only "curved," but the light "falls" toward the center (as for what happens to objects other than light, that is better left unsaid). When likened to three-dimensional formations, these objects are called "black holes."

The Schwarzschild radius is inversely proportional to the speed of light squared, so it tends to be an extremely small value. For example, the Schwarzschild radius for an object with the same mass as the moon is approximately 0.11mm. However, gravity magic can create gravity even in places where no objects with mass exist. In other words, gravity magic is the creating of curves in space-time without interposing an object with mass. Furthermore, the strength of a gravitational force F of a source of gravity is

$$F = GMm \div r^2$$

where G is the gravitational constant, M is the mass of the source of gravity, m is the mass of the object pulled by the gravity, and r is the distance between the two. As long as the gravity magic is functioning, gravity will exist there, and F will not equal zero. As long as the left side of the equation does not equal zero, then the right side will not equal zero, either, and (even without an object) the mass M in the formula will not equal zero (however, $r \neq \infty$).

From the above equation, when powerful gravity magic is at work, the value of M becomes great, and in proportion, the Schwarzschild radius becomes great as well. Gravity magic does not require a wide space to create immense gravitational force. For that reason, if one uses powerful energy to exercise gravity magic, in the end, they generate the required value M, within the Schwarzschild radius, to generate a black hole.

At the center of a black hole, gravity is infinite, and therefore the warping of space-time, or the curvature of space-time, is infinitely large, and the density of matter is infinite as well. Therefore, in regard to such unique "points" as these, (traditional) laws of physics cannot be applied. Tamaki's artifact, Encompandentia Infinita, functions to develop and control a barrier space. But that function is designed based, more than anything, on ideas of space from a system of magical culture that came at least before the Theory of Relativity, and certainly before modern physics. Ergo, it was not supposed that a warping of space-time and density of matter of infinitely high value would exist inside a barrier space that she created herself.*

Furthermore, Encompandentia Infinita uses a limited amount of magic to develop and control an infinite expanse. But its magic is too weak to control infinitely great density and space-time warp as well as the infinite expanse. In contrast, an infinite amount of gravity or magic power is not required to create a black hole. This is because, while the speed of light is a great physical quantity, it is in fact finite, and therefore the amount of gravity required to prevent light escaping is also finite. And if enough gravity to trap light is at work, from geometric inevitabilities, the center of the black hole will generate infinitely large gravity on its own. However, the extremely superior function to control infinity is Encompandentia Infinita's basic function. Therefore, as long as there are no abnormalities in its user's mental state, the artifact will work to maintain the barrier space.

Nevertheless, that does not change the fact that there is a large difference in the magical burden of controlling a barrier with a black hole inside it and that of using gravity magic to create a black hole. For this reason, powerful gravity magic is the natural enemy of magic for controlling barriers. Gravity magic has an extremely wide range of applications. Perhaps Rakan once saw Kū:nel use gravity magic to destroy a similar trap. Furthermore, a black hole only needs to exist for an instant in order to destroy the barrier, and the danger of injuring surrounding people with a wave of powerful gravity magic is minimal.

*The classical physics concept of "space" is quite different from the modern physics idea of "place." But as an exception, the concept of space in Euclidean geometry and that in modern physics are very similar.

[*Negima!* 228th Period Lexicon Negimarium]

■ Eternal Petrification

Aionion Petrosis

(ʼΑΙΩΝΙΟΝ ΠΕΤΡΩΣΙΣ)

A spell that emits a beam from the fingertips, which petrifies its targets. It is an extremely powerful and dangerous spell, and is incanted in Ancient Greek. But, while petrification from spells such as Pnoe Petras (Breath of Stone) and Kakon Omma Petroseos (Evil Eye of Petrifaction) can be undone with a certain extent of strong magic, petrification from this spell is semipermanent. For that reason, without power emitted from extremely unique and high-ranking spiritual capacity (power from a persona great enough among all the various spirits to be called a "god"), this petrification will not be undone. However, whatever damage it may take, Nodoka's artifact can recover if she only returns it to her card, so she did not get a taste of the true terror of this spell.

[*Negima!* 229th Period Lexicon Negimarium]

■ Phoenix Law Imperial Seal

Ennomos Aetosphragis

(ἔννομος ἀετοσφραγίς)

A magical seal modeled as an eagle holding scales. This seal uses powerful magic to force its target to strictly honor his word.

The eagle and the scales of this magical item's design represent power and justice, respectively.

The eagle as a symbol of power comes from the eagle being the bird sacred to the chief Greek/Roman god, Zeus/Jupiter. The ancient Roman poet P. Ovidius N. (B.C.43 - A.D.17(18)) relates the following. "Once, high and mighty lord [Jupiter] burned with the flames of love for Ganymede of Troy. Now Jupiter looked around for something he could change himself into. Jupiter must have wanted to change into something other than himself. But the one known as Jupiter would never become any bird other than one that could carry his thunderbolts. He took to the sky with his false wings and stole away the Trojan youth." (*Metamorphoses*, 10,155-160) It is not specified here, but according to Apollodoros (B.C.1C?), this bird that carries Jupiter's thunderbolts was none other than the eagle (ἀετός) (*Bibliotheca [Βιβλιοθήκη]*, 3,12,2).

Thus, the bird known as the eagle is a sacred bird with supreme divine authority. For that reason, it became the symbol of the Roman Empire, the Roman Emperor, and the Roman Empire's military. Even after the fall of the ancient Roman Empire, the western German Empire (the Holy Roman Empire) and the eastern Russian Empire each used the eagle as their national symbol, and the eagle continued to signify the highest authority (in connection with the ancient Roman Empire).

The design of the scales representing justice comes from conventions of Renaissance art. Since that time, the Roman goddess Justitia, who has become the personification of the virtue of justice, has been represented as a statue holding a sword and scales (or a book of law), and the scales are a symbol of the justice of law.

This design of power and justice is precisely what signifies the compelling force of the contract.

[*Negima!* 230th Period Lexicon Negimarium]

■ ADULTERA

The characters inscribed on the magic capsules that summon half-human, half-spirit beings such as undina. "Adultera" is a Latin word meaning "lascivious woman," and this magic item is used (mainly) to satisfy the sexual desires of men. The capsules Rakan had in 230th Period were a wood spirit (Dryas) capsule, a fire spirit (salamandra) capsule, a wind spirit (sylpha) capsule, and, for insurance, a water spirit (undina) capsule.

NEGIMA!
FAN ART CORNER

HELLO! THE CHARACTERS IN THE STORY HAVE INCREASED, AND WE'RE GETTING SUBMISSIONS OF ALL KINDS OF CHARACTERS★ ON THE OTHER HAND, WE'RE ALSO GETTING CHARACTERS THAT AREN'T IN THE STORY MUCH (LAUGH). PLEASE, SHINE LIGHT ON THEM, TOO! (^O^) (LAUGH). WELL THEN, LET'S TAKE A LOOK. ♪

TEXT BY MAX

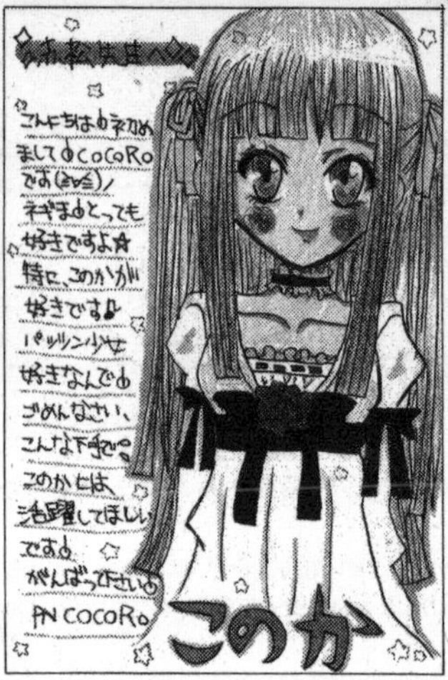
このか
PN COCORo

HOW FASHIONABLE. ▶

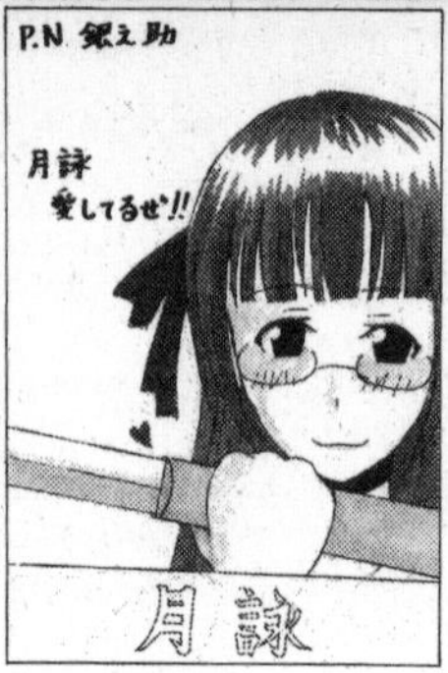
月詠
月詠

▲ WE DON'T SEE TSUKUYOMI VERY OFTEN.

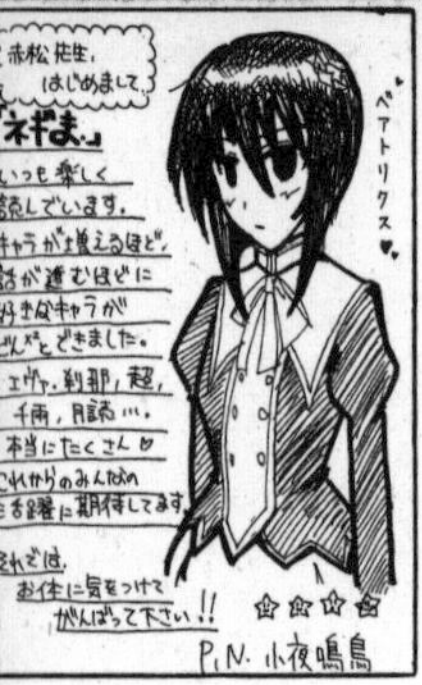
P.N. 小夜鳴鳥

▲ OHH, IT'S BEATRIX.

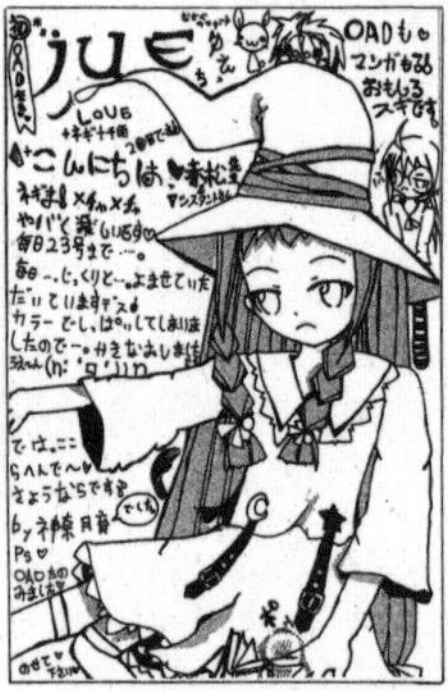
OADも マンガもめちゃおもしろスキです

▲ YUE, WITH A MYSTERIOUS EXPRESSION.

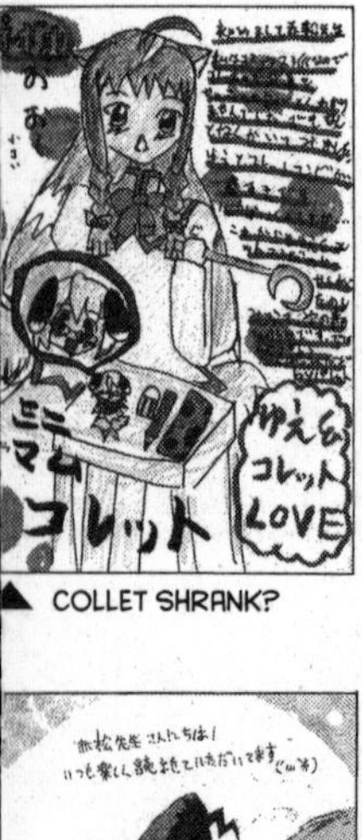
コレット
LOVE

▲ COLLET SHRANK?

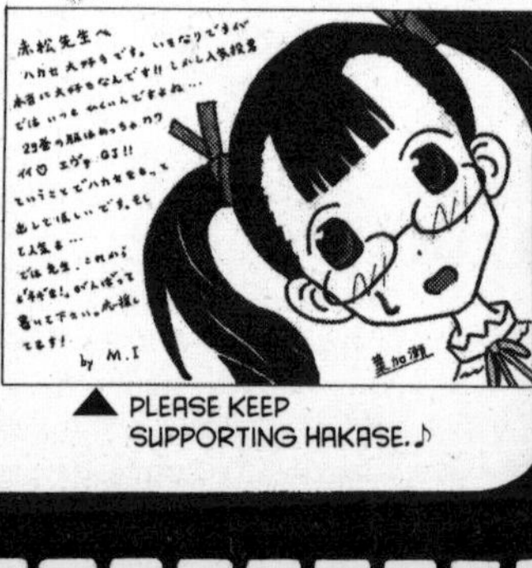
by M.I

▲ PLEASE KEEP SUPPORTING HAKASE.♪

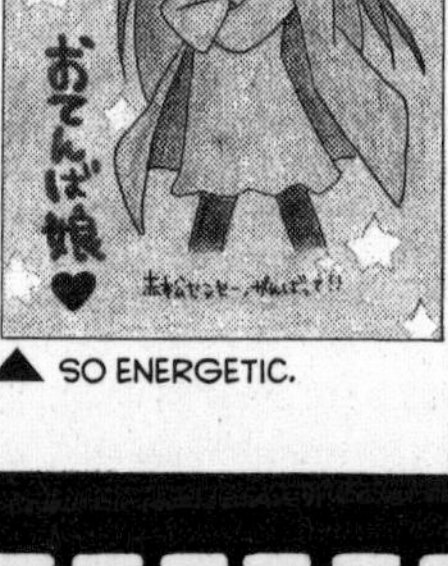
おてんば娘

▲ SO ENERGETIC.

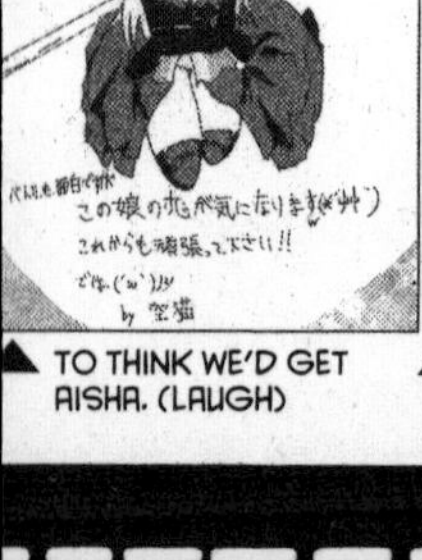

▲ TO THINK WE'D GET AISHA. (LAUGH)

NEGI MA!

MAGISTER NEGI MAGI

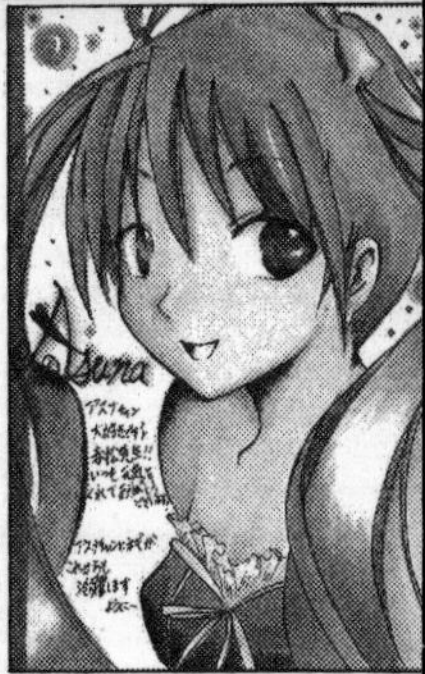
Asuna

▲ SO SEXY.

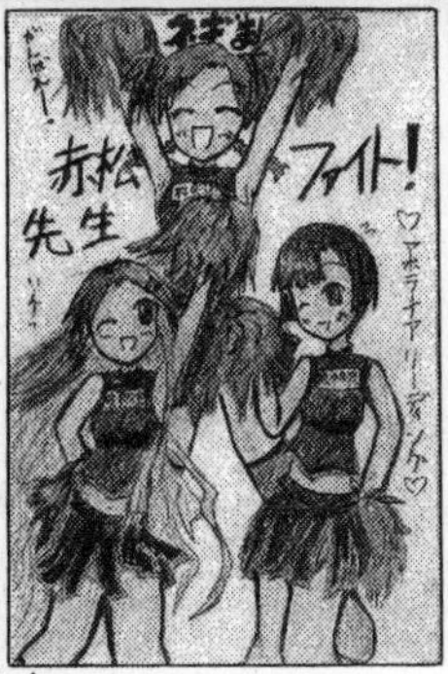
ネギま
赤松先生
ファイト！

▲ THE CHEER SQUAD IS LOOKING WELL.♪

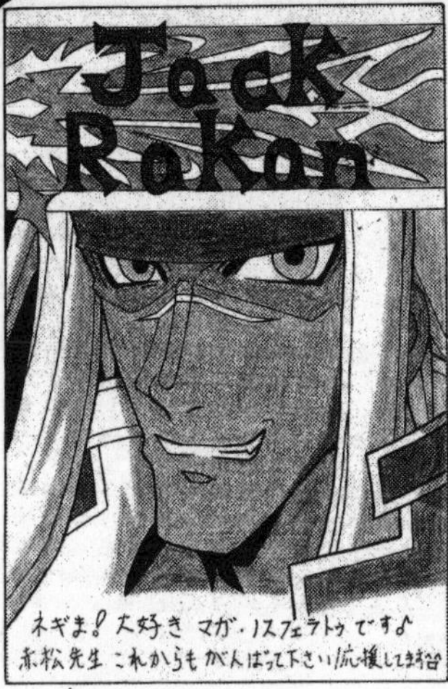
Jack Rakan
ネギま！大好き マガ・ノスフェラトゥです♪
赤松先生 これからもがんばって下さい応援してます

▲ AND HERE'S RAKAN.

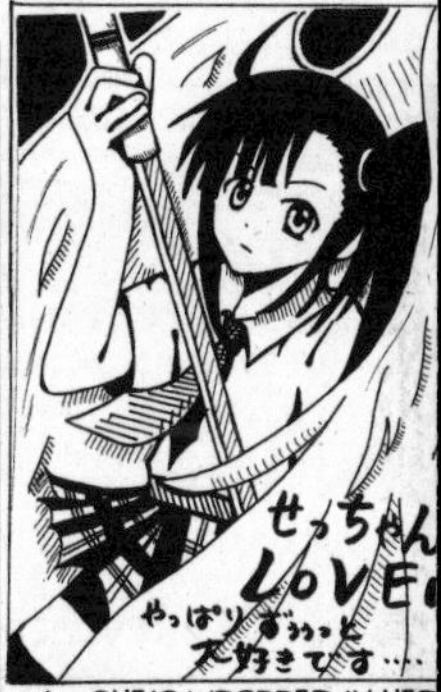
せっちゃん
LOVE
やっぱりずうっと大好きです…

▲ SHE'S WRAPPED IN HER WINGS.

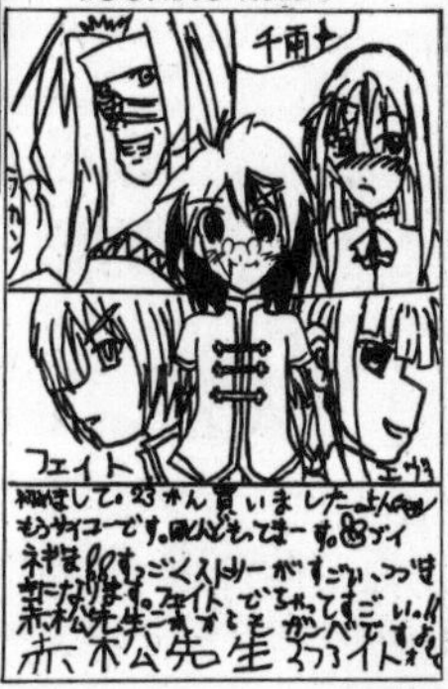
千雨
フェイト

▲ NEGI'S EXPRESSION LOOKS GOOD.

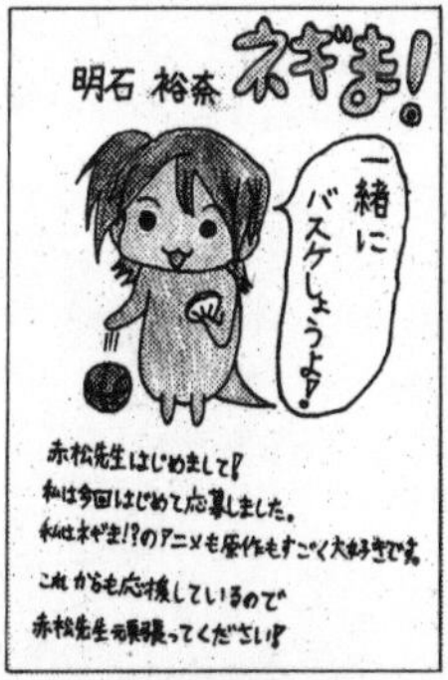
明石 裕奈
ネギま！
一緒にバスケしようよ！
赤松先生はじめまして！
私は今回はじめて応募しました。
私はネギま!?のアニメも原作もすごく大好きです。
これからも応援しているので
赤松先生頑張ってください！

SHE HAS A TAIL. ▶

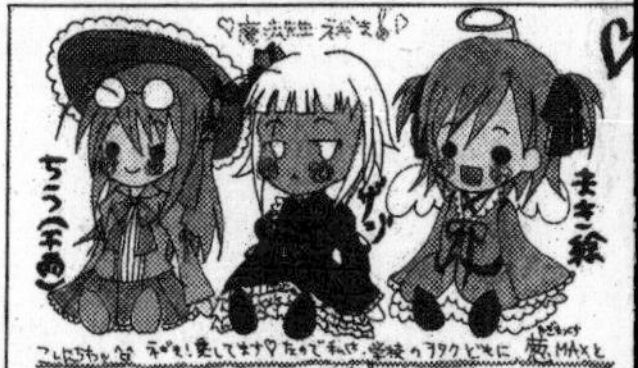
まき絵

I WANT DOLLS LIKE THIS! ▶

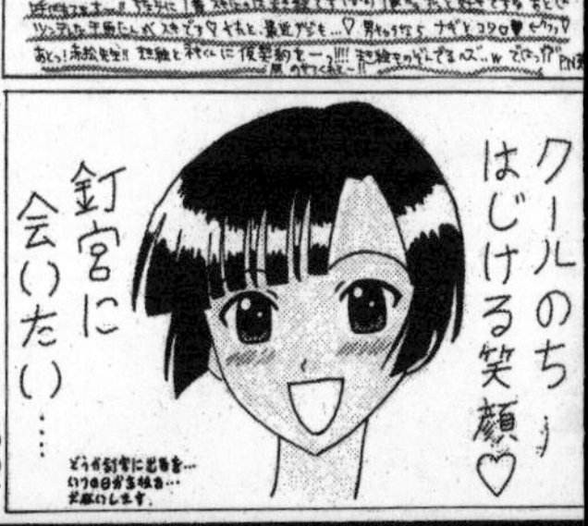
クールのちはじける笑顔♡
釘宮に会いたい…

KUGIMIYA'S POPULAR, TOO. ▶

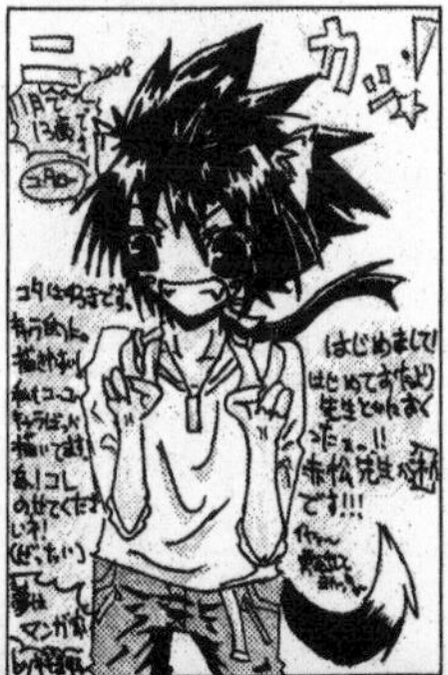
はじめまして!

HE LOOKS MISCHIEVOUS. ▶

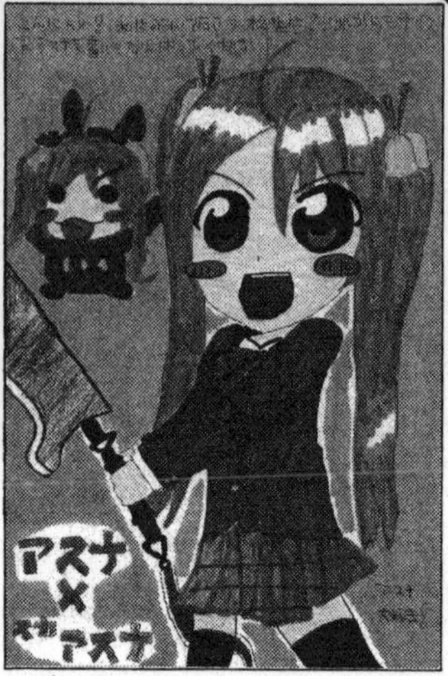
アスナ
×

▲ ADORABLE♪ ASUNA

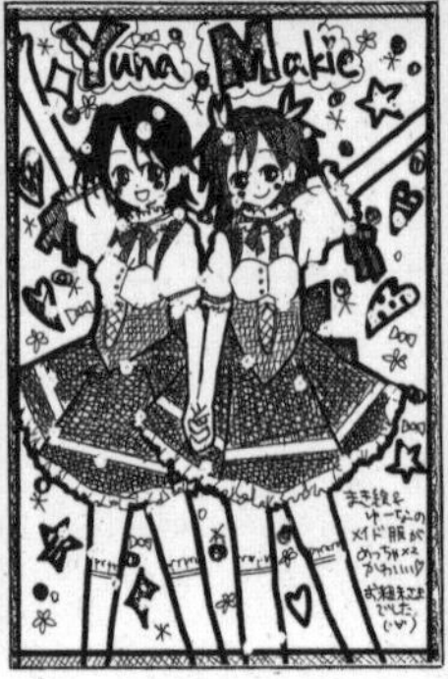
Yuna
Makie

▲ IT'S BLACK AND WHITE, BUT VERY VIBRANT.

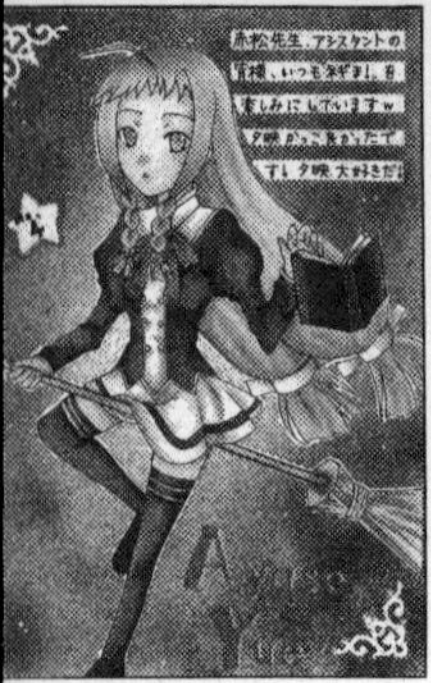

▲ THIS IS A VERY PRETTY DRAWING.

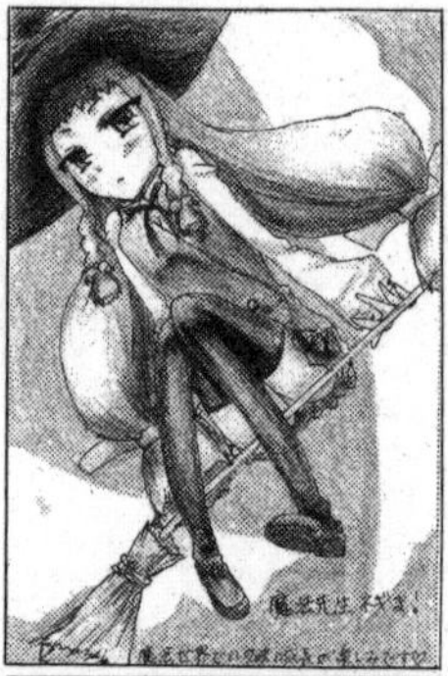

▲ YOU HAVE A DELICATE TOUCH.

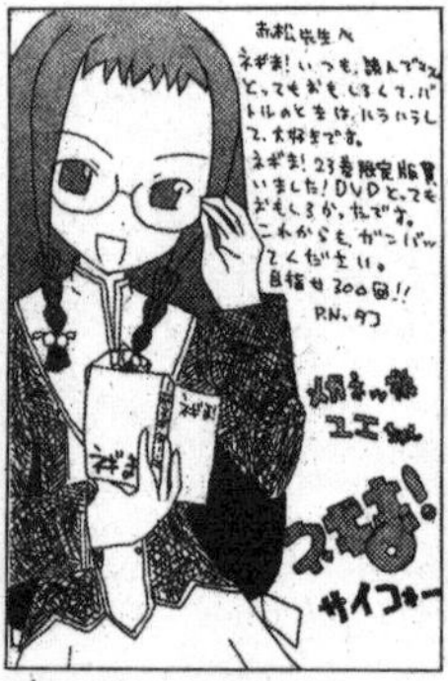

▲ SHE LOOKS VERY INTELLECTUAL.

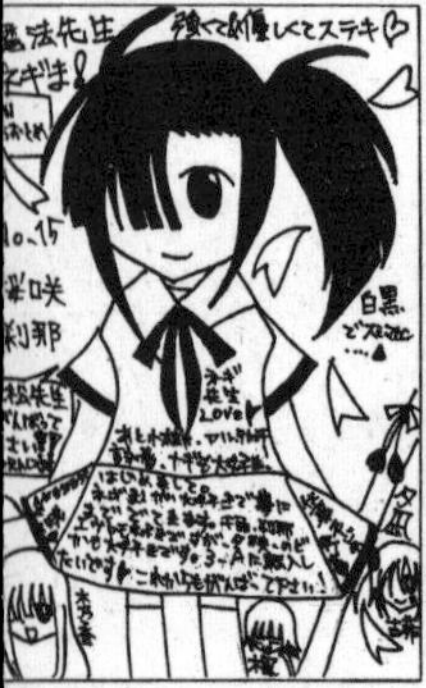
強くて優しくてステキ♡

▲ SHE LOOKS LIKE A KINDERGARTNER.

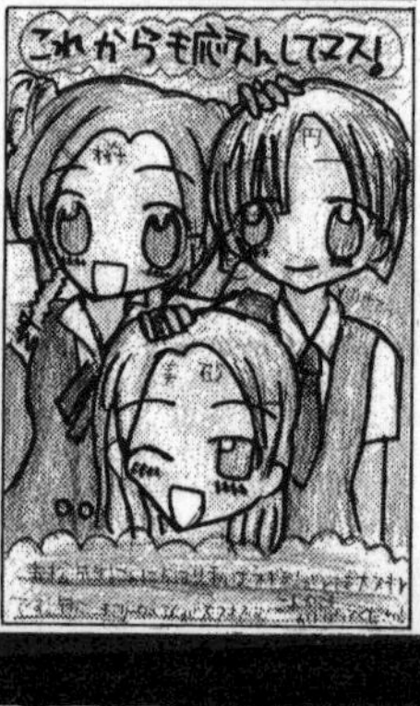
これからも応えんしてマス!

▲ THEIR NAMES ARE ON THEIR FOREHEADS. (LAUGH)

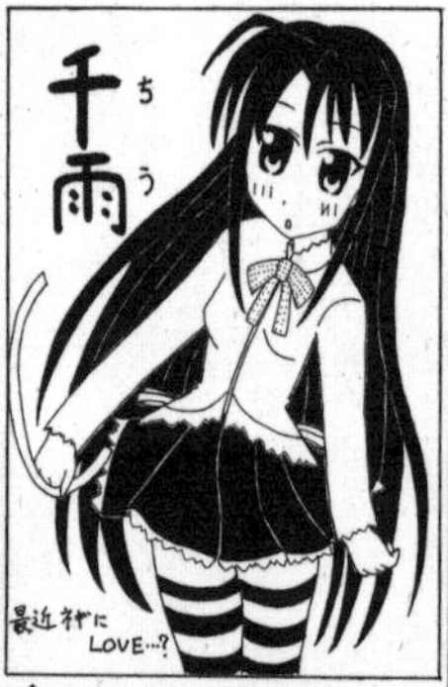
千雨
LOVE…?

▲ IT'S LOLI CHISAME. (LAUGH)

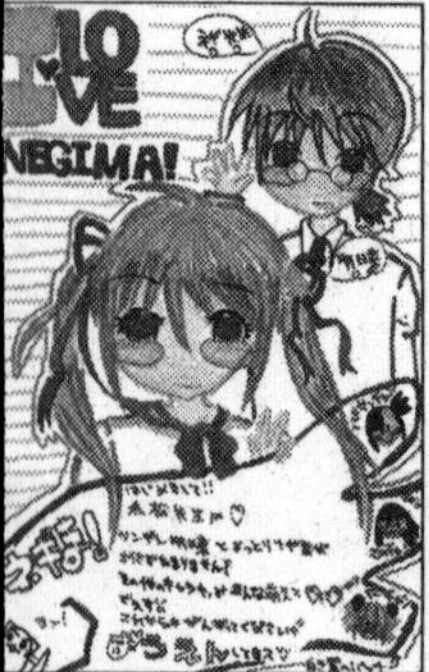
I LOVE
NEGIMA!

▲ THEY'VE BECOME SUPER CUTE.

THIS VOLUME'S

FEATURED CHARACTER

NODOKA MIYAZAKI

RANKING

MAGISTER NEGI MAGI

FIRST PLACE

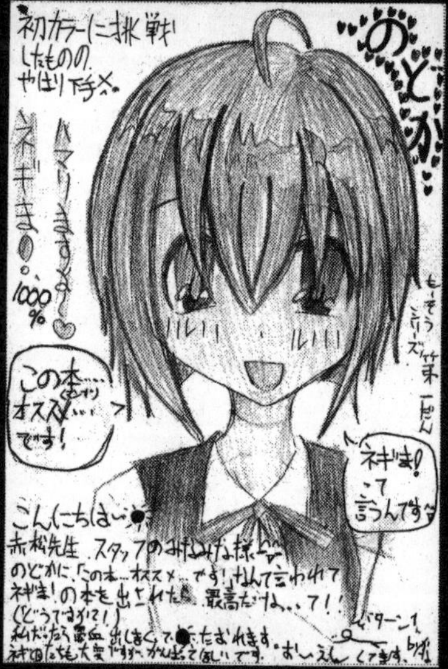

初カラーに挑戦!したものの、やはり下手×。
ネギま!ハマりますよ~
1000%
のどか
この本…オススメ…です!
ネギま!って言うんです~

A-ANOTHER AKAMATSU-SAN DREW THIS? THE SHAPE OF THE EYES IS VERY GOOD. HER EXPRESSION IS REALLY ALIVE; IT'S VERY WELL DRAWN.~♡

(AKAMATSU)

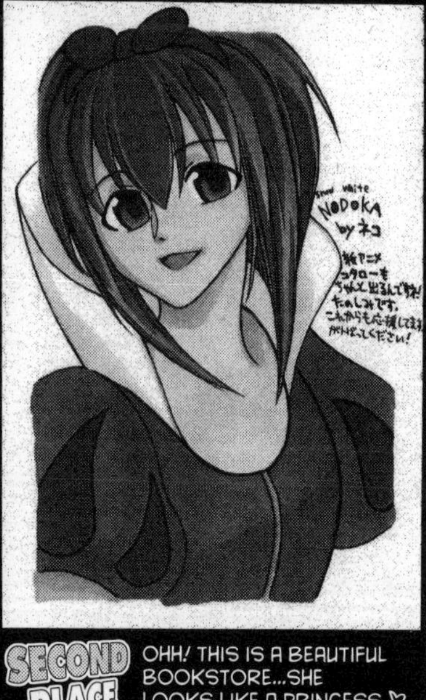

NODOKA by ネコ

SECOND PLACE

OHH! THIS IS A BEAUTIFUL BOOKSTORE...SHE LOOKS LIKE A PRINCESS.♡

THIRD PLACE

YOU WONDER WHAT HAPPENS NEXT? (LAUGH) THAT *IS* SOMETHING I'M ALWAYS CONCERNED ABOUT. THIS BOOKSTORE'S EYES ARE GOOD, TOO.

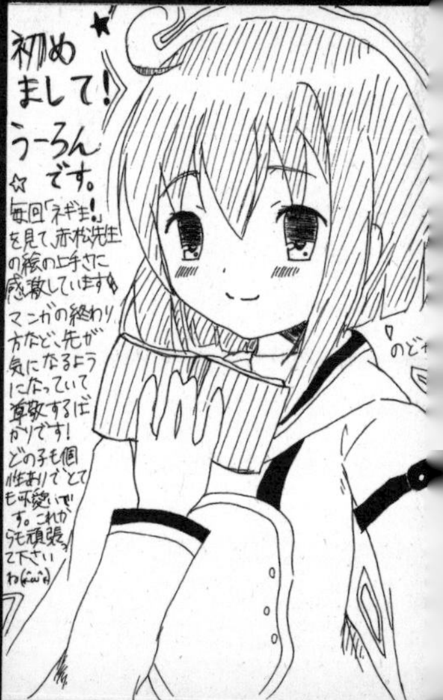

初めまして!
うーろんです。
毎回「ネギま!」を見て、赤松先生の絵の上手さに感激しています♪
マンガの終わり方など、先が気になるようになっていて尊敬するばかりです!
どの子も個性ありでとても可愛いです。これからも頑張って下さいね

MAGISTER NEGI MAGI

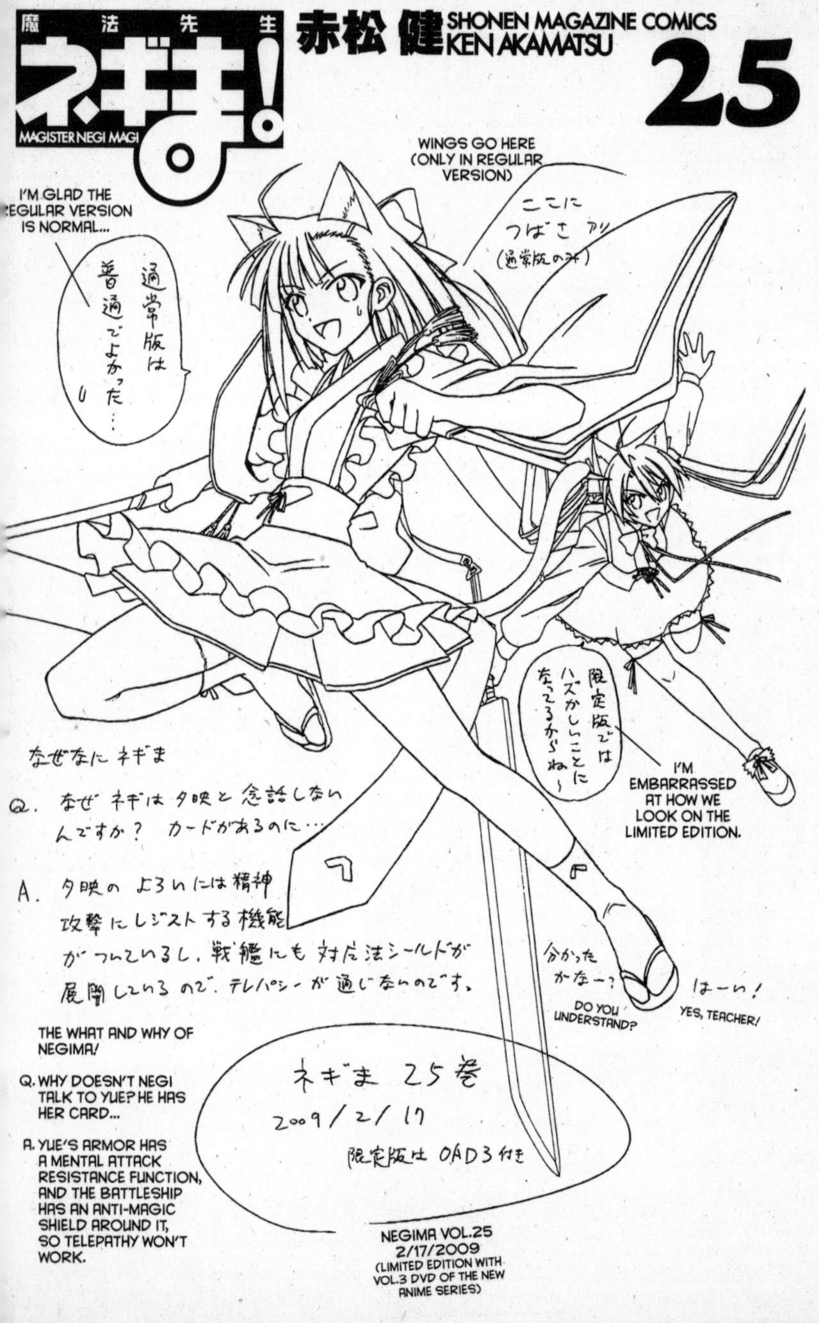

魔法先生
ネギま！
MAGISTER NEGI MAGI
赤松 健
SHONEN MAGAZINE COMICS
KEN AKAMATSU
25
ここに つばさ アリ (通常版のみ)
WINGS GO HERE (ONLY IN REGULAR VERSION)
通常版は 普通でよかった…
I'M GLAD THE REGULAR VERSION IS NORMAL...
限定版では ハズかしいことに なってるからね～
I'M EMBARRASSED AT HOW WE LOOK ON THE LIMITED EDITION.
なぜなにネギま
Q. なぜ ネギは 夕映と 念話しないんですか？ カードがあるのに…
A. 夕映の よろいには 精神攻撃にレジストする機能がついているし、戦艦にも 対魔法シールドが展開しているので、テレパシーが通じないのです。
分かったかなー？
DO YOU UNDERSTAND?
はーい！
YES, TEACHER!
THE WHAT AND WHY OF NEGIMA!
Q. WHY DOESN'T NEGI TALK TO YUE? HE HAS HER CARD...
A. YUE'S ARMOR HAS A MENTAL ATTACK RESISTANCE FUNCTION, AND THE BATTLESHIP HAS AN ANTI-MAGIC SHIELD AROUND IT, SO TELEPATHY WON'T WORK.
ネギま 25巻
2009/2/17
限定版は OAD3付き
NEGIMA VOL.25
2/17/2009
(LIMITED EDITION WITH VOL.3 DVD OF THE NEW ANIME SERIES)

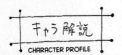

キャラ解説

CHARACTER PROFILE

㉓ 鳴滝史伽

㉓ FUMIKA NARUTAKI

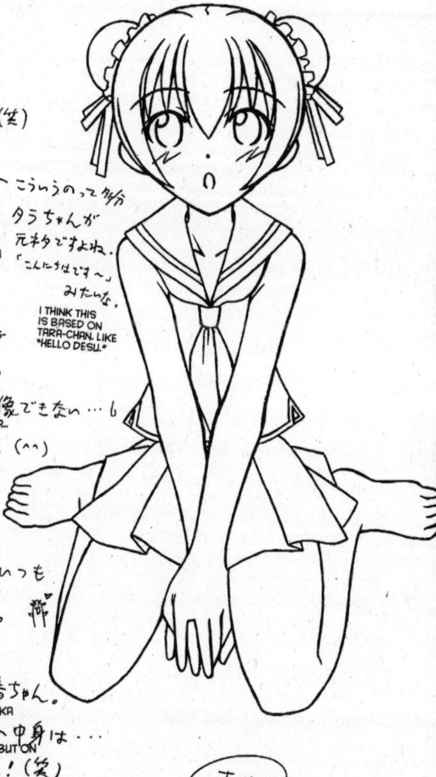

双子ちゃんの 弱気な方です。(笑)

THE TIMID ONE OF THE TWINS. (LAUGH)

夕映と同じく 丁寧語です。←

SHE SPEAKS WITH POLITE LANGUAGE, LIKE YUE.

こういうのって多分 タラちゃんが 元ネタですよね。「こんにちはですー」みたいな。

I THINK THIS IS BASED ON TARA-CHAN. LIKE "HELLO DESU."

姉より タレ目なのは おそらく 性格的なものが表情に出ている だけで、パーツ的には うりふたつ なんだと思いますよ。(一卵性だから)

I THINK THAT THE REASON HER EYES DROOP DOWN MORE THAN HER SISTER'S IS PROBABLY JUST THAT HER PERSONALITY SHOWS UP IN HER EXPRESSIONS; THE BODY PARTS OF THE SISTERS ARE AN EXACT MATCH. (SINCE THEY'RE IDENTICAL TWINS.)

姉と同じく、大人になった姿を想像できない…

LIKE WITH HER SISTER, I CAN'T IMAGINE HER HAVING GROWN UP...

でもきっと美人になるんじゃないかな。(^^) なんとなく。

BUT I'M SURE SHE'LL BE BEAUTIFUL. (^^) JUST A HUNCH.

アニメ版CVは狩野茉莉さん。ライブイベントなどの打ち上げで、いつも号泣しちゃう かわいらしい人です。守ってあげたくなっちゃう。(笑)

IN THE ANIME, SHE IS VOICED BY MARI KANŌ-SAN. SHE'S A LOVELY PERSON WHO ALWAYS BAWLS WHEN WE LAUNCH LIVE EVENTS. I JUST WANT TO PROTECT HER. (LAUGH)

ドラマ版は まなちゃこと山本真菜香ちゃん。だまってると美少女なんですが、その中身は… 私をはるかに超えるオタクです!(笑) ブログ読んでても7割くらいしか分からない…

IN THE DRAMA, SHE IS PLAYED BY MANAKA YAMAMOTO-CHAN, AKA MANACHI. WHEN SHE'S QUIET, SHE'S A BEAUTIFUL YOUNG LADY, BUT ON THE INSIDE... SHE FAR SURPASSES ME AS AN OTAKU! (LAUGH) WHEN I READ HER BLOG, I ONLY UNDERSTAND ABOUT 70% OF IT...

赤松

AKAMATSU

About the Creator

Negima! is only Ken Akamatsu's third manga, although he started working in the field in 1994 with *AI Ga Tomaranai* (released in the United States with the title *A.I. Love You*). Like all of Akamatsu's work to date, it was published in Kodansha's *Shonen Magazine*. *AI Ga Tomaranai* ran for five years before concluding in 1999. In 1998, however, Akamatsu began the work that would make him one of the most popular manga artists in Japan: *Love Hina*. *Love Hina* ran for four years, and before its conclusion in 2002, it would cause Akamatsu to be granted the prestigious Manga of the Year award from Kodansha, as well as going on to become one of the bestselling manga in the United States.

Translation Notes

Japanese is a tricky language for most Westerners, and translation is often more art than science. For your edification and reading pleasure, here are notes on some of the places where we could have gone in a different direction with our translation of the work, or where a Japanese cultural reference is used.

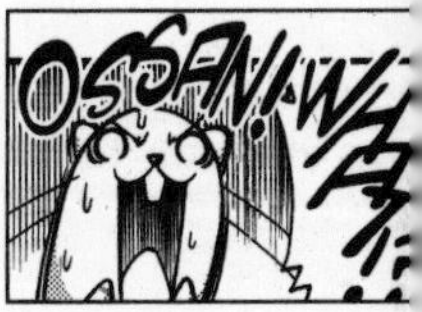
OSSAN!

Ossan, page 16

Ossan is an abbreviation of *Oji-san,* a way of addressing middle-aged men. Obviously Chamo isn't polite enough to use *Oji-san,* so *Ossan* is how he chooses to address Rakan.

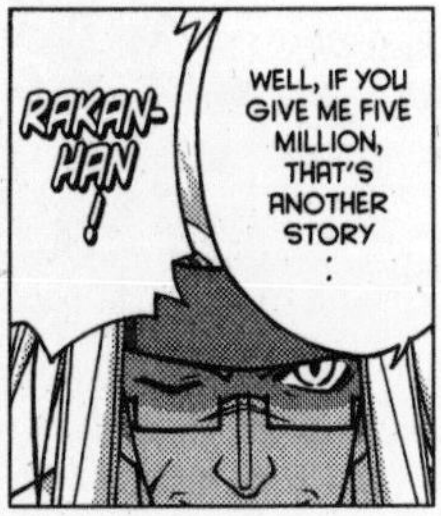
WELL, IF YOU GIVE ME FIVE MILLION, THAT'S ANOTHER STORY
RAKAN-HAN!

Rakan-han, page 16

Konoka is close enough friends with everyone that she hasn't used *-han* much until now. Being from the Kansai region, Konoka speaks with a Kansai dialect, including saying *-han* instead of *-san.*

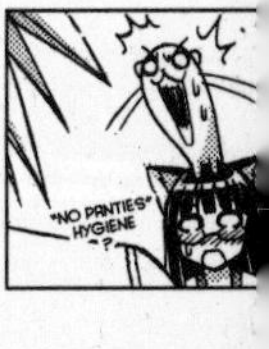
"NO PANTIES" HYGIENE ~?

No-panties hygiene, page 19

As the name suggests, "no-panties hygiene" is a method of staying healthy by removing underwear before sleeping. The theory was that the elastic band restricts the body, making it harder to relax, and that removing the panties improves ventilation, thus preventing the breeding of germs. If Tamaki does in fact believe in this method of hygiene, she has taken it so far as to use it even while awake.

Shirabe vs. Brigitte, page 24

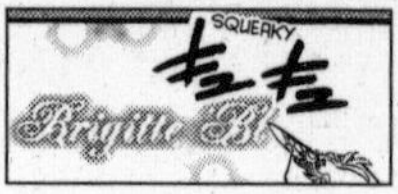
SQUEAKY

Apparently everyone in Fate's party has a code name, to protect them from having their real names used against them. Each of the girls' code names has something to do with her artifact. *Shirabe* is Japanese for "tune," *koyomi* means "calendar," and *tamaki* means "circle."

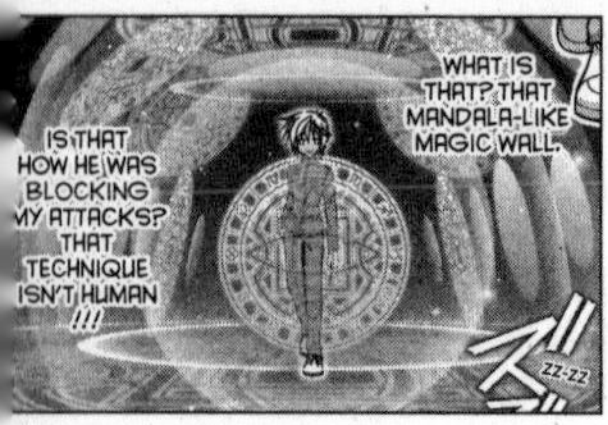
WHAT IS THAT? THAT MANDALA-LIKE MAGIC WALL.
IS THAT HOW HE WAS BLOCKING MY ATTACKS? THAT TECHNIQUE ISN'T HUMAN!!!
ZZ-ZZ

Mandala, page 89

A mandala is a set of geometric designs that represent the universe, looking much like the magic wall Fate is using. Mandalas are usually circular, and are generally used in Hinduism and Buddhism to help with meditation.

Super Kapa-kun, page 105

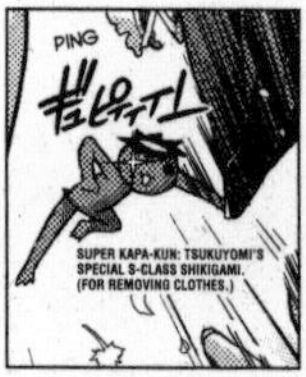
PING
SUPER KAPA-KUN: TSUKUYOMI'S SPECIAL S-CLASS SHIKIGAMI. (FOR REMOVING CLOTHES.)

As we learned when we first met Tsukuyomi, she uses various demon *shikigami*, including *kappa shikigami*. A *kappa* is a water sprite known for a whole range of evil deeds, from acts as heinous as dragging people underwater and sucking their blood to acts as mild as looking under women's skirts. Super Kapa-kun falls somewhere in the middle.

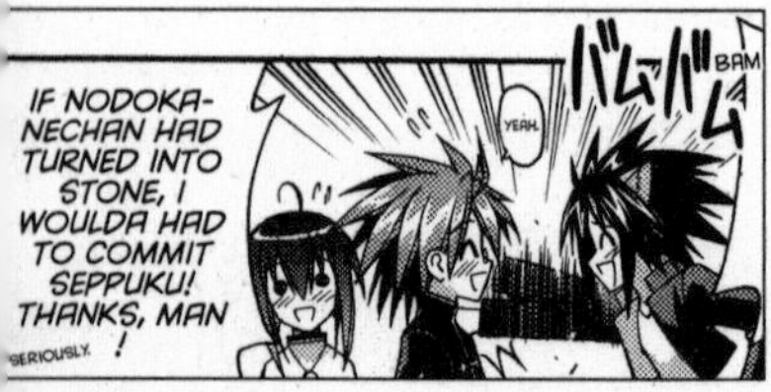
BAM
YEAH.
IF NODOKA-NECHAN HAD TURNED INTO STONE, I WOULDA HAD TO COMMIT SEPPUKU! THANKS, MAN!
SERIOUSLY.

Seppuku, page 110

Also known as *harakiri*, *seppuku* is ritual suicide committed in order to restore honor that is lost. Kotarō is saying that if he hadn't been able to prevent Nodoka's death, the only way to make up for such a serious mistake would be to kill himself.

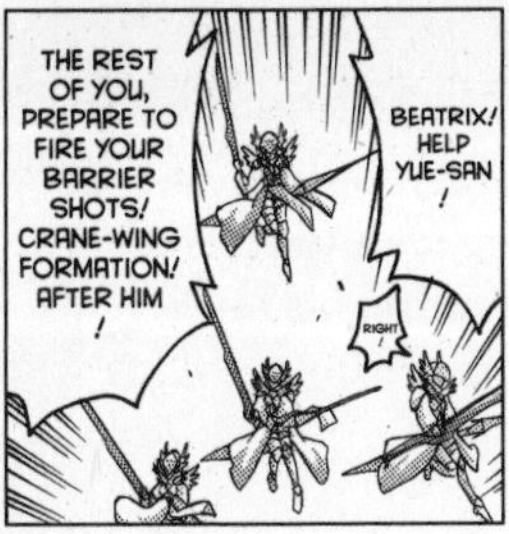
THE REST OF YOU, PREPARE TO FIRE YOUR BARRIER SHOTS! CRANE-WING FORMATION! AFTER HIM!
BEATRIX! HELP YUE-SAN!
RIGHT!

Crane-wing formation, page 116

Crane-wing is one of eight Japanese tactical formations. The soldiers line up in a V, taking the shape of a crane's spread wings. As to why the Ariadne Magic Knights would be using Japanese tactical formations—that remains a mystery.

Nabe, page 133

Nabe is Japanese for "pot," so, as expected, nabe cooking refers to cooking that is done in a pot. Meat, vegetables, etc. are all cooked together in a big pot, and those sitting around the pot take out what they want to eat.

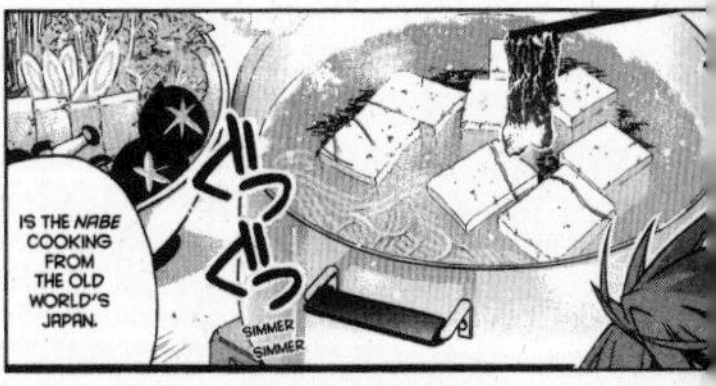
IS THE *NABE* COOKING FROM THE OLD WORLD'S JAPAN.
SIMMER
SIMMER

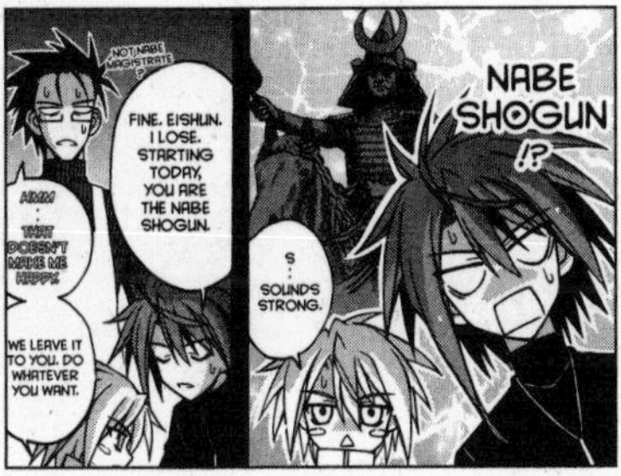
NABE SHOGUN !?
S... SOUNDS STRONG.
NOT NABE MAGISTRATE?
FINE. EISHUN. I LOSE. STARTING TODAY, YOU ARE THE NABE SHOGUN.
HMM... THAT DOESN'T MAKE ME HAPPY.
WE LEAVE IT TO YOU. DO WHATEVER YOU WANT.

Nabe Shogun, Nabe Magistrate, page 134

Nabe Bugyō, or Nabe Magistrate, is what they call someone who is very picky about how to cook the *nabe*—what ingredients to add, when to add them, etc. A Nabe Shogun is someone who is even stricter than a Nabe Magistrate.

Himeko, page 134

Himeko is the nickname Nagi has given to the Imperial Princess of Ostia. *Hime* is Japanese for "princess," and adding *ko* turns it into a cute girl's name.

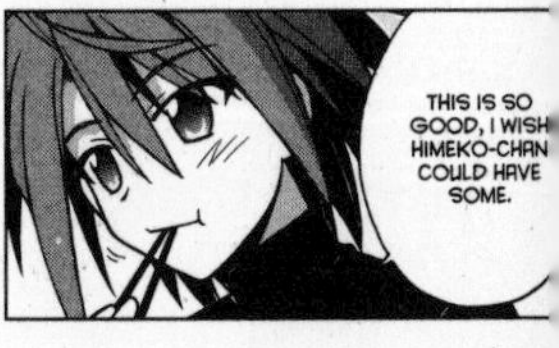
THIS IS SO GOOD, I WISH HIMEKO-CHAN COULD HAVE SOME.

Tara-chan and "Hello *desu*," page 177

Tara-chan is a character from the popular anime and manga series, *Sazae-san*. He always ends his sentences with *desu*, a polite way to end sentences, even when it is grammatically incorrect. "Hello *desu*" is an example; most Japanese people do not add *desu* to *konnichi wa* (hello).

STORY BY KEN AKAMATSU
ART BY TAKUYA FUJIMA

BASED ON THE POPULAR ANIME!

Negi Springfield is only ten years old, but he's already a powerful wizard. After graduating from his magic school in England, the prodigy is given an unusual assignment: teach English at an all-girl school in Japan. Now Negi has to find a way to deal with his thirty-one totally gorgeous (and completely overaffectionate) students—without using magic! Based on the *Negima!* anime, this is a fresh take on the beloved *Negima!* story.

Available anywhere books or comics are sold!

SAYONARA, ZETSUBOU-SENSEI

BY KOJI KUMETA

THE POWER OF NEGATIVE THINKING
VOLUME 1

Nozomu Itoshiki is depressed. Very depressed. He's certifiably suicidal, but he's also the beloved schoolteacher of a class of unique students, each charming in her own way. For all of them, it's a special time, when the right teacher can have a lasting positive effect on their lives. But is that teacher Itoshiki, a.k.a. Zetsubou-sensei, who just wants to find the perfect place to die?

Available anywhere books or comics are sold!

TOMARE!

[STOP!]

You're going the wrong way!

Manga is a completely different type of reading experience.

To start at the *beginning*, go to the *end*!

That's right! Authentic manga is read the traditional Japanese way—from right to left, exactly the *opposite* of how American books are read. It's easy to follow: Just go to the other end of the book, and read each page—and each panel—from right side to left side, starting at the top right. Now you're experiencing manga as it was meant to be.